Fodor's 91 New York City

D0242473

Fodor's Travel Publications, Inc.
New York and London

ISBN 0-679-01939-1

Grateful acknowledgment is made to the following for permission to reprint previously published material: Sterling Lord Literistic, Inc.: Excerpt from NEW YORK PROCLAIMED by V.S. Pritchett. Copyright © 1965 by V.S. Pritchett. Reprinted by permission of Sterling Lord Literistic, Inc. Random House, Inc.: Excerpt from DOWNTOWN by Michael Musto. Copyright © 1986 by Michael Musto. Reprinted by permission of Random House, Inc.

Fodor's New York City

Editor: David Low
Contributors: Michael Adams, Clair Berg, Laura Broadwell, Karen Cure, Theodore Fischer, Jane Hershey, Ann LaForge, David Laskin, John Mariani, Peter D. Meltzer, Denise Lewis Patrick, Carolyn Price, Susan Spano Wells, Todd Whitley
Art Director: Fabrizio La Rocca
Cartographer: David Lindroth
Illustrator: Karl Tanner
Cover Photograph: Francesco Ruggeri

Design: Vignelli Associates

Special Sales

Contents

Maps and Charts

Foreword

While every care has been taken to ensure the accuracy of the information in this guide, the passage of time will always bring change, and consequently, the publisher cannot accept responsibility for errors that may occur.

All prices and opening times quoted here are based on information supplied to us at press time. Hours and admission fees may change, however, and the prudent traveler will avoid inconvenience by calling ahead.

Fodor's wants to hear about your travel experiences, both pleasant and unpleasant. When a hotel or restaurant fails to live up to its billing, let us know and we will investigate the complaint and revise our entries where the facts warrant it.

Send your letters to the editors of Fodor's Travel Publications, 201 E. 50th Street, New York, NY 10022.

Highlights'91 and Fodor's Choice

Highlights '91

New York City is one of the most popular destinations in the United States, with nearly 20 million visitors arriving in 1989—36 million of them from overseas and almost 3 million of them convention delegates. Tourism figures showed for 1990 a decline for the second year in a row, perhaps a sign of the state of economic conditions across the United States. Still, the hotel occupancy rate here was hovering around 75%, so the downturn, if any, might only mean slightly less difficulty in getting reservations in this always-booked city. Visitors may even benefit from somewhat less crowded conditions at the major restaurants, attractions, and entertainment events.

A great landmark long out of commission, **Ellis Island** was scheduled to reopen in late-1990 after a $140 million restoration. The first facility to open will be the 200,000-square-foot brick-and-limestone main building, with its vast, vaulted, tiled hall, which is being converted into the Ellis Island Immigration Museum. As a federal immigration facility between 1892 and 1954, Ellis Island processed 16 million men, women, and children—the ancestors of more than 40% of all Americans living today; exhibits will document not only Ellis Island's history but the story of American immigration in general. Ferries to Ellis Island will run from Castle Clinton in Battery Park, which is also the embarkation point for ferries to the Statue of Liberty.

A renovated **Guggenheim Museum** reopens in the fall of 1991 with a restored Frank Lloyd Wright building. At the **Metropolitan Museum of Art**, the new Henry R. Kravis wing should be opening in the fall of 1992, creating a new Central Park entrance at the back of the museum. First-floor galleries will feature the European decorative arts collection, a fascinating series of period rooms, as well as an arcaded courtyard displaying European sculpture. The **Pierpont Morgan Library** is currently expanding to incorporate a 45-room brownstone, that once belonged to Morgan's son J. P. Morgan, around the corner at 37th Street and Madison Avenue. From 1991–1992, the **Jewish Museum** is closed for renovation but will still present exhibits during this period at **The New York Historical Society**. The long-orphaned **Museum of American Folk Art** has found a new home across from Lincoln Center, at Columbus Avenue and 66th Street, which will become an annex once the museum's permanent headquarters on West 53rd Street are completed in 1992.

While it's hard to predict what will still be playing in 1991 on, Off-, or Off-Off-Broadway, not to mention in downtown performance spaces, certain special dates have already been set in the arts calendar. Until May 1991, **Carnegie Hall** will be celebrating its 100th anniversary season with a gala series of events scheduled to include concerts by Luciano Pavarotti, Kathleen Battle, Yo-Yo Ma, the New York and Leningrad philharmonics, and the farewell stint of Sir Georg Solti leading the Chicago Philharmonic. The 1991 season at the **Brooklyn Academy of Music** will include a festival of plays directed by Ingmar Bergman. The **Public Theater,** downtown on Lafayette Street, continues this season its six-year Shakespeare marathon, performing all of the Bard's works with a roster of big-name stars. JoAnne Akalitis has been appointed Artistic Director. The **National Black Theater,** which produces works by contemporary black writers, has opened its new home at the intersection of 125th Street and Lenox Avenue in the heart of Harlem. Plans for expansion are underway.

The **Queens Zoo,** which had been closed for some time, will reopen in spring 1991 in Flushing Meadows Corona Park; the **Prospect Park Zoo** in Brooklyn will be closed for renovation until 1993. Also, in Prospect Park, a newly renovated, handcarved 1912 carousel, with handicap access, will be ready for operation in fall 1991.

Shoppers will note that the Herald Square area, already a prime retail area due to the presence of Macy's department store and the luxury shops in Herald Center, has added some 60 new shops and restaurants with the opening of the nine-story **A & S Plaza,** anchored by the Abraham and Straus department store.

At Trump Tower, the venerable department store **Bonwit Teller** closed in 1990. Taking its place in the fall of 1991 will be the first store in the United States run by **Galeries Lafayette,** one of France's top three department store chains.

Among the new hotels that have opened recently are the **Chatwal Inns** and **The Holiday Inn Crowne Plaza,** both reviewed in Chapter 9. There are other new properties which, though not yet open at press time, should be available to accommodate visitors by early or mid-1991. The Times Square renaissance sparked over the last four years continues with a 460-unit **Embassy Suites** at Seventh Avenue and 47th Street, which will be more upscale in price and style than its other national properties; and the 638-room **Hotel Macklowe** at 145 West 44th Street, which, along with elegant rooms starting at under $200, will feature a theater, high-tech meeting facilities, and sophisticated dining options. A 315-room **Ramada Renaissance,** to be located on the triangle formed by Broadway, Seventh Avenue, and 47th Street is slated soon to join them, as is a second major **Marriott** property, further west on Eighth Avenue. The former Royal Concordia is now the **Rihga Royal.** This 500-unit, all-suite hotel is a Japanese property, with its own restaurant, the Halcyon. The former Grand Bay at 51st Street and Seventh Avenue is now the **Parc Fifty One.** I.M.

Pei is designing what might well be New York's most expensive hotel on 57th Street between Madison and Park avenues: the 400-room **Regent of New York,** run by the same company that currently oversees the Mayfair Regent. And Marriott is planning to open a new 500-unit hotel in the Wall Street area, as is real estate giant and *New York Post* owner, Peter Kalikow.

Central Park South's **Essex House,** now a Nikko Hotel, is currently closed for a complete restoration of rooms, public areas, and restaurants; it is slated to reopen as a very expensive property by late spring 1991. Another anticipated reopening is the **Sheraton St. Regis** on Fifth Avenue, which at press time was slated to be back in business early this year. The forlorn **Hotel Tudor** has new owners, though plans for the property are still up in the air.

Despite the death of Steve Rubell—who with his Studio 54 partner, Ian Schrager, had quite an impact on the hotel scene with Morgan's and The Royalton—restoration of their other properties is continuing. **The Paramount** on West 46th Street is becoming a moderately priced "hip" hotel with Art Deco overtones, a private cinema, a restaurant, and a nightclub; the **Barbizon** on East 63rd Street will be transformed into a spa property.

Fodor's Choice

No two people will agree on what makes a perfect vacation, but it's fun and helpful to know what others think. We hope you'll have a chance to experience some of Fodor's Choices yourself while visiting New York City. For detailed information about each entry, refer to the appropriate chapters within this guidebook.

Views

The lower Manhattan skyline, seen from the Brooklyn Heights Promenade

The vista of skyscrapers ringing Central Park, best viewed from the Reservoir's northwest corner

A moonlit look at the harbor from the Staten Island Ferry

The sun setting over New Jersey and the lights of Manhattan snapping on one by one, from the World Trade Center's observation deck, 107 stories up

Architecture

The Woolworth Building, the Flatiron Building, the Empire State Building, and the World Trade Center's twin towers—each, in its time, the world's tallest building

The Chrysler Building, whose Art Deco chrome spire pierces the sky

The Dakota, grande dame of apartment buildings

The unbroken front of cast-iron beauties along Greene Street in SoHo

The graceful town houses along St. Luke's Place in the West Village

The Cathedral of St. John the Divine, an immense Gothic cathedral still abuilding

Museums

The Pierpont Morgan Library, and Morgan's personal library within

The dioramas at the American Museum of Natural History

The secluded Lehman Pavilion, among other delights at the Metropolitan Museum of Art

The medieval Cloisters, especially its unicorn tapestries

The Museum of the Moving Image, worth a foray into Queens for film lovers

Holidays and Seasonal Events

The lighting of the Christmas tree in Rockefeller Plaza

Cherry blossoms in bloom at the Brooklyn Botanic Garden

The Ninth Avenue Food Fair, a gluttonous early-May street feast

Late August afternoons when the Mets are playing at Shea and, a boardwalk's stroll away, the U.S. Open at Flushing Meadows

The San Gennaro Festival, on Little Italy's streets in September

The inflating of giant balloons the night before Macy's Thanksgiving Day Parade, on West 77th Street

Entertainment

Whatever is onstage at Playwrights' Horizons, on Theatre Row

Jazz into the wee hours at the Blue Note

Standing-room tickets for the Metropolitan Opera, obtainable the day of performance

A Woody Allen or Martin Scorcese movie, viewed along with a hometown New York audience

Standing in line at the TKTS booth—an afternoon's entertainment in itself

Restaurants

The Four Seasons *(Very Expensive)*

Le Bernadin *(Very Expensive)*

Lutèce *(Very Expensive)*

Felidia *(Expensive)*

Le Cirque *(Expensive)*

Smith & Wollensky *(Expensive)*

Gino *(Moderate)*

La Colombe D'Or *(Moderate)*

Shun Lee Palace *(Moderate)*

Union Square Café *(Moderate)*

Katz's Delicatessen *(Inexpensive)*

Shopping

Ralph Lauren's Polo store, in a superbly renovated East Side town house

Zabar's, an outstanding food store and cultural institution

Barneys New York for men's and women's clothing

The Enchanted Forest, a special SoHo toy store

An auction at Sotheby's

Hotels

The Carlyle *(Very Expensive)*

The Pierre *(Very Expensive)*

The Mark *(Expensive)*

The Mayfair Regent *(Expensive)*

The United Nations Plaza *(Expensive)*

The Algonquin *(Moderate)*

The Empire *(Moderate)*

Street Life

Itinerant musicians playing at either end of the subway shuttle between Times Square and Grand Central Terminal

The steps of the New York Public Library, weekdays at lunchtime

Lincoln Center's central plaza, just before 8 PM on concert nights

Central Park's Mall and Bethesda Terrace on weekend afternoons

Quintessentially New York

Catching sight of a dog-walker, leashed to a tangle of pooches, in Central Park

Schmoozing in the Garment District, as wheeled racks of ready-to-wear hurtle past

Watching the frenzy on the floor of the New York Stock Exchange

Gallery-hopping along West Broadway in SoHo on a Saturday afternoon (if you like trendoid crowds)

Going to a deli restaurant for a pastrami-on-rye, garlic pickles, and an egg cream

Mingling with fellow joggers at the East 90th Street entrance to Central Park

Spotting celebrities—anywhere and everywhere

New York City Area

World Time Zones

Numbers below vertical bands relate each zone to Greenwich Mean Time (0 hrs.).
Local times frequently differ from these general indications,
as indicated by light-face numbers on map.

Introduction

by Michael Adams

Senior writer for the business travel magazine Successful Meetings, *Michael Adams finally moved to his home town, New York City, 12 years ago.*

In 1925, the youthful songwriting team of Richard Rodgers and Larry Hart wrote "Manhattan," arguably the loveliest city anthem ever. "We'll have Manhattan, the Bronx, and Staten Island, too," it promises, drawing its images from the merry scramble that was the city more than 60 years ago: "sweet pushcarts," "baloney on a roll," a subway that "charms," Brighton Beach, Coney Island, and the popular comedy *Abie's Irish Rose.* "We'll turn Manhattan into an isle of joy," coos the refrain.

Several decades later, in 1989, an album called simply *New York*, by aging enfant terrible rocker Lou Reed, views the same city with glasses fogged by despair and cynicism: Drugs, crime, racism, and promiscuity reign in what Reed considers to be a sinkhole of "crudity, cruelty of thought and sound." His voice brittle with weary irony, he sings, "This is no time for celebration." Manhattan's "sweet pushcarts" now apparently overflow with deadly vials of crack.

So, whom to believe—Lou or Larry?

The truth of the matter is slippery, for New York has long been a mosaic of grand contradictions, a city for which there has never been—nor ever will be—a clear consensus. Hart himself took the city to task in another song, "Give it Back to the Indians," whose lyrics count off a litany of problems that still exist: crime, dirt, high prices, traffic jams, and all-around urban chaos. Yet for all that, millions live here, grumbling but happy, and millions more visit, curious as cats to find out what the magnificent fuss is all about.

I was in eighth grade in suburban Detroit when I first really became aware of New York. A friend's Manhattan-born mother still subscribed to the Sunday *New York Times*, and at their house I'd pore over the "Arts and Leisure" section, as rapt as an archaeologist with a cave painting. The details of what I read there have blurred, but I remember vividly the sensation I felt while reading: a combined anticipation and nostalgia so keen it bordered on pain. Although I had never been there, I was homesick for New York.

It's my home now, yet I can still understand and appreciate the impulse that draws visitors here. In a city so ripe with possibilities, we are all more or less visitors.

I think of this on an uncharacteristically warm day in late March, as I and fellow New Yorkers escape from the hives of offices and homes to celebrate spring's first preview. We unbutton our jackets, leave buses a stop or two before our usual destinations, quicken our resolve to visit that new exhibit at the Met or jog around the Central Park Reservoir. A jubilant sense of renewal infects us all, and I overhear one happy fellow saying to a friend, "I felt just like a tourist yesterday."

Whenever I get the New York blues, the best tonic for me is to glimpse the city through the eyes of a visitor. One day, after subway construction had rerouted me well out of my usual path, I found myself in the grimy Times Square station—hardly the place for a spiritual conversion. As usual I had that armor of body language that we New Yorkers reflexively assume to protect ourselves from strangers bent on (1) ripping us off, (2) doing us bodily harm, (3) converting us, (4) making sexual advances, or (5) being general pains-in-the-butt just for the hell of it. But that day, tucked away in a corner, was a group of musicians —not an uncommon sight in New York—playing the guitar, organ, and accordion with gusto and good spirits behind a homemade sign that dubbed them the "Argentinian Tango Company." Like many street musicians in Manhattan, they were *good*, but I was only half listening, too intent on cursing the city. Just as I passed the band, however, I noticed four teenagers drawn to the music—visitors surely, they were far too open and trusting to be anything else. Grinning as widely as the Argentinians, they began to perform a spontaneous imitation of flamenco dancing— clapping hands above their heads, raising their heels, laughing at themselves, and only slightly self-conscious. Passersby, myself included, broke into smiles. As I made my way to the subway platform, buoyed by the impromptu show, I once again forgave New York. This minor piece of magic was apology enough.

I wonder whether that was the moment one of those teenagers happened to fall in love with the city. It *can* happen in a single moment, to a visitor or to a longtime resident. Perhaps it hits during a stroll through Riverside Park after a blanketing snowfall, when trees have turned to crystal and the city feels a hush it knows at no other time; or when you turn a corner and spy, beyond a phalanx of RVs and a tangle of cables and high-beam lights, the filming of a new movie.

That moment could also come when the house lights begin to dim at the Metropolitan Opera, and the gaudily sparkling chandeliers make their magisterial ascent to the ceiling; or when you first glimpse the magnificently bright Prometheus statue in Rockefeller Center, gleaming like a giant present under the annual Christmas tree as dozens of skaters cut swirls of seasonal colors on the ice below. You may even be smitten in that instant when, walking along the streets in the haze of a summer afternoon, you look up above the sea of anonymous faces to see—and be astonished by—the lofty rows of skyscrapers, splendid in their arrogance and power. At times like these it is perfectly permissible to stop for a moment, take a breath, and think, "Wow! *This is New York!*" We who live here do it every so often ourselves.

For some, of course, that special moment comes with a happy shock of recognition when they spot a street or building made familiar by movies or television, anything from *I Love Lucy* to *On the Waterfront*. At the Empire State Building, who can help but remember King Kong's pathetically courageous swing from its pinnacle? Or at the brooding Dakota, the chilling destiny created for Rosemary's baby within those fortresslike walls? In the mind's eye, Audrey Hepburn is eternally pairing diamonds and a doughnut as she wends her swank way down Fifth Avenue to have breakfast at Tiffany's. And the miniature park on Sutton Place will always be where Woody Allen and Diane Keaton began their angst-ridden *Manhattan* love affair, with the 59th Street bridge gleaming beyond and Gershwin music swelling in the background.

There's a moment of sudden magic when a New York stereotype, seen so often on screen that it seems a joke, suddenly comes to life: when a gum-cracking waitress calls you "hon," or a stogie-sucking cabbie asks, "How 'bout them Yankees, Mac?" There's also the thrill of discovering one of New York's cities-within-the-city: Mulberry Street in Little Italy; Mott Street in Chinatown; Park Avenue's enclave of wealth and privilege; SoHo and TriBeCa, with their artistic types dressed in black from head to toe; or Sheridan Square, the nexus of the city's prominent lesbian and gay communities. The first glimpse of a landmark could begin the visitor's infatuation, too: frenetic Grand Central Station, abustle with suburban commuters; the concrete caverns of Wall Street, throbbing with power and ambition; or the Statue of Liberty, which neither cliché nor cheap souvenir can render common.

As you ready yourself to take on New York's contradictions, prepare to wonder and to exult. Here, on a single day, you might catch a glimpse of Jacqueline Onassis—she's been known to stop at Burger Heaven and have lunch at the counter—or Rollerena, the gloriously tacky drag-queen-cum-fairy-godmother on roller skates, who waves her magic wand to bestow blessings on select public events. Here you can eat sumptuously at a hot dog stand or at a world-celebrated gourmet shrine.

Excess and deprivation mingle here: As a limousine crawls lazily to take its pampered passengers to their luxe destination, it rolls past a threadbare beggar seeking the warmth that steams from the city's belly through an iron grate. It's a ludicrously bright cartoon and a sobering documentary, New York—almost too much for one city to be. It's maddening and it's thrilling; monstrous, yet beautiful beyond parallel.

And I envy anyone their first taste of it.

1 Essential Information

Before You Go

Visitor Information

The **New York Convention and Visitors Bureau** (2 Columbus Circle, New York, NY 10019, tel. 212/397–8222) provides a wealth of free information, including brochures, subway and bus maps, an up-to-date calendar of events, listings of hotels and weekend hotel packages, and discount coupons for Broadway shows. **The New York Division of Tourism** (1 Commerce Plaza, Albany, NY 12245, tel. 518/474–4116 or 800/225–5697) offers a free series of "I Love New York" booklets listing attractions and tour packages available in New York City.

Tour Groups

Thanks to their bulk buying power, tour operators can almost always get you better prices on air and ground transportation, hotels, and sightseeing than you can get on your own. The trade-off is that they require you to march to the beat of a tour guide's drum rather than your own. If not having to deal with the details sounds relaxing to you, an escorted tour is probably a good idea. If you yearn to have more freedom or to delve into a particular area of interest, check into an independent or special-interest tour.

When considering a tour, be sure to find out (1) exactly what expenses are included—particularly tips, taxes, side trips, meals, and entertainment; (2) the ratings of all hotels on the itinerary and the facilities they offer; (3) the cancellation policies for both you and the tour operator; (4) the number of travelers in your group; and (5) if you are traveling alone, the additional cost of single, instead of double, accommodations. Many tour operators request that packages be booked through a travel agent; there is generally no additional charge for doing so.

General-Interest Tours
Bixler Tours (P.O. Box 37, Hiram, OH 44234, tel. 216/569–3222 or 800/325–5087) offers four-night tours to New York City during the spring and fall, including Broadway shows and accommodations at the Waldorf-Astoria.
Gadabout Tours (700 E. Tahquitz Way, Palm Springs, CA 92262, tel. 619/325–5556) combines three nights in Manhattan, including dinner at Mamma Leone's and a Broadway musical, with a six-night cruise to Bermuda.
Talmage Tours (1223 Walnut St., Philadelphia, PA 19107, tel. 215/923–7100) has a variety of one- and two-day tours scheduled around popular Broadway shows.

Special-Interest Tours
Multi-Ethnic, Historic
The Lower East Side Tenement Museum (97 Orchard St., New York, NY 10002, tel. 212/431–0233) offers Sunday tours through old Jewish and Italian communities. Other tours trace the experiences of Jewish, Irish, Italian, Chinese and German immigrants.
Doorway to Design (1441 Broadway, Suite 338, New York, NY 10018, tel. 212/221–1111 or 718/339–1542) can arrange visits to unique private homes and loft spaces and private creative design firms, as well as neighborhood shopping and walking tours.

Music **Dailey-Thorp** (315 W. 57th St., New York, NY 10019, tel. 212/
307–1555) offers excellent programs, including the best of opera, ballet, and other performing arts, along with a walking
tour of the city.

Theater **Broadway Theatours, Inc.** (71 Broadway, New York, NY 10006,
tel. 212/425–6410 or 800/843–7469) and **Sutherland Travel Service, Inc.** (370 Lexington Ave., New York, NY 10017, tel. 212/
532–7732 or 800/221–2442) offer hotel/theater packages.

Seasonal **Maupintour** (Box 807, Lawrence, KS 66044, tel. 913/843–1211
or 800/255–4266) has special Thanksgiving and Christmas
tours.

Package Deals for Independent Travelers

Americantours International East (350 5th Ave., Suite 718,
New York, NY 10018, tel. 212/695–2841) offers two- and five-
night packages, including roundtrip airport transfers from
JFK, dinner at Windows on the World, and a half-day sightseeing tour of lower Manhattan. The five-night package also includes tickets to a Broadway show and admission to the Empire
State Building.
GoGo Tours (69 Spring St., Ramsey, NJ 07446, tel. 201/934–
3500 or 800/821–3731) gives you three days in New York City
with choice of hotel and sightseeing package.
Allied Tours (165 W. 46th St., New York, NY 10036, tel. 212/
869–5100) has three- and four-night packages that include a
half-day sightseeing tour.
SuperCities (1212 6th Ave., 9th fl., New York, NY 10036, tel.
212/921–5800 or 800/633–3000) offers a variety of packages
with a minimum two-night stay. Some include dinner; others
include both dinner and a show.
American Express (100 Church St., New York, NY 10007, tel.
800/241–1700) offers New York à la carte, with several options
for hotels, sightseeing, and shows.
Amtrak (tel. 800/USA–RAIL) offers rail/hotel packages as well
as an independent New York theater package.
Several major airlines also provide air/accommodations packages. Contact **American Fly AAway Vacations** (tel. 800/443–
7300); **Continental Grand Destinations** (tel. 713/821–2100 or
800/356–4080); **Delta Airlines** (tel. 404/765–2952 or 800/221–
6666); **United Vacations** (tel. 312/952–4000 or 800/328–6877).

Tips for British Travelers

Government Contact the **State of New York Division of Tourism** (25 Bedford
Tourist Office Sq., London WC1B 3HG, tel. 071/323–0648) for brochures and
tourist information.

Passports You will need a valid, 10-year passport (cost £15) to enter the
and Visas United States. You do not need a visa if you are staying for less
than 90 days and have a return ticket on a major airline. There
are some exceptions to this, so check with your travel agent or
with the **United States Embassy** (Visa and Immigration Department, 5 Upper Grosvenor St., London W1A 2JB, tel. 071/
499–3443). No vaccinations are needed for entry into the
United States.

Customs Entering the United States, you may bring 200 cigarettes, 50
cigars, or 3 pounds of tobacco; 1 U.S. quart of alcohol; duty-free
gifts up to a value of $100. Be careful not to take in meat or meat

products, seeds, plants, fruits, etc. Absolutely avoid illegal drugs.

Returning to the United Kingdom, you may take home, if you are 17 or older: (1) 200 cigarettes, 100 cigarillos, 50 cigars, or 250 grams of tobacco; (2) 2 liters of table wine and (a) 1 liter of alcohol over 22% by volume (most spirits), (b) 2 liters of alcohol under 22% by volume (fortified or sparkling wine), or (c) 2 more liters of table wine; (3) 50 grams of perfume and ¼ liter of toilet water; and (4) other goods up to a value of £32.

Insurance   We recommend that to cover health and motoring mishaps, you insure yourself with **Europ Assistance** (252 High St., Croydon, Surrey CR0 1NF, tel. 081/680–1234). It is also wise to take out insurance to cover lost luggage (if your current homeowners' policies don't cover such loss). Trip-cancellation insurance is also a good idea. **The Association of British Insurers** (Aldermary House, Queen St., London EC4, tel. 071/248–4477) will give you comprehensive advice on all aspects of holiday insurance.

Tour Operators   The on-again, off-again price battle over transatlantic fares has meant that most tour operators now offer excellent budget packages to the United States. Among those you might consider as you plan your trip are:

Albany Travel (Manchester) Ltd. (190 Deansgate, Manchester M3 3WD, tel. 061/833–0202).

American Airplan (Marlborough House, Churchfield Rd., Walton-on-Thames, Surrey KT12 2TJ, tel. 0932/246166).

Cosmosair plc (Tourama House, 17 Homesdale Rd., Bromley, Kent BR2 9LX, tel. 01/464–3400).

Jetsave (Sussex House, London Rd., East Grinstead, Sussex RH19 1LD, tel. 0342/312022).

Pan Am/Fly Drive (193 Piccadilly, London W1V 0AD, tel. 071/409–3377).

Speedbird (152 King St., London W6 0QU, tel. 01/741–8041).

Thomas Cook Ltd. (Box 36, Thorpe Wood, Peterborough PE3 6SB, tel. 0733/503202).

Airfares   Airlines flying to New York include **British Airways, TWA, Continental,** and **Virgin Atlantic.** At press time, a low-season return APEX fare was anywhere from £198 to £371.

Thomas Cook Ltd. can often book you on very inexpensive flights. Call the Cook branch nearest you and ask to be put through to the "Airfare Warehouse." Be sure to call at least 21 days in advance of when you want to travel.

Also check out the small ads in magazines such as *Time Out* and in the Sunday papers, where flights are offered for as low as £235 return.

When to Go

At one time, it seemed New York's cultural life was limited to the months between October and May, when new Broadway shows opened, museums mounted major exhibitions, and formal seasons for opera, ballet, and concerts held sway. Today, however, there are Broadway openings even in mid-July, and a number of touring orchestras and opera and ballet companies visit the city in summer. In late spring and summer, the streets and parks are filled with ethnic parades, impromptu sidewalk concerts, and performances under the stars. With the exception of regular closing days and a few holidays (such as Christmas, New Year's Day, and Thanksgiving), the city's museums are open year-round. The parks are always free, so in winter you can cross-country ski, in summer you can swim or sunbathe, and in summer and fall you can watch migrating birds make their semiannual New York visits.

Climate Although there's an occasional bone-chilling winter day, with winds blasting in off the Hudson, snow is hardly ever a problem in the city (the skyscrapers trap enough heat to melt most snowfalls). Summer is the only unpleasant time of year here, especially the humid, hot days of August, when many Manhattanites vacate the island for summer homes. Most hotels are air-conditioned, but if you're traveling in the summer and choosing budget accommodations, it's a good idea to ask whether your room has an air conditioner. Air-conditioned stores, restaurants, and museums provide respite from the heat; so do the many green expanses of parks. Subways and buses, however, do not always have functioning air-conditioning, and subway stations can be as hot as saunas (but considerably dirtier).

Because the metropolitan area's water needs are so enormous, occasional summer droughts may entail strict conservation, with the result that air-conditioning is cut back, grass goes unwatered, fountains stand dry, and restaurants serve water only upon request.

The following table shows each month's average temperatures for New York City—the daily highs and lows, expressed in both Fahrenheit and centigrade:

Jan.	41F	5C	May	70F	21C	Sept.	76F	24C
	29	−2		54	12		61	16
Feb.	43F	6C	June	81F	27C	Oct.	67F	19C
	29	−2		63	17		52	11
Mar.	47F	8C	July	85F	29C	Nov.	56F	13C
	34	1		70	21		43	6
Apr.	61F	16C	Aug.	83F	28C	Dec.	43F	6C
	45	7		68	20		31	−1

The city's weather is highly variable, however, so, shortly before your trip, check New York weather reports in your local newspaper. Updated hourly weather information for over 750 cities around the world—450 of them in the United States—can be obtained by phone from **WeatherTrak**. Dial 900/370–8725 to reach a computer, with which you can communicate by touch tone—at a cost of 75¢ for the first minute and 50¢ a minute thereafter. A taped message asks you to dial your destination's three-digit access code—either the area code, for U.S. destinations (212 for New York City), or the first three letters of the foreign city's name. For a list of all access codes, send a stamped, self-addressed envelope to Cities, Box 7000, Dallas, TX 75209. For further information, call 214/869–3035 or 800/247–3282.

Festivals and Seasonal Events

When it comes to special events, New York is indeed, as one bank's slogan puts it, "the city that never sleeps." Here is a list of some of the more important or unusual events projected to take place throughout the year; for more up-to-date information, pick up a copy of *New York* magazine, the *Village Voice*, or the Friday edition of *The New York Times* upon your arrival in the city; contact the New York Convention and Visitors Bureau (*see* Visitor Information, above); or contact the event sponsor noted at the end of some listings.

Dec. 31–Jan. 1: New Year's Eve is marked by the famous countdown in Times Square; expect throngs of somewhat unruly revelers waiting for the ball to drop. Fireworks and a midnight run are held in Central Park.

Jan.: Ice Capades makes its regular winter appearance at Madison Square Garden. Tel. 212/563–8300.

Jan. 3–13: The National Boat Show, at the Jacob K. Javits Convention Center, gives the public a look at all sorts of seagoing vessels and related equipment. Tel. 212/684–6622.

Jan.: The Winter Antiques Show, an exhibition of 17th- and 18th-century furniture, paintings, and statues, is held at the Seventh Regiment Armory, Park Avenue at 67th Street. Tel. 212/439–0300.

Late Jan.–Feb.: The Chinese New Year crackles with fireworks and energy as the Chinatown community prepares for and celebrates the lunar New Year.

Mid-Feb.: The Westminster Kennel Club Dog Show showcases top-of-the-line pooches at Madison Square Garden. Tel. 212/563–8300.

Feb.: The Millrose Games, an international track-and-field competition, is held at Madison Square Garden. Tel. 212/563–8300.

Late Mar.–Apr.: The New York City Opera begins its spring musical comedy season at the New York State Theater in Lincoln Center. Tel. 212/870–5570.

Early Mar.: The International Cat Show, at Madison Square Garden, displays favorite breeds along with varieties you've never heard of. Tel. 212/563–8300.

Mar.: Big East Basketball Championships at Madison Square Garden provide some exciting basketball action, with the Big East colleges usually in the national rankings. Tel. 212/563–8300.

Mar. 17: St. Patrick's Day Parade, a classic parade down Fifth Avenue, reflects the vitality of the Irish and Irish-American sector of the city's population.

Mar. 25: Greek Independence Day Parade breaks out along Fifth Avenue from 62nd to 79th streets.

Mid-Mar.–Apr.: Ringling Bros. Barnum & Bailey Circus brings its three-ring act to Madison Square Garden. Tel. 212/563–8300.

Apr.–June: The New York City Ballet (tel. 212/496–0600) and **American Ballet Theatre** (tel. 212/362–6000) launch the spring season with performances in Lincoln Center.

Apr.–Oct.: The major-league baseball season sees the Yankees play their home games at Yankee Stadium in the Bronx, while the Mets hold court at Shea Stadium, Queens.

Apr. 11–15: Artxpo NY at the Javits Convention Center. Tel. 212/216–2282.

Apr. 15: Easter Parade, with all its finery, is celebrated along Fifth Avenue from 49th to 59th streets. Tel. 212/397–8222.

Late Apr.: The Cherry Blossom Festival is in full bloom at the Brooklyn Botanic Garden. Tel. 718/622–4433.

May: Brooklyn Heights Promenade Art Show lines the Promenade with artists and their works, with the panorama of Manhattan across the river as a spectacular backdrop.

May: Ukrainian Festival, held on 7th Street between Second and Third avenues, is a refreshingly homespun event with what is probably the best food of any of the street fairs. Tel. 212/228-6840.

May: Martin Luther King, Jr., Parade marches down Fifth Avenue in memory of the civil rights leader.

May 18–19: The Ninth Avenue International Food Festival features food and merchandise from 32 countries. Tel. 212/581-7217.

Late May–early June: Washington Square Art Show is celebrated in Greenwich Village. Tel. 212/982-6255.

June: Metropolitan Opera performs free on weekday evenings in parks throughout the five boroughs.

June: Welcome Back to Brooklyn Day is a gala celebration along Eastern Parkway from Grand Army Plaza to Washington Avenue. Tel. 718/643-5102.

Early–mid-June: Feast of St. Anthony, a 10-day festival, spills over from Little Italy to SoHo. Tel. 212/777-2755.

Early June: Museum Mile Festival takes over Fifth Avenue from 82nd to 105th streets, with an evening of free or reduced admission to all 10 museums there.

Mid-June: Puerto Rican Day Parade proceeds down Fifth Avenue with floats, marching bands, and merrymakers. Tel. 212/665-1600.

Late June: Lesbian and Gay Pride Day Parade runs down Fifth Avenue to Washington Square.

Late June: JVC Jazz Festival features vintage stars and newcomers at venues all around town.

July 4: Independence Day is celebrated with fireworks and street fairs in various locations.

Early–mid-July: American Crafts Festival is held on weekends at Lincoln Center. Tel. 212/877-2011.

July–Aug.: Shakespeare in the Park presents two free productions at the Delacorte Theater in Central Park. Tel. 212/598-7100.

July–Aug.: Summergarden Concerts are performed free by Juilliard School students at the Museum of Modern Art. Tel. 212/708-9480.

July–Aug.: The New York Philharmonic chips in with free concerts in various city parks. Tel. 212/360-1333.

Mid-July–Aug.: Mostly Mozart Festival presents a distinguished series of classical concerts at Avery Fisher Hall in Lincoln Center. Tel. 212/874-2424.

Late July: The New York Track and Field Games bring an international roster of competitors to Wein Stadium, Columbia University. Tel. 212/860-4455.

July–Nov.: New York City Opera runs its second season at the New York State Theater in Lincoln Center. Tel. 212/870-5570.

Mid-Aug.: Harlem Week presents a series of workshops, street fairs, gospel festivals, and cultural events. Tel. 212/427-7200.

Late Aug.: Festival of the Americas brings Latin festivities to Sixth Avenue, otherwise known as Avenue of the Americas.

Late Aug.–Sept.: Lincoln Center Out-of-Doors hosts a variety of cultural events on the complex's plazas.

Late Aug.–early Sept.: U.S. Open Tennis Championships bring world-class excitement to the National Tennis Center in Flushing Meadows, Queens. Tel. 718/271-5100.

Late Aug.–early Sept.: Washington Square Art Fair makes its second yearly appearance.

Aug. 30–Sept. 2: Caribbean Festival brings a touch of carnival to Eastern Parkway in Brooklyn. Tel. 718/773–4052.

Mid-Sept.: New York Is Book Country transforms Fifth Avenue into a reader's paradise. Tel. 212/984–7616.

Mid-Sept.: Feast of San Gennaro, a popular, somewhat over-crowded 10-day extravaganza in Little Italy, features games, vendors, and fabulous food. Tel. 212/226–9546.

Sept. 21–Oct. 7: New York Film Festival features an eclectic mix of new and notable international films at Lincoln Center's Alice Tully Hall. Tel. 212/877–1800.

Sept.–Apr.: Metropolitan Opera (tel. 212/362–6000) and **New York Philharmonic** (tel. 212/874–2424) hold their seasons at Lincoln Center.

Early Oct.: Brooklyn Heights Promenade Art Show returns to the Promenade for an autumn exhibition.

Oct. 7: Pulaski Day Parade commemorates Polish hero Casimir Pulaski in a festive event up Fifth Avenue.

Oct. 8: Columbus Day Parade gives New York's Italian-Americans a chance to strut their stuff.

Oct.–Apr.: New York Rangers Hockey cuts the ice at Madison Square Garden. Tel. 212/563–8300.

Oct. 31: Halloween Parade, New York's most outrageous parade, is held in Greenwich Village.

Nov.–Apr.: New York Knicks Basketball should make for an interesting season at Madison Square Garden. Tel. 212/563–8300.

Nov. 3: New York City Marathon starts at the Verazzano Bridge in Staten Island and proceeds through all five boroughs. Tel. 212/860–4455.

Nov. 24: Macy's Thanksgiving Day Parade sends giant balloons and a sleigh-borne Santa from Central Park West at 77th Street to Broadway and 34th Street.

Mid-Nov.–Jan.: Christmas Spectacular, a musical performance featuring the high-kicking Rockettes, hits the Radio City Music Hall stage. Tel. 212/757–3100.

Late Nov.–early Jan.: Lord & Taylor and **Saks Fifth Avenue** present animated window displays.

Dec.–early Jan.: The New York City Ballet's *Nutcracker* performances are a seasonal fixture at Lincoln Center. Tel. 212/870–5570.

What to Pack

New York City has many restaurants that require men to wear jackets and ties. For sightseeing and casual dining, jeans and sneakers are acceptable just about anywhere in the city. Sneakers seem to be the universal walking shoe; you'll even see businesspeople in button-down office attire lacing them on for the sprint from one appointment to another.

An extra pair of glasses, contact lenses, or prescription sunglasses is always a good idea; it is important to pack any prescription medicines you use regularly, as well as any allergy medication you may need.

Pack light, because porters and luggage trolleys can be hard to find at New York airports.

Carry-on Luggage Passengers on U.S. airlines are limited to two carry-on bags. For a bag you wish to store under the seat, the maximum dimensions are 9″ × 14″ × 22″. For bags that can be hung in a closet or on a luggage rack, the maximum dimensions are 4″ × 23″ × 45″. For bags you wish to store in an overhead bin, the maximum dimensions are 10″ × 14″ × 36″. An airline can adapt the rules to circumstances, so on a crowded flight you may be allowed only one carry-on bag. In addition to carryons, you may bring aboard a handbag (pocketbook or purse); an overcoat or wrap; an umbrella; a camera; a reasonable amount of reading material; an infant bag; and crutches, a cane, braces, or other prosthetic device. Infant/child safety seats can also be brought aboard if parents have purchased a ticket for the child, or if there is space in the cabin.

Foreign airlines generally allow only one piece of carry-on luggage in tourist class, in addition to handbags and bags filled with duty-free goods. Passengers in first and business class are allowed to carry on one garment bag as well. Call your airline to find out its current policy.

Checked Luggage Luggage allowances vary slightly from airline to airline. Many carriers allow three checked pieces, but some allow only two, so check before you go. In all cases, check-in luggage cannot weigh more than 70 pounds per piece or be larger than 62 inches (length + width + height).

What It Will Cost

There's no doubt that New York is an expensive city to visit. Hotel rooms with views of Central Park can easily run as high as $250 a night; dinner for two at a *moderate* restaurant, plus orchestra seats at a Broadway show, can set you back $150 (*see* Chapters 8, 9, and 10). But the Big Apple is still cheaper to visit than many other world capitals. The Union Bank of Switzerland, in a recent survey of 52 major cities, placed New York 10th—behind such places as Tokyo, London, Milan, Paris, and Copenhagen. The survey estimated New York's per diem rate at $344.03, which covered a double hotel room, dinner with wine for two, short-distance car rental or public transportation, and miscellaneous expenses such as color film and phone calls. While these estimates may daunt the cost-conscious traveler, there's no cause for despair. New Yorkers themselves know how to find bargains; they comb discount clothing outlets, grab food at corner delis, walk just about everywhere, and attend free concerts and plays in the parks. You, too, can moderate the cost of your visit if you do as they do (*see* Manhattan for Free in Chapter 3 and Discount Tickets in Chapter 10).

The city's sales tax is 8 ¼%; hotel taxes add up to 13 ¼% plus a $2 occupancy tax. The customary tipping rate is 15%–20% for taxi drivers and waiters (*see* Chapter 8 for further tipping advice), and bellhops are usually given $2 in luxury hotels, $1 elsewhere. Hotel maids should be tipped around $1 per day of your stay.

Cash Machines

Virtually all U.S. banks now belong to a network of Automatic Teller Machines (ATMs) that dispense cash 24 hours a day. There are eight major networks in the United States, the largest of which are Cirrus, owned by MasterCard, and Plus, affiliated with Visa. Some banks belong to more than one network. Each network has a toll-free number you can call to locate its machines in a given city: the Cirrus number is 800/424–7787; the Plus number is 800/843–7587. Note that "cash cards" are not issued automatically—they must be requested at your local bank.

Cards issued by Visa, American Express, and MasterCard can also be used in the ATMs, but the transaction fees are usually higher than those on bank cards (and there is a daily interest charge on the "loan"). All three companies issue directories of national and international outlets that accept their cards. You can pick up a Visa or MasterCard directory at your local bank; for an American Express directory, call 800/CASH–NOW (this number can also be used for general inquiries). Contact your bank for information on fees and the amount of cash you can withdraw on any given day. Although each bank levies a charge when you withdraw money with a charge or credit card, using your American Express, Visa, or MasterCard at an ATM can be cheaper than exchanging money in a bank because of variations in exchange rates.

Traveling with Film

If your camera is new, shoot and develop a few rolls of film before leaving home. Pack some lens tissue and an extra battery for your built-in light meter. Invest about $10 in a skylight filter and screw it onto the front of your lens; it will protect the lens and reduce haze.

Film doesn't like hot weather. If you're driving in summer, don't store film in the glove compartment or on the shelf under the rear window. Put it behind the front seat on the floor, on the side opposite the exhaust pipe.

On a plane trip, never pack unprocessed film in check-in luggage; if your bags are X-rayed, you can say good-bye to your pictures. Always carry undeveloped film with you through security and ask to have it inspected by hand. (It helps to isolate your film in a plastic bag, ready for quick inspection.) Inspectors at American airports are required by law to honor requests for hand inspection; abroad, you'll have to depend on the kindness of strangers.

The machines used in U.S. airports are safe for scanning film anywhere from five to 500 times, depending on the speed of the film. After five scans, however, you may be asking for trouble. If your film gets fogged and you want an explanation, send it to the National Association of Photographic Manufacturers (550 Mamaroneck Ave., Harrison, NY 10528), which will try to determine what went wrong, at no charge.

Traveling with Children

There are many free and exciting activities for children in the Big Apple (*see* What to See and Do with Children in Manhattan in Chapter 3, What to See and Do with Children in the Other Boroughs in Chapter 4, Toys in Chapter 7, and The Arts for Kids in Chapter 10). Several local publications, including the *Village Voice*, *New York* magazine, and the Friday edition of the *New York Times*, offer up-to-date calendars of happenings for children, as does **New York Family**, a magazine published eight times a year by New York Family Publications (420 E. 79th St., Suite 9E, New York, NY 10021, tel. 212/744–0309).

Another good source of information is the weekly *Big Apple Parents' Paper* published by Buffalo-Bunyip Inc. (67 Wall St., Suite 2411, New York, NY 10005, tel. 212/533–2277).

Publications *Family Travel Times,* a newsletter published 10 times a year, also offers ideas for having fun with children, though not all data is specific to the New York City area. (To order the newsletter, contact Travel with Your Children, 80 8th Ave., New York, NY 10011, tel. 212/206–0688.) A $35 yearly subscription includes access to back issues and twice-weekly opportunities to call in for specific information. Send $1 for a sample issue.

Great Vacations with Your Kids, by Dorothy Jordon and Marjorie Cohen, offers complete advice on planning a trip with children (from toddlers to teens), with a special section on New York City vacations ($12.95 paperback, E.P. Dutton, 2 Park Ave., New York, NY 10016, tel. 212/725–1818).

Kids and Teens in Flight is a U.S. Department of Transportation brochure about children flying alone. To order a free copy, call 202/366–2220.

Home Exchange Exchanging homes is a low-cost way to enjoy a vacation in another part of the country. **Vacation Exchange Club, Inc.** (12006 111th Ave., Unit 12, Youngstown, AZ 85363, tel. 602/972–2186) specializes in domestic home exchanges. The club publishes one directory in February and a supplement in April which together cost $16. Membership is $24.70 per year, for which you receive one listing. **Loan-a-Home** (2 Park Ln., Mount Vernon, NY 10552) is popular with the academic community on sabbatical and businesspeople on temporary assignment. There's no annual membership fee or charge for listing your home, however the directory and supplement cost $30.

Getting There On domestic flights, children under two not occupying a seat travel free. Various discounts apply to children two to 12 years of age. If you want to be sure your infant is secure and traveling in his or her own safety seat, you must buy baby a separate ticket and bring your own infant car seat. (Check with the airline in advance; certain seats aren't allowed.) Some airlines allow babies to travel in their own car seats at no charge if there's a spare seat available, otherwise safety seats will be stored and the child will have to be held by a parent. If you opt to hold your baby on your lap, do so with the infant outside the seatbelt so he or she won't be crushed in case of a sudden stop. For the booklet *Child/Infant Safety Seats Acceptable for Use in Aircraft,* write to the **Federal Aviation Administration,** APA–200, 800 Independence Ave. SW, Washington, DC 20591, tel. 202/267–3479.

Also inquire about special children's meals or snacks. See the February 1990 and 1992 issues of *Family Travel Times* for "TWYCH's Airline Guide," which contains a rundown of the children's services offered by 46 airlines.

Baby-sitting Services You can usually make child-care arrangements through your hotel's concierge or housekeeper. New York City agencies include **Babysitter's Guild** (60 E. 42nd St., Suite 912, New York, NY 10017, tel. 212/682–0227), with a multilingual staff that can take your children on sightseeing tours; **Gilbert Child Care Agency** (119 W. 57th St., Suite 912, New York, NY 10019, tel. 212/757–7900); and the **Avalon Registry** (250 W. 57th St., Suite 723, New York, NY 10107, tel. 212/245–0250).

Around Town Children under age 6 travel free on subways and buses; children age 6 and older must pay full fare. Clean rest rooms are often difficult to find; your best bet is to use the washrooms at museums, department stores, hotels, and restaurants while you are there.

If you find you need a stroller once you get here, ask your hotel concierge to find one for you, or contact **AAA-U-Rent** (861 Eagle Ave., Bronx, NY 10456, tel. 212/923–0300 or 212/665–6633).

Hints for Disabled Travelers

Many buildings in New York City are now wheelchair-accessible. The subway is still hard to navigate, however; people in wheelchairs do better on public buses, most of which "kneel" to facilitate getting on and off. For brochures and further information, contact the **Mayor's Office for the Handicapped** (52 Chambers St., Office 206, New York, NY 10007, tel. 212/566–3913).

The Information Center for Individuals with Disabilities (Fort Point Pl., 1st floor, 27–43 Wormwood St., Boston, MA 02210, tel. 617/727–5540) offers useful problem-solving assistance, including lists of travel agents who specialize in tours for the disabled.

Moss Rehabilitation Hospital Travel Information Service (12th St. and Tabor Rd., Philadelphia, PA 19141, tel. 215/329–5715) provides information on tourist sights, transportation, and accommodations in destinations around the world for a small fee.

Travel Industry and Disabled Exchange (TIDE, 5435 Donna Ave., Tarzana, CA 91356, tel. 818/368–5648), for a $15 per person annual membership fee, provides a quarterly newsletter and information on travel agencies and tours.

Mobility International (Box 3551, Eugene, OR 97403, tel. 503/343–1284) is an internationally affiliated organization with 500 members. For a $20 annual fee, it coordinates exchange programs for disabled people around the world and offers information on accommodations and organized study programs.

The Society for the Advancement of Travel for the Handicapped (26 Court St., Penthouse Suite, Brooklyn, NY 11242, tel. 718/858–5483) offers access information. Annual membership costs $40; $25 for senior travelers and students. Send $2 and a stamped, self-addressed envelope for a list of tour operators who arrange travel for the disabled.

Greyhound/Trailways (tel. 800/531–5332) will carry a disabled person and companion for the price of a single fare. **Amtrak** (tel. 800/USA–RAIL) requests 72 hours' notice to provide redcap service, special seats, or wheelchair assistance at stations that are equipped to provide these services. All handicapped passengers are entitled to a 25% discount on regular, discounted coach fares. A special children's handicapped fare is also available, offering qualifying kids ages 2–11 a 25% discount on already discounted children's fares. There are exceptions to these discounts on certain prescribed days with various routes; always check with Amtrak first. For a free copy of *Access Amtrak*, a guide to its services for elderly and handicapped travelers, write to Amtrak (National Railroad Corp., 400 N. Capitol St. NW, Washington, DC 20001).

Publications The New York Division of Tourism (1 Commerce Plaza, Albany, NY 12245, tel. 518/474–411 or 800/225–5697) offers the *I Love New York Travel and Adventure Guide,* which includes ratings of various facilities' accessibility. The New York State Parks Department (State Parks, Albany, NY 12238, tel. 518/474–0456) provides information on handicapped facilities in the *Guide to New York State Parks, Historic Sites and Programs.*

The Itinerary (Box 2012, Bayonne, NJ 07002, tel. 201/858–3400) is a bimonthly travel magazine for the disabled. Call for a subscription ($10 for one year, $18 for two); it's not available in stores.

Travel for the Disabled, by Helen Hecker, is a handbook of travel resources that includes advice on all modes of transportation and lists more than 500 access guides for specific destinations around the world ($9.95). *Wheelchair Vagabond,* by John G. Nelson, contains valuable information for independent travelers planning extended trips in a car, van, or camper ($9.95 paperback, $14.95 hardcover). *The Directory of Travel Agencies for the Disabled,* by Helen Hecker, can lead you to agencies both at home and at your destination that will provide information on resources for travelers with special needs ($12.95). These publications are available through your local bookstore or directly from the publisher (Twin Peaks Press, Box 129, Vancouver, WA 98666, tel. 800/637–2256). Add $2 shipping for one book; $1 each additional book.

Access to the World: A Travel Guide for the Handicapped, by Louise Weiss, provides general information on transportation, hotels, travel agents, tour operators, and travel organizations. It is available at your local bookstore or from Henry Holt & Co. for $12.95 plus $2 shipping (tel. 800/247–3912; the order number is 0805 001417).

Hints for Older Travelers

The **American Association of Retired Persons** (AARP, 1909 K St. NW, Washington, DC 20049, tel. 202/872–4700) has two programs for independent travelers: (1) the Purchase Privilege Program, which offers discounts on hotels, airfare, car rentals, and sightseeing; and (2) the AARP Motoring Plan, which furnishes emergency aid (road service) and trip-routing information for an annual fee of $33.95 per person or married couple. The AARP Travel Service (4801 W. 110th St., Overland Park, KS 66211, tel. 800/365–5358) arranges group tours and cruises at reduced rates. AARP members must be at least 50 years old. Annual dues are $5 per person or per couple.

If you're planning to use an AARP or other senior-citizen identification card to obtain a reduced hotel rate, mention it at the time you make your reservation rather than when you check out. At restaurants, show your card to the maître d' before you're seated; discounts may be limited to certain menus, days, or hours. Your AARP card will identify you as a retired person but will not ensure a discount in all hotels and restaurants. For a free list of hotels and restaurants that offer discounts, call or write the AARP and ask for the "Purchase Privilege" brochure, or call the AARP Travel Service. When renting a car, remember that economy cars, priced at promotional rates, may cost less than the cars that are available with your ID card.

National Council of Senior Citizens (925 15th St. NW, Washington, DC 20005, tel. 202/347–8800) is a nonprofit advocacy group with some 5,000 local clubs across the country. Annual membership is $12 per person or per couple. Members receive a monthly newspaper with travel information and an ID for reduced rates on hotels and car rentals.

Mature Outlook (6001 N. Clark St., Chicago, IL 60660, tel. 800/336–6330), a subsidiary of Sears, Roebuck & Co., is a travel club for people over 50 years of age, offering discounts at Holiday Inns and a bimonthly newsletter. Annual membership is $9.95 per person or couple. Instant membership is available at participating Holiday Inns.

Elderhostel (80 Boylston St., Suite 400, Boston, MA 02116, tel. 617/426–7788) is an innovative educational program for people 60 or over (only one member of a traveling couple has to qualify). Participants live in dormitories on some 1,200 campuses around the world. Mornings are devoted to lectures and seminars; afternoons to sightseeing and field trips. The fee for a trip includes room, board, tuition (in the United States and Canada), and round-trip transportation (overseas). Special scholarships are available for those who qualify financially in the United States and Canada.

Saga International Holidays (120 Boylston St., Boston, MA 02116, tel. 800/343–0273) specializes in group travel for people over 60. A selection of variously priced tours allows you to choose the package that meets your needs.

September Days Club (tel. 800/241–5050) is run by the moderately priced Days Inns of America. The $12 annual membership fee for individuals or couples over 50 entitles them to reduced car rental rates and to reductions of 15%–50% at 95% of the chain's more than 350 motels.

The **Golden Age Passport** is a free lifetime pass to all parks, monuments, and recreation areas run by the federal government. Permanent U.S. residents over 62 may pick them up in person at any of the national parks that charge admission. The passport covers the entrance fee for the holder and anyone accompanying the holder in the same private (noncommercial) vehicle. It also provides a 50% discount on camping, boat launching, and parking (lodging is not included). Proof of age is necessary.

Greyhound/Trailways (tel. 800/531–5332) offers special fares for senior citizens, subject to date and destination restrictions. **Amtrak** (tel. 800/USA–RAIL) requests 72 hours' notice to provide redcap service, special seats, or wheelchair assistance at stations that are equipped to provide these services. Elderly passengers are entitled to a 25% discount on regular, non-discounted coach fares. It should be noted that there are exceptions to these discounts on certain prescribed days with various routes; always check with Amtrak first. For a free copy of *Access Amtrak*, a guide to its services for elderly and handicapped travelers, write to Amtrak (National Railroad Passenger Corp., 400 N. Capitol St. NW, Washington, DC 20001).

Publications *The International Health Guide for Senior Citizen Travelers,* by Dr. W. Robert Lange, MD, and *The Senior Citizens Guide to Budget Travel in the United States and Canada,* by Paige Palmer, are available for $4.95 and $3.94, respectively, plus $1 for shipping, from Pilot Books (103 Cooper St., Babylon, NY 11702, tel. 516/422–2225).

The Discount Guide for Travelers Over 55, by Caroline and Walter Weintz, lists helpful addresses, package tours, reduced-rate car rentals, etc., in the United States and abroad. To order, send $7.95 plus $1.50 shipping and handling to NAL/Cash Sales (Bergenfield Order Dept., 120 Woodbine St., Bergenfield, NJ 07621, tel. 800/526–0275).

Further Reading

Many a famous writer has set down his or her impressions of this fascinating city. Some of the best full-length accounts are *Christopher Morley's New York*, a mid-1920s essay recently republished; *Cecil Beaton's New York*, a 1938 volume with photographs; *New York Proclaimed* by V. S. Pritchett, also lavishly illustrated; *Brendan Behan's New York*, a highly personal memoir written in 1964; *Walker in the City* by Alfred Kazin; and *Apple of My Eye*, a 1978 account of writing a New York guidebook, by Helene Hanff. Perhaps the best of all is E. B. White's 1949 essay *Here's New York*, recently reissued.

The early history of New York is wittily told in the classic *Knickerbocker's History of New York*, by Washington Irving. For a fine historical introduction to the city, find the heavily illustrated *Columbia Historical Portrait of New York*, by John Kouwenhoven. *You Must Remember This*, by Jeff Kisseloff, is an oral history of ordinary New Yorkers early in this century.

Imperial City by Geoffrey Moorhouse is an insightful, no-holds-barred recent portrait. *The Power Broker* by Robert Caro is a fascinating biography of Robert Moses, one of the city's most influential parks commissioners. Robert Daley's *Prince of the City* is a true-life drama of New York police corruption. Highly critical accounts of the city's recent politics can be found in *The Streets Were Paved with Gold*, by Ken Auletta, and *The Rise and Fall of New York City*, by Roger Starr.

Theater lovers may want to read *Act One*, the autobiography of playwright Moss Hart. *The Kingdom and the Power* by Gay Talese offers a behind-the-scenes look at *The New York Times;* life at one of the city's most venerable magazines is recounted in *Here at the New Yorker* by Brendan Gill.

The Architecture of New York City by Don Martin Reynolds is a good introduction to the city's many building styles; Paul Goldberger's *The City Observed* describes Manhattan building by building. *City: Rediscovering the Center* by William H. Whyte illuminates urban street life and the use of public space, principally in New York. John Kieran's *A Natural History of New York* explores the wildlife of the city's parks.

Perhaps because so many writers have lived in New York City, there is a wealth of fiction set here. Jack Finney's *Time and Again* is a delightful time-travel story illustrated with 19th-century photos; *Winter's Tale* by Mark Helprin uses surreal fantasy to create a portrait of New York's past. Authentic 19th-century novels of New York include Henry James's *Washington Square*, Edith Wharton's *The Age of Innocence*, and Stephen Crane's *Maggie, A Girl of the Streets*. O. Henry's short stories depict the early years of this century, while Damon Runyon's are set in the raffish underworld of the 1930s and 1940s. F.

Scott Fitzgerald (*The Beautiful and the Damned*, 1922),
John Dos Passos (*Manhattan Transfer*, 1925), John O'Hara
(*Butterfield 8*, 1935), and Mary McCarthy (*The Group*, 1938)
also wrote about this city. J. D. Salinger's *Catcher in the Rye*
(1951) partly takes place here, as does Thomas Pynchon's *V*
(1965). Truman Capote's 1958 novella *Breakfast at Tiffany's* is
a special favorite of many New Yorkers.

More current New York novels include *Bonfire of the Vanities*
by Tom Wolfe, *I'll Take Manhattan* by Judith Krantz, and *People Like Us* by Dominick Dunne. For portraits of gay life, try
Larry Kramer's *Faggots*, David Leavitt's *The Lost Language of
Cranes*, or Sarah Schulman's *After Delores*. The downtown
scene is depicted in Tama Janowitz's *Slaves of New York* and
Jay McInerny's *Bright Lights, Big City*.

The black experience in Harlem has been chronicled in Ralph
Ellison's *Invisible Man*, James Baldwin's *Go Tell It On the
Mountain*, and Claude Brown's *Manchild in the Promised
Land*. For a portrait of Harlem during the 1920s, there's *When
Harlem Was In Vogue* by David Levering Lewis. The history of
New York's Jewish population can be traced through such
books as *World of Our Fathers* by Irving Howe, *Call It Sleep* by
Henry Roth, *The Promise* by Chaim Potok, *Enemies, A Love
Story* by Isaac Bashevis Singer, and *Our Crowd* by Stephen
Birmingham.

Francine Prose's *Household Saints* is a fictional portrait of life
in Little Italy; *The New Chinatown* by Peter Kwong is a recent
study of the community across Canal Street. Kate Simon's
memoir *Bronx Primitive*, Laura Cunningham's autobiographical *Sleeping Arrangements*, and E. L. Doctorow's novel
World's Fair are set in the Bronx. Betty Smith's touching prewar novel *A Tree Grows in Brooklyn* is counterbalanced by the
searing 1960s portrait of Hubert Selby Jr.'s *Last Exit to Brooklyn*. Bernard Malamud's *The Assistant* is another portrait of
Brooklyn neighborhoods.

Mysteries set in New York City range from Dashiell
Hammett's urbane 1933 novel *The Thin Man*, to Rex Stout's series of Nero Wolfe mysteries, to more recent picks: *While My
Pretty One Sleeps* (Mary Higgins Clark), *Sixth Precinct* (Christopher Newman), and *Saturday Night Dead* (Richard Rosen).

To get children psyched up for a New York trip, give them
Eloise by Kay Thompson, *Harriet the Spy* by Louise Fitzhugh,
or *Stuart Little* by E. B. White.

Arriving and Departing

By Plane

Airports Virtually every major U.S. and foreign airline serves one or
more of New York's three airports: **LaGuardia Airport** and **John
F. Kennedy International Airport,** both in the borough of
Queens, and **Newark International Airport** in New Jersey.

Airlines Carriers serving the New York area include America West
(tel. 800/247–5692); American (tel. 800/433–7300); Braniff
(tel. 800/BRANIFF); Continental (tel. 800/525–0280); Delta (tel. 800/221–1212); Midway (tel. 800/621–5700); Northwest (tel. 800/ 225–2525); Pan Am (tel. 800/442–5896); TWA

(tel. 800/221–2000); United (tel. 800/241–6522); and USAir (tel. 800/428–4322).

When choosing a flight, be sure to distinguish among (a) *non-stop flights*—no stops or changes of aircraft; (b) *direct flights*—one or more stops but no change of aircraft; and (c) *connecting flights*—at least one change of aircraft and possibly several stops as well.

Smoking As of late-February 1990, smoking is banned on all scheduled routes within the 48 contiguous states; within the states of Hawaii and Alaska; to and from the U.S. Virgin Islands and Puerto Rico; and on flights of under six hours to and from Hawaii and Alaska. The rule applies to the domestic legs of all foreign routes but does not affect international flights.

On a flight where smoking is permitted, you can request a nonsmoking seat during check-in or when you book your ticket. If the airline tells you there are no seats available in the nonsmoking section, insist on one: Department of Transportation regulations require U.S. carriers to find seats for all non-smokers, provided they meet check-in time restrictions.

Lost Luggage Luggage loss is usually covered in comprehensive travel insurance packages that include personal accident, trip cancellation, and sometimes default and bankruptcy protection. Several companies offer comprehensive policies:

Access America, Inc., a subsidiary of Blue Cross-Blue Shield (600 3rd Ave., Box 807, New York, NY 10163, tel. 212/490–5345 or 800/284–8300).

Near Services (450 Prairie Ave., Suite 101, Calumet City, IL 60409, tel. 708/868–6700 or 800/654–6700).

Travel Guard International, underwritten by Transamerica Occidental Life Companies (1100 Centerpoint Dr., Stevens Point, WI 54481, tel. 715/345–0505 or 800/782–5151).

Carefree Travel Insurance (Box 310, 120 Mineola Blvd., Mineola, NY 11501, tel. 516/294–0220 or 800/343–3553).

Luggage Insurance Airlines are responsible for lost or damaged property only up to $1,250 per passenger on domestic flights, or $9.07 per pound ($20 per kilo) for checked baggage and $400 per passenger for unchecked baggage on international flights. If you're carrying valuables, either take them with you on the airplane or purchase additional insurance for lost luggage. Some airlines will issue additional insurance when you check in, but many do not. Rates are $1 for every $100 valuation, with a maximum of $25,000 valuation per passenger; carry-on luggage is not covered.

Insurance for lost, damaged, or stolen luggage is available through travel agents or directly through various insurance companies. Two companies that issue luggage insurance are:

Tele-Trip (3201 Farnam St., Omaha, NE 68131, tel. 800/228–9792), a subsidiary of Mutual of Omaha, which operates sales booths at airports and also issues policies through travel agents. It will insure checked luggage for up to 180 days and for a $500–$3,000 valuation. For one to three days, the rate for a $500 valuation is $8.25; for 180 days, $100.

The Travelers Insurance Co. (Ticket and Travel Dept., 1 Tower Sq., Hartford, CT 06183, tel. 203/277–0111 or 800/243–3174) insures checked or carry-on luggage for a $500–$2,000 valuation per person; also for a maximum of 180 days. Rates for up to five days for a $500 valuation are $10; for 180 days, $85. Both companies offer the same rates on domestic and international flights. Check the travel pages of your local newspaper for the names of other companies that insure luggage.

Before you go, itemize the contents of each bag in case you need to file an insurance claim. Be certain to put your home address on each piece of luggage, including carry-on bags. If your luggage is stolen and later recovered, the airline must deliver the luggage to your home free of charge.

Between the Airports and Manhattan
LaGuardia Airport

Taxis cost $12–$18 plus tolls (up to $2.50) and take 20–40 minutes. Group taxi rides to Manhattan are available at taxi dispatch lines just outside the baggage-claim areas during most travel hours (except on Saturdays and holidays). Group fares range from $7–$9 per person (plus a share of tolls) depending on your destination. Call 718/784–4343 for more information.

Carey Airport Express buses (tel. 718/632–0500) depart for Manhattan every 20–30 minutes from 6:45 AM to midnight. It's a 20- to 30-minute ride to 42nd Street and Park Avenue, directly opposite Grand Central Terminal. A shuttle bus runs from there to the New York Hilton, Sheraton City Squire, and Marriott Marquis hotels. Other midtown hotels are a short cab ride away. The bus fare is $7.50; pay the driver. **The Gray Line Air Shuttle Minibus** (tel. 212/581–3929) serves major Manhattan hotels directly to and from the airport. The fare is $10 per person; make arrangements at the airport's ground transportation center or use the courtesy phone.

The most economical way to reach Manhattan is to ride the Q-33 bus (there are no luggage facilities on this bus) to either the Roosevelt Avenue–Jackson Heights station, where you can catch the E or F subway, or the 74th Street–Broadway station (it's the same station), where you can catch the No. 7 subway. Allow 90 minutes for the entire trip to midtown; the total cost is two tokens ($2.30 at press time). You can use change for your bus fare but will have to purchase a token to enter the subway.

JFK International Airport

Taxis cost $24–$30 plus tolls (up to $2.50) and take 35–60 minutes.

Carey Airport Express buses (tel. 718/632–0500) depart for Manhattan every 20–30 minutes, from 6 AM to midnight, from all JFK terminals. The ride to 42nd Street and Park Avenue (Grand Central Terminal) takes about one hour. A shuttle bus runs from there to the New York Hilton, Sheraton City Squire, and Marriott Marquis hotels; it's a short cab ride to other midtown hotels. The bus fare is $9.50; pay the driver. **The Gray Line Air Shuttle Minibus** (tel. 212/581–3929) serves major Manhattan hotels directly from the airport; the cost is $13 per person. Make arrangements at the airport's ground transportation counter or use the courtesy phone.

New York Helicopter (tel. 800/645–3494) offers daily flights between the airport and the JFK Heliport at East 34th Street and First Avenue. Planes leave every half hour for the 10-minute flight between 1:30 PM and 7:30 PM. The one-way fare is $61 per person; reservations are recommended.

The **JFK Express** is a special subway service from the Howard Beach station near JFK airport to Brooklyn and Manhattan.

The train stops at the Chambers Street and Broadway–Nassau Street stations in downtown Brooklyn, and in Manhattan along Sixth Avenue at West 4th Street, 34th Street, 42nd Street, Rockefeller Center, and 57th Street. Shuttle buses from JFK terminals to the Howard Beach station depart every 20 minutes from 6:06 AM to 12:56 AM. The ride to the 57th Street terminus takes 50 minutes. Trains have luggage space and plenty of transit police. The fare is $6.50, including a connection to the entire subway system; pay on the train. (To reach JFK, you use a token to enter the subway and pay the remainder on board the train.)

The cheapest but slowest route to Manhattan is to take the Q-10 bus (there are no luggage facilities on this bus) to the Union Turnpike–Kew Gardens station, where you can catch the E or F subway, or to the Lefferts Boulevard station, where you can catch the A subway. Allow at least two hours for the trip; the total cost is two tokens ($2.30 at press time). You can use change for your fare on the bus, but you will need to purchase a token to enter the subway.

Newark Airport **Taxis** cost $28–$30 plus tolls ($3) and take 20–45 minutes. "Share and Save" group rates are available for up to four passengers between 8 AM and midnight; make arrangements with the airport's taxi dispatcher.

NJ Transit Airport Express buses (tel. 201/460–8444) depart every 15–30 minutes for the Port Authority Bus Terminal, at Eighth Avenue and 42nd Street. From there it's a short cab ride to midtown hotels. The ride takes 30–45 minutes. The fare is $7; buy your ticket inside the airport terminal.

Olympia Airport Express buses (tel. 212/964–6233) leave for Grand Central Terminal and 1 World Trade Center (next to the Vista hotel) about every 15 minutes from 6 AM to midnight. The trip takes 35 minutes to Grand Central, 20 minutes to WTC. The fare is $7.

Newark Airport/NYC Minibus departs for major Manhattan hotels approximately every 30 minutes; schedules vary according to passenger demand. The fare is $15; make arrangements at the ground transportation counter in Newark terminal.

Passengers arriving in Newark can also take New Jersey Transit's **Airlink buses,** leaving every 20 minutes from 6:15 AM to 2 AM, to Penn Station in the city of Newark. The ride takes about 25 minutes; the fare is $4. From there they can catch **PATH Trains** (tel. 212/466–7649), which run to Manhattan 24 hours a day. The trains run every 10 minutes on weekdays, every 15–30 minutes on weeknights, every 20–30 minutes on weekends, and stop at the World Trade Center and at five stops along Sixth Avenue—Christopher Street, 9th Street, 14th Street, 23rd Street, and 33rd Street. The fare is $1.

By Limousine Car services must be licensed by the New York City Taxi and Limousine Commission and can pick up riders only by prior arrangement. It is recommended that passengers call at least 24 hours in advance for reservations. The following companies are among those that serve all three metropolitan airports:

A-Marquis Limousine Service (tel. 212/466–6332); **Airway Express Limousine and Car Service** (tel. 800/528–8989); **All State Car and Limo** (tel. 212/ 741–7440); **Carey Limousines** (tel. 212/ 599–1122); **Carmel Car and Limousine Service** (tel. 212/662–

2222); **Eastside Limo Service** (tel. 212/744–9700); **Exec-U-Ride Ltd.** (tel. 212/279–1710); **La Limousine** (tel. 212/736–0484); **London Towncars** (tel. 212/988–9700); **New York Continental Limousine Inc.** (tel. 212/617–0212); **Silver Bay Limousine Service** (tel. 212/838–2707); **Wall Chauffeured Limousine Service** (tel. 212/695–7266); **Wheels of New York** (tel. 212/465–1630).

Airline Ticket Offices Many airlines have ticket offices in convenient midtown and lower-Manhattan locations. American, Continental, Delta, Eastern, Pan Am, TWA, United, and USAir, for example, all have offices at the **Airlines Building** (100 E. 42nd St.). Offices are generally open weekdays 8–7 and weekends 9–5, but hours vary among carriers.

Ticket offices are also clustered in three other Manhattan locations: the New York Hilton Hotel at 1335 Sixth Avenue (American, Continental, Delta, Eastern, and TWA); the Waldorf-Astoria Hotel at 301 Park Avenue (American, Continental, Eastern, and TWA); and 1 World Trade Center (American, British Airways, Continental, Delta, Eastern, Lufthansa, Pan Am, Swissair, TWA, United, and USAir). Many foreign carriers have ticket offices along Fifth Avenue north of 50th Street.

By Car

The **Lincoln Tunnel** (I–495), **Holland Tunnel,** and **George Washington Bridge** (I–95) connect Manhattan with the New Jersey Turnpike system and points west. The Lincoln Tunnel comes into midtown Manhattan; the Holland Tunnel into lower Manhattan; and the George Washington Bridge into northern Manhattan. Each of the three arteries requires a toll ($3 for cars) eastbound into New York, but no toll westbound.

From Long Island, the **Midtown Tunnel** (I–495) and **Triborough Bridge** (I–278) are the most direct links to Manhattan. Both require tolls ($2.50 for cars) in both directions.

From upstate New York, the city is accessible via the **New York (Dewey) Thruway** (I–87) (toll) to the **Major Deegan Expressway** (I–87) through the Bronx and across the **Triborough Bridge** (toll), or via the **Taconic State Parkway** to the **Saw Mill River Parkway** into upper Manhattan.

From New England, the **Connecticut Turnpike** (I–95) connects with the **New England Thruway** (I–95) (toll) and then the **Bruckner Expressway** (I–278). Take the Bruckner to the **Triborough Bridge** (toll) or to the **Cross Bronx Expressway,** which enters upper Manhattan on the west side.

Manhattan has two major north–south arteries that run the length of the island. The **West Side Highway** skirts the Hudson River from Battery Park (where it's known as West Street) through midtown (where it becomes the Henry Hudson Parkway north of 72nd Street) and past the George Washington Bridge. Both the Holland and Lincoln tunnels enter Manhattan just a few blocks east of this route; the Cross Bronx Expressway connects with the Henry Hudson Parkway in northern Manhattan at the George Washington Bridge. **Franklin D. Roosevelt Drive** (FDR Drive) runs along the East River from Battery Park into upper Manhattan, where it becomes Harlem River Drive north of 125th Street. Both the Queens Midtown Tunnel (East 36th Street) and the Queensboro Bridge (East 59th Street) can be entered a few blocks west of FDR Drive, which connects with the Triborough Bridge at East 125th Street.

Be forewarned: Driving within Manhattan can be a nightmare of gridlocked streets and predatory motorists. Free parking is almost impossible to find in midtown, and violators may be towed away literally within minutes. All over town, parking lots charge exorbitant rates—as much as $15 for two hours in some neighborhoods. If you do drive, don't plan to use your car much for traveling within Manhattan.

Car Rentals

If you find you absolutely need a car—perhaps for a weekend escape or because Manhattan is part of a longer trip—you'll have to sort out Manhattan's confusing array of car-rental possibilities. Although rates were once cheaper out of Newark airport, that is no longer the case; prices charged by national firms are the same at Newark, Kennedy, and LaGuardia, as well as at Manhattan rental locations. For a subcompact, expect to pay $45–$55 per day, with 70–100 free miles and 30¢ per additional mile. Companies with multiple Manhattan and airport locations include **Avis** (tel. 800/331–1212); **Budget** (tel. 800/527–0700); **Dollar** (tel. 800/421–6868); **Hertz** (tel. 800/654–3131); **National** (tel. 800/328–4567); and **Thrifty** (tel. 800/367–2277). Some regional budget companies, such as **American International** (tel. 800/527–0202) and **Rent-A-Wreck** (tel. 800/221–8282), offer lower rates. If you are flying into LaGuardia or Kennedy, you might look into some local Queens agencies with lower rates, such as **ABC** (tel. 800/247–6110) or **Universal** (tel. 718/786–0786). **Sunshine Rent-A-Car** (tel. 212/989–7260) is good for budget rentals in Greenwich Village.

Whomever you rent from, get a reservation number and ask whether there is free mileage and whether you must pay for a full tank of gas even if you don't use it. Also, find out what you're responsible for if you don't sign a collision-damage waiver: This can add $9–$12 daily to your bill. Be aware that many rental companies are redefining customer responsibility to include loss of the car from theft or vandalism.

By Train

Amtrak (tel. 800/872–7245) offers frequent service within the Northeast Corridor, between Boston and Washington, DC. Trains arrive at and depart from **Pennsylvania Station** (31st–33rd Sts., between 7th and 8th Aves.). Amtrak trains serve Penn Station from the Southeast, Midwest, and Far West. Penn Station also handles **Long Island Railroad** trains (tel. 718/454–5477), with service to and from all over Long Island, and **New Jersey Transit** trains (tel. 201/460–8444), with frequent service from the northern and central regions of New Jersey.

Amtrak service from Montreal and upstate New York and the *Lake Shore Limited* train from Chicago both use **Grand Central Terminal** (42nd St. and Park Ave.). **Metro-North Commuter Railroad** (tel. 212/532–4900) serves the northern suburbs and Connecticut from Grand Central Terminal as far east as New Haven. The other Metro-North Manhattan stop is at 125th Street and Park Avenue in East Harlem—not a good place to get off the train unless you are visiting this neighborhood.

PATH Trains (tel. 212/466–7649) run 24 hours a day to New York City from terminals in Hoboken, Jersey City, Harrison, and Newark, New Jersey; they connect with seven major New Jersey Transit commuter lines at Hoboken Station, Broad Street Station (Newark), and Penn Station (Newark). PATH trains stop in Manhattan at the World Trade Center and along Sixth Avenue at Christopher Street, 9th Street, 14th Street, 23rd Street, and 33rd Street. They run every 10 minutes on weekdays, every 15–30 minutes on weeknights, and every 20–30 minutes on weekends. The fare is $1.

By Bus

All long-haul and commuter bus lines feed into the **Port Authority Terminal,** a mammoth multilevel structure that occupies a nearly 2-square-block area between 40th and 42nd streets and Eighth and Ninth avenues. Though it was recently modernized and is fairly clean, large numbers of vagrants make the terminal an uncomfortable place to spend much time. Especially with night arrivals, plan to move through the terminal swiftly. Beware of hustlers trying to help you hail a cab on Eighth Avenue—they will demand a tip for performing this unnecessary service and can be hostile and aggressive if crossed.

For information on any service into or out of the Port Authority Terminal, call 212/564–8484. Some of the individual bus lines serving New York include **Greyhound-Trailways** (consult local information for a number in your area); **Adirondack** and **Pine Hill Trailways** from upstate New York (tel. 914/339–4230); **Bonanza Bus Lines** from New England (tel. 401/331–7500); **Martz Trailways** from northeastern Pennsylvania (tel. 717/821–3838); **New Jersey Transit** from around New Jersey (tel. 201/460–8444); **Peter Pan Bus Lines** from New England (tel. 413/781–2900); and **Vermont Transit** from New England (tel. 802/862–9671).

The **George Washington Bridge Bus Station** is located at Fort Washington Avenue and Broadway between 178th and 179th streets in the Washington Heights section of Manhattan. Six bus lines, serving northern New Jersey and Rockland County, New York, make daily stops there from 5 AM to 1 AM. The terminal connects with the 175th Street station on the A subway, making it slightly more convenient for travelers going to the Upper West Side.

Staying in New York

Important Addresses and Telephone Numbers

Tourist Information New York Convention and Visitors Bureau. The main office is at 2 Columbus Circle (tel. 212/397–8222) and is open weekdays 9–6.

Emergencies Dial 911 for **police, fire,** or **ambulance** in an emergency.

Deaf Emergency Teletypewriter (tel. 800/342–4357), for medical, fire, and ambulance emergencies.

Doctor **Doctors On Call, 24-hour house-call service** (tel. 212/737–2333). Near midtown, 24-hour emergency rooms are open at **St. Luke's-Roosevelt Hospital** (458 W. 59th St., tel. 212/523–4000) and **St. Vincent's Hospital** (7th Ave. and 11th St., tel. 212/790–7000).

Dentist The **Dental Emergency Service** (tel. 212/679–3966; after 8 PM, tel. 212/679–4172) will make a referral.

24-Hour Pharmacy **Kaufman's Pharmacy** (Lexington Ave. and 50th St., tel. 212/755–2266).

Hotlines The New York Telephone Company lists important emergency and community services numbers in the front of its white-pages directory. Here are some numbers that may come in handy:

Better Business Bureau of Metropolitan New York (tel. 212/533–6200).

Crime Victims' Hotline (tel. 212/577–7777).

NYC On Stage (tel. 212/587–1111) provides up-to-the-minute information on tickets for music and dance performances.

Sex Crimes Report Line (tel. 212/267–7273).

Sportsphone (tel. 212/976–1313).

Time of Day (tel. 212/976–1616).

Weather (tel. 212/976–1212).

Telephones

There are more than 58,000 public telephones in New York City, nearly 25,000 of which are in Manhattan. A visitor should never have to hunt more than three or four blocks before finding a coin-operated phone. If you're making a brief call—and don't mind the cacophonous sound of traffic or subways rumbling in the background—street phones are probably your best bet. If you want to consult a directory or make a more leisurely call, pay phones in the lobbies of office buildings or hotels (some of which take credit cards) are a better choice.

The area code for Manhattan and the Bronx is 212; for Brooklyn, Queens, and Staten Island, it's 718. Pay telephones cost 25¢ for the first three minutes of a local call (this includes calls between 212 and 718 area codes); an extra deposit is required for each additional minute.

Rest Rooms

Public rest rooms in New York run the gamut when it comes to cleanliness. Facilities in Penn Station, Grand Central Terminal, and the Port Authority bus terminal are often quite dirty and are inhabited by homeless people. Rest rooms in subway stations are even more filthy and are often downright unsafe.

As a rule, the cleanest bathrooms are in midtown department stores such as Macy's, Lord & Taylor, and Bloomingdale's, or in the lobbies of large hotels. Public atriums, such as the Citicorp Center and Trump Tower, also provide good public facilities. Restaurants, too, have rest rooms, but usually just for patrons. Be aware that cinemas, Broadway theaters, and concert halls have limited amenities, and there are often long lines before performances, as well as during intermissions.

Crime

New York's bad reputation in this area is not deserved—most people live here for years without being robbed or assaulted. Nevertheless, travelers make particularly easy marks for pickpockets and hustlers, so caution is advised. Someone who appears to have had an accident at the exit door of a bus may flee with your wallet or purse if you attempt to give aid; the individual who approaches you with a complicated story is probably playing a confidence game and hopes to get something from you. Keep jewelry and valuables out of sight on the street and do not venture down deserted blocks in out-of-the-way neighborhoods, especially after dark. Beware of strangers jostling you in crowds. Women should never hang their purse on a chair in a restaurant or on a hook in a rest-room stall. Men are advised to carry wallets in their front pants pockets rather than in their hip pockets.

Opening and Closing Times

New York is very much a 24-hour city. Its subways and buses run around the clock, and plenty of services are available at all hours and on all days of the week. To compensate for being open at odd times, however, many businesses close during what one would expect to be their normal workweek, so it's always a good idea to check ahead.

Banks are open weekdays 9–3 or 9–3:30, although a few branches in certain neighborhoods may stay open late on Friday or are open on Saturday mornings.

Post offices are generally open weekdays 10–5. The main post office on Eighth Avenue between 31st and 33rd streets is open 24 hours, Monday–Saturday.

Museum hours vary greatly, but most of the major ones are open Tuesday–Sunday and keep later hours on Tuesday or Thursday evenings.

Stores are normally open Monday–Saturday 10–5 or 10–6. Major department stores usually have late hours at least one evening a week. In business districts, stores may open earlier, while in neighborhoods such as the Village and SoHo, they open later and close later. Many stores in residential neighborhoods are open on Sundays.

Changing Money

Foreign travelers visiting New York can exchange foreign currency and traveler's checks at a number of offices around Manhattan. Large banks—Bank Leumi, Chase Manhattan, Chemical, Citibank, and Manufacturers Hanover Trust, for example—accommodate travelers during weekday business hours. Other companies provide exchange services up to seven days a week and often quote rates over the phone. They include:

American Express Travel Service, with nine Manhattan locations including: 822 Lexington Avenue, tel. 212/758–6510; Bloomingdale's, 59th Street and Lexington Avenue, tel. 212/705–3171; 150 E. 42nd Street, tel. 212/687–3700; 374 Park Avenue, tel. 212/421–8240; American Express Tower, 200 Vesey

Street, tel. 212/640–2000; and Macy's Herald Square, 151 W. 34th Street, tel. 212/695–8075. Hours vary among locations.

Chequepoint USA, 551 Madison Avenue, tel. 212/980–6443. Open weekdays 8–6, weekends 10–6.

Deak International (tel. 212/757–6915) has branches at 630 Fifth Avenue in Rockefeller Center; 1 Herald Center at 33rd Street and Sixth Avenue; 41 E. 42nd Street; 875 Third Avenue; and 29 Broadway. Open weekdays 9–5, Saturdays 10–3.

Freeport Currencies, 3 W. 46th Street, tel. 212/221–2000. Open weekdays 9–6, Saturdays 10–3.

Harold Reuter & Co., Pan Am Building, 200 Park Avenue, Room 332 East, tel. 212/661–0826. Open weekdays 8–5. At Abraham & Straus, 32nd Street and Sixth Avenue, 6th fl. Open Mon.–Sat., 10–6.

New York Foreign Exchange, 61 Broadway, Suite 805, tel. 212/248–4700. Open weekdays 9–5.

People's Foreign Exchange, 104 E. 40th Street, Suite 114, tel. 212/983–4727. Open weekdays 9–6, Saturdays 10:30–3.

Getting Around

On Foot The cheapest, sometimes the fastest, and usually the most interesting way to explore this city is by walking. Because New Yorkers by and large live in apartments rather than in houses, and travel by cab, bus, or subway rather than by private car, they end up walking quite a lot. As a result, street life is a vital part of the local culture. On crowded sidewalks, people gossip, snack, sunbathe, browse, buy drugs, cement business deals, make romantic rendezvous, encounter long-lost friends, and fly into irrational quarrels with strangers. It's a wonderfully democratic hubbub.

The typical New Yorker, if there is such an animal, walks quickly, dodging around cars, buses, bicycle messengers, construction sites, and other pedestrians. Yet although the natives seem hurried and rude, they will often cheerfully come to the aid of a lost pedestrian, so don't hesitate to ask passersby for directions.

Before you start out, keep a few simple rules in mind: Above 14th Street, the city is planned along a grid, with Fifth Avenue marking the dividing line between east and west. The streets, numbered from 1 to 228, are straight lines running east to west. The avenues—from First to Twelfth—run north to south. Below 14th Street, however, chaos reigns (*see* Orientation in Chapter 3).

By Subway The 230-mile subway system operates 24 hours a day and, especially within Manhattan, serves most of the places you'll want to visit. It's cheaper than a cab and, during the workweek, often faster than either cabs or buses. The trains have finally been rid of their graffiti (some New Yorkers, of course, perversely miss the colorful old trains) and sleek new air-conditioned cars predominate on many lines. The New York subway deserves much of its negative image, however. Many trains are crowded, dirty, and noisy, and even occasionally unsafe. Although trains are scheduled to run frequently, especially during rush hours, you never know when some incident somewhere on the line may stall traffic indefinitely. Unsavory characters lurk around certain stations, and panhandlers frequently work

Manhattan Address Locator

To locate avenue addresses, take the address, cancel the last figure, divide by 2, add or subtract the key number below. The answer is the nearest numbered cross street, approximately. To find addresses on numbered cross streets, remember that numbers increase east or west from 5th Ave., which runs north–south.

Ave. A... *add 3*

Ave. B...*add 3*

Ave. C...*add 3*

Ave. D...*add 3*

1st Ave....*add 3*

2nd Ave....*add 3*

3rd Ave....*add 10*

4th Ave....*add 8*

5th Ave.

Up to 200...*add 13*

Up to 400...*add 16*

Up to 600...*add 18*

Up to 775...*add 20*

From 775 to 1286...
cancel last figure and subt. 18

**Ave. of the
Americas**...*subt. 12*

7th Ave....*add 12*

Above 110th St... *add 20*

8th Ave....*add 9*

9th Ave....*add 13*

10th Ave....*add 14*

Amsterdam Ave.
...*add 59*

Audubon Ave.
...*add 165*

**Broadway
(23–192 Sts.)**...*subt. 30*

Columbus Ave.
...*add 60*

Convent Ave....*add 127*

Central Park West...
*divide house number by
10 and add 60*

Edgecombe Ave.
...*add 134*

Ft. Washington Ave.
...*add 158*

Lenox Ave.....*add 110*

Lexington Ave....*add 22*

Madison Ave....*add 27*

Manhattan Ave.
...*add 100*

Park Ave....*add 34*

Park Ave. South
...*add 8*

Pleasant Ave....*add 101*

Riverside Drive...
*divide house number
by 10 and add 72 up to
165 Street*

St. Nicholas Ave.
...*add 110*

Wadsworth Ave.
...*add 173*

West End Ave.
...*add 59*

York Ave....*add 4*

their way through the cars. Don't write off the subway—millions ride it every week without incident—but stay alert at all times.

The subway fare is $1.15. Reduced fares are available for handicapped people and senior citizens during nonrush hours. You must use a token to enter; they are sold at token booths that are *usually* open at each station. It's advisable to buy several tokens at one time to prevent waiting in line later (it always seems the lines are longest just as your train is roaring into the station). A token permits unlimited transfers within the system.

This book's subway map covers the most-visited parts of Manhattan. Maps of the full subway system are posted on many trains and at some stations, but don't rely on finding one when you need it. You may be able to pick up free maps at token booths, too, but they are often out of stock. Make sure the map you refer to is up-to-date—lengthy repair programs can cause reroutings that last long enough for new "temporary" maps to be printed.

For route information, ask the token clerk or a transit policeman. Call 718/330–1234 (a local call, 25¢ from pay phones) for 24-hour information. And don't hesitate to ask any knowledgeable-looking fellow rider for directions: Once New Yorkers realize you're "harmless," most bend over backward to be helpful.

Most midtown stops are crowded until fairly late at night, so for safety's sake, stay among the crowds on the center of the platforms. Avoid empty or nearly empty cars. During off-peak hours, try to ride in the same car as the conductor: It will stop near a line of light bulbs mounted above the edge of the platform. When disembarking from a train, stick with the crowd until you reach the comparative safety of the street.

By Bus Most buses follow easy-to-understand routes along the Manhattan grid. Routes go up or down the north–south avenues, or east and west on the major two-way crosstown streets. Most bus routes operate 24 hours, but service is infrequent late at night. Buses are great for sightseeing, but traffic jams—a potential threat at any time or place in Manhattan—can make rides maddeningly slow.

Bus fare is the same as subway fare: $1.15, at press time, in coins (no pennies) or a subway token. When you get on the bus you can ask the driver for a free transfer coupon, good for one change to an intersecting route. Legal transfer points are listed on the back of the slip. Transfers have time limits of at least two hours, often longer. You cannot use the transfer to enter the subway system.

Guide-A-Rides, which consist of route maps and schedules, are posted at many bus stops in Manhattan and at major stops throughout the other boroughs. Each of the five boroughs of New York has a separate bus map, and they are scarcer than hens' teeth. They are occasionally available in subway token booths, but never on buses. The best places to obtain them are the Convention and Visitors Bureau at Columbus Circle or the information kiosks in Grand Central Terminal and Penn Station.

Manhattan Subways

86th St Bway ① ② ③ ⑨
79th St Bway

72nd St Bway

66th St/Bway Lincoln Center

Ⓐ Ⓑ Ⓒ Ⓓ

CENTRAL PARK

86th St Central Park W

81st St Museum of Natural History

59th St Columbus Circle

50th St 8th Ave

42nd St 8th Ave

Times Sq

Penn Station

34th St 8th Ave

28th St

23rd St 8th Ave Ⓐ Ⓒ Ⓔ

14th St 8th Ave ⓁⓁ

Christopher St Sheridan Sq

Houston St Varick St

Holland Tunnel

Canal St Varick St

Franklin St Varick St.

Chambers St

Chambers St Varick St

Cortland St World Trade Center

Rector St Greenwich St

Rector/Trinity Pl

South Ferry

Lincoln Tunnel

86th St Lexington Ave ④ ⑤ ⑥

77th St Lexington Ave

68th St Lexington Ave

Roosevelt Island

63rd St Lexington Ave TRAMWAY Ⓑ Ⓠ ⓇⓃ

5th Ave 60th St **59th St Lexington Ave** Queensboro Bridge

Ⓓ 5th Ave

57th St/Bway

50th St/7th Ave

Ⓓ Ⓕ

Ⓢ

5th Ave 42nd St **Grand Central**

Lexington Ave/53rd St. ⒺⒻ

Lexington Ave 52nd St.

QUEENS

23rd St Ely Ave

Vernon Blvd Jackson Ave ⑦

Queens-Midtown Tunnel

34th St Herald Sq

33rd St Park Ave S

28th St Park Ave S ④ ⑤ ⑥

23rd St Park Ave S

① Ⓑ Ⓡ
② Ⓓ Ⓝ
③ Ⓕ
   Ⓠ

18th St

6th Ave 3rd Ave

14th St Union Sq 1st Ave ⓁⓁ

8th St/Astor Pl

W 4th St

Bleecker St Lafayette St

2 Ave/E Houston St Ⓜ Ⓙ Ⓩ

Williamsburg Br.

Prince Spring

Spring

Delancey St/Essex St
Delancey St/Spring St
Grand/Christie

E. B'way

Canal Bway

Manhattan Bridge

City Hall Bway

Park Pl

Fulton

Brooklyn Bridge

Ⓕ BROOKLYN

ⒹⒷⓆ York St

Fulton

High St

Ⓐ Ⓒ

Broad/Wall ② ③ Clark

Borough Hall

ⓂⓃⓇ

Whitehall ④ ⑤

Jay St Borough Hall

Brooklyn Battery Tunnel

Subway Lines

——————— BMT

=========== IND

•••••••••• IRT

By Taxi Taxis are usually easy to hail on the street or from a taxi rank in front of major hotels. You can tell if a cab is available by checking its rooftop light; if the center panel is lit, the driver is ready to take passengers. Taxis cost $1.50 for the first 1/8 of a mile, 25¢ for each 1/8 of a mile thereafter, and 25¢ for each minute not in motion. A 50¢ surcharge is added to rides begun between 8 PM and 6 AM. There is no charge for extra passengers. Taxi drivers also expect a 15% tip. Barring performance above and beyond the call of duty, don't feel obliged to give them more.

To avoid unhappy taxi experiences, try to have a general idea of where you want to go. A few cab drivers are dishonest; some are ignorant; some can barely understand English. If you have no idea of the proper route, you may be taken for a long and costly ride.

By Trolley The Manhattan Neighborhood Trolley, a 1900 vintage red-and-green car seating 30 passengers runs Monday–Sunday, 12 PM–6 PM, making stops every hour at South Street Seaport, Battery Park, the World Trade Center, the World Financial Center, City Hall Park, Chatham Square in Chinatown, Grand Street in Little Italy, and Orchard Street on the Lower East Side. Tickets, which are valid for boarding and reboarding all day, cost $3.50 for adults, $2.50 for senior citizens and children under age 12, and must be purchased in advance, at the Seaport, at major hotels, or by mail (Manhattan Neighborhood Trolley, Box 1053, Knickerbocker Station, New York, NY 10002, tel. 212/677–7268).

By Limousine If you want to ride around Manhattan in style, you can rent a chauffeur-driven car from one of many limousine services. Companies usually charge by the hour or offer a flat fee for sightseeing excursions. The Manhattan yellow pages provides a full listing of limousine operators, but here are several recommended companies: **A-Marquis Limousine Service** (tel. 212/466–6332); **All State Car and Limo** (tel. 212/741–7440); **Bermuda Limousine International** (tel. 212/249–8400); **Carey Limousines** (tel. 212/599–1122); **Carmel Car and Limousine Service** (tel. 212/662–2222); **Concord Luxury Limousine** (tel. 212/230–1600); **Eastside Limo Service** (tel. 212/744–9700); **Exec-U-Ride Ltd.** (tel. 212/279–1710); **Gordon's Limousine Service** (tel. 212/921–0081); **La Limousine** (tel. 212/736–0484); **London Towncars** (tel. 212/988–9700); **New York Continental Limousine Inc.** (tel. 212/617–0212); **Silver Bay Limousine Service** (tel. 212/838–2707); **Wall Chauffeured Limousine Service** (tel. 212/695–7266); **Wheels of New York** (tel. 212/465–1630).

Guided Tours

Orientation Tours The most pleasant way to get a crash orientation to Manhattan is aboard a **Circle Line Cruise.** Once you've finished the three-hour, 35-mile circumnavigation of Manhattan, you'll have a good idea of where things are and what you want to see next. Narrations are as interesting and individualized as the guides—often moonlighting actors—who deliver them. *Pier 83, west end of 42nd St., tel. 212/563–3200. Fare: $15 adults, $7.50 children under 12. Operates early Mar.–Dec., daily.*

For a shorter excursion, the **TNT EXpress,** a new hydroliner, will show you the island of Manhattan in an hour. *Pier 11, 2 blocks south of South Street Seaport, tel. 212/244–4770. Fare: $15 adults, $13 senior citizens, $8 children under 12, children under 5 free. Boats depart weekdays and Sat. 12 noon and 2 PM.*

At South Street Seaport's Pier 16 you can take two- or three-hour voyages to New York's past aboard the iron cargo schooner *Pioneer* (tel. 212/669–9416). You can take 90-minute tours of New York Harbor aboard the sidewheeler *Andrew Fletcher* or the re-created steamboat *DeWitt Clinton*.

Gray Line (900 8th Ave. at 53rd St., tel. 212/397–2600) offers a number of standard city bus tours, plus cruises and day trips to Brooklyn and Atlantic City. **Short Line Tours** (166 W. 46th St., tel. 212/354–5122) offers a number of tour options. **Manhattan Sightseeing Bus Tours** (150 W. 49th St., tel. 212/869–5005) has 10 different tours.

Island Helicopter (heliport at E. 34th St. and East River, tel. 212/683–4575) offers a number of fly-over options, from $36 (for 16 miles) to $89 (for more than 75 miles). From the west side, **Manhattan Helicopter Tours** (heliport at W. 30th St. and Hudson River, tel. 212/247–8687) has tours ranging from $35 to $144.

Special-Interest Tours **Backstage on Broadway** (tel. 212/575–8065) takes you behind the scenes of a Broadway show and lets you mingle with show people. Reservations are mandatory. **Art Tours of Manhattan** (tel. 609/921–2647) provides an inside view of museum and gallery exhibits. **Gallery Passports** (tel. 212/288–3578) admits you to artists' studios, lofts, and other art attractions in Manhattan. **Soho Art Experience** (tel. 212/219–0810) offers tours of SoHo's architecture, galleries, shops, and artists' lofts. **Doorway to Design** (tel. 212/221–1111) tours fashion and interior design showrooms, as well as artists' private studios. **Harlem Your Way!** (tel. 212/690–1687), **Harlem Spirituals, Inc.** (tel. 212/302–2594), and **Penny Sightseeing Co., Inc.** (tel. 212/410–0080), offer walking tours and Sunday gospel trips to Harlem. **Brooklyn Connoisseur's Choice Tours** (tel. 718/857–7811) organizes a tour of the Brooklyn Museum and Brooklyn Botanic Garden.

Walking Tours **Sidewalks of New York** (33 Alan Terr., Suite 2, Jersey City, NJ 07306, tel. 212/517–0201) hits the streets from various thematic angles—Historic Church tours, Ye Old Tavern tours, Celebrity Home tours, Final Resting Places of the Rich and Famous tours. These walks are offered on weekends, both days and evenings, year-round. Tours last 2–2½ hours and cost $15; no reservations are required. **Adventure on a Shoestring** (300 W. 53rd St., New York, NY 10019, tel. 212/265–2663) is a 27-year-old organization that explores New York neighborhoods. Tours are scheduled periodically for $5 per person. The **Municipal Art Society** (tel. 212/935–3960) operates a series of bus and walking tours. The **Urban Park Rangers** (tel. 212/397–3080) offer weekend walks and workshops, most of them free, in city parks. The **92nd Street YMHA** (tel. 212/996–1105) always has something special to offer on weekends. **The Streets Where We Lived** is a multiethnic historic walking tour given by The Lower East Side Tenement Museum (tel. 212/431–0233). Other knowledgeable walking-tour guides include **Michael Levin** (tel. 212/924–7187), **Michael George** (tel. 212/975–4114), **Joyce Gold** (tel. 212/242–5762), **Arthur Marks** (tel. 212/673–0477), **Ginter-Gotham Urban History** (tel. 212/496–6859), and **Pete Salwen** (tel. 212/873–1944).

The most comprehensive listing of tours offered during a particular week is published in the "Other Events" section of *New York* magazine.

Self-Guided The **New York Convention and Visitors Bureau** provides three
Walking Tours pamphlets that cover historical and cultural points of interest
in Manhattan and Brooklyn: "I Love New York Visitors Guide
and Map," "42nd Street—River to River," and "Brooklyn on
Tour." These materials are available at the bureau's information center (2 Columbus Circle, tel. 212/397–8222).

The **Municipal Art Society of New York** has prepared a comprehensive "Juror's Guide to Lower Manhattan: Five Walking
Tours" for the benefit of jurors who are often required to kill
time while serving in downtown courthouses. Along with an
explanation of the New York jury system, the pamphlet includes tours of lower Manhattan and Wall Street, the City Hall
district, Chinatown and Little Italy, South Street Seaport, and
TriBeCa. Nonjurors can purchase copies at Urban Center
Books (457 Madison Ave. at 51st St., tel. 212/935–3595).

A free "Walking Tour of Rockefeller Center" pamphlet is available from the information desk in the lobby of the RCA building
(30 Rockefeller Plaza).

2 Portraits of New York City

The New York Babel

by V. S. Pritchett

One of the great living masters of English prose, V. S. Pritchett expounds delightfully on his impressions of the city in New York Proclaimed. Here are some choice passages from the book.

If Paris suggests Intelligence, if London suggests Experience, then the word for New York is Activity. York itself is an almost intolerably famous name, but adding New to it was one of the lucky prophetic insights of nomenclature, for newness, from day to day, was to be the moral essence of the place. There is no place where newness is so continuously pursued.

What is not naturally active in New York soon has to turn to and become so. There is not an inactive man, woman, or child in the place. It might be thought that a contemplative, passive New Yorker, one who is inhabited by his feelings and his imaginings, who lives in an inner world, or was born torpid, must be immune to the active spirit. This is not so in New York, where states like passivity, contemplation, vegetativeness, and often sleep itself are active by prescription. Pragmatism sees to that. The prime example is the bum or derelict. There he lies asleep or drunk on the doorstep or props himself against a wall in the Bowery, an exposed, accepted, but above all an established figure of a 51st state. In a city where all activity is specialized, he has his specialty: he must act in protest against activity, which leads him from time to time on a chase for alcohol, a smoke, or a coin as persistent as a salesman's, but in solitude. Virginia Woolf used to ask where Society was; the notion was metaphysical to her. But Skid Row exists as a recognized place. You go there when the thing comes over you. You graduate in dereliction. You put in a 20-hour day of internal fantasy-making in your studied rejection of the New York norm. The Spanish mendicant has his rights and takes his charity with condescension; the bum grabs with resentment. He is busy. You have upset his dream. The supremely passive man in theory, he will stop in the middle of the street as he crosses the Bowery, holding up his dirty hand at the traffic, and scream in the manner of madness at the oncoming driver. Screaming like that—and New York is dotted with screamers on a scale I have seen in no other city in the world, though Naples has its share—reveals the incessant pressure of the active spirit.

For ourselves who are trying to settle first what we see before our eyes, this active, practical spirit has curious manifestations. New York City is large, but Manhattan is small in extent, so small that a large part of its population has to be pumped out of it every night by bridges and tunnels. Despite the groans about the congestion of its traffic, it is easy to dash from one end to the other of the island and to drive fast all around it. And most people do dash. The only real difficulty is in the downtown tangle of named streets in old New York; the grid has settled the rest. The grid is an un-

lovely system. It is not originally American: Stuttgart and
Berlin hit upon this method of automatically extending cities in the 17th century. By the 18th century Europe had discovered that cities must be designed before they are
extended: mere pragmatism and planning will not do. It absolutely will not do if left to engineers, soldiers, or what are
called developers. The makers of the New York grid confused the idea that parallel lines can be projected into infini-
ty without meeting, with the idea of design. The boredom
this has inflicted upon the horizontal life of Manhattan has
turned out to be endurable to the primarily active man who
is impatient of the whole idea of having neighbors. The
striping, unheeding avenues of the grid have given one superb benefit. They cut through long distances, they provide
long vistas that excite the eye, and these are fine where the
buildings are high, if they are featureless where the buildings are low. No other city I can think of has anything like
the undulating miles that fly down Park Avenue from 96th
Street to Grand Central, blocked now though it is by the
brutal mass of the Pan Am Building—a British affront to
the city and spoken of as a revenge for Suez—or the longer
streak of Madison. These two avenues impress most as a
whole, other avenues in part, by their assurance as they
cleave their way through the cliffs.

O f course, being a stranger, you have been living it
up, for if you want a night city, this is preeminent-
ly the one. There is a large fluorescent population
of pale faces—who is that old man sitting alone in the Automat at this late hour? Where are all those taxis streaking to
endlessly through the night? You have been listening to the
jazz in Birdland perhaps, listening to the long drumming
that says "Encroach, encroach, encroach, encroach, over-
come, come!" or to that woman with the skirling voice
which is shoving, pushing, and struggling cheerfully to get
all her energy out of her body and into her mouth as she
sings what is really the theme song of the city: "And it's
good. It's all good, good, good." She was wired in to some
dynamo.

Those words never fade from the mind. In sleep you still
hear them. You are a receiving station for every message
Babel sends out day and night. The sirens of the police cars,
the ambulances and fire engines, mark the hours, carrying
the mind out to fantasies of disaster. I say "fantasies," for
surely all these speeding crews are studiously keeping alive
the ideal of some ultimate dementia while the rest of us
sleep. New York demands more than anything else that one
should never fail to maintain one's sense of its drama; even
its social manners, at their most ceremonious, have this
quality. Where the crowds of other cities are consolidating
all day long, filling up the safes and cellars of the mind, the
New York crowd is set on the pure function of self-
dispersal. A couple of cops idling through the night in a police car will issue their noise as if it were part of the uniform

and to keep up their belief in their own reality and in the sacred notion of the Great Slaying or the Great Burglarization. Then there is light traffic on the highways, with its high, whipping, cat-gut whine. On 104th Street on the West Side I used to have the sensation of being flayed alive all night by knives whipping down Riverside Drive; it was not disagreeable. City life is for masochists. On many other avenues the trucks bulldozed the brain. There were bursts of noctambulist shouting off Madison and 60th at 3 or 4; followed by the crowning row of the city, the clamor of the garbage disposers, successors to Dickens's gentlemanly swine, that fling the New York garbage cans across the pavement and grind the stuff to bits on the spot. Often I have sat at my window to watch these night brutes chew up the refuse. The men have to rush to keep up with its appetite. As a single producer of shindy this municipal creature is a triumph.

The only way of pinning some sort of identity onto the people is to think of them as once being strangers like yourself and trace them to their districts. The man who used to bring my breakfast, saying, every morning, "Lousy day," was a 115th Street Puerto Rican, of five years' standing. You learn to distinguish. You know where the Ukrainians, the Sephardic Jews, early and late Italians, degrees of Irish, live. You build up a map of the black and Puerto Rican pockets. You note the Germans are at 86th Street and yet the Irish are there, too; that, at the bottom, on East End Avenue, the neighborhood has become suddenly fashionable. The Greenwich Village Italians are pretty fixed; the several Harlems have established their character, for they have stuck to their district for 60 years, which must be a record for New York. You know the Greeks are on Ninth Avenue. The Lower East Side, now largely transformed, is Jewish and Puerto Rican. But large groups break away; poor give place to poorer. Sometimes poor give place to rich. In Sutton Place they cleared the poor away from that pleasant little cliff on the East River. But one must not understand these quarters as being the old parishes or the ancient swallowed-up villages of European cities, though they were sometimes the sites of farms. Topographically they are snippings of certain avenues and cross streets. For the avenues stripe the city and the groups live on a block or two along or across the stripe. One would have to analyze New York street by street, from year to year, to know the nuances of racial contact.

Statistics deceive, but it is clear that the oldest American stock of Dutch, British, and German, though dominant in wealth and traditional influence, is a small minority in New York. The question no one can answer is how far the contents of the melting pot have really melted and whether a new race has yet been created. For a long time the minorities resist, huddle into corners. Some foreign groups of New Yorkers melt slowly or not at all. O. Henry in his time called Lower Manhattan "Bagdad-on-the-Subway," thinking then of the unchanging Syrians and Armenians around Rector Street, but they have almost vanished. The Ukrainians still have their shops and churches near Avenue A. The Russian Orthodox priest walks down the street. The Poles shout from their windows or sit on the cagelike fire escapes east of Greenwich Village. Slowly these people, no doubt, merge; but the tendency for social classes to be determined by race is marked. Many groups of Orthodox Jews remain untouched. Over in Williamsburg you see a sect wearing beards, the men in black hats and long black coats, their hair often long, with curls at the ears, walking with a long loping shuffle as if they traveled with knees bent. They look like a priesthood, and the boys, curled in the same way, might be their acolytes. You will meet them with their black cases of treasure between their feet, standing on the pavement outside the diamond markets of 47th Street.

The foreign are tenacious of their religions—there must be more Greek Orthodox and Russian Orthodox churches than in any other city outside of Europe—and of their racial pride. The old Romanian who cleans your suit has never seen Romania, but he speaks with his old accent; as one looks at his settled, impersonal, American face, one sees the ghost person of another nation within its outlines, a face lost, often sad and puzzled. The Italian cop stands operatically in the full sun at the corner of Union Square; the nimble Greek with his four pairs of hands in the grocer's has the avidity of Athens under that slick, standard air of city prosperity. It occasionally happens that you go to restaurants in New York kept by the brother-in-law or uncle, say, of the man who has the founding place in London, Naples, or Paris; you fall into family gossip, especially with Italians, who are possibly more recent but who are still entangled in the power politics of the European family system. I once talked to an Irish waiter who rushed away into the bar crying, "D'ye see that bloody Englishman? He knows me father." I didn't, but I did know that his father was a notorious leader of one of those "columns" of the I.R.A. in the Irish Civil War.

In this quality of being lost and found there is the mixture of the guilt, the sadness, the fading mind of exile with the excited wonder at life which is an essential New York note. New York tolerance allows the latitude to civilization. People are left alone and are less brutally standardized than in other cities. "Clearly"—these foreigners tell you with resignation—"this is not Europe. But"—they suddenly brighten, tense up, and get that look of celebration in their eyes—"it is New York." That is to say, the miracle. Although New Yorkers of all kinds curse the city for its expense and its pressures, and though all foreigners think it is the other foreigners who make it impossible, they are mad about the place. There is no place like it in the world. And although a Londoner or a Parisian will think

the same about their cities, here the feeling has a special
quality: that of a triumphant personal discovery of some
new thing that is getting bigger, richer, higher, more various as every minute of the day goes by. They have come to a
ball. And this is felt not only by the New Yorker with the
foreign strain, but also by the men and women who come in
from the other states, drawn by its wealth but even more by
the chances, the freedom, and the privacy that a metropolis
offers to human beings. Its very loneliness and ruthless-
ness are exciting. It is a preemptive if not a literal capital.
Scott Fitzgerald speaks of his wife Zelda coming up because she wanted "luxury and largeness beyond anything
her world provided," and that precisely describes the general feeling of many a newcomer.

Let There Be Downtown

by Michael Musto

As a columnist for The Village Voice, *Michael Musto has been a front-line observer of the downtown scene. This excerpt is from his book* Downtown, *a wry, if already dated, insider's view of the ever-changing world below 14th Street.*

hen you're alone and life is making you lonely, you can always go downtown . . . if you're on the list. (Preferably the *A* list.)

Oh sure, anyone can hop into a Porsche—or a Sherman tank —and drive through the chicest rubble in town to gape and gawk at New York's young, gifted and broke, but to go beyond touristy and be welcomed into the downtown elite, you have to observe a few thousand rules. First, realize that there *are* no rules; you just look and do as you feel. Second, be incredibly rebellious and angry, but not to the point where it might hurt your career. Walk around with a huge chip on your shoulder, but only if the chip looks fabulous. Feel a constant, driving creativity—rather than throw out a beer can, you should feel the urge to make an earring out of it. Above all, get bored so easily that by the time a trend you started becomes accepted, you should be willing to let someone else cash in on it just so you can move on to the next three trends. Always be a member of the vanguard, even if you have to pay dues to join.

The downtown scene is so transient that just as you discover a club, you find it's been turned into a pizzeria, but that's okay; wait fifteen minutes and it'll be a club again. There's such a need for constant stimulation that hair salons have art on the walls and art galleries can have hair on the walls if they like. Clubs become showrooms, American Legion offices become clubs, and the only thing certain is that nothing is certain. Roller discos suddenly change into gay Arab-biker sushi bars just for the sake of change, and no one questions the transformation as long as free drink tickets are still available.

Downtown parties are exercises in sensory stimulation. A rat put in a hot club instead of a Skinner box would probably go borderline psychotic from all the fabulous stimuli. Club regulars have seen it all, and want more. Just dancing is boring, especially since no one dances anymore, and dancing with video monitors in the background is irritating, especially since a video you don't like could put your dancing feet to sleep. But dancing with video and live bands and fashion shows and art installations might hold some people's attention until the next complimentary cocktail comes along. The clubs, with all these elements thrown together, are a microcosm of the whole outlandish mish-mosh that is downtown, a best-of-the-wildest vaudeville revue that starts at midnight and ends when everyone feels like it.

This mercurial quality has given downtown a fascinating luster as insiders and outsiders alike knock each other down to discover a trend that might still be viable by five-thirty.

Downtown has caught the public's imagination so intensely that many people are content just to observe this three-ring circus of bearded fashion victims, fake unicorns with swelled heads grafted on and incredibly acrobatic young creative types from afar—it's less exhausting that way. Mainstream America is fascinated with the idea of a scene in which seemingly everyone is an artist, musician, designer or "beauty engineer" (i.e., a hairdresser) and keeps such unusual office hours—from dusk to dawn. The media has latched onto and glorified the scene's peculiarities, making yesterday's societal outcasts today's luminaries of fashion and fabulousness. This wasn't always the case. Except for an occasional "Real People" segment on someone with pink hair, downtowners had long been left to their own devices in the relative obscurity of the Lower East Side. But as these outcasts became noticed, their image ascended from that of freaks to that of freaks with talent, with mixed results. The Felliniesque cast of characters was finally accepted, but along with that acceptance came crass commercialism in the guise of gentrification. The neighborhood they created in the Lower East Side was invaded by not very creative franchises and money-hungry real estate agents.

That's one of the paradoxes of the downtown scene—the more recognition it gets, the less of a definable entity it becomes as outside forces pounce on it and put it out of the financial range of the people who prompted the whole scene in the first place. *People* wrote about it in the summer of 1984 and rents went up. *Life* covered it in the summer of 1985 and by then the scene was so ready to be shipped for mass consumption, it's a wonder creativity was still part of the package. But despite their surface antiauthoritarian attitudes, a lot of downtown people would love a crack at fame and a chance to go mainstream, even if it means their environs are losing a little bit of funk appeal. "Gentrification!" many of them scream as they arrange their press clippings into neat little portfolios.

The battle between rebelliousness and career ambitions helps make downtown a hotbed of volatility. The fact that every day there's a whole new legion of artists, musicians and designers—Where do they come from?—keeps everyone on his and her creative toes. If you don't continually push and innovate, you could find yourself a has-been in your early twenties, enjoying a cup of mud ("Clink, clink, darling!") with the local degenerates, which is not as appalling as it may sound. Even the local degenerates have attained a patina of semichic—they seem to be destroying themselves in more glamorous ways than before. Fortunately, they're outnumbered by the artists, and the artists are outnumbered by people interested in their art. Curiosity about the scene has reached such a feverish pitch that when Cyndi Lauper—rock's queen to glad rags and crazy colors—revealed to the world that some of her brilliantly hideous ensembles of bargain wear were procured at various downtown thrift shops, people started shopping in this long-ignored area for their own perfect mismatches. When Keith Haring and Jean Michel Basquiat, one-time bad boys of public chalk and spray-can statements, started commanding high five-figure prices for their paintings, the downtown scene went over the top. It wasn't just chic anymore, it was profitable, and that makes it chicer than ever.

I n fact, downtown's so chic it's not just downtown anymore. It's a feeling, a style, a sensibility that's invaded popular culture, no matter where it might be located. No longer do downtowners get nosebleeds above 14th Street, now they're pretty safe all the way up to 23rd and maybe even beyond that. Department stores feature downtown-style displays. Large magazines prey off the glamor and vogue of downtown mademoiselles while avant-garde publications skyrocket from Avenue A to Madison Avenue. Formerly subterranean personalities appear in MTV videos and East Village annoyances become international superstars. Suddenly the scene is turned into what cynics might liken to one big Haring canvas of faceless creatures feeding off each other until everyone has hollowed-out middles. But at least the canvas is worth five figures.

You come to realize just how loose the geographical parameters of the scene are when you learn that one of Lauper's favorite "downtown" vintage clothing shops is Screaming Mimi's, on the Upper West Side. As spiraling rents force a lot of young artists out of the Lower East Side, downtown becomes anywhere they can get a reasonable apartment, even if that includes Hoboken, New Jersey, or Long Island City, Queens—places they would have retched at a few years ago. Downtown is a state of mind so fabulous that, until there's a guest list for public transportation too, all it needs to travel is a token.

We've already said that downtown is no longer a location, it's a state of mind. But let's face it—that state of mind began and happens to exist mostly . . . downtown.

Walk down St. Marks Place and you're on the Champs Elysées of life below 14th Street. Local kids in illfitting overcoats covering purposely mismatched outfits peer through their fifties nerd glasses (without lenses—a fashion, not vision, statement). If they could see, they'd notice a procession of glamor ghouls wearing black from head to toe and wielding Madonna-inspired crosses to ward off vampires (and Madonna). No one even notices the handful of punk survivors standing around wondering what happened to their movement. Though thinking about that makes those survivors angry and keeps them punk for a while longer.

Punk or not, the East Villagers are so emaciated—either from bulimia, fashion consciousness or malnutrition—that the only way they can gain weight is to cut themselves and hope a scab will form. They follow the Edie Sedgwick diet —drugs and occasional free buffets—until they look like severe and gorgeous wire hangers. Then they shop around furiously looking for cheap long-sleeved items to hang on themselves. You'll find them, and everything else, in the East Village. Vintage clothing shops sell some of the most expensive cheap clothing in New York, while newer boutiques sell cheap expensive clothing. St. Marks Bookshop offers every esoteric book imaginable for those who don't necessarily believe that *Hollywood Wives* is a seminal 20th-century work. Sushi joints litter the streets—Japan's revenge for losing the war, some say—but a slice of pizza with extra cheese is more to the local taste. You can spend your daily $2 luxury allowance on a morning cup of coffee and the monthly paper (*East Village Eye*). Morning, by the way, is about one in the afternoon.

At night all the downtowners swarm the streets with the incredibly natural glow that only comes from doing very hard drugs. Neatly coiffed gays file into Boybar, where they cruise their own reflections and go home alone (they're afraid of that new disease—personal interaction), but the reflections are generally attractive. Boybar emphasizes a much more aesthetic and imaginative image than the down-and-dirty bars further west, where there *are* no mirrors.

Not that St. Marks Place is totally pristine: it's only half pristine, the other half you wouldn't want to test with a white glove. Ironically, though, it's the slightly ragged half the neighborhood is fighting for, because that's the "authentic" half. The rest is the result of outsiders coming in with aerosol cans and making it all lilac-scented and lovely. To most of the real East Villagers, just the words "lilac-scented and lovely" are enough to warrant a barf bag.

But that hasn't stopped the well-fed middle-class professionals from swarming into this last residential horizon, the Shangri-la-de-da of commercial exhilaration. The lack of available rental housing in New York has forced tens of thousands of them to invade previously déclassé areas, revamping them into places where a Yuppie might get inspired, not mugged. It happened to East LA and the East End of London. In New York it happened to Park Slope, Chelsea and Columbus Avenue; in the mid- to late 1970s, it happened to SoHo, which went from a decaying manufacturing area to a spruced-up, expensive culture-vulture haven that teems with tourists on the weekends. Now, the East Village is going through a similar transition, and residents are simultaneously thrilled to see their neighborhood becoming more livable and appalled to find a lot of the character moving out along with the rubble.

The East Village is technically the area between 14th Street and Houston, bounded by the Bowery and the East

River. A melting pot for immigrants for 150 years, it's now a
melting pot for real estate dealers like Harry Helmsley who
are closing in with $ signs in their eyes. The neighborhood's
become so profitable that one dilapidated 16-story building
on Avenue B—the Christodora—was recently sold for a
2000% profit. When *New York* magazine subtitled their
Lower East Side cover story "There goes the neighborhood," they weren't kidding. But a whole new neighborhood was coming in.

The touristy transformation of the neighborhood into
an artsy-fartsy Coney Island is undeniable. But what
all the people shedding crocodile tears over the good
old days forget is that in the good old days you couldn't even
enter Tompkins Square Park unless you were a world-class
runner, and Alphabetland was a no-man's-land of burnt-out
buildings and bodegas that bustled with creative energy
only because you *had* to be creative to survive in such a slum
center. Now, some of the locals who fought with their land-
lords for years over bathroom facilities have actually gotten
to take a bath.   The rubble is still ominously visible—the
city, which owns many of the dilapidated buildings, is waiting for optimum prices before cleaning them up. But in between the garbage heaps are new, funky boutiques and
galleries that have redefined the neighborhood with their
idiosyncratic and comfortable ambience and affordable
chic. These small, offbeat, living room-style spots are a far
cry from their larger, more sterile SoHo equivalents,
where a graffiti board with crayons in the back seems so
calculated it must have been drawn up by an interior designer. Not surprisingly, just as SoHo once thumbed its
nose at the uptown establishment, a lot of the East Village's
appeal stems from its disdain of SoHo, which it feels has
been about as avantgarde as Times Square since the late
seventies.

The East Villagers say their neighborhood is more spontaneous, more combustible, and as much as some residents
may complain, still pulsing with a twenty-four-hour creative vitality that makes it throb. The complaints are only
because the youthquake of the sixties is registering on the
seismograph again, and downtowners are afraid that too
much commercialization of it might turn the tremors into
arthritic pains.

Here you can buy dresses for men, cowboy boots for women
and books on outer-body experiences—or the experiences
themselves. You can pick up the *Julia* lunchbox you lost as a
kid, that Twister game you bring out when you want the
guests to leave and that adorable retro, and adorably useful, TV tray you pull out afterwards. Here when someone
says, "Why don't you come up and see my etchings," he really means it.

3 Exploring Manhattan

Manhattan is, above all, a walker's city. Along its busy streets there's something else to look at every few yards. Attractions, many of them world-famous, are crowded close together on this narrow island, and because it has to grow up, not out, new layers are simply piled on top of the old. The city's character changes every few blocks, with quaint town houses shouldering sleek glass towers, gleaming gourmet supermarkets sitting around the corner from dusty thrift shops, and soot-smudged warehouses inhabited at street level by trendy neon-lit bistros. Many a visitor has been beguiled into walking a little farther, then a little farther still—"Let's just see what that copper dome and steeple belongs to . . ."—and ending up with a severe case of blisters. So be warned: Wear your most comfortable shoes, preferably sneakers, and take time along the way to stop and rest.

Our walking tours cover a great deal of ground, yet they only scratch the surface. If you plod dutifully from point to point, nose buried in this book, you'll miss half the fun. Look up at the tops of skyscrapers and you'll see a riot of mosaics, carvings, and ornaments. Go inside an intriguing office building and study its lobby decor; read the directory to find out what sorts of firms have their offices there. Peep around corners, even in crowded midtown, and you may find fountains, greenery, and sudden bursts of flowers. Find a bench or ledge to perch on, and take time just to watch the street life. New York has so many faces that every visitor can discover a different one.

Orientation

The map of Manhattan bears a Jekyll-and-Hyde aspect. The rational, Dr. Jekyll part prevails above 14th Street, where the streets form a regular grid pattern, imposed in 1811. Consecutively numbered streets run east and west (crosstown), while broad avenues, most of them also numbered, run north (uptown) or south (downtown). The chief exceptions are Broadway (which runs on a diagonal from East 14th to West 79th streets) and the thoroughfares that hug the shores of the Hudson and East rivers.

Fifth Avenue is the east–west dividing line for street addresses: in both directions, they increase in regular increments from there. For example, on 55th Street, the addresses 1–99 East 55th Street run from Fifth, past Madison, to Park (the equivalent of Fourth) avenues, 100–199 East 55th would be between Park and Third avenues, and so on; the addresses 1–99 West 55th Street are between Fifth and Sixth avenues, 100–199 West 55th would be between Sixth and Seventh avenues, and so forth. Above 59th Street, where Central Park interrupts the grid, West Side addresses start numbering at Central Park West, an extension of Eighth Avenue. Avenue addresses are much less regular, for the numbers begin wherever each avenue begins and increase at different increments. An address at 552 Third Avenue, for example, will not necessarily be anywhere near 552 Second Avenue. New Yorkers themselves cannot master the complexities of this system, so in their daily dealings they usually include cross-street references along with avenue addresses (as far as possible, we follow that custom in this book). New Yorkers also rely on the handy Manhattan Address Locator (*see* Chapter 1), found in the front of the local phone book.

Manhattan Neighborhoods

Below 14th Street—the area that was already settled before the 1811 grid was decreed—Manhattan streets reflect the disordered personality of Mr. Hyde. They may be aligned with the shoreline or they may twist along the route of an ancient cow path. Below 14th Street you'll find West 4th Street intersecting West 11th Street, Greenwich Street running roughly parallel to Greenwich Avenue, Leroy Street turning into St. Luke's Place for one block and then becoming Leroy again. There's an East Broadway and a West Broadway, both of which run north–south and neither of which is an extension of plain old Broadway. Logic won't help you below 14th Street; only a good street map and good directions will.

You may also be confused by the way New Yorkers use "uptown" and "downtown." These terms refer both to locations and to directions. Uptown means north of wherever you are at the moment; downtown means to the south. But Uptown and Downtown are also specific parts of the city (and, some would add, two very distinct states of mind). Unfortunately, there is no consensus about where these areas are: Downtown may mean anyplace from the tip of Lower Manhattan through Chelsea; it depends on the orientation of the speaker.

A similar situation exists with "East Side" and "West Side." Someone may refer to a location as "on the east side," meaning somewhere east of Fifth Avenue. A hotel described as being "on the west side" may be on West 42nd Street. But when New Yorkers speak of the East Side or the West Side, they usually mean the respective areas above 59th Street, on either side of Central Park. Be prepared for misunderstandings.

Exploring

Highlights for First-time Visitors

Rockefeller Center, Tour 1
Times Square, Tour 3
The United Nations, Tour 3
The Metropolitan Museum of Art, Tour 5
Central Park, Tour 7
The American Museum of Natural History, Tour 8
The Statue of Liberty, Tour 17
The World Trade Center, Tour 17
South Street Seaport, Tour 18
The Brooklyn Bridge (*see* Chapter 4)

Tour 1: Rockefeller Center

Numbers in the margin correspond with points of interest on the Midtown map.

When movies and TV shows are set in Manhattan, they often start with a panning shot of Rockefeller Center, for no other city scene—except perhaps the downtown skyline—so clearly says "New York." Begun during the Great Depression of the 1930s by John D. Rockefeller, this 19-building complex occupies nearly 22 acres of prime real estate between Fifth and Seventh avenues and 47th and 52nd streets. Its central cluster of buildings are smooth shafts of warm-hued limestone, streamlined with glistening aluminum, but the real genius of the complex's design was its intelligent use of public space: plazas, concourses, and street-level shops that create a sense of community for the nearly quarter of a million human beings who use it daily. Restaurants, shoe-repair shops, doctors' offices, barbershops, banks, a post office, bookstores, clothing shops, variety stores—all are accommodated within the center, and all parts of the complex are linked by underground passageways.

Rockefeller Center helped turn midtown into New York City's second "downtown" area, which now rivals the Wall Street area in the number of its prestigious tenants. The center itself is a capital of the communications industry, containing the headquarters of a TV network (NBC), several major publishing companies (Time Inc., McGraw-Hill, Simon & Schuster, and Warner Books), and the world's largest news-gathering organization, the Associated Press.

In many ways, Rockefeller Center is the heart of New York City. Close to the majority of hotels, this is a logical first stop for any visitor to the city.

Let's begin the tour with a proud symbol of the center's might: the huge statue of Atlas supporting the world that stands
❶ sentry before the **International Building** (5th Ave. between 50th and 51st Sts.). The building, with a lobby inspired by ancient Greece and fitted with Grecian marble from the island of Tenos, houses many foreign consulates, international airlines, and a passport office from which lines of last-minute applicants overflow into Fifth Avenue throughout the summer.

One block south on Fifth Avenue, between 49th and 50th streets, you'll come to the head of the **Channel Gardens,** a promenade with six pools surrounded by flowerbeds filled with seasonal plantings, conceived by artists, floral designers, and sculptors—10 shows a season. They are called the Channel Gardens because they separate the British building to the north from the French building to the south (above each building's entrance is a coat of arms bearing that country's national symbols). The French building contains among other shops the **Librairie de France,** which sells French-language books, periodicals, and records; its surprisingly large basement contains a Spanish bookstore and a dictionary store.

At the foot of the Channel Gardens is perhaps the most famous sight in Rockefeller Center (if not all of New York): the great gold-leaf statue of the fire-stealing Greek hero **Prometheus,**
❷ sprawled on his ledge above the **Lower Plaza.** A quotation from Aeschylus is carved into the red granite wall behind, and 50 jets of water spray around the statue. The plaza's trademark ice-skating rink is open from late September through April; the rest of the year, it becomes an open-air café. In December the plaza is decorated with an enormous live Christmas tree. Around the rim of the Lower Plaza you'll see the flags of all the members of the United Nations.

The backdrop to the Lower Plaza is the center's tallest tower,
❸ the 70-story **RCA Building,** occupying the block bounded by Rockefeller Plaza, Avenue of the Americas (which New Yorkers call Sixth Avenue), and 49th and 50th streets. The block-long street called Rockefeller Plaza, officially a private street (to maintain that status, it closes to all traffic on one day a year), is often choked with celebrities' black limousines, for

this is the headquarters of the NBC television network. From this building emanated some of the first TV programs ever; the "Today" show has been broadcast from here since 1952, and a shot of this building is included in the opening credit sequences of "Saturday Night Live" and "Late Night with David Letterman," both taped here.

One way to see what goes on inside is to request free tickets to one of the three New York–produced NBC shows with audiences (besides "Saturday Night" and "Letterman," there's also "Donahue") by sending a postcard to NBC Tickets (30 Rockefeller Plaza, New York, NY 10112). Unfortunately, the first two shows are usually booked for more than a year in advance, "Donahue" for about six months. Another way to get behind the scenes is to spend $7 to take a tour of the NBC studios: One leaves every 15 minutes, 9:30–4:00, Monday through Saturday, and on Sundays during the summer; Thursdays 9:30–8.

You can also buy a T-shirt, ashtray, Frisbee, or other paraphernalia bearing the logos of your favorite NBC programs at a boutique in the magnificent black granite lobby. As you enter the building from Rockefeller Plaza, look up at the ceiling mural above the entrance: Wherever you stand, the figure seems to be facing you. Take time also to study the allegorical murals above the entrance on Sixth Avenue. The old rooftop observation deck is, unfortunately, closed now, but you can take an elevator to the top floor to enjoy the spectacular view with drinks or a meal at the **Rainbow Room** (*see* Chapter 8).

Escalators in the RCA Building will take you down to the marbled catacombs that connect the various components of Rockefeller Center. There's a lot to see down under: restaurants in all price ranges, from the chic American Festival Cafe to McDonald's; the Rockefeller Center Museum; a post office and clean public rest rooms (scarce in midtown); and just about every kind of store. To find your way around, consult the strategically placed directories or obtain the free "Shops and Services Guide" at the RCA Building reception desk. *Center*, a free quarterly magazine containing articles about Rockefeller Center, a calendar of events, and capsule descriptions of its restaurants, is available in the lobbies of most of the complex's buildings.

If you're intent on seeing network TV, look around Rockefeller Center for pages distributing free tickets to screenings of shows contemplated for broadcast by not only NBC but also CBS and ABC, whose headquarters are nearby. (CBS is located in a black monolith, popularly called Black Rock, at Sixth Avenue and 53rd Street, while ABC's offices are one block farther north at Sixth Avenue and 54th Street).

❹ Across 50th Street from the RCA Building is America's largest indoor theater, the 6,000-seat **Radio City Music Hall.** Home of the fabled Rockettes chorus line (which actually started out in St. Louis in 1925), Radio City was built as a movie theater with a stage suitable for live shows as well. Its days as a first-run movie house are long over, but after an announced closing in 1978 Radio City has had an amazing comeback, producing concerts, awards presentations, and special events, along with its own Christmas and Easter extravaganzas. When there's no show you can tour the premises for $6 (tel. 212/632-4041).

Tours 1-3: Midtown

Columbus Circle

W. 57th St.

W. 56th St.

Carnegie Hall

W. 55th St.

W. 54th St.

W. 53rd St.

W. 52nd St.

W. 51st St.

Radio City Music Hall

W. 50th St.

THEATER DISTRICT

W. 49th St.

W. 48th St.

W. 47th St.

W. 46th St.

W. 45th St.

W. 44th St.

Times Square

W. 43rd St.

Port Authority Bus Terminal

W. 42nd St.

W. 41st St.

Bryant Park

W. 40th St.

W. 39th St.

W. 38th St.

Ninth Ave.

Eighth Ave.

Seventh Ave.

Broadway

Avenue of the Americas (Sixth Ave.)

Fifth Ave.

Algonquin Hotel, **26**
American Craft Museum, **9**
AT&T World Headquarters, **18**
Bryant Park, **24**
Celanese Building, **5**
Chrysler Building, **29**
Daily News Building, **30**
Duffy Square, **23**

Exxon Building, **7**
Ford Foundation Building, **31**
General Motors Building, **16**
Grand Central Terminal, **28**
IBM Building, **17**
International Building, **1**
ICP Mid-Town, **25**
Lever House, **19**

Lower Plaza, **2**
McGraw-Hill Building, **6**
Museum of Broadcasting, **11**
Museum of Modern Art, **10**
New York Public Library, **27**
The Plaza, **15**
Radio City Music Hall, **4**

RCA Building, **3**
St. Bartholomew's Church, **21**
St. Patrick's Cathedral, **12**
St. Thomas's Church, **13**
Seagram Building, **20**
Time-Life Building, **8**
Times Square, **22**
Trump Tower, **14**
United Nations Headquarters, **32**

E. 58th St.

E. 57th St.

0   880 yards

0   800 meters

E. 56th St.

E. 55th St.

E. 54th St.

E. 53rd St.

TURTLE BAY

E. 52nd St.

E. 51st St.

E. 50th St.

Madison Ave.

Park Ave.

E. 49th St.

E. 48th St.

E. 47th St.

E. 46th St.

Lexington Ave.

Third Ave.

Second Ave.

First Ave.

Sutton Pl.

FDR Drive

E. 45th St.

E. 44th St.

E. 45th St.

E. 44th St.

Vanderbilt Ave.

E. 43rd St.

Queens
Midtown
Tunnel

E. 42nd St.

E. 41st St.

Tudor City Pl.

E. 40th St.

Park Ave.

E. 39th St.

E. 38th St.

East River

Later additions to Rockefeller Center include Sixth Avenue's skyscraper triplets—the **Celanese Building** (6th Ave. between 47th and 48th Sts.), the **McGraw-Hill Building** (6th Ave. between 48th and 49th Sts.), and the **Exxon Building** (6th Ave. between 49th and 50th Sts.)—and their cousin immediately to the north, the **Time-Life Building** (6th Ave. between 50th and 51st Sts.). All have street-level plazas, but the most interesting is McGraw-Hill's, where a 50-foot steel sun triangle points to the seasonal positions of the sun at noon and a pool demonstrates the relative size of the planets.

Time Out For supercasual eating when the weather is good, the **Sixth Avenue food vendors** near Rockefeller Center offer the best selection in the city. These "à la cart" diners offer far more than trite hot dogs—there's a truly international menu of tacos, falafel, souvlaki, tempura, Indian curry, Afghani kofta kebabs, or Caribbean beef jerky. Food carts are licensed and inspected by the Department of Health, and the price is right: No dish is more than $5, and most cost much less.

Fifty-third Street between Sixth and Fifth avenues is a mini-Museum Row. The **American Craft Museum** spotlights the work of contemporary American and international craftspersons working in clay, glass, fabric, wood, metal, or paper. *40 W. 53rd St., tel. 212/956–3535. Admission: $3.50 adults, $1.50 students and senior citizens. Open Tues. 10–8, Wed.– Sun. 10–5.*

The **Museum of Modern Art** (MOMA) is a bright and airy six-story structure built around a secluded sculpture garden. All the important movements of art since 1880 are represented here, and the collection includes not only painting and sculpture but also photography, architecture, decorative arts, drawings, prints, illustrated books, and films. After only a quick look-see, you'll be able to drop terms such as Cubism, Surrealism, Abstract Expressionism, Minimalism, and Post-Modernism as though you'd known them all your life. Some of the world's most famous paintings are displayed on the second floor: Van Gogh's *Starry Night*, Picasso's *Les Demoiselles d'Avignon*, Matisse's *Dance*. The superstars of American art appear on the third floor: Andrew Wyeth, Andy Warhol, Jackson Pollock, Frank Stella, and Mark Rothko, to name but a few. Leave time to sit outside in the Sculpture Garden, and don't miss the classic office furniture and Paris subway bench in the fourth-floor Architecture and Design Collection. Afternoon and evening film shows, mostly foreign films and classics, are free with the price of admission; tickets are distributed in the lobby on the day of the performance, and often they go fast. Programs change daily; call 212/708–9500 for a schedule. *11 W. 53rd St., tel. 212/708–9400. Admission: $6 adults, $3.50 students, $3 senior citizens, under 16 free. Pay what you wish Thurs. 5–9. Open Fri.–Tues. 11–6, Thurs. 11–9.*

On the same side of Fifth Avenue, the **Museum of Broadcasting** presents special screenings, usually retrospectives of the work of a particular radio or TV star or of an era in TV and radio history. Visitors can also screen items from the museum's stupendous collection of more than 25,000 TV shows, 10,000 commercials, and 15,000 radio programs. *23 W. 52nd St., tel. 212/752–7684. Suggested donation: $4 adults, $3 stu-*

dents, *$2 senior citizens and under 13. Open Tues. noon–8, Wed.–Sat. noon–5.*

Tour 2: Midtown from Fifth to Park Avenues

Numbers in the margin correspond with points of interest on the Midtown map.

The stretch of Fifth Avenue upward from Rockefeller Center glitters with world-famous shops, but the rents are even higher along East 57th Street, a parade of very exclusive smaller shops and upmarket art galleries (*see* Chapter 7). The area is also studded with handsome churches—relics of an era when this was a district of millionaires' mansions—as well as some of the most striking skyscrapers of the later 20th century.

The string of stores begins right across the street from Rockefeller Center's Channel Gardens (*see* Tour 1, above), with no less than **Saks Fifth Avenue** (5th Ave. and 50th St.), the flagship of the national department store chain. On the next block is Gothic-style **St. Patrick's,** the Roman Catholic Cathedral of New York. Dedicated to the patron saint of the Irish—then and now one of New York's principal ethnic groups—the white marble and stone structure was begun in 1858, consecrated in 1879, and completed in 1906. Among the statues in the alcoves around the nave is a striking modern interpretation of the first American-born saint, Mother Elizabeth Seton. From outside, catch one of the city's most photographed views: the ornate white spires of St. Pat's against the black glass curtain of **Olympic Tower,** a multiuse building of shops, offices, and luxury apartments.

Cartier, Inc. displays its wares in a jewel box of a turn-of-the-century mansion on the southeast corner of 52nd Street and Fifth Avenue; similar houses used to line this street, many of their occupants parishioners of **St. Thomas's Church** (5th Ave. at 53rd St.), an Episcopal institution that has occupied the site since 1911. The impressive huge stone reredos behind the altar holds the statues of more than 50 apostles, saints, martyrs, missionaries, and church figures. Upon entering, look to the far right to see enameled discs representing the branches of the armed forces, and carved busts of four U.S. military chiefs-of-staff.

On the northwest corner of Fifth Avenue and 54th Street, you'll see the imposing bulk of the **University Club,** a granite palace built by New York's leading turn-of-the-century architects McKim, Mead & White, for this exclusive midtown men's club, one of several that only recently have begun accepting women members. Pick out the crests of various prestigious universities above its windows. On two other corners of this intersection you'll find two branches of the **Gucci** leather and clothing enterprise.

Fifth Avenue Presbyterian Church, a grand brownstone church (1875), sits on the northwest corner of Fifth Avenue and 55th Street. **Steuben Glass** occupies a ground-floor showroom in the green-glass tower at Fifth Avenue and 56th Street; across the street, **Harry Winston** (718 5th Ave.) has fabulous jewelry but does not encourage browsers. Despite its Fort Knox–like art deco entrance, **Tiffany & Co.** (727 5th Ave. at 57th St.) is less intimidating and perhaps somewhat less expensive than you may fear. One quintessential New York movie, *Breakfast at Tiffany's*, opens with Audrey Hepburn, dressed in an evening gown, emerging from a yellow cab at dawn to stand here window-shopping with a coffee and Danish.

⑭ Trump Tower, on Fifth Avenue between 56th and 57th streets, an exclusive 68-story apartment house that bears the name of its celebrity developer, Donald Trump. The grand Fifth Avenue entrance leads into a glitzy six-story shopping atrium paneled in pinkish-orange marble and trimmed with lustrous brass. A fountain cascades against one wall, drowning out the clamor of the city. In further contrast to the real world, every inch of Trump Tower is kept gleaming, and security is omnipresent but discreet. Shops are chic and tony, among them Cartier, Bucellati, and Abercrombie & Fitch.

Returning to Fifth Avenue, cross 57th Street to visit **Bergdorf Goodman,** which contains designer boutiques and a surprisingly complete men's department. **Van Cleef & Arpels** jewelers is located within Bergdorf's 57th Street corner.

Cross 58th Street to **Grand Army Plaza,** the open space along Fifth Avenue between 58th and 60th streets. The southern block features the Pulitzer Fountain, donated by publisher Joseph Pulitzer of Pulitzer Prize fame. Appropriately enough for this ritzy area, the fountain is crowned by a female figure representing Abundance. When the fountain is dry (as it is much of the time), its rim becomes a perch for tourists and office workers pausing to get a bit of sun. The block to the north holds an equestrian statue of Civil War general William Tecumseh Sherman; beyond it is a grand entrance to Central Park (*see* Tour 7, below).

⑮ Appropriately named **The Plaza,** the famous hotel (*see* Chapter 9) at the western edge of this square is a registered historical landmark built in 1907, now owned by Donald Trump. Its architect, Henry Hardenbergh, was the same man who designed the rather dour Dakota apartment building (*see* Tour 8, below), but here he achieved a sprightly birthday-cake effect with white-glazed brick busily decorated and topped off with a copper-and-slate mansard roof. The hotel has been featured in many movies, from Alfred Hitchcock's *North by Northwest* to more recent films such as *Arthur* and *Crocodile Dundee*. Among the many upper-crust parties that have taken place in the Plaza's ballroom was Truman Capote's Black and White Ball of 1966, attended by everyone who was anyone—all dressed, naturally, in black and white.

Time Out | The intimate front bar at **Jean Lafitte** (68 W. 58th St., tel. 212/751–2323) is an unusually relaxed place in this busy area of New York. While waiting for a table at this pleasant French bistro, you can sip your drink for as long as you like.

⑯ Adjacent to Grand Army Plaza stands the **General Motors Building,** a 50-story tower of Georgia marble. One section of the main-floor lobby displays a dozen or so shiny new GM vehicles. The other part of the lobby is the flagship of the legendary **F.A.O. Schwarz** toy store, with its fantastic mechanical clock right inside the front doors. Bigger than it looks from outside, the toy-o-rama offers a vast, wondrously fun selection, although it definitely tends toward expensive imports. Browsing here should bring out the child in everyone, as it did in the movie *Big*, when Tom Hanks and his boss got caught up in tap-dancing on a giant keyboard.

Return to 57th Street and Fifth Avenue, and head east. Stay on the north side of the street to visit **Chanel** (appropriately located at No. 5 E. 57th St.), **Burberry's Ltd.** (9 E. 57th St.), **Hermès,** (11 E. 57th St.), **Louis Vuitton** (51 E. 57th St.), and gizmo shop supreme, **Hammacher Schlemmer** (145 E. 57th St.). In two sleekly art deco subterranean levels, **Place des Antiquaires** (125 E. 57th St.) is an ultrahigh-class shopping mall where several dozen of the city's top art and antiques dealers operate out of plate-glass stalls. Some shops have very narrowly defined specialties: Lune, for example, sells almost nothing but antique fans. Whether or not you're in the market for these pricey items, browsing can be fun.

⑰ At Madison Avenue and 57th Street, look up at the **IBM Building,** a five-sided sheath of dark gray-green granite and glass. On the ground level there's the **IBM Gallery of Science and Art,** which presents a variety of temporary shows and the permanent science exhibition *Think,* including lasers, magnets, and superconductors. *Tel. 212/745-3500. Admission free. Open Tues.–Sat. 11–6.*

Time Out At the 56th Street corner, step into IBM's high, cool atrium, one of the most inviting public spaces in town. Small marble-topped tables and wrought-iron chairs are provided, and a small café serves those who've come without their brown-bag lunch.

⑱ At Madison Avenue and 55th Street, pop into the **AT&T World Headquarters,** designed by architect Philip Johnson. Unlike the sterile ice-cube-tray buildings of Sixth Avenue, AT&T's rose granite columns, its regilded statue of the winged *Golden Boy* in the lobby, and its peculiar Chippendale roof have made it an instant landmark for New Yorkers, who consider it the first postmodern skyscraper. An adjacent structure houses the **AT&T InfoQuest Center,** a postmodern museum of telecommunications technology. Entrants receive an access card on which they encode their names; they then use the card to operate displays on lightwave communication, microelectronics, and computer software. Displays are neither terribly technical nor (on behalf of AT&T) self-serving. Some exhibits—such as those where you program your own music video and rearrange a scrambled picture of your face—are downright entertaining. *Madison Ave. and 56th St., tel. 212/605-5555. Admission free. Open Tues. 10–9, Wed.–Sun. 10–6.*

If you head west on 55th Street, you'll pass a narrow limestone town house that's home to the New York **Friars Club,** a venerable show-biz institution founded in 1956, best known for its banquets at which celebrity guests of honor are mercilessly "roasted" by their peers. Friars have included Frank Sinatra, Milton Berle, Sammy Davis, Jr., and Henny Youngman.

Turn right onto broad Park Avenue to see some of the most important buildings in modern architecture. On the corner of 54th Street, peer to your left (east) toward Lexington Avenue, where you can see the soaring, luminescent white shaft of the **Citicorp Center** (1977), designed by Hugh Stubbins & Associates. Its most striking feature is the angled top, originally intended to carry an immense solar-energy collector that was never installed. At street level, the Citicorp Center has a pleasant mall of restaurants and shops.

19 Directly in front of you, on the west side of Park Avenue between 53rd and 54th streets, is **Lever House,** a 1952 creation by Skidmore, Owings, & Merrill. It's basically a sheer, slim glass box, resting on one end of a one-story-thick shelf that seems to float above the street, balanced on square chrome columns. Because the tower occupies only half of the space above the lower floors, a great deal of air space is left open, and the tower's side wall displays a reflection of its neighbors.

20 On the other side of Park Avenue, one block south between 52nd and 53rd streets, the **Seagram Building** is the only New York building by German architect Mies van der Rohe, a leading interpreter of the International Style. This, too, is a simple boxlike tower, although the black metal and bronze glass exterior looks more severe than Lever House's cool blue-green. Built in 1958, it created a sense of spaciousness with its ground-level plaza, an innovation at the time that has since become a common element in urban skyscraper design. Inside is one of New York's most venerated restaurants, **The Four Seasons** (*see* Chapter 8).

21 For a pleasing contrast, walk down to 51st Street, where you'll see **St. Bartholomew's Church** nestled amid the skyscrapers. Built in 1919, it has rounded arches, while its intricate tiled dome is Byzantine. Church fathers have been eager to sell the air space over St. Bart's, to take advantage of the fabulous property values in this part of town, but landmark preservation forces have so far prevented any such move, thereby protecting this welcome gulp of sky in midtown.

Tour 3: Across 42nd Street

Numbers in the margin correspond with points of interest on the Midtown map.

As midtown Manhattan's central axis, 42nd Street ties together several major points of interest, from the United Nations on the East River, past the Grand Central railroad terminal, to Times Square. (The crosstown bus route continues on to the Jacob Javits Convention Center near the Hudson River.) While it's never less than a busy commercial thoroughfare, a few blocks of 42nd Street are downright disreputable, living up to the often-held image of New York as a den of pickpockets, porno houses, prostitutes, and destitutes. An ambitious plan to redevelop Times Square is currently fighting for approval, but in the meantime try to imagine West 42nd Street as a scene out of the movie *Taxi Driver*, lyrical in its squalor.

22 While it may not exactly be the Crossroads of the World, as it is often called, **Times Square** is one of New York's principal energy centers. It's one of many New York City "squares" that are actually triangles formed by the angle of Broadway slashing across a major avenue—in this case, crossing Seventh Avenue at 42nd Street. The square itself is occupied by the former Times Tower, now resheathed in white marble and called **One Times Square Plaza.** When the *New York Times* moved into its new headquarters on December 31, 1904, it publicized the event with a fireworks show at midnight, thus starting a New

Year's Eve tradition. Each December 31, workmen on this roof lower a 200-pound ball down the flagpole by hand, just as they have since 1908. The huge intersection below is mobbed with revelers, and when the ball hits bottom on the stroke of midnight, pandemonium ensues.

The present headquarters of the *New York Times* (229 W. 43rd St.) occupies much of the block between Seventh and Eighth avenues; look for the blue delivery vans lined up along 43rd Street. From 44th to 51st streets, the cross streets west of Broadway are lined with some 30 major theaters (*see* Chapter 10). This has been the city's main theater district since the turn of the century; movie theaters joined the fray beginning in the 1920s. As the theaters drew crowds of people in the evenings, advertisers began to mount huge electric signs here, which gave the intersection its distinctive nighttime glitter. Even the developers who want to change this area intend to preserve the signs, making them bigger and brighter with new technology (much of it developed for Tokyo's night-lit Ginza district).

The northern triangle of the intersection, which reaches up to 47th Street, is named **Duffy Square** after World War I hero Father Francis P. Duffy, the "Fighting Chaplain," who later was pastor of a theater district church on West 42nd Street. Besides the suitably military statue of Father Duffy, there's also one of George M. Cohan, the indomitable trouper who wrote "Yankee Doodle Dandy." Today Duffy Square is an important place to visit for the **TKTS discount ticket booth,** which sells half-price tickets to Broadway and some Off-Broadway shows (*see* Chapter 10). Some days it seems that almost every show in town is up for grabs; at other times there may be nothing available but a few long-running hits and some sleepers. The lines may look long, but they move surprisingly fast.

The only live theater on 42nd Street itself is provided by a group of thriving Off-Broadway playhouses, often called **Theatre Row** (*see* Chapter 10), between Ninth and Tenth avenues. The block between Seventh and Eighth avenues that was once the heart of the theater district is now a sleazy strip of X-rated bookstores, peep shows, and theaters that specialize in skin flicks and kung fu movies; the sidewalks are full of loiterers and panhandlers who drift between here and the Port Authority bus station at 42nd Street and Eighth Avenue. The most prominent vestige of the old 42nd Street is the **New Amsterdam** (214 W. 42nd St.), a designated landmark that opened in 1903. Today the New Amsterdam is "dark"—lying fallow in anticipation of the area's redevelopment—but in its prime it was an opulent two-theater facility that showcased the likes of Eddie Cantor, Will Rogers, Fanny Brice, and the Ziegfeld Girls.

Heading east on 42nd Street, you'll pass **Hotaling's News** (142 W. 42nd St., tel. 212/840–1868), a bustling little shop that carries more than 220 daily newspapers from throughout the United States, most issues only a day or two old. The rear section stocks current newspapers, magazines, and foreign-language books from more than 40 countries.

At Sixth Avenue you'll see steps rising into the shrubbery and trees of **Bryant Park,** named for the poet and editor William Cullen Bryant (1794–1878). This was the site of America's first World's Fair, the Crystal Palace Exhibition of 1853–54; today it's the backyard of the New York Public Library's central research branch. A program of landscaping and tightened security has helped to improve this park, but it is still somewhat of a hangout for undesirables, and its long-term fate is still in question. One reason to enter the park, however, is to visit the **Bryant Park Discount Dance and Music Ticket Booth,** which, in a setup similar to TKTS, sells tickets for music and dance performances throughout the city (*see* Chapter 10).

A ground-level passage through the **City University Graduate Center** (33 W. 42nd St.) connects 42nd and 43rd streets; walk through to look at the art exhibits. At the northeast corner of Sixth Avenue and 43rd Street, the International Center of Photography (*see* Tour 5, below) has a relatively new branch, **ⅆ ICP Mid-Town,** which presents several photographic shows a year in an ultracontemporary, multilevel space. *Tel. 212/768–4683. Admission: $2 adults, $1 students and senior citizens. Open Tues.–Sun. 11–6.*

㉖ A block north, you'll see the **Algonquin Hotel** (59 W. 44th St.; *see* Chapter 9), which is surprisingly unpretentious considering its history as a haunt of well-known writers and actors. Its most famous association is with a witty group of literary Manhattanites who gathered in its dining room in the 1920s—a clique that included short-story writer Dorothy Parker, humorist Robert Benchley, playwright George S. Kaufman, and actress Tallulah Bankhead. One reason they met here was the hotel's proximity to the offices of *The New Yorker* magazine (*see* below).

Next door to the Algonquin is the somewhat dingier (and cheaper) **Iroquois Hotel** (49 W. 44th St.), where struggling actor James Dean lived in the early 1950s. Across the street is the **Royalton Hotel** (44 W. 44th St.; *see* Chapter 9), chicly redone by former Studio 54 hosts Ian Schrager and the late Steve Rubell. You might want to step into its lobby for a peek, but unless your clothes are suitably trendy, you may be hustled along by the staff. Next door, at 42 West 44th Street, is the **Association of the Bar of the City of New York,** with a neoclassical facade resembling the courthouses where its members spend so much of their time.

Back on the north side of the street, at 37 West 44th Street is the **New York Yacht Club,** former longtime home of the America's Cup trophy. Notice its swelling windowfronts, looking just like the sterns of ships, complete with stone-carved water splashing over the sill. The redbrick **Harvard Club** (27 W. 44th St.) echoes the Harvard campus with its modest Georgian-style architecture. Across the street at 28 West 44th Street is the unprepossessing entrance to the building where *The New Yorker* magazine is put together; inside, the magazine's offices are just as unpretentious, even a little dowdy. At 20 West 44th, the **Mechanics' and Tradesmen's Institute Building,** in a turn-of-the-century prep school building, has a wonderful library in a three-story-high hall; here you'll also find the intriguing **Mossman Collection of Locks,** open free to the public (tel. 212/840–1840; open weekdays 11–1, 2–4, except the first Wed. of every month).

At the corner of Fifth Avenue, look left to notice the large clock on a pedestal set in the Fifth Avenue sidewalk, a relic of an era when only rich people could afford watches. Then turn right and walk south. Between 40th and 42nd streets on Fifth Ave-

㉗ nue, you'll find the central research building of the **New York Public Library**. This 1911 masterpiece of Beaux Arts design was financed largely by John Jacob Astor, whose previous library building downtown has since been turned into the Public Theater (*see* Tour 13, below). Its grand front steps are guarded by two crouching marble lions—dubbed "Patience" and "Fortitude" by former Mayor Fiorello LaGuardia, who said he visited the facility to "read between the lions." After admiring the white marble neoclassical facade (crammed with statues, as is typical of Beaux Arts buildings), walk through the bronze front doors into the grand marble lobby with its sweeping double staircase. Take a (quiet) look upstairs at the huge, high-ceilinged main reading room, a haven of scholarly calm, or visit the current exhibit in the art gallery. Among the library's treasures on display are Gilbert Stuart's portrait of George Washington, Charles Dickens's desk, and Jefferson's own handwritten copy of the Declaration of Independence. Free one-hour tours, each as individual as the library volunteer who leads it, are given Monday through Saturday at 11 AM and 2 PM. *Tel. 212/930–0800. Open Mon.–Wed. 10–9, Thurs.–Sat. 10–6.*

㉘ Continue east on 42nd Street to **Grand Central Terminal** (not a "station," as many people call it, since all runs begin or end here). Constructed between 1903 and 1913, this Manhattan landmark was originally designed by a Minnesota architectural firm and later gussied up with Beaux Arts ornamentation. Stop on the south side of 42nd Street to admire the three huge windows separated by columns, and the Beaux Arts clock and sculpture crowning the facade above the elevated roadway (Park Avenue is routed around Grand Central's upper story). Go in the side doors on Vanderbilt Avenue to enter the cavernous main concourse, with its 12-story-high ceiling displaying the constellations of the zodiac. Unfortunately, the terminal has in recent years become a magnet for homeless people, and the once-grand waiting rooms and rest rooms have become shabby indeed. But it's worth a visit, especially at rush hour, when this immense room crackles with the frenzy of scurrying commuters, dashing every which way. *Free tours Wed. at 12:30 PM, tel. 935–3960.*

On the southwest corner of Park Avenue and 42nd Street, directly opposite Grand Central, the **Whitney Museum of American Art at Philip Morris** (120 Park Ave.) occupies the ground floor of the Philip Morris Building. Each year this free branch of the Whitney Museum (*see* Tour 5, below) presents five successive exhibitions of 20th-century painting and sculpture. An espresso bar and seating areas make it a much more agreeable place to rest than anywhere else in Grand Central.

The southeast corner of 42nd and Park is a major departure point for buses to the three New York area airports, and upstairs at 100 East 42nd Street you'll find ticket counters for most major U.S. airlines. Around the corner is the main office of the **Bowery Bank** (110 E. 42nd St.), whose massive arches and 70-foot-high marble columns give it a commanding presence. At the end of the block is the **Chanin Building** (122 E. 42nd St.), notable for the geometric Art Deco patterns that adorn its facade. Across the street you'll see the **Grand Hyatt** (*see* Chapter 9), which was created by wrapping a new black glass exterior around the former Commodore Hotel.

㉙ Ask New Yorkers to name their favorite skyscraper and most will choose the Art Deco **Chrysler Building** at 42nd Street and Lexington Avenue. Although the Chrysler Corporation itself moved out a long time ago, this graceful shaft culminating in a stainless-steel spire still captivates the eye and the imagination. The building has no observation deck, but you can go inside its elegant dark lobby, which is faced with African marble and covered with a ceiling mural that salutes transportation and human endeavor.

Time Out The **Automat** (southeast corner of 3rd Ave. and 42nd St.) is the last survivor of the world's first fast-food chain. Patrons can use coins or tokens to extract dishes—baked beans and macaroni-and-cheese are perennial favorites—from glass-fronted cubbyholes, and to crank coffee out of fish-head spouts. Authentic automat facilities are confined to one wall (a cafeteria, sandwich bar, and bakery occupy the rest of the space), but the sleek contours of Art Deco styling prevail throughout.

㉚ New York's biggest-selling newspaper is produced in the **Daily News Building** (220 E. 42nd St.), an Art Deco tower designed with brown-brick spandrels and windows to make it seem loftier than its 37 stories. Step into the lobby for a look at its revolving illuminated globe, 12 feet in diameter; the floor is laid out as a gigantic compass, with bronze lines indicating air mileage from principal world cities to New York. A small gallery displays *News* photos.

㉛ The **Ford Foundation Building** (320 E. 43rd St., with an entrance on 42nd St.) encloses a 12-story, ⅓-acre greenhouse. With a terraced garden, a still pool, and a couple of dozen full-grown trees as centerpieces, the Ford garden is open to the public—for tranquil strolling, not for picnics—weekdays from 9 to 5.

Climb the steps along 42nd Street between First and Second avenues to enter **Tudor City,** a self-contained complex of a dozen buildings featuring half-timbering and lots of stained glass. Constructed between 1925 and 1928, the apartments of this residential enclave originally had no east-side windows, lest the tenants be forced to gaze at the slaughterhouses, breweries, and glue factories then located along the East River. Today, however, they're missing a wonderful view of the United Nations Headquarters; you'll have to walk to the terrace at the end of 43rd Street to overlook the UN. This will place you at the head of the **Sharansky Steps** (named for Natan, formerly Anatoly, Sharansky, the Soviet dissident), which run along the **Isaiah Wall** (inscribed "They Shall Beat Their Swords Into Plowshares"); you'll also look down into **Ralph J. Bunche Park** (named for the black American former UN undersecretary) and **Raoul Wallenberg Walk** (named for the Swedish diplomat and World War II hero).

㉜ The **United Nations Headquarters** complex occupies a lushly landscaped 18-acre riverside tract just east of First Avenue between 42nd and 48th streets. Its rose garden is especially pleasant to stroll in, although picnicking is strictly forbidden. A line of flagpoles with banners representing the current roster of 159 member nations stands before the striking 550-foot-high slab of the Secretariat Building, with the domed General Assembly Building nestled at its side. The headquarters was designed in 1947–53 by an international team of architects, led by Wallace Harrison. You can enter the General Assembly Building at the 46th Street door; the interior corridors overflow with imaginatively diverse artwork donated by member nations. Free tickets to most sessions are available on a first-come, first-served basis 15 minutes before sessions begin; pick them up in the General Assembly lobby. Visitors can take early luncheon in the Delegates Dining Room or eat anytime in the public coffee shop. *Tel. 212/963–7539. Open daily 9:15–4:45. 1–hr. tours leave the General Assembly lobby every 20 min. Tour admission: $5.50 adults, $3.50 students. Children under 5 not permitted.*

Tour 4: Murray Hill to Union Square

Numbers in the margin correspond with points of interest on the Murray Hill to Union Square map.

As the city grew progressively north throughout the 19th century, one neighborhood after another had its fashionable heyday, only to fade from glory. But these three neighborhoods, east of Fifth Avenue roughly between 20th and 40th streets, have preserved much of their historic charm, in Murray Hill's brownstone mansions and town houses, Madison Square's classic turn-of-the-century skyscrapers, and Gramercy Park's London-like leafy square. The only "must-see" along this route is the Empire State Building, but the walk as a whole is worth taking for the many moments en route when you may feel as if you've stepped back in time.

❶ Begin on East 36th Street, between Madison and Park avenues, at the **Pierpont Morgan Library.** The core of this small, patrician museum is the famous banker's own study and library, completed in 1906 by McKim, Mead & White. If you walk east past the entrance to admire its neoclassical facade, look for what is believed to be McKim's face on the sphinx in the right-hand sculptured panel. The rest of Morgan's mansion was torn down after his death and replaced with exhibition space for his collection of drawings, manuscripts, and rare books. (His son, J. P. Morgan, lived in a 45-room brownstone around the corner, which you can see with a quick stroll to 37th and Madison; the library recently bought that mansion and is in the process of renovating and incorporating it.) You enter the library on 36th Street, through the exhibition wing; whether or not you are interested in the current show, go down the corridor on your right to see Morgan's study, its red-damask-lined walls hung with first-rate paintings, and his majestic personal library with its dizzying tiers of handsomely bound rare books, letters, and illuminated manuscripts. *29 E. 36th St., tel. 212/685–0610. Suggested donation: $3 adults, $1 students and senior citizens. Open Tues.–Sat. 10:30–5, Sun. 1–5.*

❷ As you proceed south on Madison Avenue, at 35th Street you'll pass the **Church of the Incarnation,** a broodingly dark brownstone version of a Gothic chapel. Inside, however, there's enough jewel-like stained glass to remedy the dour effect. Look especially for the north aisle's 23rd Psalm Window, by the Tiffany Glass works, or the south aisle's two Angel windows dedicated to infants, which are by the 19th-century English writer-artist William Morris.

Tour 4: Murray Hill to Union Square

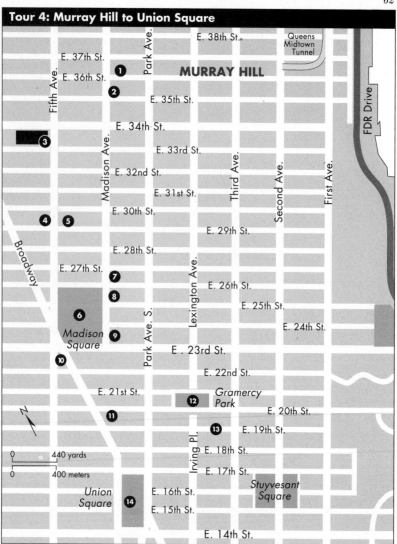

At 35th Street and Madison Avenue, veteran globe-trotters will enjoy a stop at **The Complete Traveller Bookstore** (199 Madison Ave., tel. 212/679–4339), a comprehensive shop for travel literature.

Walk west from Madison Avenue to Fifth Avenue and continue south on the west side of the street; at 34th Street, you'll reach the **Empire State Building**; it may no longer be the world's tallest building, but it is certainly one of the world's best-loved skyscrapers. The Art Deco playground for King Kong opened in 1931 after only about a year of construction. The crowning spire was originally designed as a mooring mast for dirigibles, but none ever docked there; in 1951, a TV transmittal tower was added to the top, raising the total height to 1,472 feet. Today more than 15,000 people work in the building, and more than 2.5 million people a year visit the 86th- and 102nd-floor Observatories. At night the top 30 stories are illuminated with colors appropriate to the season (red and green around Christmas; orange and brown for Halloween). In 1956, revolving beacons named the "Freedom Lights" were installed. These lights are illuminated from dusk to midnight.

Pass beneath the stainless-steel canopy on 34th Street to enter the three-story-high marbled lobby, where illuminated panels depicting the Seven Wonders of the World brazenly add the Empire State as the Eighth Wonder. Go to the concourse level to buy a ticket for the observation decks. The 102nd-floor spot is glassed in; the 86th floor is open to the air. In the movie *An Affair to Remember*, Cary Grant waited here impatiently for his rendezvous with Deborah Kerr, unaware that she had just been hit by a car on the busy avenue far below. *5th Ave. and 34th St., tel. 212/736–3100. Admission: $3.50 adults, $1.75 children under 12. Open daily 9:30 AM–midnight.*

Also on the concourse level of the Empire State Building, you'll find the **Guinness World Records Exhibit Hall**, where clever displays tell the story of various unusual record-holders. *Tel. 212/947–2335. Admission: $4.50 adults, $2.75 children. Open Mon.–Thurs. 9–8, Fri.–Sun. 9 AM–10 PM.*

Continue south on Fifth Avenue to 29th Street and the **Marble Collegiate Church** (1854), a marble-fronted structure built for the Reformed Protestant Dutch Congregation first organized in 1628 by Peter Minuit, the canny Dutchman who bought Manhattan from the native Indians for $24. In recent times its pulpit was occupied by Dr. Norman Vincent Peale *(The Power of Positive Thinking)*, Marble Collegiate's pastor from 1932 to 1984.

Go east on 29th Street to the **Church of the Transfiguration** (1 E. 29th St.), which is better known as the Little Church Around the Corner. Set back in a shrub-filled New York version of an old English churchyard, it won its memorable appellation in 1870 when other area churches refused to bury actor George Holland, a colleague of well-known thespian Joseph Jefferson. Jefferson was directed to the "little church around the corner" that did that sort of thing, and the Episcopal institution has welcomed literary and show-biz types ever since. Go inside to see the south transept's stained-glass window, by John LaFarge, depicting 19th-century superstar actor Edwin Booth in his most famous role, Hamlet.

❻ Bordered by Fifth Avenue, Broadway, Madison Avenue, 23rd and 26th streets, **Madison Square** was the site (circa 1845) of New York's first baseball games. On the north end, an imposing 1881 statue by Augustus Saint-Gaudens memorializes Civil War naval hero Admiral Farragut. A somewhat less successful statue at the south end is of William Henry Seward, the Secretary of State who bought Alaska in 1867; the sculptor apparently took a statue he'd made of Lincoln signing the Emancipation Proclamation and simply switched the head for Seward's. The square has recently been rehabilitated with modern sculpture, new benches, and a playground, but there may still be unsavory types about. Many of the once-posh hotels in the neighborhood, having gone to seed, now provide temporary housing for homeless families, and at night, after the office workers have deserted the area, prostitutes ply their trade nearby. It's safe by day, however, and new luxury apartment towers like the one just south of the square are helping to change the neighborhood.

❼ The block at 26th Street and Madison Avenue is now occupied by the ornate **New York Life Insurance Building,** designed in 1928 by Cass Gilbert, who also did the Woolworth Building (*see* Tour 17, below). Its birthday-cake top is capped by a gilded pyramid that is stunning when lit at night. Go inside to admire the soaring lobby's coffered ceilings and ornate bronze doors. This was formerly the site of the second (1890–1925) Madison Square Garden, designed by architect and playboy Stanford White, who was shot in the Garden's roof garden by Harry K. Thaw, the jealous husband of actress Evelyn Nesbit—a lurid episode more or less accurately depicted in the movie *Ragtime.*

❽ Coincidentally, other scenes in *Ragtime* were filmed in front of the **Appellate Division of the State Supreme Court,** which is at Madison Avenue and 25th Street. The roof balustrade of this imposing white marble Corinthian structure depicts great lawmakers of the past: Moses, Justinian, Confucius, and others, although a statue of Mohammed had to be removed because it offended the Islamic religion to present an image of the prophet.

❾ The **Metropolitan Life Insurance Tower** (Madison Ave. between 23rd and 24th Sts.) made this building the world's tallest when it was added in 1909. The 700-foot tower re-creates the campanile of St. Mark's in Venice. The four dials of its clock are each three stories high; wait for the quarter hour to hear it chime. Met Life's North Building, between 24th and 25th streets, is connected by a skywalk. Its Art Deco loggias have attracted many film crews—it appeared in such recent films as *Eyewitness, After Hours,* and *Radio Days.*

❿ The Renaissance-style **Flatiron Building** occupies the triangular lot formed by Broadway, Fifth Avenue, and 23rd Street. This, too, was the tallest building in the world when it opened (1902). Its rounded front point is only six feet wide, but gentle waves built into the molded limestone-and-terra-cotta side walls soften the wedge effect. Winds invariably swooped down its 20-story height, billowing up the skirts of women pedestrians on 23rd Street, and local traffic cops had to shoo away male gawkers—coining the phrase "23 Skiddoo." Originally named the Fuller Building, it was instantly rechristened by the public because of its resemblance to a flatiron, and eventually the nickname became official. It has also lent its name to the Flatiron District that lies to the south, an area of photographers' studios, residential lofts, and advertising agencies.

Continue south on Broadway and turn east on 20th Street to ⓫ the **Theodore Roosevelt Birthplace,** a reconstruction of the Victorian brownstone where Teddy lived until he was 15 years old. Before becoming president, Roosevelt was New York City's police commissioner and the governor of New York State. The house contains Victorian period rooms and Roosevelt memorabilia; a selection of videos about the namesake of the teddy bear can be seen on request. *28 E. 20th St., tel. 212/260–1616. Admission: $1. Open Wed.–Sun. 9–5.*

Time Out   Open 24 hours a day, **Miss Kim's** (270 Park Ave. S) is a combination grocery store, salad bar, and cafeteria of a type that flourishes all over town. You can fill up a container with food from a huge 50-item salad bar or a steam table with hot foods, paying for it by the pound. There's also a pastry counter and sandwich bar; countermen serve hot drinks, including espresso, while cold drinks (including beer) can be taken straight from the cooler. There's seating on a mezzanine, but most people just take their meals outside.

Just east of Park Avenue South between 20th and 21st streets ⓬ lies **Gramercy Park,** a picture-perfect city park complete with flowerbeds, bird feeders, sundials, and cozy benches. It stays nice largely because it's surrounded by a locked cast-iron fence, and only residents of the property around the park can obtain keys. Laid out in 1831 according to a design inspired by London's residential squares, Gramercy Park is surrounded by interesting buildings.

Walk to the northeast corner and head clockwise. The white terra-cotta apartment building at **36 Gramercy Park East** is guarded by concrete knights in tarnished armor. The turreted redbrick building at **34 Gramercy Park East** was one of the city's first cooperative apartment houses; its tenants have included actors James Cagney, John Carradine, and Margaret Hamilton, who played the Wicked Witch in *The Wizard of Oz.* The austere gray Friends Meeting House at 28 Gramercy Park South has lately become **The Brotherhood Synagogue,** and a narrow plaza just east of the synagogue contains a Holocaust memorial. Society doyenne Mrs. Stuyvesant Fish, a fearless iconoclast who reduced the time of formal dinner parties from several hours to 50 minutes, resided at **19 Gramercy Park South** in the 1880s.

As you cross Irving Place on the south side of the square, peek inside the park and you'll see a statue of actor Edwin Booth playing Hamlet. Booth lived at No. 16, which he remodeled in the early 1880s to serve as an actors' club, **The Players Club.** Stanford White, the architect for the renovation, was a member of the club, as were many other nonactors. Members over the years have included Mark Twain, Booth Tarkington, John and Lionel Barrymore, Irving Berlin, Winston Churchill, Lord Laurence Olivier, Frank Sinatra, Walter Cronkite, Jack Lemmon, Richard Gere, and Raul Julia.

The **National Arts Club** (15 Gramercy Park S) was once the home of Samuel Tilden, a governor of New York and the Democratic presidential candidate who, in 1876, received more popular votes than Rutherford B. Hayes, although Hayes won the electoral college vote. Calvert Vaux, codesigner of Central Park, remodeled this building in 1874, conjoining two houses. Among its Victorian Gothic decorations are medallions portraying Goethe, Dante, John Milton, and Benjamin Franklin.

On the west end of the square, note the row of redbrick Greek Revival town houses, with their fanciful cast-iron verandas looking like something out of New Orleans's French Quarter. Mayor James Harper (elected in 1888) lived at No. 4, behind the pair of street lanterns. The actor John Garfield died in 1952 while staying at No. 3.

Return to Irving Place and head south to 19th Street, where the tree-lined block running to your left, toward Third Avenue, **⑬** has been called **"The Block Beautiful"** for its fine small 19th-century houses and stables. Silent-film star Theda Bara lived at No. 132; later, so did Mrs. Patrick Campbell, one of George Bernard Shaw's favorite actresses. Painter George Bellows (1882–1925) lived at No. 10.

Time Out | **Pete's Tavern** (18th St. and Irving Pl.) claims to be the oldest saloon in New York (1864), and also claims that O. Henry wrote "The Gift of the Magi" while sitting in the second booth to the right. Both facts are disputed, but stop here anyway for a quick burger or a casual beer, and absorb the atmosphere of the Gaslight Era.

O. Henry, whose real name was William Sidney Porter, lived nearby, at 55 Irving Place, although the building he lived in no longer stands. A plaque on the redbrick house at 17th Street and Irving Place proclaims it as the home of Washington Irving, for whom the street is named, but it was his nephew's house, though the famous writer did visit there often. At 40 Irving Place, you'll see a huge bust of the writer outside **Washington Irving High School,** alma mater of Claudette Colbert and Whoopi Goldberg.

At the foot of Irving Place is the **Palladium** (126 E. 14th St.), a former movie palace turned into a cavernous, innovative disco—now well past its brief "in" moment—by Ian Schrager and the late Steve Rubell, of Studio 54 fame.

⑭ Turn left and head west to **Union Square,** the area between Park Avenue South and Broadway and 14th and 17th streets. Its name, originally signifying the fact that two main roads merged here, proved doubly apt in the early 20th century when the square became a rallying spot for labor protests and mass demonstrations; many unions, as well as fringe political parties, moved their headquarters nearby. Over the years the area deteriorated into a habitat of drug dealers and kindred undesirables, until a massive renewal program in the 1980s transformed it. If possible, visit on Greenmarket day (Wednesday, Friday, and Saturday), when farmers from all over the Northeast, including some Pennsylvania Dutch and latter-day hippies, bring their goods to the big town: fresh produce, homemade bakery goods, cheeses, cider, New York State wines, even fish and meat. If the prices aren't much lower than those in stores, the quality and freshness are much higher. The benches of Union Square make a great site for a city-style picnic.

Tour 5: Museum Mile

Numbers in the margin correspond with points of interest on the Museum Mile, Upper East Side map.

Once known as Millionaire's Row, the stretch of Fifth Avenue between 79th and 104th streets has been fittingly renamed Museum Mile, for it now contains an impressive cluster of cultural institutions. The connection is more than coincidental: Many museums are housed in what used to be the great mansions of merchant princes and wealthy industrialists. In 1979 a group of 10 Fifth Avenue institutions formed a consortium that, among other activities, sponsors a Museum Mile Festival each June. The Frick Collection and the Whitney Museum are not officially part of the Museum Mile Consortium, but they're located close enough to be added to this tour.

It would be impossible to do justice to all these collections in one outing; the Metropolitan Museum alone contains too much to see in a day. You may want to select one or two museums to linger in and simply walk past the others, appreciating their exteriors (this in itself constitutes a minicourse in modern architecture). Save the rest for another day—or for your next trip to New York.

Be sure to pick the right day of the week for this tour: Most of these museums are closed on Mondays, but many have free admission during extended hours on Tuesday or Thursday evenings.

❶ Begin at Fifth Avenue and 70th Street with **The Frick Collection,** housed in an ornate, imposing Beaux Arts mansion built in 1914 for coke-and-steel baron Henry Clay Frick, who wanted the superb art collection he was amassing to be kept far from the soot and smoke of Pittsburgh, where he'd made his fortune. The mansion was designed by architects Carrère and Hastings (also responsible for the Public Library on Fifth Avenue at 40th Street); opened as a public museum in 1935 and expanded in 1977, it still has the appearance of a gracious private home, albeit one with a bona fide masterpiece in almost every room. Strolling through the mansion, one can imagine how it felt to live with Vermeers by the front stairs, Gainsborough and Reynolds portraits in the dining room, canvases by Constable and Turner in the library, and Titians, Holbeins, a Bellini, and an El Greco in the living room. Some of the collection's best pieces include Pierre Renoir's *Mother and Children* and Jean-Honoré Fragonard's *The Progress of Love.* Even the resting area is a masterpiece: a tranquil indoor court with a fountain and glass ceiling. *1 E. 70th St., tel. 212/288–0700. Admission: $3 adults, $1.50 students and senior citizens. Children under 10 not admitted. Open Tues.–Sat. 10–6, Sun. 1–6, closed holidays.*

❷ Walk one block east to Madison Avenue and head up to 75th Street to **The Whitney Museum of American Art.** This museum grew out of a gallery in the studio of the sculptor and collector Gertrude Vanderbilt Whitney, whose talent and taste were fortuitously accompanied by the wealth of two prominent families. The current building, opened in 1966, is a minimalist gray granite vault, separated from Madison Avenue by a dry moat; it was designed by Marcel Breuer, a member of the Bauhaus

Americas Society, **15**
Asia Society, **16**
Bloomingdale's, **12**
Carl Schurz Park, **19**
Conservatory
Garden, **11**
Cooper-Hewitt
Museum, **6**
El Museo Del
Barrio, **10**
Frick Collection, **1**
Gracie Mansion, **20**
Guggenheim
Museum, **4**
Henderson Place
Historic District, **18**
International Center
of Photography, **8**
Jewish Museum, **7**
Metropolitan Museum
of Art, **3**
Museum of the City of
New York, **9**
National Academy of
Design, **5**
Ralph Lauren, **17**
Seventh Regiment
Armory, **14**
Temple Emanu-El, **13**
Whitney Museum of
American Art, **2**

Tours 5 and 6: Museum Mile, Upper East Side

E. 106th St.
E. 105th St.
E. 104th St.
E. 103rd St.
E. 102nd St.
E. 101st St.
E. 100th St.
E. 99th St.
E. 98th St.
E. 97th St.
E. 96th St.
E. 95th St.
E. 94th St.
E. 93rd St.
E. 92nd St.
E. 91st St.
E. 90th St.
E. 89th St.
E. 88th St.
E. 87th St.
E. 86th St.
E. 85th St.
E. 84th St.
E. 83rd St.
E. 82nd St.
E. 81st St.
E. 80th St.
E. 79th St.
E. 78th St.
E. 77th St.
E. 76th St.
E. 75th St.
E. 74th St.
E. 73rd St.
E. 72nd St.
E. 71st St.
E. 70th St.
E. 69th St.
E. 68th St.
E. 67th St.
E. 66th St.
E. 65th St.
E. 64th St.
E. 63rd St.
E. 62nd St.
E. 61st St.
E. 60th St.
E. 59th St.

Fifth Ave.
Madison Ave.
Park Ave.
Lexington Ave.
Third Ave.
Second Ave.
First Ave.
York Ave.
East End Ave.
First Ave.
FDR Dr.

CENTRAL PARK

East River

Queensboro
Bridge

0   440 yards
0   400 meters

school, which prized functionality in architecture. The mono-lithic exterior is much more forbidding than the interior, where changing exhibitions offer an intelligent survey of 20th-century American works; a third-floor gallery features a sample of the permanent collection, including Edward Hopper's haunting *Early Sunday Morning* (1930), Georgia O'Keeffe's *White Cali-co Flower* (1931), and Jasper Johns's *Three Flags* (1958). Alex-ander Calder's *Circus*, a playful construction he tinkered with throughout his life (1898–1976), stands near the front en-trance. The Whitney has also opened branches throughout the city: across from Grand Central Terminal, on Seventh Avenue at 51st Street, and downtown at the Federal Reserve Plaza. *945 Madison Ave. at 75th St., tel. 212/570–3676. Admission: $4.50 adults, $2.50 senior citizens; free for students with valid I.D. and children at all times, and for everyone Tues. 6–8. Open Tues. 1–8, Wed.–Sat. 11–5, Sun. noon–6.*

Cut back to Fifth Avenue and walk north to **The American-Irish Historical Society,** in a town house once owned by U.S. Steel president William Ellis Corey, who scandalized his social class by marrying musical comedy star Mabelle Gilman. With its or-namentation and mansard roof, this is another fine example of the French-influenced Beaux Arts style that was so popular at the turn of the century. The society's library holdings chronicle people of Irish descent who became successful in the United States. *991 5th Ave. at 81st St., tel. 212/288–2263. Admission free by appointment. Open Tues.–Fri. 10:30–5, Sat. 10:30–4:30.*

❸ **The Metropolitan Museum of Art** has valid evidence for billing itself as "New York's number-one tourist attraction." It's the largest art museum in the Western Hemisphere (1.6 million square feet), and its permanent collection of 3.3 million works of art from all over the world includes items from prehistoric to modern times. The museum, founded in 1870, moved to this lo-cation in 1880, but the original redbrick building by Calvert Vaux has since been encased in other architecture. The majes-tic Fifth Avenue facade, designed by Richard Morris Hunt, was built in 1902 of gray Indiana limestone; later additions eventually surrounded the original building on the sides and back.

The Fifth Avenue entrance leads into the Great Hall, a soaring neoclassical chamber that has been designated a landmark in its own right. Past the admission booths, a vast marble stair-case leads up to the European painting galleries, whose high-lights include Botticelli's *The Last Communion of St. Jerome,* Pieter Bruegel's *The Harvesters,* El Greco's *View of Toledo,* Jo-hannes Vermeer's *Young Woman with a Water Jug,* and Rem-brandt's *Aristotle with a Bust of Homer.* Nearby in the André Meyer Galleries, a large central salon full of Impressionist paintings is surrounded by smaller rooms displaying the Im-pressionists' precursors and successors (with one long gallery devoted to the sculpture of Auguste Rodin).

American art has its own wing, back in the northwest corner; the best approach is on the first floor, where you enter through a refreshingly light and airy garden court graced with Tiffany stained-glass windows, cast-iron staircases by Louis Sullivan, and a marble Federal-style facade taken from the Wall Street branch of the United States Bank. Take the elevator to the third floor and begin working your way down through the rooms decorated in period furniture—everything from a Shaker retiring room to a colonial ballroom to the living room of a Frank Lloyd Wright house—and excellent galleries of American painting.

In the realm of 20th-century art, the Met was a latecomer, allowing the Museum of Modern Art and the Whitney to build their collections with little competition until the Metropolitan's contemporary art department was finally established in 1967. The big museum has been trying to make up for lost time, however, and in 1987 it opened the three-story Lila Acheson Wing, in the southwest corner. Pablo Picasso's 1906 portrait of Gertrude Stein is the centerpiece of this collection.

There is much more to the Met than paintings, however. Visitors with a taste for classical art should go immediately to the left of the Great Hall on the first floor to see the Greek and Roman statuary, not to mention a large collection of rare Roman wall paintings excavated from the lava of Mount Vesuvius. Directly above these galleries, on the second floor, you'll find room after room of Grecian urns and other classical vases. The Met's awesome Egyptian collection, spanning some 3,000 years, lies on the first floor directly to the right of the Great Hall. Its centerpiece is the Temple of Dendur, an entire Roman temple (circa 15 BC) donated by the Egyptian government in thanks for U.S. help in saving ancient monuments. Placed in a specially built gallery with views of Central Park to refresh the eye, the temple faces east, as it did in its original location, and a pool of water has been built at the same distance from it as the river Nile once stood. Another spot deserving of contemplation is directly above the Egyptian treasures, in the Asian galleries: The Astor Court Chinese garden reproduces a Ming Dynasty (1368–1644) scholar's courtyard, complete with water splashing over artfully positioned rocks.

There's also a fine arms and armor exhibit on the first floor (go through the medieval tapestries, just behind the main staircase, and turn right). Or keep going straight from the medieval galleries until you enter the cool skylit white space of the Lehman Pavilion, where the small but exquisite personal collection of the late donor, investment banker Robert Lehman, is displayed in rooms resembling those of his West 54th Street town house. This is one of the lesser-known wings of the Met (perhaps because it's tucked away behind so many other galleries), so it's a good place to go when the other galleries begin to feel crowded.

The new Henry R. Kravis wing should be opening in the spring of 1991, creating a new Central Park entrance at the back of the museum. Its first-floor galleries will feature the European decorative arts collection—a fascinating series of period rooms—as well as an arcaded courtyard displaying European sculpture.

Although it exhibits only a portion of its vast holdings, the Met offers more than can reasonably be seen in one visit. Choose what you want to see, find a map, and plan your tour accordingly—or, if you're not compulsive about seeing the "major pieces," wander wherever your fancy takes you. Either way, your time will not be wasted. Walking tours and lectures are free with your admission contribution. Tours covering various sections of the museum begin about every 15 minutes on weekdays, less frequently on weekends; they depart from the Tour Board in the Great Hall. Self-guided audio tours can also be rented at a desk in the Great Hall.

Lectures, often related to temporary exhibits, are given on Sundays, Tuesdays, and Fridays. *5th Ave. at 82nd St., tel. 212/535-7710. Suggested contribution: $5 adults, $2.50 students and senior citizens, children free. Open Tues.–Thurs. and Sun. 9:30–5:15, Fri. and Sat. 9:30–8:45.*

Time Out | Across from The Met is the Stanhope Hotel's sidewalk café, **The Terrace** (5th Ave. and 81st St.), open May through October, a convenient spot to take an elegant break after a day at the museum—to sip a cocktail and enjoy light Continental-American fare while you people-watch.

Across from the Met, between 82nd and 83rd streets on Fifth Avenue, one Beaux Arts town house stands its ground amid newer apartment blocks. It now belongs to the Federal Republic of Germany, which has installed a branch of the Goethe Institute here. **Goethe House** (tel. 212/972–3960; call for schedules) offers a changing series of art exhibitions as well as lectures, films, and chamber music concerts; its extensive library (closed in the summer) includes current issues of German newspapers and periodicals. Up at 86th and Fifth, a brightly embellished limestone-and-redbrick mansion, designed by Carrère and Hastings to echo the Place des Vosges in Paris, was once the home of Mrs. Cornelius Vanderbilt III. It now houses the **Yivo Institute for Jewish Research** (tel. 212/535–6700; open weekdays 9:30–5:30), with exhibitions focusing on Eastern European and American Jewish history.

④ Frank Lloyd Wright's **Guggenheim Museum** (opened in 1959) is a controversial work of architecture—even many of those who like its assertive six-story spiral rotunda will admit that it does not result in the best space in which to view art. A newly expanded and fully restored Guggenheim is scheduled to reopen in the fall of 1991 after being closed for half a year. A new tower and expanded gallery space will display the newly acquired Panza Collection of minimalist art, among other works. Inside, under a 92-foot-high glass dome, a quarter-mile-long ramp spirals down past changing exhibitions of modern art. The museum has especially strong holdings in Vasily Kandinsky (1866–1944), Paul Klee (1879–1940), and Pablo Picasso (1881–1973); the oldest pieces are from the French Impressionists. *1071 5th Ave. at 89th St., tel. 212/360–3500. Admission: $4.50 adults, $2.50 students and senior citizens; free Tues. 5–7:45. Open Tues. 11–7:45, Wed.–Sun. 11–4:45.*

⑤ A block north is **The National Academy of Design,** housed in a stately 19th-century mansion and a pair of town houses on 89th Street. The academy itself, which was founded in 1825, required each elected member to donate a representative work of art, which has resulted in a strong collection of 19th- and 20th-century art. (Members have included Samuel F. B. Morse, Winslow Homer, John Singer Sargent, Augustus Saint-Gaudens, and Thomas Eakins.) *1083 5th Ave. at 89th St., tel. 212/369–4880. Admission: $2.50 adults, $2 students and senior citizens; free Tues. 5–8. Open Tues. noon–8, Wed.–Sun. noon–5.*

At 91st Street you'll find the former residence of industrialist
⑥ Andrew Carnegie, now the home of the **Cooper-Hewitt Museum** (officially the Smithsonian Institution's National Museum of Design). Carnegie sought comfort more than show when he

built this 64-room house on what was the outskirts of town in 1901; he administered his extensive philanthropic projects from the first-floor study. (Note the low doorways—Carnegie was only five feet two inches tall.) The core of the museum's collection was begun in 1897 by the three Hewitt sisters, granddaughters of inventor and industrialist Peter Cooper; major holdings include drawings, prints, textiles, furniture, metalwork, ceramics, glass, woodwork, and wall coverings. The Smithsonian rescued their museum from financial ruin in 1963, and the Carnegie Corporation donated the mansion in 1972. The changing exhibitions, which focus on various aspects of contemporary or historical design, are invariably well researched, enlightening, and often amusing. *2 E. 91st St., tel. 212/860–6868. Admission: $3 adults, $1.50 students and senior citizens; free Tues. 5–9. Open Tues. 10–9, Wed.–Sat. 10–5, Sun. noon–5.*

Across 91st Street from the Cooper-Hewitt, the **Convent of the Sacred Heart** is in a huge Italianate mansion originally built in 1918 for financier Otto Kahn, a noted patron of the arts.

Time Out **Jackson Hole** (Madison Ave. and 91st St.) is a cheerful spot that serves the great American hamburger plus other sandwiches, omelets, chicken, and salads. Ski posters evoke the mood of the eponymous Wyoming resort. Prices are reasonable; beer and wine are available.

---

❼ **The Jewish Museum** (1109 5th Ave. at 92nd St., tel. 212/860–1889), set in a gray stone Gothic-style château built in 1908, usually holds the largest collection of Jewish ceremonial objects in the Western Hemisphere. The museum is closed for renovation for 1991–1992. During this time period, it will present exhibitions at the New-York Historical Society (77th St. and Central Park West; *see* Tour 8, below).

❽ The handsome, well-proportioned Georgian-style mansion on the corner of Fifth Avenue and 94th Street was built in 1914 for Willard Straight, founder of *The New Republic* magazine. Today it is the home of **The International Center of Photography** (ICP), a relatively young institution—founded in 1974—building a strong collection of 20th-century photography. Its changing exhibits often focus on the work of a single prominent photographer or one photographic genre (portraits, architecture, etc.). The bookstore carries an impressive array of photography-oriented books, prints, and postcards. *1130 5th Ave. at 94th St., tel. 212/860–1777. Admission: $3 adults, $1.50 students and senior citizens, $1 children under 12; free Tues. 5–8. Open Tues. noon–8, Wed.–Fri. noon–5, weekends 11–6.*

As you proceed north on Fifth Avenue, you may want to walk a few paces east on 97th Street to see the onion-domed tower of the **Russian Orthodox Cathedral of St. Nicholas,** built in 1902. Between 98th and 101st streets, Fifth Avenue is dominated by the various buildings of **Mount Sinai Hospital,** which was founded in 1852 by a group of wealthy Jewish citizens and moved here in 1904. The 1976 addition, the Annenberg Building, is a looming tower of Cor-Ten steel, which has deliberately been allowed to develop a patina of rust.

❾ **The Museum of the City of New York** traces the course of Big Apple history, from the Dutch settlers of Nieuw Amsterdam to the present day, with period rooms, dioramas, slide shows, and clever displays of memorabilia. An exhibit on the Port of New York illuminates the role of the harbor in New York's rise to greatness; the noteworthy Toy Gallery has several meticulously detailed dollhouses. Weekend programs appeal especially to children. *5th Ave. at 103rd St., tel. 212/534–1672. Suggested contribution: $3 adults, $1.50 students and senior citizens, $1 children. Open Tues.–Sat. 10–5, Sun. and all legal holidays (not Mon.) 1–5.*

El Museo Del Barrio, founded in 1969, concentrates on Latin culture in general, with a particular emphasis on Puerto Rican art. ("El Barrio" means "the neighborhood," and the museum is positioned on the edge of Spanish Harlem.) The permanent collection includes numerous pre-Columbian artifacts. *1230 5th Ave. at 104th St., tel. 212/831–7272. Suggested contribution: $2. Open Wed.–Sun. 11–5.*

Having completed this long walk, you may want to reward yourself by crossing the street to Central Park's **Conservatory Garden.** The entrance, at 105th Street, is through elaborate wrought-iron gates that once graced the mansion of Cornelius Vanderbilt II. In contrast to the deliberately rustic effect of the rest of the park, this is a symmetrical, formal garden. The central lawn is bordered by yew hedges and flowering crab apple trees, leading to a reflecting pool flanked by a large wisteria arbor. To the south is a high-hedged flower garden named after Frances Hodgson Burnett, author of the children's classic *The Secret Garden.* To the north is the Untermeyer Fountain, with its three spirited girls dancing at the heart of a huge circular bed where 20,000 tulips bloom in the spring, and 5,000 chrysanthemums in the fall.

Tour 6: The Upper East Side

Numbers in the margin correspond with points of interest on the Museum Mile, Upper East Side map.

The Upper East Side epitomizes the high-style, high-society way of life most people associate with the Big Apple. Between Fifth and Lexington avenues, up to about 86th Street, is an elegant enclave of wealth. Luxury co-ops and condominiums, exquisite town houses, private schools, posh galleries, and international shops line streets where even the sidewalks seem more sparkling clean than any others in Manhattan. You may find the people who live and work in this neighborhood a bit snobbish compared with other New Yorkers, but take it in stride—they treat everybody that way.

A fitting place to begin your exploration of the moneyed Upper East Side is that infamous shrine to conspicuous consumption, **Bloomingdale's** (59th St. between Lexington and 3rd Aves., tel. 212/705–2000). This block-long behemoth is noisy, trendy, and crowded; you'll find everything from designer clothes to high-tech teakettles in slick, sophisticated displays. Not one to shrink from the spotlight, Bloomie's has appeared in more than a few Manhattan movies. Diane Keaton and Michael Murphy shared a perfume-counter encounter here in Woody Allen's *Manhattan;* Robin Williams, playing a Russian musician, defected to the West in *Moscow on the Hudson;* and mermaid Darryl Hannah, in *Splash,* took a crash course in human culture in front of a bank of TVs in the appliance department.

Time Out On Bloomingdale's sixth floor, frazzled shoppers can take a break at **Le Train Bleu** restaurant (tel. 212/705–2100), decorated like a snappy Pullman car and overlooking the 59th Street Bridge. Besides à la carte snacks, it offers one of the best bargains in town for afternoon tea.

Leaving Bloomingdale's, head west on 60th Street toward Fifth Avenue. As you cross Park Avenue, stop for a moment on the wide, neatly planted median strip. Look south toward midtown and you'll see the Pan Am Building, towering over the gilded peaked roof of the Helmsley Building at the foot of the avenue. Then turn to look uptown, and you'll see a thoroughfare lined with massive buildings that are more like mansions stacked atop one another than apartment complexes. As you proceed into the Upper East Side, observe the trappings of wealth: well-kept buildings, children in private school uniforms, nannies wheeling grand baby carriages, dog-walkers, limousines, doormen in braided livery. This is the territory where Sherman McCoy, protagonist of Tom Wolfe's *Bonfire of the Vanities*, lived in pride before his fall.

On the northwest corner of 60th Street and Park Avenue is **Christ Church United Methodist Church** (520 Park Ave.), built during the Depression but designed to look centuries old, with its random pattern of limestone blocks. Inside, the Byzantine-style sanctuary (open Sundays and holidays) glitters with golden hand-laid mosaics.

Continue west on 60th Street to pass a grouping of very different kinds of clubs. A French flag flutters over the doorway of the scholarly **Grolier Club** (47 E. 60th St.), founded in 1884 and named after the 16th-century French bibliophile Jean Grolier. Its members are devoted to the bookmaking crafts; one of them, Bertram Grosvenor Goodhue, designed this neatly proportioned redbrick building in 1917. The club presents public exhibitions and has a specialized reference library open by appointment only to scholars, collectors, and students. On the next block over, at 10 East 60th Street, a red canopy shelters the entrance to the **Copacabana,** the once-swanky nightclub commemorated in the Barry Manilow song "Lola." From the time it opened in 1940 until well into the 1950s, the Copa was one of Manhattan's most glamorous night spots, featuring such performers as Ella Fitzgerald, Sid Caesar, Frank Sinatra, Tony Bennett, Sammy Davis, Jr., Nat King Cole, Jimmy Durante, and Lena Horne. The club closed in 1973, although it has since had various comebacks, currently keeping a low profile as a discotheque and group-function space. Right next door is the exclusive **Harmonie Club** (4 E. 60th St.), one of several private men's social clubs (many of which now admit women) in this area. Built in 1905 by McKim, Mead & White, this pseudo-Renaissance palace, awkwardly stretched to high-rise proportions, is closely guarded by an unfriendly doorman, so it's best to admire it from afar. Across the street is the **Metropolitan Club** (1 E. 60th St.), an even more lordly neoclassical edifice built in 1893, also by McKim, Mead & White. J. P. Morgan established this club when a friend of his was refused membership in the Union League Club; its members today include rulers of foreign countries and presidents of major corporations.

Take a right at Fifth Avenue. On the next block you'll pass the **Hotel Pierre** (*see* Chapter 9), which opened in 1930; notice its lovely mansard roof and tower. As you cross 62nd Street, take a look at the limestone-and-brick mansion at 2 East 62nd, the home of the **Knickerbocker Club,** another private social club. You may want to detour down this elegant block of town houses; take special note of No. 11, which has elaborate Corinthian pilasters and an impressive wrought-iron entryway.

Across the street is the **Fifth Avenue Synagogue** (5 E. 62nd St.), a limestone temple built in 1959. Its pointed oval windows are filled with stained glass in striking abstract designs.

⓭ Continue up Fifth Avenue to 65th Street, where you'll see **Temple Emanu-El,** the world's largest Reform Jewish synagogue (it has seats for 2,500 worshipers). Built in 1929 of limestone, it is covered with mosaics and designed in the Romanesque style with Byzantine influences; the building features Moorish and art-deco ornamentation. *1 E. 65th St., tel. 212/744–1400. Services Mon.–Thurs. 5:30 PM, Fri. 5:15 PM, Sat. 10:30 AM. Guided group tours by appointment.*

Head east across the avenues on 65th Street, taking in their different character. Fifth Avenue, once lined with the mansions of millionaires, is now lined with the co-ops of millionaires. Madison Avenue started out as a commercial street to serve Fifth Avenue patrons, and its somewhat smaller buildings almost all contain shops or businesses at street level. Railroad tracks once ran down the middle of Park Avenue; they were covered with a roadway just after World War I and the grand sweeping street that resulted became a distinguished residential address. Continue on to Lexington Avenue, another commercial street, and you'll see low-rise brownstones whose street-level shops are generally less posh and more practical than those on Madison Avenue.

Between Madison and Park avenues on 65th Street, you'll pass a pair of town houses (45–47 E. 65th St.) built in 1910 for Sara Delano Roosevelt and her son, Franklin, who later became president of the United States. No. 47, where FDR once lay recovering from polio, is now the **Sara Delano Roosevelt Memorial House,** part of Hunter College. Across the street and toward Park Avenue is **Le Cirque** restaurant (*see* Chapter 8), one of the city's gourmet shrines, located in the **Mayfair Regent Hotel** (*see* Chapter 9). On the next block, a pair of fierce, fat stone lions guard the doorway of the **China Institute,** in its pleasant and unpretentious redbrick town house. Changing public exhibitions of Chinese art are held here. *125 E. 65th St., tel. 212/744–8181. Suggested contribution: $1. Open Mon.–Sat. 10–5.*

Backtrack to Park Avenue and head north toward the red Victorian castle-fortress at 66th Street, the **Seventh Regiment Armory** (643 Park Ave.). This huge structure is still used as a military headquarters (you can see soldiers in camouflage uniforms manning the driveway on Lexington Avenue), but it has plenty of meeting and social space as well, which is used for a tennis arena, a theater, a shelter for homeless people, and an exhibit hall that hosts, among other events, a posh annual antiques show. Both Louis Comfort Tiffany and Stanford White helped design its surprisingly residential interior; go up the front stairs into the wood-paneled lobby and take a look around.

On the west side of Park Avenue, a pair of grand mansions face each other across 68th Street. Though houses have generally been replaced by apartment buildings along Park Avenue, these survivors give you an idea of how the neighborhood once looked. The grandly simple silvery limestone palace on the southeast corner, built in 1920, now houses the prestigious **Council on Foreign Relations** (58 E. 68th St.). The dark-red brick town house on the northwest corner was built in 1909–1911 by McKim, Mead & White for Percy Pyne, the grandson of noted financier Moses Taylor. From 1948 to 1963, this mansion was the Soviet Mission to the United Nations; when the Russians moved out, developers wanted to raze the town house, but in 1965 Marquesa de Cuevas acquired the property and presented it to the Center for Inter-American Relations. Now **⑮** called the **Americas Society**, it has an art gallery that's open to the public. *680 Park Ave., tel. 212/249–8950. Suggested donation: $2. Open Tues.–Sun. noon–6.*

Note how the three houses to the north—built during the following decade, and designed by three different architects—carried on the Pyne mansion's Georgian design to create a unified block. Today these buildings hold the **Spanish Institute** (684 Park Ave.), the **Instituto Italiano di Cultura** (Italian Institute, 686 Park Ave.), and the **Italian Consulate** (690 Park Ave.).

⑯ Two blocks north, on the east side of Park Avenue, is the **Asia Society,** a museum and educational center in an eight-story red granite building in striking contrast to the older, more traditional architecture of the street. While this is the headquarters of a nonprofit educational society, not technically a museum, it does offer public exhibitions of Asian art, including South Asian stone and bronze sculptures; art from India, Nepal, Pakistan, and Afghanistan; bronze vessels, ceramics, sculpture, and paintings from China; Korean ceramics; and paintings, wood sculptures, and ceramics from Japan. *725 Park Ave., tel. 212/288–6400. Admission: members free, $2 nonmembers, $1 students and senior citizens. Open Tues.–Sat. 11–6, Sun. noon–5.*

New York has been used as a locale for many a movie, and film buffs may enjoy prowling around this neighborhood past some notable location shots. The house at **162 East 70th Street,** near Lexington Avenue, is where mild-mannered Manhattan psychiatrist Dr. Robert Elliot (played by Michael Caine) worked, in the basement office, in Brian DePalma's 1980 suspense film *Dressed to Kill.* A block farther north, at **171 East 71st Street,** the white town house with the green striped awning was where Holly Golightly (played by Audrey Hepburn) lived in *Breakfast at Tiffany's.* And at **114 E. 72nd Street,** you'll find the modern white brick apartment tower where Sylvia Miles slipped Jon Voight past the doorman after picking him up on the street in *Midnight Cowboy.*

At this point, shoppers may want to double back to Madison Avenue and get down to shopping business (*see* Chapter 7). The catchphrase "Madison Avenue" no longer refers to the midtown advertising district (most major agencies have moved away from there anyway) but instead to uptown's fashion district: Madison Mile, between 59th and 79th streets, an exclusive area of haute couture designer boutiques, patrician art galleries, and unique specialty stores. For the most part, these shops are small, intimate, expensive—and almost invariably closed on Sundays. Even if you're just window-shopping, it's fun to step inside the tony digs of **Ralph Lauren** (867 Madison Ave. at 72nd St.), which hardly seems like a store at all. In fact, it's in the landmark Rhinelander Mansion and has preserved the grand house's walnut fittings, oriental carpets, and family portraits as an aristocratic setting in which to display high-style preppy clothing (it's draped about casually, as though waiting to be put away). Be sure to visit the fourth-floor home furnishings section, where merchandise is arrayed in to-the-manor-born dream suites.

Just east of Madison Avenue, at 35 E. 76th Street, is the **Car-lyle Hotel,** one of the city's most elite and discreet properties (*see* Chapter 9). In the early 1960s President John F. Kennedy frequently stayed here; rumor has it that he entertained Marilyn Monroe in his rooms when Mrs. Kennedy was not around. The hotel's current roster of rich-and-famous guests includes Elizabeth Taylor, George C. Scott, Steve Martin, Paul Newman, and Warren Beatty.

West of Madison is the so-called **Gucci Town House** (16 E. 76th St.), the former Gucci family mansion, which in 1988 sold for $7 million, at the time the most ever paid for a New York town house.

Time Out Stop in at the homey, casual **Kalinka Cafe** (1067 Madison at 80th St., tel. 212/472–9656) for a bit of borscht or some chicken Kiev. This narrow restaurant features fresh flowers and delicious Russian entrées ranging from $9 to $20.

Continue north on Madison Avenue past the **Frank E. Camp-bell Funeral Chapel** (1076 Madison Ave. at 81st St.), *the* place for fashionable funerals since 1898. The somber chocolate-colored edifice has seen massive funeral events for Rudolph Val-entino (1926) and Judy Garland (1969), and more recent cere-monies for Robert Kennedy, John Lennon, and Rita Hayworth.

If you've still got the energy, head up to 86th Street and walk east all the way over to York Avenue, a far more modest and ethnic part of town. In the **Henderson Place Historic District,** you'll find 24 small-scale town houses built in the 1880s in the Queen Anne style, which was developed in England by Richard Norman Shaw. Designed to be comfortable yet romantic dwell-ings, they combine elements of the Elizabethan manor house with classic Flemish details. Note, especially, the lovely bay windows, the turrets marking the corner of each block, and the symmetrical roof gables, pediments, parapets, chimneys, and dormer windows.

Until the 1830s, when the New York & Harlem Railroad and a stagecoach line began racing through the area, this neighbor-hood was the quiet, remote hamlet of **Yorkville,** a predomi-nantly German community. Over the years it has also welcomed waves of immigrants from Austria, Hungary, and Czechoslova-kia, and local shops and restaurants still bear reminders of this European heritage.

When you reach East End Avenue, you'll be facing **Carl Schurz Park,** overlooking the East River. Stand by the railings and look out at the Triborough and Hell's Gate bridges, Ward's and Randall's islands, and, on the other side of the river, Astoria,

Queens. During the American Revolution, a house on this promontory was used as a fortification by the Continental army, then was taken over as a British outpost. In more peaceful times, the land became known as East End Park. It was renamed in 1911 to honor Carl Schurz (1829–1906), a famous 19th-century German immigrant who eventually served the United States as a minister to Spain, a major general in the Union Army, and a senator of Missouri. During the Hayes administration Schurz was Secretary of the Interior; he later moved back to Yorkville and worked as editor of the *New York Evening Post* and *Harper's Weekly*.

Stroll up Carl Schurz Park to reach one of the city's most famous residences, **Gracie Mansion,** the official home of the mayor of New York. Surrounded by a small lawn and flowerbeds, this Federal-style yellow frame house still feels like a country manor house, which is what it was built as in 1779 by wealthy merchant Archibald Gracie. The Gracie family entertained many notable guests at the mansion, including Louis Philippe (later king of France), President John Quincy Adams, the Marquis de Lafayette, Alexander Hamilton, James Fenimore Cooper, Washington Irving, and John Jacob Astor. The city purchased Gracie Mansion in 1887, and, after a period of use as the Museum of the City of New York (now at Fifth Ave. and 103rd St.—*see* Tour 5, above), Mayor Fiorello H. LaGuardia made it the official mayor's residence.

Tour 7: Central Park

Numbers in the margin correspond with points of interest on the Central Park map.

It's amazing that 843 acres of the world's most valuable real estate should be set aside as a park, yet the city's 1856 decision to do so has proved to be marvelous wisdom, for Central Park contributes mightily toward helping New Yorkers maintain their sanity. It provides space large enough to get lost in (the entire principality of Monaco would fit within its borders), space where you can escape from the rumble of traffic to hear a bird sing or watch an earthworm tumble through the soil.

Although it appears to be simply a swath of rolling countryside exempted from urban development, Central Park is in fact one of the most cunningly planned artificial landscapes ever built. When they began in 1858, designers Frederick Law Olmsted and Calvert Vaux were presented with a swampy neighborhood of a few farms, houses, and a church. It took them 16 years, $14 million, and 5 million cubic yards of moved earth to create this playground of lush lawns, thick forests, and quiet ponds. Hills and tunnels artfully conceal transverse roads (66th, 79th, 86th, and 96th streets) so crosstown traffic will not disturb park goers, and a meandering circular drive carries vehicular traffic in the park (the drive is closed to auto traffic on weekends year-round).

Today Central Park hosts just about any activity that a city dweller might engage in outdoors: jogging, cycling, horseback riding, softball, ice skating, croquet, tennis, bird-watching, boating, chess, checkers, theater, concerts, skateboarding, and break dancing. If you're traveling with children, you'll especially appreciate how much there is to do and see. Try to come on a weekend, when local residents gratefully flock here to play—free entertainment is on tap, and the entire social microcosm is on parade.

Weekend crowds also make it safe to go into virtually any area of the park, although even on weekdays you should be safe anywhere along this tour. Despite its bad reputation, Central Park has the lowest crime rate of any precinct in the city—which is probably helped by the fact that respectable New Yorkers (except for dog-walkers and dedicated runners) stay out of it at night. You should do the same.

Our route covers a lot of territory, but Olmsted and Vaux scattered their attractions so generously that there's something to see or do at almost every turn. One caveat, however: Although there are cafés connected with several attractions, as well as food stands near many entrances, the range of food is limited and predictable. Do as most New Yorkers do and stop beforehand at a deli or gourmet food shop for a picnic to carry in with you. *Tel. 212/397–3156 for general information, 212/360–1333 for a recorded message on city park events, 212/397–3080 for information on weekend walks and talks led by Urban Park Rangers. Bus tours are offered on Tues. and Thurs.*

At Grand Army Plaza, or any intersection of Central Park South (59th Street's name between Fifth and Eighth avenues), you can hire a ride in a horse-drawn carriage. Recently, carriages were restricted by law to ramble only in the park. Carriages operate all year, except in extremely hot or cold weather, and blankets are provided when it's cool. The official rates are $34 for the first half hour and $10 for each additional 15 minutes, although drivers will often try to get more, so be sure to agree on a price in advance. And be forewarned: Only tourists ride in these carriages, so once you get in, you're marked.

To explore the park on foot, begin at Grand Army Plaza. Enter the park along the main road (East Drive), turning down the first path to your left to the **Pond.** Walk along the shore to the Gapstow Bridge (each of the park's 30 bridges has its own name and individual design), where you can look back at the often-photographed view of midtown skyscrapers reflected in the pond. From left to right, you'll see the peak-roofed brown Sherry-Netherland hotel, the black-and-white General Motors building, the rose-colored Chippendale top of the AT&T building, the black glass shaft of Trump Tower, and in front the green gables of the white Plaza Hotel.

Return to the main path and continue north to **Wollman Memorial Rink,** a skating rink that has become a symbol of municipal inefficiency to New Yorkers. Fruitless and costly attempts by the city to repair the deteriorated facility had kept it closed for years, until builder Donald Trump adopted the project and quickly completed it. Even if you don't want to join in, you can stand on the terrace here to watch the skaters—ice-skating throughout the winter, roller-skating April to October. The blaring loudspeaker system in this otherwise quiet park makes the rink hard to ignore. *Tel. 212/517–4800. Admission: $5 adults, $2 children under 12. Skate rental: $2.50. Open Mon.–Thurs. 10–9:30, Fri. and Sat. 10 AM–11 PM, Sun. 10–5.*

Adjacent to the rink is a recent Trump addition: the **Gotham Miniature Golf** course, where putters manoeuvre around scale models of various city landmarks. *Tel. 212/517–4800. Admis-*

Tour 7: Central Park

sion: $4 adults, $2 children under age 12. Open Mon.–Thurs. 10–9:30, Fri. and Sat. 10 AM–11 PM, Sun. 10–5.

Turn your back to the rink and you'll see the brightly painted ❸ eaves, steeple, and high-pitched slate roof of the **Dairy,** originally an actual dairy built in the 19th century when cows grazed here. Today it's the park's Visitor Center, offering maps, brochures, videos, children's programs, and some very interesting hands-on exhibits. *Tel. 212/397–3156. Open Tues.–Sun. 11–5, Fri. 1–5.*

As you leave the Dairy, follow the path to your right, which passes under the Playmates Arch—aptly named, because it leads to a large area of ballfields and playgrounds. Coming ❹ through the arch, you'll hear the jaunty music of the **Carousel.** Although this isn't the park's original one, it is an authentic antique, built in 1908 and later moved here from Coney Island. Its 58 ornately hand-carved steeds are three-quarters the size of real horses, and the organ plays an astonishing variety of tunes, new and old. *Tel. 212/879–0244. Admission: 75¢. Open weekdays 10:30–4:30, weekends 10:30–5:30.*

Climb the slope to the left of the Playmates Arch and walk along beside the Circular Drive. From here you can choose between two parallel routes: Turn left onto the paved path that ❺ runs alongside the chain-link fence of the **Sheep Meadow,** or go ❻ all the way to the circular flowerbed at the foot of the **Mall.** The broad formal walkway of the Mall called **"The Literary Walk"** is a peaceful spot, lined with the largest group of American elms in the northeast and statues of famous men, including Shakespeare, Robert Burns, and Sir Walter Scott. The other path, however, buzzes on weekends with human activity: volleyball games, roller-skating, impromptu music fests. By contrast, the 15 grassy acres of the Sheep Meadow make an ideal spot for picnicking or sunbathing. It's an officially designated quiet zone, where the most vigorous sports allowed are kite-flying and Frisbee-tossing. This lawn was actually used for grazing sheep until 1934; the nearby sheepfold was turned into the Tavern on the Green restaurant (*see* Tour 8, below).

The gravel path that borders the Sheep Meadow on the north is ❼ heady with the scent of lilacs in spring; it leads to the **Mineral Springs Pavilion,** where there's a snack bar. Behind it are the beautifully manicured **Lawn Bowling Greens** and **Croquet Grounds.** Peer through gaps in the high hedges to watch the players, usually dressed in crisp white. To obtain a permit, call 212/360–8133. (Programming here is questionable for the next two years due to reconstruction).

Both the Sheep Meadow path and the Mall eventually lead to ❽ the **Bandshell,** site of summer concerts, speeches, and performance art. (In December 1980, just after John Lennon's assassination, thousands of mourners stood here in an emotional moment of silence to pay tribute to his memory.) The 72nd Street transverse—the only crosstown street that connects with the Circular Drive—cuts across the park just north of here, but you can pass beneath it through a lovely tiled arcade ❾ to reach **Bethesda Fountain,** set on an elaborately patterned paved terrace on the edge of the **Lake.** This ornate, three-tiered fountain is named after the biblical Bethesda pool in Jerusalem, which was supposedly given healing powers by an angel (hence the angel rising from the center). Perch on the low terrace wall or the edge of the fountain and watch the rowboaters stroke past on the lake. If you want to get out on the

⑩ water yourself, take the path east from the terrace to **Loeb Boathouse,** where in season you can rent a rowboat (or a Venetian gondola!). The boathouse also operates a bike-rental facility and a better-than-average restaurant. *Boat rental $6 per hr, gondola $20 per 30 min; tel. 212/517–2233. Bicycle rental $6 per hr, tandems $12 per hr; tel. 212/861–4137.*

⑪ The path to the west of the terrace leads to **Bow Bridge,** a splendid cast-iron bridge arching over a neck of the lake. The view from either side is postcard-perfect, with the water reflecting a quintessentially New York image of vintage apartment buildings peeping above the treetops. If you continue across

⑫ the bridge, you'll enter the **Ramble,** a heavily wooded 37-acre area laced with twisting, climbing paths. This is prime bird-watching territory; a rest stop along a major migratory route, it shelters many of the 269 species of birds that have been sighted in the park. Because it is so dense and isolated, however, it may not be a good place to wander alone.

If you don't venture into the Ramble, recross Bow Bridge and

⑬ continue west on the lakeside path to **Cherry Hill,** where a circular plaza sets off a wrought-iron-and-gilt fountain that is smaller, but no less lovely, than Bethesda Fountain. This area was originally a carriage turnaround and watering area for horses. The path will lead you back to the 72nd Street transverse; on the rocky outcrop directly across the road, you'll see a statue of a falconer gracefully lofting his bird. Turn to the right and you'll see a more prosaic statue, a pompous bronze figure of Daniel Webster with his hand thrust into his coat. Cross the Circular Drive behind Webster, being careful to watch for bikes hurtling around the curve.

⑭ You've now come to **Strawberry Fields,** the "international peace garden" memorializing singer John Lennon. Climbing up a hill, its curving paths, shrubs, trees, and flowerbeds create a deliberately informal pastoral landscape, reminiscent of the English parks Lennon may have been thinking of when he wrote the Beatles song "Strawberry Fields." A black-and-white mosaic set into one of the sidewalks contains simply the word "Imagine," another Lennon song title. Just beyond the trees, at 72nd Street and Central Park West, is the Dakota (*see* Tour 8, below), where Lennon and his wife Yoko Ono lived at the time of his death.

From the top of Strawberry Fields' hill, turn right through a rustic wood arbor thickly hung with wisteria vines, then head back down the hill and follow the Circular Drive north (cross the drive as soon as possible so you can walk along the lake). Shortly past the lake, you'll see on your right a dark wood chalet that looks like something straight out of Germany's Black

⑮ Forest. This is the **Swedish Cottage,** where weekly marionette shows are staged. *Tel. 212/988–9093. Admission: $2. Call for schedule and reservations.*

⑯ Turn right and walk past the cottage to the little-known **Shakespeare Garden,** one of the park's few formal flower plantings, tucked onto terraces on the side of a relatively steep hill. In the garden, you'll find plants that William Shakespeare mentioned in his writings. (It is just one of the many Shakespeare Gardens

⑰ throughout the world.) The open-air **Delacorte Theater,** where the New York Shakespeare Festival performs each summer, is just around the corner. But for the best view of the Delacorte, head for the top of the hill, aptly called **Vista Rock.**

⓲ Vista Rock is dominated by **Belvedere Castle,** built in 1872 of the same gray Manhattan schist that thrusts out of the soil in dramatic outcrops throughout the park. If you step through the pavilion out onto the lip of the rock, you can examine some of this schist, polished and striated by Ice Age glaciers. From here you can look down directly upon the stage of the **⓳** Delacorte; you can also see the **Great Lawn** stretching beyond, a series of softball fields that hum with action on weekends and most summer evenings. In summer, should you see a few hundred people picnicking in a row around the oval edge of the lawn, you'll know they're waiting to pick up free tickets to a Shakespeare performance at the Delacorte.

The castle itself, a typically 19th-century mishmash of styles—Norman, Gothic, Moorish—was deliberately kept small so that when it was viewed from across the lake, the lake would seem bigger. (The Ramble's forest now obscures the lake's castle view.) Since 1919 it has been a measurement station of the U.S. Weather Bureau; look up to see the twirling meteorological instruments atop the tower. Climb out onto its balconies for a dramatic view, or get a minilesson in geology from the exhibits within. If you've got children with you, visit the ground-floor learning center. *Tel. 212/772-0210. Admission free. Open Tues.–Thur. and weekends 11–5, Fri. 1–5.*

From the castle's plaza, take a left and follow the path along **⓴** **Turtle Pond,** populated by fish, ducks, and dragonflies, as well as turtles. At the east end of the pond you'll pass a statue of King Jagiello of Poland; groups gather here for folk-dancing on **㉑** weekends. Follow the path north to nearby **Cleopatra's Needle,** a somewhat worn obelisk covered with hieroglyphics; it was a gift to the city in 1881 from the khedive of Egypt. The copper crabs supporting the huge stone at each corner almost seem squashed by its weight. If you look just past the trees, you can see the glass-enclosed wing of the Metropolitan Museum (*see* Tour 5, above) that holds the Egyptian Temple of Dendur.

Vigorous walkers may want to continue north to the **Reservoir,** popular with New Yorkers for the running track that surrounds it, and, in springtime, for its fragrant flowering trees. The city's main reservoirs are upstate; this one is more or less a holding tank.

Others can return south from Cleopatra's Needle, following the path to the left under Greywacke Arch, which leads around the back corner of the Metropolitan Museum. This side of the park, perhaps in keeping with its proximity to the East Side, has a tamer landscape than the west side, and here you'll see more uniformed nannies and fussy little dogs on leashes. A few minutes' walk will take you to one of the park's most formal areas: **㉒** the symmetrical stone basin of the **Conservatory Water,** where you can watch some very sophisticated model boats being raced each Saturday morning at 10 AM. (Unfortunately, model boats are not for rent here.) At the north end of the pond is one of the park's most beloved statues, José de Creeft's 1960 sculpture of **Alice in Wonderland,** sitting on a giant mushroom with the Mad Hatter, White Rabbit, and leering Cheshire Cat in attendance. On the west side of the pond, a bronze statue of **Hans Christian**

Andersen, the Ugly Duckling at his feet, is the site of storytelling hours on summer weekends.

Climb the hill at the far end of the Conservatory Water, cross the 72nd Street transverse, and follow the path south to the **23 Children's Zoo.** Although small, it's friendly—mostly barnyard animals, but a few more exotic critters as well, housed in colorfully designed enclosures that allow the little ones to see up close. *Tel. 212/408–0271. Admission: 10¢. Open daily 10–4:30.*

24 Pass under the Denesmouth Arch to the **Delacorte Clock,** a delightful glockenspiel set above a redbrick arch. Every hour its six-animal band circles around and plays a tune, while monkeys on the top hammer their bells.

25 Just past the clock is the **Central Park Zoo,** recently reopened after years of renovation. Clustered around the central Sea Lion Pool are separate exhibits for each of the Earth's major environments; the Polar Circle features a huge penguin tank and polar-bear floe; the open-air Temperate Territory is highlighted by a pit of chattering monkies; and the Tropic Zone contains the flora and fauna of a miniature rain forest. This is a good zoo for children and adults who like to take time to watch the animals; even a leisurely visit will take only about an hour, for there are only about 100 species on display. Go to the Bronx Zoo (*see* Chapter 4) if you need tigers, giraffes, and elephants— the biggest specimen here is the polar bear. *Tel. 212/439–6500. Admission: $1 adults, 50¢ senior citizens, 25¢ children 3–12. Open Apr.–Oct., weekdays 10–5, Tues. 10–8, weekends and holidays 10–5:30; Nov.–Mar., daily 10–4:30.*

Tour 8: The Upper West Side

Numbers in the margin correspond with points of interest on the Upper West Side, Columbia map.

The Upper West Side has never been as fashionable as the East Side, despite the fact that it has a similar mix of real estate— large apartment buildings along Central Park West, West End Avenue, and Riverside Drive; and town houses on the shady, quiet cross streets. Once a haven for the Jewish intelligentsia, by the 1960s the West Side had become a rather grungy multiethnic community. In the 1970s gentrification began slowly, with actors, writers, and gays as the earliest settlers. Today, however, this area almost rivals the East Side in attracting high-powered Yuppies who can afford to live anywhere. There seems to be scaffolding everywhere, as landmark brownstones are meticulously restored and new windows installed in huge apartment blocks (a sure sign of impending co-opping). Young families have gravitated to its large apartments; on weekends, the sidewalks are crowded with couples pushing babies around in their imported strollers. Columbus Avenue is a trendy boutique-and-restaurant strip, somewhat hipper and more dynamic than Madison Avenue; Amsterdam Avenue is slowly following suit, although its architecture is still largely tenement-style, its shopfronts an uneasy mix of bodegas and boutiques. Along upper Broadway, new luxury apartment towers are slowly blocking in the horizon. Many longtime Westsiders decry the "yuppification" of their neighborhoods, but the good news is that small businesses now thrive on blocks that a few years ago were not safe to walk on.

❶ The West Side story begins at **Columbus Circle,** where a statue of Christopher himself crowns a stately pillar at the intersection of Broadway, Eighth Avenue, Central Park West, and Central Park South. Columbus Circle is a good place to begin any tour of New York, for it is the headquarters of the **New York Convention and Visitors Bureau,** located in a weird pseudo-Moorish structure locally nicknamed "the Lollipop Building." Count on the bureau for brochures; bus and subway maps; hotel, restaurant, and shopping guides; a seasonal calendar of events; free TV-show tickets and discounts on Broadway theater; and sound advice. The New York City Department of Cultural Affairs operates an art gallery on the second floor. *2 Columbus Circle, tel. 212/397–8222. Open weekdays 9–6.*

On the southwest quadrant of the circle, the **New York Coliseum,** a blank functional-looking white brick building, was the city's chief convention and trade-show venue before the opening of the Jacob Javits Center. A soaring multiuse complex proposed for the site was bitterly opposed by New Yorkers determined not to let its huge shadow be cast across Central Park; the project was scaled down considerably, and construction may even have begun by the time you read this. On the northeast corner of the circle, an entrance to Central Park is presided over by the Maine Monument, with its florid bronze figures atop a stocky limestone pedestal. The pie-shape wedge of land between Central Park West and Broadway holds the **Paramount Communications Building,** formerly the Gulf & Western Building. The box office of the subterranean Paramount movie theater juts above the ground on the Broadway side of the plaza.

At the world headquarters of the **American Bible Society** (1865 Broadway at 61st St., tel. 212/581–7400), ascend red-carpeted stairs to a little-known second-floor library (open weekdays 9–4:30), which displays, among other things, Helen Keller's massive 10-volume braille Bible, a replica of the original Gutenberg press, and a Torah (Jewish scriptures) from China. Four blocks up the street, the **Mormon Visitors Center** (Broadway and 65th St., tel. 212/595–1825; open daily 10–8) has a free guided tour and films explaining the beliefs of the Church of Jesus Christ of Latter-day Saints.

❷ Covering an eight-block area west of Broadway between 62nd and 66th streets, **Lincoln Center** is the home of New York's major-league performing arts institutions. This unified complex of pale travertine marble was built during the 1960s to supplant an urban ghetto (*West Side Story* was filmed on the slum's gritty, deserted streets just before the demolition crews moved in). Lincoln Center can seat nearly 15,000 spectators at one time in its various halls (*see* Chapter 10).

Stand on Broadway, facing the central court with its huge fountain, which Mel Brooks fans may recognize as the spot where Zero Mostel and Gene Wilder danced exuberantly in *The Producers.* The three concert halls on this plaza clearly relate to each other architecturally, with their symmetrical bi-level facades, yet each has slightly different lines and different details. To your left, huge honeycomb lights hang on the portico of the **New York State Theater,** home to the New York City Ballet and the New York City Opera. Straight ahead, at the rear of the plaza, is the **Metropolitan Opera House,** its brilliant-colored

American Museum of
Natural History
and Hayden
Planetarium, **8**

Barnard College, **12**

Cathedral of St. John
the Divine, **11**

Columbia
University, **10**

Columbus Circle, **1**

Dakota, **6**

Grant's Tomb, **14**

Jewish Theological
Seminary, **16**

Lincoln Center, **2**

Museum of American
Folk Art, **3**

New-York Historical
Society, **7**

Riverside Church, **13**

Riverside Park, **9**

Spanish and
Portuguese
Synagogue, Shearith
Israel, **4**

Teachers College, **17**

Union Theological
Seminary, **15**

Verdi Square, **5**

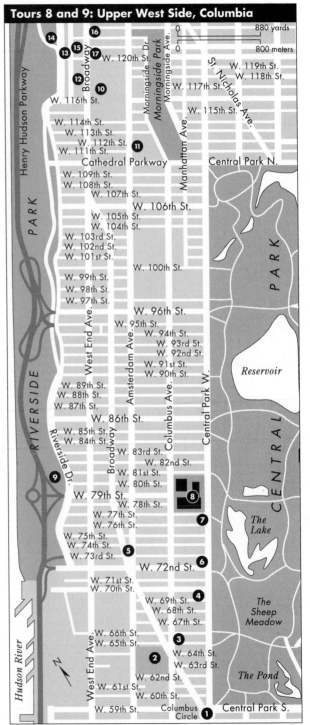

Tours 8 and 9: Upper West Side, Columbia

Chagall tapestries visible through the arched lobby windows; the Metropolitan Opera and American Ballet Theatre perform here. To your right, abstract bronze sculptures distinguish **Avery Fisher Hall,** named after the founder of Fisher Radio and host to the New York Philharmonic Orchestra.

Wander through the plaza, then angle to your left between the New York State Theater and the Metropolitan Opera House into **Damrosch Park,** where summer open-air festivals are often accompanied by free concerts at the **Guggenheim Bandshell.** Angle to your right from the plaza, between the Metropolitan and Avery Fisher, and you'll come to the North plaza, with a massive Henry Moore sculpture reclining in a reflecting pool. To the rear is the **Library and Museum of the Performing Arts,** a branch of the New York Public Library with an extensive collection of books, records, and scores on music, theater, and dance; visitors can listen to any of 42,000 records and tapes, or check out its four galleries. Next to the library is the wide glass-walled lobby of the **Vivian Beaumont** and **Mitzi E. Newhouse theaters,** officially considered Broadway houses although far removed from the theater district.

An overpass leads from this plaza across 65th Street to the world-renowned **Juilliard School** (for music and theater); its ground floor houses **Alice Tully Hall,** home of the Chamber Music Society of Lincoln Center and the Film Society of Lincoln Center.

Visitors can wander freely through the lobbies of all these buildings. A one-hour guided "Take-the-Tour" covers all the grand theaters. *Tel. 212/877–1800, ext. 512, for schedule. Admission: $6.25 adults, $5.25 students and senior citizens, $3.50 children.*

Conveniently close to Lincoln Center, at the northwest corner of Broadway and 66th Street, you'll find **Tower Records,** the uptown branch of that vast emporium of records, tapes, and CDs. The checkout lines are long and slow, but there's always a good soundtrack to browse by, and you can find something here for every musical taste—opera, jazz, rock, gospel, early music, new music, you name it.

❸ Across the busy intersection, the long-orphaned **Museum of American Folk Art** has found a new home at Columbus Avenue and 66th Street. (This gallery will become an annex once the museum's permanent headquarters on West 53rd Street are completed in 1992.) Its collection includes primitive paintings, quilts, carvings, dolls, trade signs, painted wood carousel horses, and a giant Indian-chief copper weathervane. *2 Lincoln Sq., tel. 212/977–7298. Admission free. Open daily 9–9.*

Turn onto West 67th Street and head toward Central Park along one of the city's most handsome blocks. Many of the apartment buildings here were designed as "studio buildings," with immense windows that make them ideal for artists; look up at the facades and imagine the high-ceilinged spaces within. Also notice the Gothic motifs, carved in white stone or wrought in iron, that decorate several of these buildings at street level. Perhaps the finest apartment building on the block is the **Hotel des Artistes** (1 W. 67th St.), built in 1918, with its elaborate mock-Elizabethan lobby. Its tenants have included Isadora Duncan, Rudolph Valentino, Norman Rockwell, Noël Coward, Fannie Hurst, and contemporary actors Joel Grey and Richard

Thomas; another tenant, Howard Chandler Christy, designed the lush, soft-toned murals in the excellent ground-floor restaurant, **Café des Artistes** (*see* Chapter 8), where Louis Malle's *My Dinner with André* was filmed.

Another dining landmark is just inside Central Park at 66th Street, **Tavern on the Green** (*see* Chapter 8). Originally built as a sheepfold, in the days when sheep grazed on the meadows of the park, it was converted into a restaurant in the 1930s. Many of its dining rooms have fine park views, and at night white lights strung through the surrounding trees create an undeniably magical effect.

Movie buffs may want to detour down to 65th Street, where you'll find the art deco building that was supposedly **"Spook Central"** in the movie *Ghostbusters* (55 Central Park West).

➍ If you return to Broadway via 70th Street, you'll pass **The Spanish and Portuguese Synagogue, Shearith Israel,** at the southwest corner of 70th and Central Park West, a temple built in 1897 as the fifth home of the oldest Jewish congregation in the United States (founded in 1655). The adjoining "Little Synagogue" is a replica of Shearith Israel's Georgian-style first synagogue; inside are many furnishings from that 1730 temple. On the next block, at 135 West 70th Street, is a startling Egyptian-style facade, built in 1926 as the grand lodge of a fraternal organization, the **Knights of Pythias Temple.** Recently converted into a condo, it has been toned down somewhat from the original multicolored King Tut fantasy.

At Broadway and 70th Street, look north to view the uptown skyline. Slightly ahead and to your right you'll see the **Dorilton,** an ornate redbrick apartment building with an odd buttress flying from one wing to another; this was supposedly the home of the news anchor played by Sigourney Weaver in *Eyewitness*. Beyond, at the square's north end, is an imposing gray bank building, now a branch of the Apple Bank for Savings but originally the **Central Savings Bank,** built to resemble the Federal Reserve Bank downtown. The **subway kiosk** on the traffic island south of 72nd Street is an official city landmark, a structure with rounded neo-Dutch moldings that was the first express station north of 42nd Street. Rising behind and to the left of it you'll see the white facade and fairy-castle turrets of the **Ansonia Hotel** (73rd St. and Broadway), a turn-of-the-century luxury building whose thick, soundproof walls made it attractive to musicians; once home to Enrico Caruso, Igor Stravinsky, Arturo Toscanini, Florenz Ziegfeld, Theodore Dreiser, and Babe Ruth, today it is decidedly down-at-heel.

Time Out   Keep to your right, staying on the east side of this hectic intersection, and head up to **Gray's Papaya King** (southeast corner of 72nd St. and Amsterdam Ave., tel. 212/799–0243), a New York quasi-institution that pairs the sacred (health-enriching papaya and other natural juices) and the profane (hot dogs smothered in sauerkraut and onions).

Officially, the triangle south of 72nd Street is **Sherman Square** (named for the Union Civil War general, William Tecumseh **➎** Sherman), while the triangle north of 72nd is **Verdi Square** (for Italian opera composer Giuseppe Verdi). A decade ago, however, Verdi Square was better known as "Needle Park" because of the drug addicts who hung out there. While the neighborhood has vastly improved, Verdi Square is still unverdant and unwelcoming, but at long last the benches where vagrants congregated were torn out in 1989.

❻ Head east on 72nd Street, to where the stately **Dakota** presides over the corner of 72nd and Central Park West. When this was first built in the 1880s, rich people did not live in apartment buildings, and no one lived this far north (it seemed as far away as the Dakotas, hence the name). But with its lavish flats, reasonable rents, and attentive staff, the Dakota made apartment living chic. Its tenants have included Boris Karloff, Judy Holliday, José Ferrer and Rosemary Clooney, Lauren Bacall, Rex Reed, Gilda Radner, and John Lennon and Yoko Ono. Soot has darkened the building's yellow brick, stone trim, and copper turrets, and this slightly spooky appearance was played up in the movie *Rosemary's Baby*, filmed here. Stop by the gate on 72nd Street; this is the spot where, in December 1980, a deranged fan shot John Lennon as he came home from a recording session. Lennon is memorialized in Central Park's Strawberry Fields, across the street (*see* Tour 7, above).

Proceed up Central Park West and you'll see several other famous apartment buildings, including **The Langham** (135 Central Park West), where Mia Farrow's apartment was featured in Woody Allen's film *Hannah and Her Sisters;* the twin-towered **San Remo** (145-146 Central Park West), over the years home to Rita Hayworth, Dustin Hoffman, Raquel Welch, Paul Simon, Tony Randall, and Diane Keaton—but not to Madonna, whose application was rejected because of her flamboyant lifestyle; and **The Kenilworth** (151 Central Park West), with its immense pair of ornate front columns, once home to Basil Rathbone, film's quintessential Sherlock Holmes.

❼ The city's oldest museum, **The New-York Historical Society,** preserves within its stern gray granite home what was unique about the city's past, including the quaint hyphen in "New-York." Along with changing exhibits of American history and art, the museum displays original Audubon watercolors, early American toys, Tiffany lamps, antique vehicles, and Hudson River School landscapes. **The Jewish Museum** will present exhibits here on the first and second floors through 1992. *170 Central Park West and 77th St., tel. 212/873-3400. Admission: $3 adults, $2 senior citizens, $1 children under 12; pay what you wish Tues. Open Tues.-Sun. 10-5.*

❽ The **American Museum of Natural History,** the attached **Hayden Planetarium,** and their surrounding grounds occupy a four-block tract bounded by Central Park West, Columbus Avenue, and 77th and 81st streets. As you approach at 77th Street, you can see the original architecture in the pink granite corner towers, with their beehive crowns. A more classical facade was added along Central Park West, with its centerpiece an enormous equestrian statue of President Theodore Roosevelt, naturalist and explorer. Enter the museum on 81st Street.

With a collection of more than 36 million artifacts, the museum displays something for every taste, from a 94-foot blue whale to the 563-carat Star of India sapphire. Among the most enduringly popular exhibits are the wondrously detailed dioramas of animal habitat groups, on the first and second floors just behind the rotunda, and the fourth-floor halls full of dinosaur skeletons. In the new Hall of South American Peoples, opened in 1989, bird calls and monkey howls provide a soundtrack for a look at the Amazon rain forest. The Naturemax Theater projects films on a giant screen; the Hayden Planetarium (on 81st Street) has two stories of exhibits, plus Sky Shows projected on 22 wraparound screens; its rock-music Laser Shows draw crowds of teenagers on Friday and Saturday nights. *Museum: tel. 212/769–5100. Suggested contribution: $4 adults, $2 children. Open Sun.–Tues. and Thurs. 10–5:45; Wed., Fri., and Sat. 10–9. Planetarium: tel. 212/769–5920. Admission: $4 adults, $3 senior citizens, members, and students; $2 children; $6 for laser show. Open weekdays 12:30–4:45, Sat. 10–6, Sun. 12–6. Naturemax Theater film admission: single feature—$4 adults, $2 children; double feature—$6 adults, $3 children; discounts for members, senior citizens, and groups. Call 212/ 769–5920 for show times.*

Directly behind the museum is Columbus Avenue, where shoppers may want to forsake this tour for boutique-shopping. If you do, work your way up one side of the street and back down the other, going north to 86th Street and south to 67th Street (*see* Chapter 7).

Return to Broadway via 77th Street to join New Yorkers in a pilgrimage to some of the city's greatest food shrines, all on the west side of the street. The fresh produce in the bountiful but unpretentious **Fairway Market** (2127 Broadway at 74th St.) literally bursts onto the street. Have a look at the handmade signs describing the produce and cheeses; they can be as fresh as the merchandise itself. **Citarella's** fish store at 75th Street and Broadway features intricate, often absurd arrangements of seafood on shaved ice in the front window. At the southwest corner of Broadway and 80th Street, **H & H Bagels** sells several varieties of huge, chewy bagels hot from the oven, along with juices, cream cheese, and lox (but no coffee—and they will not dress your bagel in any way). On the next block, **Zabar's** offers exquisite delicatessen items, prepared foods, gourmet groceries, coffee, and cheeses; a mezzanine level features cookware, dishes, and small appliances. Be prepared to muscle a lot of pushy strangers for elbow room, for Zabar's prides itself on carrying a vast range of hard-to-get foods, and at prices that are very reasonable.

9 Having bought your picnic lunch, you may now want to head west to **Riverside Park,** a long, slender green space along the Hudson River landscaped by Central Park architects Olmsted and Vaux. Enter at 80th Street and Riverside Drive and wander to your right, heading for the **Promenade,** a broad formal walkway with a stone parapet looking out over the river. Before strolling along the Promenade, however, you may want to descend the steps here and go through the underpass beneath Riverside Drive, to reach the **79th Street Boat Basin,** a rare spot in Manhattan where you can walk right along the river's edge, smell the salt air, and watch a flotilla of houseboats bob on the water.

If you walk to the end of the Promenade, you'll see a patch of its median strip exploding with flowers tended by nearby residents. Look up to your right, where the Civil War **Soldiers' and Sailors' Monument,** a tight circle of white marble columns, crests a hill along Riverside Drive. Climb to the monument for a refreshing view of Riverside Park, the Hudson River, and the New Jersey waterfront.

Tour 9: Columbia University and Environs

Numbers in the margin correspond with points of interest on the Upper West Side, Columbia map.

On the high ridge just north and west of Central Park, a cultural outpost grew up at the end of the 19th century, spear-headed by a triad of institutions: Columbia University, which developed the mind; St. Luke's Hospital, which cared for the body; and the Cathedral of St. John the Divine, which tended the soul. Idealistically conceived of as an American Acropolis, the cluster of academic and religious institutions that developed here managed to keep these blocks stable during years when neighborhoods on all sides were collapsing into decay. In the past decade, West Side gentrification has reclaimed the area to the south, while the Harlem areas north and east of here remain problematic. Yet within the gates of the Columbia or Barnard campuses, or inside the hush of the cathedral or Riverside Church, the pace of life seems kinder, gentler, more contemplative. Being a student neighborhood, the area has a casual atmosphere, hip and yet whole-earth, friendly, and fun.

🔟 A logical starting point is on the east side of Broadway at 116th Street, right in front of the campus gates of **Columbia University,** a wealthy, private, coed institution that is New York City's only Ivy League school. The gilded crowns on the black wrought-iron gates serve as a reminder that this was originally King's College when it was founded in 1754, before American independence. Walk along the herringbone patterned brick paths of College Walk into the refreshingly green main quadrangle, dominated by massive neoclassical **Butler Library** to your right (south) and the rotunda-topped **Low Memorial Library** to your left (north). Butler, built in 1934, holds the bulk of the university's 4.5 million books; Low, built in 1895–97 by McKim, Mead & White (who laid out the general campus plan when the college moved here in 1897), is now mostly offices, but on weekdays you can go inside to see its domed, templelike former Reading Room. The steps of Low Library, presided over by Daniel Chester French's statue *Alma Mater*, have been a focal point for campus life, not least during the student riots of 1968. Here Dan Aykroyd and Bill Murray, playing recently fired Columbia research scientists, hit upon the idea of going into business as *Ghostbusters*.

Before Columbia moved here, this land was occupied by the Bloomingdale Insane Asylum; the sole survivor of those days is **Buell Hall,** the gabled orange-red brick house just past Low Library. Just north is **St. Paul's Chapel** (1907), an exquisite little Byzantine-style domed church laid out in the shape of a cross. Step inside to admire the newly renovated tiled vaulting. *Tel. 212/854-3574. Open Sept.–May, Mon.–Fri. 10–4; Sat. 11–2; Sun. for services, 8:30–1 and 6–9. Call ahead for hours June–Aug.*

A student-run art gallery has been opened downstairs in the chapel's Postcrypt. *Tel. 212/854-1953. Admission free. Open Tues.–Fri. 2–6 and Sat. 9–12:30 as a coffee house, offering poetry readings and folk music.*

Cross Amsterdam Avenue, either through the second set of campus gates at the other end of College Walk, or by taking the overpass. The rather grim white building on the northeast corner of 116th Street and Amsterdam Avenue features a massive, muscular statue of the Greek prince Bellerophon taming the winged horse Pegasus; this is sculptor Jacob Lipchitz's metaphor for the force of law overcoming disorder, an appropriate sentiment for the front of the **Law School.** Walk east to Morningside Drive, where on your left you'll see the redbrick Georgian-style **President's House** (1912), another McKim, Mead & White design. Across the street you may want to pause on the overlook to gaze into **Morningside Park,** tumbling steeply into a wooded gorge. Designed by Central Park's Olmsted and Vaux, it's a lovely landscape, but bordered as it is by some rough blocks of Harlem, it's not safe to walk in.

As you proceed south on Morningside Drive you'll pass, at 114th Street, the graceful pillared portico of **Eglise de Notre Dame,** a Roman Catholic church that features, behind the altar, a replica of the French grotto of Lourdes; stop in, if possible, during one of the frequent daily services. Around the corner on 113th Street you can still see the baroque 1896 core of **St. Luke's Hospital,** which has grown rather awkwardly into a jumble of newer buildings.

⓫ A chain-link fence runs along 113th Street beside the **Cathedral of St. John the Divine,** New York's major Episcopal church and, when completed, to be the largest cathedral in the world (St. Peter's of Rome is larger, but it's technically a basilica). Here you can have a rare, fascinating look at a Gothic cathedral in progress. Before you go to the main entrance on Amsterdam Avenue, peer into this side lot—the cathedral's **stone-cutting yard,** the only such operation in the United States. This immense limestone-and-granite church has been built in spurts. Its first cornerstone was laid in 1892 and a second in 1925, but with the U.S. entry into World War II, construction came to a "temporary" halt that lasted until 1982. St. John's follows traditional Gothic engineering—it is supported by stonemasonry rather than by a steel skeleton—so new stonecutters had to be trained before the current work could proceed on the two front towers, which will be followed by the transept and, finally, the great central tower. A model in the superb gift shop inside shows what the cathedral will look like when completed, probably several years in the future. The shop is known for its fine selection of international crafts and ecological literature. Open daily, 9–5.

On the wide steps climbing to the Amsterdam Avenue entrance, you'll see five portals arching over the entrance doors; the central one shows St. John having his vision of the Lord in glory, but statuary is still being slowly added to the other portals. Before you go inside, take a closer look at the facade's huge blocks of limestone: Each one carries a pattern of rough chisel marks called "boasting," the individual mason's distinctive signature.

Inside is a vast nave, the length of two football fields, which can seat 5,000 worshipers. The small chapels that border the nave have a surprisingly contemporary outlook. The one immediately to your left celebrates athletes and sports, and just past it is the only **Poet's Corner** in the United States; the right-hand aisle's chapels movingly mourn tragedies such as the Holocaust and the spread of AIDS.

Beneath the 155-foot-high central dome, which could comfortably contain the Statue of Liberty, you can see another quirk of the cathedral: Its original Romanesque-Byzantine design was scrapped in 1907, when architect Ralph Adams Cram took over and instated a Gothic style. Here, where the transept will someday cross the nave, note the rough granite walls of the original scheme (they will eventually be covered with limestone); note also that the side nearer the entrance has a pointed Gothic arch, while the arch near the altar is still rounded Romanesque. The altar area itself expresses the cathedral's interfaith tradition with menorahs, Shinto vases, and golden chests presented by the king of Siam; the church's international mission is represented in the ring of chapels behind the altar, dedicated to various ethnic groups. The **Baptistry,** to the left of the altar, is an exquisite octagonal chapel with a 15-foot-high marble font and a polychrome sculpted frieze commemorating New York's Dutch heritage.

To the south of the cathedral itself is the **cathedral close,** a peaceful precinct of Gothic-style châteaus that include the Bishop's House, the Deanery, and the Cathedral School. A circular plaza just off Amsterdam at 111th Street features the Peace Fountain, which despite its rather grotesque central sculpture is interesting for the outer rim decorated with small bronzes designed by local schoolchildren.

Along with Sunday services (8, 9, and 11 AM, and 7 PM), the cathedral operates a score of community outreach programs and presents a full calendar of nonreligious (classical, folk, winter solstice) concerts. *Amsterdam Ave. and 112th St., tel. 212/316–7400. Tours Mon.–Sat. 11, Sun. 12:45.*

Time Out   On the other side of Amsterdam Avenue, between 111th and 112th streets, you'll find two casual restaurants: **V & T Restaurant** (1024 Amsterdam, tel. 212/663–1708) for spicy pizza and Italian cooking; and the **Hungarian Pastry Shop** (1030 Amsterdam Ave., tel. 212/866–4230) for luscious desserts and coffees.

Walk west to Broadway and back up to 117th Street, where ⑫ across from Columbia is its sister institution, **Barnard College,** established in 1889. One of the former Seven Sisters of women's colleges, Barnard has steadfastly remained a single-sex institution and has maintained its independence from Columbia, although its students can take classes there (and vice versa). The main gates face **Barnard Hall,** its brick-and-limestone design echoing Columbia's buildings. Turn right to follow the path north through the narrow but neatly landscaped campus. The student center and the science tower, a striking pair of modern white limestone buildings, face each other across a short flight of stairs; beyond them is **Milbank Hall,** another stately brick structure in the neoclassical mode. Note the bear (the college's mascot) on the carved stone seal to the left of the central window.

A narrow iron-barred gate to the left (closed on weekends, unfortunately) leads onto Claremont Avenue. Follow either Claremont or Broadway north to 120th Street, where a left-⑬ hand turn takes you to Riverside Drive. On your right, **Riverside Church** is a modern (1930) Gothic-style edifice whose smooth, pale limesto e walls seem the antithesis of St. John the Divine's rough gray hulk; in fact, it feels more akin to Rockefeller Center, not least because John D. Rockefeller was a major benefactor of the church. While most of the building is refined and restrained, the main entrance, on Riverside Drive, explodes with elaborate stone carving (modeled after the French cathedral of Chartres, as are many other decorative details here). Inside, look at the handsomely ornamented main sanctuary, which seats only half as many people as St. John the Divine does; take the elevator to the top of the 22-story, 356-foot tower (admission: $1), with its 74-bell carillon, the largest in the world. Affiliated with the Baptist church and the United Church of Christ, Riverside is basically nondenominational, interracial, international, extremely political, and socially conscious. Its calendar includes political and community events, dance and theater programs, and concerts, along with regular Sunday services at 10:45 AM. *Tel. 212/222–5900. Open daily 10–5; Sun. service 10:45.*

Across Riverside Drive, in Riverside Park, stands the General Grant National Memorial Monument, commonly known as ⓴ **Grant's Tomb,** where Civil War general and two-term president Ulysses S. Grant rests beside his wife, Julia Dent Grant. The white granite mausoleum, with its imposing columns and classical pediment, is much smaller inside than its model Les Invalides in Paris, where Napoleon is buried. Under a small white dome, the Grants' twin black marble sarcophagi are sunk into a deep circular chamber, which you view from above; minigalleries to the sides display photographs and Grant memorabilia. In contrast to this austere monument, the surrounding plaza features wacky 1960s-era mosaic benches, designed by local schoolchildren. *Riverside Dr. and 122nd St., tel. 212/666–1640. Admission free. Open Wed.–Sun. 9–4:30.*

You may want to sit for a moment in Sakura Park, a quiet formal garden on the other side of Riverside Drive, to admire **International House** (1924), an elegant, ornate, pale building that houses many foreign students enrolled in the area. Then walk back east on 122nd Street; across Claremont Avenue, you'll see the prestigious **Manhattan School of Music** (*see* Chapter 10) in the modern block on your left, and the interdenominational ⓯ **Union Theological Seminary** in the rough gray collegiate Gothic quadrangle on your right (the main entrance is at Broadway and 120th Street). Founded in 1836, the seminary moved here in 1910; it has one of the world's finest theological libraries.

At the corner of 122nd Street and Broadway, a large blank-walled redbrick tower fronts the intersection at an angle. This ⓰ is the **Jewish Theological Seminary,** founded in 1887 as a training ground for rabbis, cantors, and scholars of Conservative Judaism. This complex was built in 1930, although the tower, which housed part of the seminary's excellent library, was extensively renovated after a fire in 1966.

As you head back south on Broadway, on your left you'll see the ⓱ redbrick Victorian buildings of Columbia University's **Teachers College,** founded in 1887 and today the world's largest graduate school in the field of education. Notice the band of stone along the Broadway facade, inscribed with the names of famous teachers throughout history—a fitting comment upon this entire academically oriented neighborhood.

Tour 10: Harlem

Numbers in the margin correspond with points of interest on the Harlem map.

Harlem has been the mecca for black American culture and life for nearly a century. Originally called "Nieuw Haarlem" and settled by Dutch farmers, Harlem was a well-to-do suburb in the 19th century; black New Yorkers began settling here in large numbers in about 1900, moving into a surplus of fine apartment buildings and town houses built by real-estate developers for a middle-class white market that never materialized. By the 1920s, Harlem (with one "a") had become the most famous black community in the United States, perhaps in the world. In an astonishing confluence of talent, known as the Harlem Renaissance, black novelists, playwrights, musicians, and artists gathered here. Black performers starred in chic Harlem jazz clubs—which, ironically, only whites could attend. Throughout the Roaring Twenties, while whites flocked here for the infamous parties and nightlife, blacks settled in for the opportunity this self-sustaining community represented. But the Depression hit Harlem hard. By the late 1930s, it was no longer a popular social spot for downtown New Yorkers, and many successful black families began moving out to homes in the suburbs of Queens and New Jersey.

By the 1960s, Harlem's population had dropped dramatically, and many of those who remained were disillusioned enough to join in civil rights riots. A vicious cycle of crowded housing, poverty, and crime was choking the neighborhood, turning it into a simmering ghetto. Today, however, Harlem is well on its way to restoring itself. Mixed in with some of the seedy remains of the past are old jewels such as the refurbished Apollo Theatre and such new attractions as the Studio Museum. A great number of Harlem's classic brownstone and limestone homes are being restored and lived in by young families, bringing new life to the community.

Deserted buildings, burned-out shopfronts, and yards of rubble still scar certain parts; although a few whites have begun to move in here, some white visitors may feel conspicuous in what is still a largely black neighborhood. But Harlemites are accustomed to seeing tourists on their streets; only common traveler's caution is necessary during daytime excursions to any of the places highlighted, although for nighttime outings it's smart to take a taxi. Bus tours may be a good alternative way to see Harlem, because they cover more areas than the central Harlem walk outlined below (*see* Special-Interest Tours in Chapter 1).

Sunday is a good time to tour Harlem, because that's when you can listen to gospel music at one of the area's many churches. Soulful, moving, often joyous, gospel music blends elements from African songs and chants, American spirituals, and rhythm and blues. Gospel fans and visitors are welcome at the **Canaan Baptist Church of Christ**, where Wyatt Tee Walker is pastor. *132 W. 116th St., Sun. services 10:45 AM.*

As you head east from the church, notice on the southwest corner of 116th Street and Lenox Avenue the aluminum onion dome of the **Malcolm Shabazz Mosque** (102 W. 116th St.), a former casino that was converted in the mid-1960s to a black Mus-

lim temple (Malcolm X once preached here). Several Muslim stores are located nearby.

On weekdays you may want to begin your tour at the next stop, **Marcus Garvey Park**, which interrupts Fifth Avenue between 120th and 124th streets. Renamed after Marcus Garvey (1887–1940), who led the back-to-Africa movement, this rocky plot of land is interesting less for itself than for the handsome buildings of the surrounding Mount Morris Historic District (Mount Morris Square was the park's original name). Walk up the west side of the park to admire the fine town houses facing the park or on the side streets.

Between the brownstones on 120th Street you'll see **20 West Home of Black Cinema** (20 W. 120th St., tel. 212/410–2101), a private, black-owned movie theater that specializes in films written, produced, and directed by black artists. The owners, who live in the upper part of the house, have created a cozy basement theater and a comfortable sitting area where the artists often appear in person to discuss their films after the showing. Call to reserve a seat for one of the nighttime screenings.

Time Out At the other end of Marcus Garvey Park is **La Famille** (2017 5th Ave., between 124th and 125th Sts., tel. 212/722–9806), a bar and restaurant that serves great food upstairs and a changing nighttime menu of jazz downstairs. La Famille offers standard soul-food fare plus a more Continental menu—although, unfortunately, it's not open for lunch on weekends.

Harlem's main street is **125th Street,** the chief artery of its cultural, retail, and economic life. Real-estate values here have never come close to those downtown along Fifth Avenue or even Broadway, and many of the commercial buildings rise only a few stories. New businesses have been moving in of late, however, bringing smart new shopfronts along a retail row that until recently saw many "For Rent" signs. Among the revitalization projects is the new building that should be open as of June 1990 on the northeast corner of Fifth Avenue and 125th Street: Above the street-level stores will be the new home of the **National Black Theater** (tel. 212/722–3800), which produces new works by contemporary black writers.

The pivotal intersection of 125th Street and Lenox Avenue has been glorified with the name **Africa Square,** as part of that civic policy that often gives uptown streets different names (Seventh Avenue becomes Adam Clayton Powell, Jr., Boulevard, Eighth Avenue becomes Frederick Douglass Boulevard, Sixth Avenue is called Lenox Avenue) to reflect black heritage. Except in the case of Lenox Avenue, however, just about everybody still uses the streets' former names.

Time Out Between 126th and 127th streets is **Sylvia's Soul Food Restaurant** (328 Lenox Ave., tel. 212/996–0660), owned by Sylvia Woods, the self-proclaimed "Queen" of soul food in New York. Sylvia has earned that title with such mouth-watering entrées as her spicy barbecued ribs and crispy fried pork chops. On Thursdays, don't miss the juicy peach cobbler for dessert. And if you're an early bird, try the hearty, country-style breakfast.

❸ **The Studio Museum in Harlem**, one of the community's show-places, is a small art museum that houses a large collection of paintings, sculpture, and photographs (including historic photographs of Harlem by James Van DerZee, popular in the 1930s). The museum often offers special lectures and programs, and its gift shop (open seven days a week) is full of black American and African-inspired books, posters, and jewelry. *144 W. 125th St., tel. 212/865–2420 or 864–0014. Admission: $2 adults; $1 students, senior citizens, and children. Free on Wed. for senior citizens. Open Wed.–Fri. 10–5, weekends 1–6.*

❹ A fantastic restoration brought the **Apollo Theatre**, one of Harlem's greatest landmarks, back to life in 1986. When it opened in 1913 it was a burlesque hall for white audiences only, but after 1934, music greats such as Billie Holiday, Ella Fitzgerald, Duke Ellington, Count Basie, and Aretha Franklin performed here. The theater fell on hard times and closed for a while in the early 1970s. The current Apollo's roster of stars isn't as consistent as it was in the past, but its regular Wednesday night amateur performances are as wild and raucous as they were in the theater's heyday. *253 W. 125th St., tel. 212/ 749–5838. Call for performance schedules.*

Return to Seventh Avenue and head east to 126th Street, ❺ where the **Black Fashion Museum** is housed in a brownstone. Costumes from black theater and films are displayed, and the work of black fashion designers of the past century is highlighted. *155 W. 126th St., tel. 212/666–1320. Suggested donation: $1.50 adults, $1 students, 50¢ children under age 13. Open weekdays noon–8 by appointment.*

As you head up Seventh Avenue, between 131st and 132nd streets you'll pass what is today the Williams Christian Methodist Church. In its former life, this was the **Lafayette Theater,** which presented black revues in the 1920s and housed the WPA's Federal Negro Theater in the 1930s. A tree outside the theater was considered a lucky charm for black actors; having fallen victim to exhaust fumes, it has been replaced by the abstract metal "tree" on the traffic island in the center of Seventh Avenue.

At 135th Street, cross back to Lenox Avenue, where you'll find ❻ the **Schomburg Center for Research in Black Culture**. In 1926 the New York Public Library's Division of Negro History acquired the vast collection of Arthur Schomburg, a scholar of black and Puerto Rican descent. In 1940, after Schomburg died, this collection, which includes over 100,000 books, documents, and photographs recording black history, was named after him. In 1972, the ever-growing collection was designated a research library and in 1980 it moved into this modern redbrick building from the ivy-covered Victorian one next door (designed by McKim, Mead & White), which is now a branch library. The expansion and renovation of the original Schomburg building will be completed sometime in 1991 and will include the new **American Negro Theater**, with seating for 380, and increased gallery space. The center's resources include rare manuscripts, art and artifacts, motion pictures, records, and videotapes. Regular exhibits, performing arts programs, and lectures continue to contribute to Harlem culture. *515 Lenox Ave., tel. 212/862–4000. Admission free. Open Mon.–Wed. noon–8, Thurs.–Sat. 10–6.*

❼ Founded downtown in 1808, the **Abyssinian Baptist Church** was one of the first black institutions to settle in Harlem when it moved here in the 1920s. The Gothic-style bluestone church was further distinguished by its famous family of ministers— Adam Clayton Powell, Sr., and his son, Adam Clayton Powell, Jr., the first black U.S. congressman. Stop in on Sunday to hear the gospel choir and the fiery sermon of its present minister, Rev. Calvin Butts. *132 W. 138th St. Sun. services 11 AM.*

❽ Across Seventh Avenue from the church is a handsome set of town houses known as **Striver's Row** (W. 138th and W. 139th Sts. between 7th and 8th Aves.). Since 1919, black doctors, lawyers, and other middle-class professionals have owned these elegant homes, designed by famous period architects such as Stanford White (his contributions are on the north side of 139th Street). Musicians W. C. Handy ("The St. Louis Blues") and Eubie Blake ("I'm Just Wild About Harry") were among the residents here. The area became known as Striver's Row because less affluent Harlemites felt its residents were "striving" to become well-to-do. These quiet, tree-lined streets are a remarkable reminder of the Harlem that used to be.

Tour 11: Chelsea

Numbers in the margin correspond with points of interest on the Chelsea map.

Like the London district of the same name, New York's Chelsea has preserved its villagelike personality. Both have their quiet nooks where the 19th century seems to live on; both have been havens for artists, writers, and bohemians. Although London's Chelsea is a much more upscale chunk of real estate, New York's Chelsea is catching up, with town-house renovations reclaiming block after block of the side streets. Seventh, Eighth, and Ninth avenues may never be the shopping mecca that King's Road in London's Chelsea has been, but they have plenty of hip, one-of-a-kind boutiques sprinkled among the grubby grocery stores and other remnants of the neighborhood's immigrant tenement past.

Precisely speaking, the New York neighborhood was named not after Chelsea itself but after London's Chelsea Royal Hospital, an old soldiers' home. Running from 14th to 24th streets, from Eighth Avenue west, it was one family's country estate until the 1830s, when Clement Clarke Moore saw the city moving north and decided to divide his land into lots. With an instinctive gift for urban planning, he dictated a pattern of development that ensured street after street of graceful row houses. A clergyman and classics professor, Moore is probably best known for his 1822 poem "A Visit from St. Nicholas," which he composed while bringing a sleigh full of Christmas treats from lower Manhattan to his Chelsea home.

Begin your tour of Chelsea at the corner of Sixth Avenue and 18th Street. In the latter part of the 19th century, when the elevated tracks of the Sixth Avenue El train still cast their shadow along this street, the blocks between 18th and 23rd streets were a veritable fashion row. Stand on the west side of the avenue and look across at the elaborately embellished, glazed terra-cotta building just north of 18th Street. Originally the

❶ **Siegel-Cooper Dry Goods Store**, built in 1895, it contains 15½ acres of space, yet it was built in only five months. In its retail

Tour 11: Chelsea

heyday, the store's main floor featured an immense fountain—a circular marble terrace with an enormous white-marble-and-brass replica of *The Republic*, the statue Daniel Chester French displayed at the 1983 Chicago World's Fair—which became a favorite rendezvous point for New Yorkers. During World War II, the building was a military hospital. Today it houses the Chelsea Racquet & Fitness Club, a variety of button companies, and a number of graphics and printing firms. Ignore the ugly graffiti and dirt-smudged windows on the lower levels and look up at the building's splendid ornamentation: round wreathed windows, Corinthian and Doric pilasters, Romanesque rounded arches, lion heads, and more.

Now cross Sixth Avenue and take a look at the building on the west side: the original **B. Altman Dry Goods Store,** built in 1876 with additions in 1887 and 1910. Look closely at the exposed columns at the base of the building—it's constructed of cast iron. B. Altman moved out of this giant in 1906 to set up shop in imposing quarters at Fifth Avenue and 34th Street. The latter store closed in 1990.

On the east side of Sixth Avenue at 20th Street is the Gothic-style **Church of the Holy Communion,** an Episcopal house of worship built in 1846 by church architect Richard Upjohn. To the horror of some preservationists, it was converted a few years ago into **Limelight,** a nightclub with state-of-the-art sound and video systems.

On the west side of Sixth Avenue between 20th and 21st streets stands another former retail palace, the **Hugh O'Neill Dry**

Goods Store. Constructed in 1875, this cast-iron building features Corinthian columns and pilasters; its corner towers were once topped off with huge bulbous domes. Look up at the pediment and you'll see the name of the original tenant proudly displayed.

❺ Turn left on 21st Street for a look at **The Third Cemetery of the Spanish & Portuguese Synagogue, Shearith Israel**, a private green oasis with a hardy old ailanthus tree. In use from 1829 to 1851, it is one of three graveyards created in Manhattan by this congregation *(see* Tour 8, above, and Tour 16, below).

Walk back to 20th Street and take a right, heading west. Beginning at Eighth Avenue is the **Chelsea Historic District,** packed with examples of all of Chelsea's architectural periods: Greek and Gothic Revival, Italianate, and 1890s apartment buildings. At 344 West 20th Street, between Eighth and Ninth avenues,
❻ you'll find **St. Peter's Church,** built between 1836 and 1838. The Greek Revival–style **rectory** (1832) to the right of the main church originally served as the sanctuary. Four years after it was built, the congregation had already laid foundations for a bigger church when, it is said, a vestryman returned from England bursting with excitement over the Gothic Revival that had just taken hold there. The fieldstone **church** that resulted ranks as one of New York's earliest examples of Gothic Revival architecture, although its floor plan is still that of a Greek temple rather than the typical Gothic cross shape. To the left of the church, the brick **parish hall** is an example of the so-called Victorian Gothic style; its churchlike front was added in 1871. The wrought-iron fence framing the three buildings once enclosed St. Paul's Chapel downtown *(see* Tour 17, below).

When Clement Clarke Moore divided up his estate, he began by
❼ deeding a large section to the **General Theological Seminary**, where he taught Hebrew and Greek. At Ninth Avenue and 20th Street, the Episcopal seminary still occupies a block-long stretch. The stoutly fenced campus is accessible through the modern building on Ninth Avenue on Sundays and by appointment (tel. 212/243–5150); at other times, you can view the grounds from West 20th Street. The **West Building** (1836) is another early example of Gothic Revival architecture in the city. Most of the rest of the complex was completed in 1883–1902, when Eugene Augustus Hoffman, the school's third dean, hired architect Charles Coolidge Haight to design a campus that would rival most American colleges of the day, in the style known as English collegiate Gothic, which Haight had pioneered. The general campus plan is in an "E" shape, with the spine facing 21st Street. In the center is the **Chapel of the Good Shepherd,** with its 161-foot-high bell tower modeled after the one at Magdalen College, Oxford. **Sherred Hall,** a three-story classroom building flanked by dormitories, expresses beautifully the simple quality and uniform look Haight strove for. **Hoffman Hall,** the refectory-gymnasium, has an enormous dining hall that resembles a medieval knight's council chamber. A 1960s-era building facing Ninth Avenue houses administrative offices and the 210,000-volume **St. Mark's Library,** generally considered the nation's greatest ecclesiastical library; it has the world's largest collection of Latin Bibles.

Across the street from the seminary, at **404 West 20th Street,** is the oldest house in the historic district. Built between 1829 and

1830 in the Federal style, it still has one clapboard side wall, although over the years it acquired a Greek Revival doorway and Italianate windows on the parlor floor, and the roof was raised one story. The houses next door, from 406 to 418 West 20th, are **Cushman Row**, some of the country's most perfect examples of Greek Revival town houses. Built by dry-goods merchant Don Alonzo Cushman, a friend of Clement Clarke Moore who became a millionaire by developing Chelsea, the houses retain such details as the tiny wreath-encircled attic windows, deeply recessed doorways with brownstone frames, and handsome iron balustrades, newels, and fences. Notice the pineapples, a traditional symbol of welcome, atop the newels in front of Nos. 416 and 418.

Farther down West 20th Street, at **Nos. 446 to 450,** you'll find some exceptional examples of Italianate houses. The arched windows and doorways are hallmarks of this style, which prized circular forms—not least because, being expensive to build, they showed off the owner's wealth.

When you reach Tenth Avenue, turn right and walk north (uptown). Movie buffs might make a quick detour right onto 21st Street to take a peek at **467 West 21st Street,** where, in the 1960s and '70s, Anthony Perkins of *Psycho* was the live-in landlord.

At 22nd Street, on the east side of Tenth Avenue, is **Clement Clarke Moore Park**, a friendly, understated area of greenery that complements the row-house district.

Time Out On the northeast corner of this intersection, the **Empire Diner** (210 10th Ave., tel. 212/243–2736), an Art Deco classic with its stainless-steel interior set off by black-and-chrome furnishings, is open 24 hours a day and even features live music. Entrée prices range from $6.95 to $15, but there's plenty on the milk-shake and dessert list for under $4. A full bar is available.

West 22nd Street also has a string of handsome old row houses just east of Tenth Avenue. **No. 435** was the longtime residence of actors Geraldine Page and Rip Torn, who were married in 1961; they nicknamed this Chelsea town house "The Torn Page." In 1987, a year after winning an Oscar for *The Trip to Bountiful*, Page suffered a fatal heart attack here.

On the block spanning 23rd and 24th streets, between Tenth and Ninth avenues, you can't miss the **London Terrace Apartments**, a huge complex containing 1,670 apartments. When it first opened in 1930, the doormen dressed as London bobbies. It's actually made up of two rows of interconnected apartment buildings, which enclose a block-long private garden. As you walk along 23rd Street, notice the lions on the arched entryways: From the side they look as though they're snarling, but from the front they display wide grins.

The site of the Clarke family manor (where Clement Clarke Moore was born in 1779) was just across 23rd Street here, on what was then a high bluff overlooking the Hudson.

During the 1880s and Gay '90s, 23rd Street was the heart of the entertainment district, lined with theaters, music halls, and beer gardens. Today it is an undistinguished, even rundown, commercial thoroughfare, but there is one relic of its once-proud past: the **Chelsea Hotel**, at 222 West 23rd Street. Built of red brick with lacy wrought-iron balconies and a mansard roof, it opened in 1884 as a cooperative apartment house and became a hotel in 1905, although it has always catered to long-term tenants, with a tradition of broad-mindedness that has attracted many creative types. Its literary roll call of former tenants includes Mark Twain, Eugene O'Neill, O. Henry, Thomas Wolfe, Tennessee Williams, Vladimir Nabokov, Mary McCarthy, Brendan Behan, Arthur Miller, Dylan Thomas, William S. Burroughs, and Arthur C. Clarke (who wrote the script for *2001: A Space Odyssey* while living here). In 1966, Andy Warhol filmed artist Brigid Polk in her Chelsea hotel room, which eventually became *The Chelsea Girls*, considered by many to be Warhol's best film. More recently, the hotel was seen on screen in *Sid and Nancy* (1986), a dramatization of a true-life Chelsea Hotel murder, when drugged punk rocker Sid Vicious accidentally stabbed to death his girlfriend Nancy Spungeon. The shabby, seedy aura of the Chelsea Hotel is part of its allure. Step into the lobby to read its commemorative plaques and look at its unusual artwork, some of it donated in lieu of rent by residents down on their luck.

Tour 12: Greenwich Village

Numbers in the margin correspond with points of interest on the Greenwich Village and the East Village map.

Greenwich Village, which New Yorkers almost invariably speak of simply as "the Village," enjoyed a raffish reputation for years. Originally a rural outpost of the city—a haven for New Yorkers during early 19th-century smallpox and yellow fever epidemics—many of its blocks still look somewhat pastoral, with brick town houses and low-rises, tiny green parks and hidden courtyards, and a crazy-quilt pattern of narrow, tree-lined streets. In the mid-19th century, however, as the city spread north of 14th Street, the Village became the province of immigrants, bohemians, and students (New York University, today the nation's largest private university, was planted next to Washington Square in 1831). Its politics were radical and its attitudes tolerant, which is one reason it is home to such a large gay community today.

A lot has changed in the past 20 years, though. Today Village apartments and town houses go for high rents, and several posh restaurants have put down roots. Except for the isolated western fringe, where a string of tough gay bars along West Street attracts some drug traffic and prostitution, the Village is about as safe and clean as the Upper East Side. Nevertheless, something about the tangled street plan and the small buildings encourages anarchy. Shabby shopfronts, hole-in-the-wall restaurants, and nonmainstream arts groups persist and thrive here. There's still a large student population, and several long-time residents remain, paying cheap rents thanks to rent-control laws. The Village is no longer dangerous, but it still feels bohemian.

Several generations of writers and artists have lived and worked here: in the 19th century, Henry James, Edgar Allan Poe, Mark Twain, Walt Whitman, and Stephen Crane; at the turn of the century, O. Henry, Edith Wharton, Theodore Dreiser, and Hart Crane; and during the 1920s and '30s, John Dos Passos, Norman Rockwell, Sinclair Lewis, John Reed, Eugene O'Neill, Edward Hopper, and Edna St. Vincent Millay. In the late 1940s and early 1950s, the abstract impressionist painters Franz Kline, Jackson Pollock, Mark Rothko, and Willem de Kooning congregated here, as did the Beat writers Jack Kerouac, Allen Ginsberg, and Lawrence Ferlinghetti. The 1960s brought folk musicians and poets, notably Bob Dylan and Peter, Paul, and Mary.

❶ Begin a tour of Greenwich Village at Washington Arch in **Washington Square** at the foot of Fifth Avenue. Designed by Stanford White, a wood version of Washington Arch was built in 1889 to commemorate the 100th anniversary of George Washington's presidential inauguration and was originally placed about half a block north of its present location. The arch was reproduced in stone in 1892, and the statues—*Washington at War* on the left, *Washington at Peace* on the right—were added in 1913. Body builder Charles Atlas modeled for *Peace*.

Washington Square started out as a cemetery, principally for yellow fever victims, and an estimated 10,000–22,000 bodies lie below. In the early 1800s it was a parade ground and the site of public executions; bodies dangled from a conspicuous Hanging Elm that still stands at the northwest corner of the square. Later Washington Square became the focus of a fashionable residential neighborhood and a center of outdoor activity.

By the early 1980s, Washington Square had deteriorated into a tawdry place only a drug dealer could love. Then community activism motivated a police crackdown that sent the drug traffic elsewhere and made Washington Square comfortable again for Frisbee players, street musicians, skateboarders, jugglers, stand-up comics, sitters, strollers, and a huge outdoor art fair each spring and fall.

Most of the buildings bordering Washington Square belong to New York University. **The Row,** a series of Federal-style town houses along Washington Square North between Fifth Avenue and University Place, now serves as faculty housing. At 7–13 Washington Square North, in fact, only the fronts were preserved, with a large Fifth Avenue apartment building taking over the space behind. Developers were not so tactful when they demolished 18 Washington Square, once the home of Henry James's grandmother, which he later used as the setting for his novel *Washington Square* (Henry himself was born just off the square, in a long-gone house on Washington Place). The house at 20 Washington Square North is the oldest building (1820) on the block. Notice its Flemish bond brickwork— alternate bricks inserted with the smaller surface facing out— which before 1830 was considered the only way to build walls that would stand.

❷ On the east side of the square, NYU's main building contains the **Grey Art Gallery**, whose intelligent changing exhibitions usually focus on contemporary art. *33 Washington Pl., tel. 212/ 998–6780. Admission free. Open Sept.–May, Tues., Thurs. and Fri., 11–6:30, Wed. 11–8:30, Sat. 11–5; June–Aug., weekdays 11–7.*

On the south side of the square, a trio of red sandstone hulks represents an abortive 1960s attempt to create a unified campus look for NYU, as envisioned by architects Philip Johnson and Richard Foster. At one time, plans called for all of the Washington Square buildings to be refaced in this red stone; fortunately, the cost proved prohibitive. On LaGuardia Place,

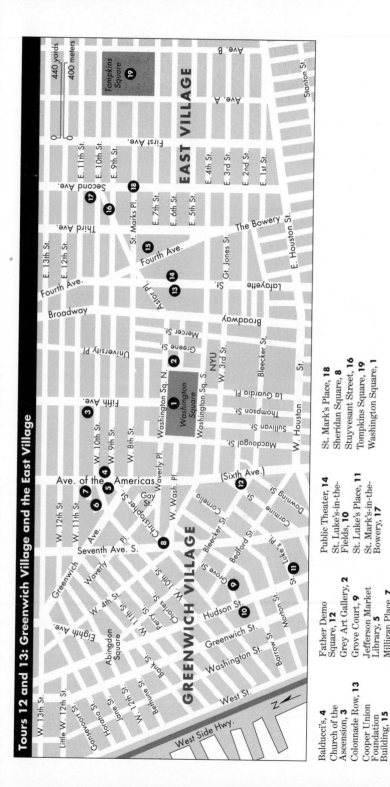

Tours 12 and 13: Greenwich Village and the East Village

GREENWICH VILLAGE

EAST VILLAGE

Tompkins Square, 19

440 yards
400 meters

Balducci's, 4
Church of the Ascension, 3
Colonnade Row, 13
Cooper Union Foundation Building, 15

Father Demo Square, 12
Grey Art Gallery, 2
Grove Court, 9
Jefferson Market Library, 5
Milligan Place, 7
Patchin Place, 6

Public Theater, 14
St. Luke's-in-the-Fields, 10
St. Luke's Place, 11
St. Mark's-in-the-Bowery, 17

St. Mark's Place, 18
Sheridan Square, 8
Stuyvesant Street, 16
Tompkins Square, 19
Washington Square, 1

the undistinguished modern **Loeb Student Center** stands on the site of a famous boardinghouse, nicknamed the House of Genius for the talented writers who had lived there over the years: Theodore Dreiser, Stephen Crane, Willa Cather, O. Henry, and Eugene O'Neill, among others. Next door is the square-towered **Judson Memorial Church** (the tower is now an NYU dormitory), designed by McKim, Mead & White.

Go up Fifth Avenue half a block to **Washington Mews,** a cobblestoned private street lined on one side with the former stables of the houses on The Row. Writer Walter Lippmann and artist-patron Gertrude Vanderbilt Whitney (founder of the Whitney Museum) once had homes in the mews; today it's most-ly owned by NYU. A similar mews, gaslit **MacDougal Alley,** can be found between Eighth Street and the square just off MacDougal Street, one block west.

Eighth Street, the main commercial strip of Greenwich Village, is not the "real" Greenwich Village but a compendium of fast-food purveyors, poster and record shops, and clothing and shoe stores. The crowds along this street are often the "bridge and tunnel people"—a disparaging term Manhattanites use for those who come to the city, via bridge or tunnel, from the other boroughs or suburbs.

On the southwest corner of Fifth Avenue and West 10th Street, the **Church of the Ascension** is a Gothic-style brownstone de-signed by Richard Upjohn. Inside, you can admire stained-glass windows by John LaFarge and a marble altar sculpture by Augustus Saint-Gaudens. In 1844, President John Tyler married Julia Gardiner here.

Walk west on **11th Street,** one of the best examples of a Village town house block. One exception to the general 19th-century redbrick look is the modern, angled front window of 18 West 11th Street, usually occupied by a stuffed bear whose outfit changes from day to day. This house was built after the original was destroyed in a 1970 explosion; the owners' radical daugh-ter, Kathy Boudin, had started a bomb factory in the basement with her Weathermen friends. At the time, actor Dustin Hoff-man lived next door at No. 16; he was seen on TV news trying to rescue his personal possessions. Hoffman's costar in *The Grad-uate,* Anne Bancroft, later lived down at 52 West 11th Street with her husband, director Mel Brooks.

Time Out Don't miss **Patisserie Lanciani** (271 W. 4th St., between W. 11th and Perry Sts., tel. 212/929–0739), a tiny black-and-white café where writers gain inspiration as they sample the freshly baked pastries and the excellent coffee.

On Sixth Avenue, turn left to sample the wares at **Balducci's** (6th Ave. and 9th St.), a full-service gourmet food store that sprouted from the vegetable stand of the late Louis Balducci, Sr. Along with more than 80 Italian cheeses and 50 kinds of bread, this family-owned enterprise features imported Italian specialties and a prodigious selection of fresh seafood.

Directly opposite, the triangle formed by West 10th Street, Sixth Avenue, and Greenwich Avenue originally held a greenmarket, a jail, and the magnificent towered courthouse that is now the **Jefferson Market Library**. Critics variously termed the courthouse's hodgepodge of styles Venetian, Victorian, or Italian; Villagers, noting the alternating wide bands of red brick and narrow strips of granite, dubbed it the Lean Bacon Style. Over the years, the structure has housed a number of government agencies (public works, civil defense, census bureau, police academy); it was on the verge of demolition when public-spirited citizens saved it and turned it into a public library in 1967. Note the fountain at the corner of West 10th Street and Sixth Avenue, and the seal of the City of New York on the east front; inside, look at the handsome interior doorways and climb the graceful circular stairway. If the gate is open, visit the flower garden behind the library, a project run by local green thumbs.

❻ Just west of Sixth Avenue on 10th Street is the wrought-iron gateway to a tiny courtyard called **Patchin Place**; around the corner, on Sixth Avenue just north of 10th Street, is a similar **❼** cul-de-sac, **Milligan Place**, which few New Yorkers even know is there. Both were built around 1850 for the waiters (mostly Basques) who worked at the high-society Brevoort Hotel, long ago demolished, on Fifth Avenue. Patchin Place later became home to several writers, including Theodore Dreiser, e.e. cummings, and Djuna Barnes.

Take Christopher Street, which veers off from the southern end of the library triangle, a few steps to **Gay Street.** A bending lane lined with small row houses circa 1810, Gay Street was originally a black neighborhood and later a strip of speakeasies. Ruth McKinney lived and wrote *My Sister Eileen* in the basement of No. 14, and Howdy Doody was designed in the basement of No. 12.

At the end of Gay Street go west on Waverly Place to the mid-street island occupied by the **Northern Dispensary**, an institution that from 1827 provided health care (first free, then inexpensive) for the needy. In 1988, the debt-ridden clinic, which by then performed only dental services, was heavily fined for refusing to treat two men infected with AIDS and finally had to close its doors. Ironically, the Roman Catholic Archdiocese, which took over the site, decided to turn it into a nursing home for AIDS patients.

As you go west on Christopher Street, you'll pass steps leading down to the **Lion's Head** (59 Christopher St.), a longtime hangout for literary types. Before she found stardom, Jessica Lange was a waitress here. The restaurant faces onto a green triangle that's technically called **Christopher Park,** but it contains a statue of Civil War general Philip Sheridan; this confuses New Yorkers, because there's another triangle to the south (between Washington Place, Barrow Street, and Seventh Avenue) **❽** called **Sheridan Square.** Formerly covered with asphalt, Sheridan Square was recently landscaped following an extensive dig by urban archaeologists, who unearthed artifacts dating back to the Dutch and Native American eras.

Sheridan Square was the site of a nasty 1863 riot in which a group of freed slaves were nearly lynched; in 1969, gays and police clashed nearby during a protest march that galvanized the gay rights movement. Across the busy intersection of Seventh Avenue, **Christopher Street** comes into its own as the symbolic heart of New York's gay community. Many bars and stores along here cater to that clientele, although the street is by no means off-limits to other people.

West of Seventh Avenue, the Village turns into a picture-book town of twisting, tree-lined streets, quaint houses, and tiny restaurants. Follow Grove Street from Sheridan Square past the boyhood home of poet Hart Crane (45 Grove St.) to the crossing of Grove and Bedford streets, a secluded intersection that seems to have fallen through a time warp into the 19th century. On the northeast corner stands one of the few remaining clapboard structures in the city (17 Grove St.); wood construction was banned as a fire hazard in 1822, the year it was built. The house has since served many functions; it housed a brothel during the Civil War. Behind it, at 102 Bedford Street, is **Twin Peaks,** an 1835 house that was rather whimsically altered in the 1920s, with stucco, half-timbers, and a pair of steep roof peaks added on.

9 Grove Street curves in front of the iron gate of **Grove Court,** an enclave of brick-fronted town houses from the mid-1800s. Built originally as apartments for employees at neighborhood hotels, Grove Court used to be called Mixed Ale Alley because of the residents' propensity to pool beverages brought from work. It now houses a more affluent crowd: A town house there recently sold for $3 million.

Time Out Where Christopher meets Grove and Waverly Place, **Pierre's** (170 Waverly Pl., tel. 212/929–7194) is everyone's favorite little French corner bistro. The sumptuous couscous and the profiterole are two specialties. Music may include guitar or piano during dinner at this relaxed, friendly place.

The building at 77 Bedford Street is the oldest house in the Village (1799). The place next door, 75½ Bedford Street, has an even greater claim to fame: Not only was it the residence (at different times) of both Edna St. Vincent Millay and John Barrymore, it is also, at 9½ feet wide, New York's narrowest house. The lot was an alley until rising real-estate prices inspired construction in 1873.

Heading west on Commerce Street, you soon reach the **Cherry Lane Theater,** one of the original Off-Broadway houses and the site of American premieres of works by O'Neill, Beckett, Ionesco, and Albee. Across the street stand two nearly identical brick houses separated by a garden. Popularly known as the **Twin Sisters,** the houses were said to have been built by a sea captain for two daughters who loathed each other. Historical record insists that they were built by a milkman who needed the two houses and an open courtyard for his work.

Follow Barrow Street to Hudson Street, so named because this was originally the bank of the Hudson River. The block to the **10** northwest is owned by **St. Luke's-in-the-Fields,** built in 1822 as a country chapel for downtown's Trinity Church; its first warden was Clement ("'Twas the Night Before Christmas") Clarke Moore, who figured so largely in Chelsea's history (*see* Tour 11, above). An unadorned structure of soft-colored brick, St. Luke's was nearly destroyed by fire in 1981, but a flood of donations, many quite small, from residents of the West Village financed restoration of the square central tower. A gem of a garden is hidden behind the brick wall; although it is supposed to be open only to residents of the row houses along Hudson Street, which are owned by the church, discreet visitors will not be disturbed—provided they can find their way in past the school behind the church. Bret Harte once lived at 487 Hudson Street, at the end of the row.

Walk south to Leroy Street, which on the east side of Hudson **⑪** becomes **St. Luke's Place**, a row of classic 1860s town houses shaded by graceful gingko trees. Novelist Theodore Dreiser wrote *An American Tragedy* at No. 16; poet Marianne Moore lived at No. 14, playwright Sherwood Anderson at No. 12. Mayor Jimmy Walker (first elected in 1926) lived at No. 6; the lampposts in front are "mayor's lamps," which were sometimes placed in front of the residences of New York mayors. This block is often used as a film location, too: No. 12 is shown as the Huxtables' home on "The Cosby Show" (although the family supposedly lives in Brooklyn), while No. 4 was the setting of the movie *Wait Until Dark*. Before 1890 the playground on the south side of the street was a graveyard where, according to legend, the dauphin of France—the lost son of Louis XVI and Marie Antoinette—is buried.

Across Seventh Avenue, St. Luke's Place becomes Leroy Street again, which terminates in an old Italian neighborhood at Bleecker Street. Amazingly unchanged amid all the Village gentrification, Bleecker between Sixth and Seventh avenues seems more vital these days than Little Italy does. Stop into one of the fragrant Italian bakeries (**Zito's**, 259 Bleecker St., and **Rocco's**, 243 Bleecker St.), or look inside the old-style butcher shops (**Ottomanelli's**, 281 Bleecker St., and **Faicco's**, 260 Bleecker St.). **John's Pizzeria** (278 Bleecker St.) is one of those places that locals swear by. You may also be tempted to stop in at the **Lafayette Bakery** (298 Bleecker St.); it's French rather than Italian, but the treats are luscious all the same. The **⑫** activity here focuses on **Father Demo Square** (Bleecker St. and 6th Ave.), once a cluster of pushcarts and now the site of the **Church of Our Lady of Pompeii,** where Mother Cabrini, a naturalized Italian immigrant who became the first American saint, often prayed.

Head up Sixth Avenue to Third Street and check out the playground caged there within a chain-link fence. NBA stars of tomorrow learn their moves on this patch of asphalt, where citystyle basketball is played all afternoon and evening in all but the very coldest weather. Across the street, the **Waverly Theater** (323 6th Ave.), a former church converted to a cinema in 1937, is popular with movie goers for its cult films and midnight shows.

Return along Washington Square South to MacDougal Street and turn right. The **Provincetown Playhouse** (133 MacDougal St.) premiered many of Eugene O'Neill's plays. The two houses at 127 and 129 MacDougal Street were built for Aaron Burr in 1829; notice the pineapple newel posts, a symbol of hospitality. Louisa May Alcott wrote *Little Women* while living at 130-132 MacDougal Street.

At **Minetta Tavern** (113 MacDougal St.), a venerable Village watering hole, turn right onto **Minetta Lane,** which leads to narrow **Minetta Street,** another former speakeasy alley. Both streets follow the course of Minetta Brook, which once flowed through this neighborhood and still bubbles deep beneath the pavement.

The foot of Minetta Street returns you to the corner of Sixth Avenue and Bleecker Street, where you reach the stomping grounds of 1960s-era folksingers (many of them performed at the now-defunct Folk City one block north on West 3rd Street). This area still attracts a young crowd—partly because of the proximity of NYU—to its cafés, bars, jazz clubs, coffeehouses, theaters, and cabarets (*see* Chapter 11), not to mention its long row of unpretentious ethnic restaurants.

Time Out Turn back up MacDougal to stop at the neighborhood's oldest coffeehouse, **Caffe Reggio** (119 MacDougal St., tel. 212/475–9557), where an antique machine steams forth espresso and cappuccino. The tiny tables are close together, but the crowd usually makes for interesting eavesdropping.

Farther east on Bleecker Street, the **Bleecker Street Cinema** (144 Bleecker St., tel. 212/674–2560) was converted from a pair of row houses to a famous 1880s Italian restaurant to a cinema (*see* Chapter 10). This is the theater where Aidan Quinn was a projectionist in *Desperately Seeking Susan*.

Beyond LaGuardia Place (named after the same Mayor Fiorello LaGuardia as the airport) loom the modern dorms of New York University. Turn to the left and you're back at Washington Square.

Tour 13: The East Village

Numbers in the margin correspond with points of interest on the Greenwich Village and the East Village map.

The gritty tenements of the East Village—an area bounded by 14th Street on the north, Fourth Avenue or the Bowery on the west, Houston Street on the south, and the East River—provided inexpensive living places for artists, writers, and actors until very recently. Now the East Village can be as costly a place to live as anywhere else south of 96th Street.

In a way, the area has the best of both worlds. New residents have brought in their wake new restaurants, shops, and somewhat cleaner streets, while the old East Villagers maintain the trappings of the counterculture. Longtime iconoclastic theaters such as CSC Repertory and LaMama (*see* Chapter 10) continue to thrive, although the "hot" art galleries that opened in narrow East Village storefronts a couple of years ago have already deserted this no-longer-a-bargain neighborhood, seeking more floor space in other parts of town.

To explore the East Village, begin at the intersection of East 8th Street, Fourth Avenue, and Astor Place. Sculpture adorns two traffic islands here: One island contains *Alamo*, a massive black cube sculpted by Bernard Rosenthal; another bears an ornate cast-iron replica of a Beaux Arts subway entrance, providing access to the uptown No. 6 line. Go down into the station to see the authentically reproduced wall tiles.

Just west of the intersection, **Astor Wine and Spirits** (12 Astor Pl.) is one of New York's most comprehensive liquor stores, offering good prices on imports and even better deals on house brands. (New York State has unexpectedly restrictive liquor-control laws: Liquor and wine can be sold only in liquor stores, which sell *only* liquor and wine—no beer, soda, ice, or glasses—and must close on Sundays.)

Continue west on Astor Place to **Astor Place Hair Designers** (2 Astor Pl.), where lines of people stretch out to the sidewalk awaiting service. Choose your cut from Polaroids in the window—maybe the Village Cut, a Guido, or a L'il Tony. It costs only $10 for men and $12 for women, and it's open every day.

Continue west to Broadway, where you turn left to hit a trendy downtown shopping strip, especially strong in funky second-hand and surplus clothing stores. Above street level, the old warehouses here have mostly been converted into residential lofts. Walk south to 4th Street, where you'll see **Tower Records** (692 Broadway, tel. 212/505–1500), a very big and very good record-tape-and-CD store that also serves as a mingling place for young hipsters (or would-be hipsters).

13 Go west on 4th Street to Lafayette Street and turn left. The long block ahead of you on your left contains **Colonnade Row** (1833), a grand sweep of four houses (originally nine) fronted by marble Corinthian columns. Although sadly run-down today, in their time these houses were home to millionaires John Jacob Astor and Cornelius Vanderbilt; writers Washington Irving, William Makepeace Thackeray, and Charles Dickens all stayed here at one time or another.

14 In 1854 Astor opened the city's first free library in the impo ing Italian Renaissance–style structure directly across the street, which was renovated in 1967 to serve as the New York Shakespeare Festival's **Public Theater**. Under the leadership of producer Joseph Papp, the Public's six playhouses and one cinema present a broad-based repertoire (*see* Chapter 10); the long-running hit *A Chorus Line* had its first performances here, but so have many less commercial plays. The New York Shakespeare Festival is in the middle of a six-year marathon that, for the first time in America, will present in turn all of Shakespeare's plays. *425 Lafayette St., tel. 212/598–7150. Theater tickets: $10–$20 for regular performances, $30 for Shakespeare Marathon productions. Some half-price tickets for most performances available at 6 PM (matinees, 1 PM); the line forms 1–2 hrs earlier.*

15 Return to Astor Place and turn right, heading toward the massive brownstone **Cooper Union Foundation Building**. This college was founded in 1859 by industrialist Peter Cooper, who wanted to provide a forum for public opinion and free technical education for the working class; it still offers tuition-free education and an active public affairs program. Cooper Union was the first structure to be supported by steel railroad rails—rolled in Cooper's own plant. A basement art gallery presents changing exhibits on history and design. Walk south along the building to **Cooper Square,** the large open space created where Fourth and Third avenues merge into the Bowery. A statue of Peter Cooper by Augustus Saint-Gaudens presides over the square.

Musicians may want to stop in at the **Carl Fischer Music Store** (62 Cooper Sq., tel. 212/677–1148) to select from the infinitude of sheet music, confer with the knowledgeable staff, and hang out with the other musicians there.

A few steps east of Cooper Square on 7th Street, **Surma, The Ukrainian Shop** (11 E. 7th St.) celebrates this neighborhood's tightly knit Ukrainian community. (Across the street, look for the mosaic dome of **St. George's Ukrainian Catholic Church.**) Surma's exotic stock includes Ukrainian books, magazines, and cassette tapes; greeting cards; musical instruments; colorful painted eggs and Surma's own brand of egg coloring; honey; and an exhaustive selection of peasant blouses.

McSorley's Old Ale House (15 E. 7th St.), one of several claimants to the distinction of being New York's oldest bar, is often crammed with collegiate types enticed by McSorley's own brands of ale. McSorley's opened in 1854 but didn't admit women until 1970.

🔟 Return to Third Avenue and walk north to **Stuyvesant Street**, basically a block-long continuation of Astor Place that angles up toward 10th Street, running through what was once Governor Peter Stuyvesant's "bouwerie," or farm. The house at 21 Stuyvesant Street was built in 1804 as a wedding gift for a great-great-granddaughter of the governor. The redbrick row houses at Nos. 21–35 and 42–46 were added in the 1860s; a similar one around the corner, at 118 East 10th Street, was the childhood home of architect Stanford White.

🔟 Stuyvesant Street ends in front of **St. Mark's-in-the-Bowery Church**, a 1799 fieldstone country church to which a Greek Revival steeple and a cast-iron front porch have been added. This, the city's oldest continually used church building (Governor Stuyvesant and Commodore Perry are buried here), had to be completely restored after a disastrous fire in 1978. Over the years, St. Mark's has hosted much countercultural activity. In the 1920s a forward-thinking pastor injected the Episcopalian ritual with Native American chants, Greek folk dancing, and Eastern mantras. During the hippie era, St. Mark's welcomed avant-garde poets and playwrights. Today dancers, poets, and performance artists cavort in the main sanctuary, where pews have been removed to accommodate them.

Second Avenue, which borders the church on the east, was known in the early part of this century as the Yiddish Rialto. Between Houston and 14th streets, eight theaters presented Yiddish-language productions of musicals, revues, and heart-wrenching melodramas. Today the theaters are gone; all that remains are Hollywood-style stars (Stars of David, that is) embedded in the sidewalk in front of the **Second Avenue Deli** (2nd Ave. and 10th St.) to commemorate Yiddish stage luminaries.

Time Out   For some of the best Italian pastries in the city, try **Veniero Pasticerria** (342 E. 11th St. near 1st Ave., tel. 212/674–7264), a lively café that has rows and rows of incredibly fresh cannolis, fruit tarts, cheesecakes, and other desserts on display. If you can't get in, try **Derobertis Pastry Shop** (176 1st Ave., tel. 212/674–7137); it's a more subdued neighborhood hangout.

🔟 The intersection of Second Avenue and **St. Marks Place** (the name given to 8th Street in the East Village) is the hub of the "hip" East Village. During the 1950s beatniks such as Allen Ginsberg and Jack Kerouac lived and wrote in the area; the 1960s brought Bill Graham's Fillmore East concerts, the Electric Circus, and hallucinogenic drugs. The black-clad, pink-haired or shaven-headed punks followed, and many of them remain today. St. Marks Place between Second and Third avenues is a counterculture bazaar lined with vegetarian restaurants, jewelry stalls, leather shops, haircutters, and stores selling books, posters, and weird clothing; **St. Marks Bookshop** (12 St. Marks Pl.) is excellent for browsing and for getting a sense of the neighborhood. The East Village always manages to get all the styles first; the trend that *Time* magazine will discover in six months is parading down St. Marks Place today.

On the other side of Second Avenue, **Theater 80** (80 St. Marks Pl., tel. 212/254–7400), one of New York's few remaining revival movie houses, shows a different double feature almost daily (the Friday and Saturday bills are the same). The fare includes vintage American and foreign films, some relatively recent finds, and cult classics.

P.S. 122 (150 1st Ave. at 9th St., tel. 212/477–5288) is a former public school building transformed into a complex of spaces for avant-garde entertainment. Shocking, often crude, and predictably unpredictable, P.S. 122 happenings translate the spirit of the streets into performance art. Prices are low, rarely more than $10, except for occasional benefit performances.

East of First Avenue, Manhattan avenues are designated with letters, not numbers, earning this area the nickname Alphabet City. Until relatively recently, Alphabet City also meant a burned-out territory of slums and drug haunts, but colonization by the avant-garde art community changed all that. At the height of the East Village art scene, only a few years ago, there were more than two dozen galleries here, featuring work that was often startling, innovative, or political. The art dealers, however, have either gone out of business or moved to more mainstream (and spacious) sites in SoHo or Greenwich Village.

19 A focal point for the Far East Village is **Tompkins Square**, the leafy park bordered by Avenues A and B and 7th and 10th streets. Although the square itself could use a face-lift, the restored brownstones along 10th Street are evidence that Tompkins Square is already smartly gentrified. In the past few years, however, the park has come to symbolize the tension between old and new East Villagers. As police moved to rid the park of vagrants—long a customary feature here—a bloody confrontation broke out in the summer of 1988, and the incident was nearly repeated in the summer of 1989.

Time Out   **Jerry's 103** (103 2nd Ave., at 6th St., tel. 212/777–4120) stays open until 4 AM four days a week, and until 5 AM on Fri. and Sat. Its reasonably priced menu (pizzas, pastas, salads, and seafood) and informal atmosphere make it popular at all hours, especially with young artists.

Tour 14: SoHo and TriBeCa

Numbers in the margin correspond with points of interest on the SoHo, TriBeCa, Little Italy, Chinatown map.

Today the names of these two downtown neighborhoods are virtually synonymous with a certain postmodern chic—an amalgam of black-clad artists, hip young Wall Streeters, track-lit loft apartments, new "hot" galleries, and restaurants with a minimalist approach to both food and decor. It's all very urban, very cool, very now. But 25 years ago, they were virtual wastelands. SoHo (so named because it is the district *South of Hous-*

ton Street, bounded by Broadway, Canal Street, and Sixth Avenue) was described in a 1962 City Club of New York study as "commercial slum number one." It was saved by two factors: (1) preservationists discovered here the world's greatest concentration of cast-iron architecture, and fought to prevent demolition, and (2) artists discovered the large, cheap, well-lit spaces that cast-iron buildings provide. At first it was technically illegal for artists to live in their loft studios, but so many did that eventually the zoning laws were changed to permit residence.

By 1980, the tide of loft dwellers, galleries, and trendy shops and cafés had made SoHo so desirable a residential area, despite the still-gritty look of the neighborhood, that none but the most successful artists could afford it anymore. Seeking similar space, artists moved downtown to another half-abandoned commercial district, for which a new SoHo-like name was invented: TriBeCa (the *Tri*angle *Be*low *Ca*nal Street, although in effect it goes no farther south than Murray Street and no farther east than Broadway). The same scenario played itself out again, and TriBeCa's rising rents are already beyond the means of most artists, who have moved instead to Long Island City (*see* Chapter 4) or areas of Brooklyn or New Jersey. But just because the artists have left doesn't mean that SoHo and TriBeCa aren't still a vital scene.

Perhaps the best introduction to these areas is a walk up Greene Street, where the block between Canal and Grand streets contains the longest continuous row of cast-iron buildings anywhere (Nos. 8–34 Greene St.). The architectural rage between 1860 and 1890, cast-iron buildings were popular because they did not require massive walls to bear the weight of the upper stories. With no need for load-bearing walls, they were able to have more interior space and larger windows. They were also versatile, with various architectural elements produced from standardized molds to mimic any style—Italianate, Victorian Gothic, neo-Grec, to name but a few visible in SoHo. Look, for example, at 28–30 Greene Street, an
❶ 1873 building nicknamed the **Queen of Greene Street**. Besides its blue paint job, notice how many decorative features have been applied: dormers, columns, window arches, and projecting central bays. Handsome as they are, these buildings were always commercial, housing stores and light manufacturing, principally textiles. Along this street notice the iron-loading docks and the sidewalk vault covers studded with glass disks to let light into basement storage areas. In front of 62–64 Greene Street there's one of the few remaining turn-of-the-century bishop's-crook lampposts, with various cast-iron curlicues from the base to the curved top.

❷ At 72–76 Greene Street is the so-called **King of Greene Street**, a five-story Renaissance-style building with a magnificent projecting porch of Corinthian columns. Today the King (now painted yellow) houses three art galleries—**Ariel, Condeso/ Lawler**, and **M-13**—plus **The Second Coming**, which sells vintage clothing, furniture, and other curiosities.

At the northeast corner of Prince and Greene streets, turn to look at the corner diagonally opposite for a rare glimpse of the side of an iron-front building. You'll see the same window pattern and decoration continued, with one window open and a cat sitting on the sill—where it has sat since 1973, when artist

Richard Haas first painted this meticulously realistic **mural** on the blank side wall.

Take Prince Street west to Wooster Street, which, like a few other SoHo streets, still has its 19th-century pavement of Belgian blocks, a smoother successor to traditional cobblestones. At 141 Wooster Street, one of several outposts of the DIA Art Foundation, you can visit the **New York Earth Room**, Walter de Maria's avant-garde 1977 artwork that consists of 11 tons of gently sculpted soil filling a second-floor gallery. *Tel. 212/473–8072. Admission free. Open Wed.–Sat. noon–6.*

Continue west to West Broadway (which, somewhat confusingly, runs parallel to and four blocks west of regular Broadway). This is SoHo's main drag, and on Saturday it can be crowded with smartly dressed uptowners and suburbanites who've come down for a little store- and gallery-hopping (*see* Chapter 7). In the block between Prince and Spring streets alone there are three major art stops: **420 West Broadway,** with six separate galleries including two of the biggest SoHo names, Leo Castelli and the Sonnabend Gallery; the **Mary Boone Gallery** (417 West Broadway); and another excellent cluster of galleries at **415 West Broadway.** One block south, at 383 **West Broadway,** OK Harris and DiLaurenti share digs.

Time Out   The crowded, lively **Cupping Room Cafe** (359 West Broadway, tel. 212/925–2898) specializes in comforting soups, muffins, and daily specials, as well as unusual, oversize drinks. If the cafe is packed, treat yourself to a three- or five-course classic French meal ($15–$18) at the student-operated restaurant of The French Culinary Institute, **L'École** (462 Broadway and Grand St., tel. 212/219–8890); you'll have a choice of appetizer, entrée, and dessert, served in a visually creative presentation.

Go east to Broome Street and Broadway where, on the northeast corner, you'll see the sadly unrestored classic of the cast-iron genre, the **Haughwout Building** (488 Broadway), nicknamed the Parthenon of Cast Iron. Built in 1857 to house Eder Haughwout's china and glassware business, the exterior was inspired by a Venetian palazzo. Inside, it contained the world's first commercial passenger elevator, a steam-powered device invented by Elisha Graves Otis.

Head north up Broadway, which temporarily loses its SoHo ambience in the midst of discount clothing stores. Just below Prince Street, the 1907 **Singer Building** (561 Broadway) shows the final flower of the cast-iron style, with wrought-iron balconies, terra-cotta panels, and broad expanses of windows. Across the street is one of New York's gourmet shrines, the gleaming **Dean & DeLuca** food market (560 Broadway), whose bread and produce arrangements often are worthy of still-life paintings. The smartly restored **560 Broadway** building also houses a respected multigallery exhibit space; another such space is just up the street at **568 Broadway.**

On the west side of Broadway, the **New Museum of Contemporary Art** shows experimental, often radically innovative work by unrecognized artists, none of it more than 10 years old. *583 Broadway between Prince and Houston Sts., tel. 212/219–1355. Suggested donation: $2.50 adults, $1.50 students, senior citizens, and artists. Open Wed , Thurs., and Sun. noon–6; Fri. and Sat. noon–8.*

Tours 14-16: SoHo, TriBeCa, Little Italy, Chinatown

Go one block west to stone-paved Mercer Street, where the sidewalks may be cluttered with cartons of cloth or leather remnants discarded by the sweatshops upstairs (artists find a lot of good collage material here). Between Broome and Spring streets is **Enchanted Forest** (85 Mercer St., tel. 212/925–6677), with a fanciful selection of stuffed animals, books, and hand-made toys that almost deserves to be considered an art gallery. Both kids and adults have a great time here.

❼ Two blocks farther south, **The Museum of Holography** has a permanent exhibit on the history of holograms, three-dimensional photographs created by laser beams. This combination science show and art gallery projects a film on holography and has three changing exhibits a year. The gift shop has a terrific selection of 3-D art and souvenirs. *11 Mercer St. (near Canal St.), tel. 212/925–0581. Admission: $3.50 adults, $2.50 students, children, and senior citizens. Open Tues.–Sun. 11–7.*

Walk one block to your right on Canal Street, then cross and you're officially in TriBeCa. Go south on Church Street, and **❽** turn west on White Street to visit the **Alternative Museum,** a gallery that exhibits art with a political or sociopolitical twist. *17 White St., tel. 212/966–4444. Voluntary contribution. Open Tues.–Sat. 11–6.*

Continue down West Broadway, past the life-size iron Statue of Liberty crown above the blue-tiled entrance to **El Teddy's,** a gourmet Mexican restaurant. Stop in for a drink, if only to see how the kitschy decor has been carried out inside.

In the mid-19th century, Worth Street was the equivalent of Seventh Avenue today, the center of the garment trade; the area to the west, near the Hudson River docks, became the heart of the wholesale food business. Turn right onto Duane **❾** Street to reach **Duane Park,** preserved since 1800 as a calm, shady triangle; it is still surrounded by cheese, butter, and egg warehouses (note the Land O'Lakes sign facing the south side of the park).

One block north on Hudson Street, on your right you'll see the Art Deco **Western Union Building** (60 Hudson St.), where 19 subtly shaded colors of brick are laid in undulating patterns. Turn up quiet Jay Street, and pause at narrow Staple Street, little more than an alley, where a green pedestrian walkway overhead links two warehouses. The street is named for the staple products unloaded here by ships in transit that didn't want to pay duty on any extra cargo. Framed at the end of the street is the redbrick **New York Mercantile Exchange,** its square corner tower topped by a bulbous roof. On the ground floor is an acclaimed new restaurant, **Chanterelle** (*see* Chapter 8).

If you continue west on Jay Street, you'll pass the loading docks of a very active food wholesaler, **Bazzini's Nuts and Confections.** Tucked into a corner of its extensive warehouse is its up-scale retail shop (corner of Jay and Greenwich Sts.), where you can buy nuts, coffee beans, candies, cookies, and various other delicacies.

On the corner of Greenwich and Harrison streets, a surprising row of early-19th-century town houses is nestled in the side of a huge high-rise apartment complex. These three-story redbrick houses were moved here from various sites in the neighborhood when, in the early 1970s, the food-wholesalers' central market nearby was razed and moved to the Bronx. Walk around the houses to peer into the green yard they enclose.

Time Out The long-awaited **TriBeCa Grill** (375 Greenwich St., tel. 212/ 941–3900) is located on the first floor of the old Martinson Coffee Building, which now houses actor Robert De Niro's **Tribeca Film Center**, a movie production complex. The Grill specializes in fresh grilled fish, sumptuous salads, and charcuterie. And that's the old Maxwell Plum's bar in the middle of the restaurant.

⑩ The high-rise towers belong to **Independence Plaza**, a pleasant, if somewhat utilitarian, project of the mid-1970s that was supposed to be part of a wave of demolition and construction—until the preservationists stepped in. For several years Independence Plaza remained a middle-class island stranded downtown, far from stores, schools, and neighbors; with TriBeCa's growing chic, however, plus the development of Battery Park City to the south, it has become a much more desirable address.

Movie fans may want to continue north to Moore Street, where a right turn will take you two blocks to 14 Moore Street, the firehouse (still in use) that was filmed as the **Ghostbusters' headquarters** in the movies *Ghostbusters* and *Ghostbusters II*.

⑪ If you go south on Greenwich Street, you'll soon come to the 2½-acre **Washington Market Park**, a much-needed recreation space for this neighborhood. Named after the great food market that once sprawled over this area, it is a green, landscaped oasis with tennis courts, a playground, and even a gazebo. Just across Chambers Street, P.S. 234, a public elementary school, has opened to serve TriBeCa's younger generation. At the corner, a stout little red tower resembles a lighthouse, and iron ship figures are worked into the playground fence—reminders of the neighborhood's long-gone dockside past.

Tour 15: Little Italy

Numbers in the margin correspond with points of interest on the SoHo, TriBeCa, Little Italy, and Chinatown map.

Mulberry Street is the heart of Little Italy; in fact, at this point it's virtually the entire body. In 1932 an estimated 98% of the inhabitants of this area were of Italian birth or heritage, but since then the growth and expansion of neighboring Chinatown has encroached on the Italian neighborhood to such an extent that merchants and community leaders of the Little Italy Restoration Association (LIRA) negotiated a truce in which the Chinese agreed to let at least Mulberry remain an all-Italian Street. If you want the flavor of a whole Italian neighborhood, you'd do better visiting Carroll Gardens in Brooklyn or Arthur Avenue in the Bronx (*see* Chapter 4); or rent a video of the Martin Scorsese movie *Mean Streets*, which was filmed in Little Italy back in the very early 1970s.

Start at the intersection of Grand and Mulberry streets. Facing north (uptown), on your right you'll see a series of wide, four-story houses from the early 19th century, built long before the great flood of immigration hit this neighborhood between 1890 and 1924. Turn and look south along the east side of Mulberry Street to see Little Italy's predominant architecture today:

tenement buildings with fire escapes projecting over the sidewalks. Most of these are of the late 19th-century New York style known as railroad flats: five-story buildings on 25-by-90-foot lots, with all the rooms in each apartment placed in a straight line like railroad cars. This style was common in the densely populated immigrant neighborhoods of lower Manhattan until 1901, when the city passed an ordinance requiring air shafts in the interior of buildings.

Today Mulberry Street between Broome and Canal streets is crowded with restaurants, cafés, bakeries, imported food shops, and souvenir stores. Especially on weekends, when suburbanites flock here, this is a street for strolling, gawking, and inhaling the aroma of garlic and olive oil. Some restaurants and cafés display high-tech Eurodesign; others seem dedicated to staying exactly as their old customers remember them. One block north, at the southwest corner of Broome and Mulberry streets, stairs lead down through a glass entrance to what seems to be a blue-tiled cave—and, appropriately enough, it is

12 the **Grotta Azzurra** (Blue Grotto) restaurant (387 Broome St., tel. 212/925–8775), a longtime favorite for both the hearty food and the very Italian ambience. Across Mulberry Street is **Caffe Roma** (385 Broome St., 212/226–8413), a traditional pastry shop where you can eat cannoli at postage-stamp-size wrought-iron tables. At the corner of Mulberry and Grand, **E. Rossi & Co.** (established in 1902) is an antiquated little shop that sells housewares, espresso makers, embroidered religious postcards, and jocular Italian T-shirts. Down Grand Street is **Ferrara's** (195 Grand St., tel. 212/226–6150), a nearly 100-year-old pastry shop that ships its creations—cannoli, peasant pie, Italian rum cake—all over the world. Another survivor of the pretenement era is at 149 Mulberry Street, formerly the Van Rensselaer House (built in 1816); notice its dormer windows. Today it houses **Paolucci's Restaurant.**

13 **Umberto's Clam House** (129 Mulberry St., tel. 212/431–7545) is perhaps best known as the place where mobster Joey Gallo was munching scungili in 1973 when he was fatally surprised by a task force of mob hit men. Quite peaceful now, Umberto's specializes in fresh shellfish in a spicy tomato sauce. At 247 Mulberry Street, you may get the urge to check out the doorway of the **Ravenite Social Club**, where John Gotti and his pals have been known to hang out. Turn onto Hester Street to visit yet

14 another Little Italy institution, **Puglia** (189 Hester St., tel. 212/966–6006), a restaurant where guests sit at long communal tables, sing along with house entertainers, and enjoy moderately priced Southern Italian specialties with quantities of homemade wine. (For other Little Italy restaurants, *see* Chapter 8.)

15 One street west, on Baxter Street, stands the **San Gennaro Church** (officially, Most Precious Blood Church, National Shrine of San Gennaro), which each year around September 19 sponsors Little Italy's keynote event, the annual Feast of San Gennaro. (The community's other big festival celebrates St. Anthony of Padua, in June; that church is at Houston and Sullivan streets, in what is now SoHo.) During the feasts, Little Italy's streets are closed to traffic, arches of tinsel span the thoroughfares, the sidewalks are lined with booths offering games and food, and the whole scene is one noisy, crowded, kitschy, delightful party.

Where are the cops when you need them? Certainly not in the former police headquarters, a magnificent 1909 Renaissance-style palazzo that occupies the entire block bounded by Grand, Centre, Baxter, and Broome streets. The police moved to their new quarters, the modern Police Plaza behind the Municipal Building (*see* Tour 18, below) in 1973, and this lavish domed baroque edifice has been converted into a luxury co-op project aptly called **The Police Building.** Cross to the far side of Centre Street for a good look at the columns, dome, and statuary around its main entrance, including pediment statues representing each of New York's five boroughs.

Walk up Baxter Street to Spring Street, and turn right to hit Mulberry Street. The **D & G Bakery** (45 Spring St.), one of the last coal-oven bakeries in the United States, served as Nicholas Cage's workplace in the movie *Moonstruck.*

Return to Baxter Street, which soon merges with Lafayette Street. At the corner of Lafayette and Houston streets, on your right you'll see the redbrick **Puck Building** (note the gilded figure of Shakespeare's mischievous Puck himself above the entrance). Built in 1885, it was originally headquarters for the 19th-century humor magazine *Puck;* more recently, it was home to New York City's current satire magazine, *Spy.*

Tour 16: Chinatown

Numbers in the margin correspond with points of interest on the SoHo, TriBeCa, Little Italy, and Chinatown map.

Visibly exotic, Chinatown is a popular tourist attraction, but it is also a real, vital community, where about half of the city's population of 300,000 Chinese still live. Its main businesses are restaurants and garment factories; some 55% of its residents speak little or no English. Theoretically, Chinatown is divided from Little Italy by Canal Street, the bustling artery that links the Holland Tunnel (to New Jersey) and the Manhattan Bridge (to Brooklyn). However, in recent years, an influx of immigrants from the People's Republic of China, Taiwan, and especially Hong Kong has swelled Manhattan's Chinese population, and Hong Kong residents, anticipating the return of the British colony to PRC domination in 1997, have been investing their capital in Chinatown real estate. Consequently, Chinatown now spills over its traditional borders into Little Italy to the north and the formerly Jewish Lower East Side to the east.

Originally Canal Street was a tree-lined road with a canal running its length. Today the Chinatown stretch of Canal Street is almost overwhelmed with sidewalk markets bursting with stacks of fresh seafood and strangely shaped vegetables in extraterrestrial shades of green. Food shops proudly display their wares: If America's motto is "a chicken in every pot," then Chinatown's must be "a roast duck in every window."

The slightly less frantic **Kam Man** (200 Canal St.), a duplex supermarket, sells an amazing assortment of fresh and canned imported groceries, herbs, and the sort of dinnerware and furniture familiar to patrons of Chinese restaurants. Choose from 100 kinds of noodles or such delicacies as dried starch and fresh chicken feet.

Mott Street, the principal business street of the neighborhood, looks the way you might expect Chinatown to look: narrow and twisting, crammed with souvenir shops and restaurants in funky pagoda-style buildings, crowded with pedestrians at all hours of the day or night. Within the few dense blocks of Chinatown, hundreds of restaurants serve every imaginable type of Chinese cuisine, from fast-food noodles or dumplings to sumptuous Hunan, Szechuan, Cantonese, Mandarin, and Shanghai feasts (*see* Chapter 8). Every New Yorker thinks he or she knows the absolute flat-out best, but whichever one you try, at 8 PM on Saturday, don't be surprised if you have to wait in line to get in.

As you proceed down Mott Street, take a peek down Pell Street, a narrow lane of wall-to-wall restaurants whose neon signs stretch halfway across the thoroughfare.

Time Out A few steps down Pell Street, turn onto Doyers Street to find the **Viet-Nam Restaurant** (11 Doyers St., tel. 212/693–0725), an informal, inexpensive little basement restaurant that serves spicy, exotic Vietnamese dishes.

At the corner of Mott and Mosco streets stands the **Church of the Transfiguration.** Built in 1801 as the Zion Episcopal Church, this imposing Georgian structure with Gothic windows is now a Chinese Catholic church where mass is said in Cantonese and Mandarin.

❷⓿ The **New York Chinatown History Project** (70 Mullberry St., 2nd fl., tel. 212/619–4785), between Bayard and Canal Steets, shows interactive photographic exhibits on Asian-American labor history. It also has a resource library and bookstore and offers a walking tour of Chinatown.

❷❶ At the end of Mott Street is **Chatham Square,** which is really more of a labyrinth than a square: 10 streets converge here, creating pandemonium for cars and a nightmare for pedestrians. A Chinese arch honoring Chinese casualties in American wars stands on an island in the eye of the storm. On the far end of the square, at the corner of Catherine Street and East Broadway, you'll see a branch of the Manhattan Savings Bank, built to resemble a pagoda (in this neighborhood, even some public phone booths have been styled as pagodas).

Skirting Chatham Square, head to the right to go down Worth Street. The corner of Worth, Baxter, and Park streets was once known as Five Points, the central intersection of a tough 19th-century slum of Irish and German immigrants. Today it has **❷❷** been replaced by **Columbus Park,** a shady, paved urban space where children play and elderly Chinese gather to reminisce about their homelands.

Return to Chatham Square, cross Park Row to your left, and take a sharp left turn on St. James Place to find two remnants of this neighborhood's pre-Chinatown past. On St. James Place is **❷❸** the **First Shearith Israel** graveyard (predecessor of the one in Chelsea, *see* Tour 11, above, connected with the congregation that today worships on the Upper West Side, *see* Tour 8, above). The first Jewish cemetery in the United States, this site was consecrated in 1656, when it was considered to be well outside of town. Walk a half block farther, turn left on James Street, and you'll see **St. James Church,** a stately 1837 Greek Revival edifice where Al Smith, who rose from this poor Irish neighborhood to become New York's governor and a 1928 Democratic presidential candidate, once served as altar boy.

24 Go back past Chatham Square and up the Bowery to **Confucius Plaza**, the open area monitored by a statue of Confucius and the sweeping curve of a redbrick high-rise apartment complex named for him. At 18 Bowery, at the corner of Pell Street, stands one of Manhattan's oldest homes, a Federal and Georgian structure built in 1785 by meat wholesaler Edward Mooney. For some exotic shopping, duck into the **Canal Arcade,** a passage linking Bowery and Elizabeth Streets. Just before Canal Street, at 52 Bowery, you'll see the **Silver Palace** restaurant (*see* Chapter 8), worth a peek inside for its Chinese rococo interior, complete with dragons whose eyes are blinking lights.

At the intersection of the Bowery and Canal Street, a grand arch and colonnade mark the entrance to the Manhattan Bridge, which leads to Brooklyn. This corner was once the center of New York's diamond district. Many jewelry dealers have moved uptown to 47th Street between Fifth and Sixth avenues (*see* Off the Beaten Track, below), but a substantial number still occupy shops on the Bowery and the north side of Canal. The selection is pretty good, but don't expect to pay the first price quoted to you.

Tour 17: Wall Street and the Battery

Numbers in the margin correspond with points of interest on the Lower Manhattan map.

Lower Manhattan doesn't cover many acres but it is packed with attractions, for it has always been central to the city's networks of power and wealth. It was here that the New Amsterdam colony was established by the Dutch in 1625; in 1789, the first capital building of the United States was located here. The city did not really expand beyond these precincts until the middle of the 19th century. Today lower Manhattan is in many ways dominated by Wall Street, which is both an actual street and a shorthand name for the vast, powerful financial community that clusters around the New York and American stock exchanges. Visit on a weekday to catch the district's true vitality —but expect to be jostled on the crowded sidewalks if you stand too long, peering at the great buildings that surge skyward on every corner. A different but equally awe-inspiring sight can be found on the tip of the island, as you look out across the great silvery harbor and see enduring symbols of America: the Statue of Liberty and Ellis Island, port of entry for countless immigrants to a new land.

Our tour begins at the southernmost point of Manhattan, at the **Staten Island Ferry Terminal** (for subway riders that's just outside the South Ferry station on the No. 1 line). The **Staten Island Ferry** is still the best deal in town: The 20- to 30-minute ride across New York Harbor provides great views of the Manhattan skyline, the Statue of Liberty, the Verrazano Narrows Bridge, and the New Jersey coast—and it costs only 50¢ *roundtrip*. A word of advice, however: While commuters love the ferry service's swift new low-slung craft, the boats ride low in the water and have no outside deck space. Wait for one of the higher, more open old-timers.

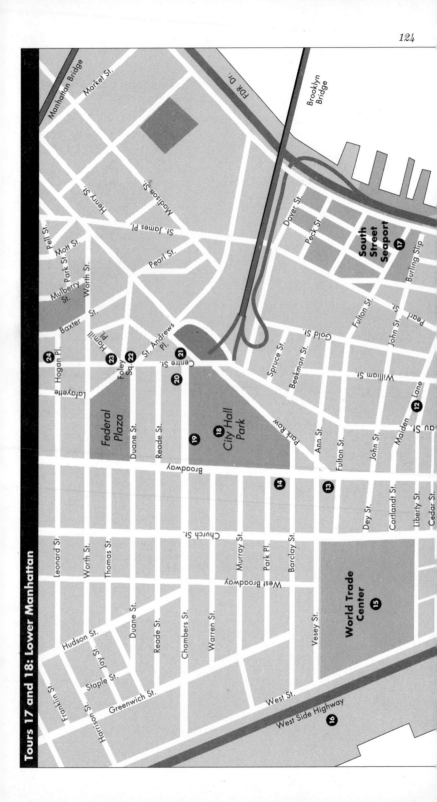

Tours 17 and 18: Lower Manhattan

East River

440 yards
400 meters

Maiden Lane

South St.

Front St.

Water St.

Wall St.

Pearl St.

Hanover Sq.

Pine St.

Nassau St.

S. William St.

Broad St.

Exchange Pl.

Water St.

Thames St.

Whitehall St.

Beaver St.

Bridge St.

Stone St.

Pearl St.

Broadway

Trinity Pl.

Battery Pl.

Rector St.

Albany St.

Battery Park

Battery Park City

Hudson River

N

Battery Park, **2**
Castle Clinton, **3**
City Hall, **18**
Criminal Court Building, **24**
Ellis Island, **5**

Federal Hall National Memorial, **9**
Federal Reserve Bank, **12**
Fraunces Tavern, **8**
Municipal Building, **21**

New York County Courthouse, **23**
New York Stock Exchange, **10**
St. Paul's Chapel, **13**

South Street Seaport Historic District, **17**
Staten Island Ferry, **1**
Statue of Liberty, **4**
Surrogate's Court, **20**
Trinity Church, **11**

Tweed Courthouse, **19**
U.S. Courthouse, **22**
U.S. Customs House, **6**
Vietnam Veterans Memorial, **7**

Woolworth Building, **14**
World Financial Center, **16**
World Trade Center, **15**

2 To the west of South Ferry lies **Battery Park,** a verdant landfill, loaded with monuments and sculpture, at Manhattan's green toe. The park's name refers to a line of cannons once mounted here to defend the shoreline (which ran along what is currently State Street). Head west along the water's edge to the **East Coast Memorial,** a statue of a fierce eagle that presides over eight granite slabs inscribed with the names of U.S. servicemen who died in the Western Atlantic during World War II. Climb the steps of the East Coast Memorial for a fine view of the main features of **New York Harbor;** from left to right: **Governors Island,** a Coast Guard installation; hilly **Staten Island** in the distance; the **Statue of Liberty** on Liberty Island; **Ellis Island,** gateway to the New World for generations of immigrants; and the old railway terminal in **Liberty Park,** on the mainland in Jersey City, New Jersey.

Continue west past a romantic **statue of Giovanni da Verrazano,** the Florentine merchant who piloted the ship that first sighted New York and its harbor in 1524. The Verrazano Narrows Bridge between Brooklyn and Staten Island—the world's longest suspension bridge—is visible from here, just beyond Governors Island.

3 Built in 1811 as a defense for New York Harbor, the circular brick fortress now called **Castle Clinton** was, when first built, on an island 200 feet from shore. In 1824 it became Castle Garden, an entertainment and concert facility that reached its zenith in 1850 when more than 6,000 people (the capacity of Radio City Music Hall) attended the U.S. debut of the "Swedish Nightingale," Jenny Lind. After landfill connected it to the city, Castle Clinton became, in succession, an immigrant processing center, an aquarium, and now a restored fort, museum, and ticket office for ferries to the Statue of Liberty and Ellis Island.

4 The popularity of the **Statue of Liberty** surged following its 100th birthday restoration in 1986. After arriving on Liberty Island, you can take an elevator 10 stories to the top of the pedestal. The strong of heart and limb can climb another 12 stories to the crown. Currently you may have to wait in line for up to three hours for the privilege. *Tel. 212/363–3200. Round-trip fare: $3.25 adults, $1.50 children. Daily departures on the hour 9–5; extended hours in summer.*

5 Castle Clinton will also be the departure point for ferries to **Ellis Island,** which opened in September 1990 to record crowds after a $140 million restoration, the largest-ever U.S. project of its kind (the fund-raising drive was headed by Chrysler Corporation chairman Lee Iacocca). Now a national monument, Ellis Island was once a federal immigration facility that processed 17 million men, women, and children between 1892 and 1954—the ancestors of more than 40% of Americans living today. *Tel. 212/883–1986. Round-trip fare: $6 adults, $3 children 3–11. Daily departures on the hour 9–4. Ellis Island Immigration Museum admission free.*

A broad mall that begins at the landward entrance to Castle Clinton leads back across the park to the **Netherlands Memorial,** a quaint flagpole depicting the bead exchange that bought from the native Indians the land to establish Fort Amsterdam in 1626. Inscriptions describe the event in English and Dutch.

6 As you leave the park, across State Street you'll see the imposing **U.S. Customs House,** built in 1907 in the ornate Beaux Arts style fashionable at the time. Above the base, the facade features massive columns rising to a pediment topped by a double row of statuary. Daniel Chester French, better known for the statue of Lincoln in the Lincoln Memorial in Washington, DC, sculpted the lower statues, which symbolize various continents (left to right: Asia, the Americas, Europe, Africa); the upper row represents the major trading cities of the world. The Customs House facade appeared in the movie *Ghostbusters II* as the fictional New York Museum of Art. Federal bankruptcy courts are currently housed in the Customs House, and a branch of the Smithsonian Institution's Museum of the American Indian will soon open on the ground floor.

The Customs House faces onto **Bowling Green,** an oval greensward at the foot of Broadway that became New York's first public park in 1733. On July 9, 1776, a few hours after citizens learned about the signing of the Declaration of Independence, rioters toppled a statue of British King George III that had occupied the spot for 11 years; much of the statue's lead was melted down into bullets. In 1783, when the occupying British forces fled the city, they defiantly hoisted a Union Jack to a greased, uncleated flagpole so it couldn't be lowered; patriot John Van Arsdale drove his own cleats into the pole to replace the flag with the Stars and Stripes.

From Bowling Green, head south on State Street. A stunning semicircular office tower in reflective glass hugs the bend of the street at 17 State Street. Next door is the **Shrine of St. Elizabeth Ann Seton** (7-8 State St.). What is now the rectory of the shrine is a redbrick Federal-style town house with a distinctive wood portico shaped to fit the curving street. This house was built in 1793 as the home of the wealthy Watson family; Mother Seton and her family lived here from 1801 to 1803. She joined the Catholic Church in 1805, after the death of her husband, and went on to found the Sisters of Charity, the first American order of nuns. In 1975 she became the first American-born saint. Masses are held here daily.

7 Turn onto Water Street, passing on your right **New York Plaza,** a complex of high-tech office towers linked by an underground concourse. Just beyond it is the **Vietnam Veterans Memorial,** where letters from servicemen and women have been etched into a wall of greenish glass.

8 Return to Broad Street and go one block inland to **Fraunces Tavern,** a complex of five 19th-century buildings housing a museum, restaurant, and bar (*see* Chapter 8). The main building is a Colonial home (brick exterior, cream-colored portico and balcony) built in 1719 and converted to a tavern in 1762. This was the site where, in 1783, George Washington delivered a farewell address to his officers celebrating the British evacuation of New York; later, the building housed some offices of the fledgling U.S. government. Today Fraunces Tavern contains two fully furnished period rooms and other displays of 18th- and 19th-century American history. *Broad and Pearl Sts., tel. 212/ 425–1778. Suggested contribution: $2.50 adults, $1 students, senior citizens, and children; free Thurs. Restaurant open weekdays. Museum open June–Sept., weekdays 10–4; Oct.– May, weekdays 10–4, Sun. noon–5.*

Walk through the lobby of the new office building at **85 Broad Street,** which, paying due homage to urban archaeology, traces the course of the old Dutch Stone Street with a line of brown paving stones. At the side of the building, on Pearl Street, peer through the transparent panel in the sidewalk to see the excavated foundations of the 17th-century Stadt Huis, the old Dutch City Hall.

Time Out   The brick plaza behind 85 Broad Street is flanked by a variety of small restaurants. Order a take-out meal or snack and eat it out here on the benches, where you can watch busy office workers milling past.

Head up Pearl Street to **Hanover Square,** a quiet tree-lined plaza that stood on the waterfront when the East River reached Pearl Street. This was the city's original printing house square; on the site of 81 Pearl Street, William Bradford established the first printing press in the colonies. The pirate Captain Kidd lived in the neighborhood, and the brownstone **India House** (1837) used to house the New York Cotton Exchange. Today it holds Harry's of Hanover Square, a vintage Wall Street bar.

Walk inland up Hanover Square to the rounded corner of South William and Beaver streets, where a graceful columned porch marks the entrance to **Delmonico's** restaurant, opened in 1888 on the site of an earlier Delmonico's founded in 1827. A pioneer in serving Continental cuisine, it was *the* place to go at the turn of the century; under different ownership, it is still a restaurant today.

Two blocks farther north, William Street crosses **Wall Street,** so called because it traces the course of a wood wall built across the island in 1653 to defend the Dutch colony against the native Indians. Arguably the most famous thoroughfare in the world, though only a third of a mile long, Wall Street began its financial career with stock traders conducting business along the sidewalks or at tables beneath a sheltering buttonwood tree. Today it's a dizzyingly narrow canyon—look to the right and you'll glimpse a sliver of East River waterfront; look to the left and you'll see the black spire of Trinity Church, tightly framed by skyscrapers at the head of The Street.

To learn the difference between Ionic and Corinthian columns, look at the **Citibank Building** to your right (55 Wall St.). The lower stories were part of an earlier U.S. Customs House, built in 1863, and it was literally a bullish day on Wall Street when oxen hauled its 16 granite Ionic columns up to the site. When the National City Bank took over the building in 1907, McKim, Mead & White added a second tier of columns, but made them Corinthian.

One block east on Wall Street, where Broad Street becomes Nassau Street, you'll find on your right a regal statue of George Washington on the steps of the **Federal Hall National Memorial.** This 1883 statue by John Quincy Adams Ward marks the spot where Washington was sworn in as the first U.S. president in 1789. After the capital moved to Philadelphia in 1790, the original Federal Hall became New York's City Hall, then was demolished in 1812 when the present City Hall (*see* Tour 18, below) was completed. The clean and simple lines of the current structure, built as (yet another) U.S. Customs House in 1842, were modeled after the Parthenon, a potent symbol for a young nation striving to emulate classical Greek democracy. It's now a museum featuring exhibits on New York and Wall Street. *26 Wall St., tel. 212/264–8711. Admission free. Open weekdays 9–5.*

In building a two-story investment bank at the corner of Wall and Broad streets, J. P. Morgan was in effect declaring himself above the pressures of Wall Street real-estate values. Now **Morgan Guaranty Trust,** the building bears pockmarks near the fourth window on the Wall Street side, created when a bomb in a pushcart exploded in 1920.

❿ Perhaps the heart of Wall Street is the **New York Stock Exchange,** which has its august Corinthian main entrance around the corner at 20 Broad Street. Compared to the Federal Hall memorial, this neoclassical building is much more elaborately decorated, as befitted the more grandiose national image of 1901, when it was designed. Inside, after what may be a lengthy wait, you can take an elevator to the third-floor visitor center. A self-guided tour, informative slide shows, video displays, and guides may help you interpret the seeming chaos you'll see from the visitors' gallery overlooking the immense (50-foot-high) trading hall. *Tickets available at 20 Broad St., tel. 212/656–5167. Free tickets are distributed at 9:30. Open weekdays 9:20–3:30.*

⓫ Jet-black **Trinity Church** (Broadway and Wall St.) was New York's first Anglican parish (1646). The present structure (1846) ranked as the city's tallest building for most of the second half of the 19th century. Its three huge bronze doors were designed by Richard Morris Hunt to recall Ghiberti's doors for the Bapistry in Florence, Italy. The church's Gothic Revival interior is surprisingly light and elegant, although you may see derelicts napping in the pews. On the church's south side is a 2½-acre graveyard: Alexander Hamilton is buried beneath a huge white pyramid; and a monument commemorates Robert Fulton, the inventor of the steamboat (he's actually buried in the Livingstone family vault, with his wife). *Tours weekdays at 2; free 30-min concerts, Tues. 12:45 PM.*

Just north of the church is tiny Thames Street, where a pair of skyscrapers playfully called the **Thames Twins**—the Trinity and U.S. Realty buildings—display early 20th-century attempts to apply Gothic decoration to skyscrapers. Across the street at 120 Broadway, the 1915 **Equitable Building** rises 30 stories straight from its base with no setback; its overpowering shadow on the street convinced the city government to pass the nation's first zoning law. Large public plazas around the bases of skyscrapers have helped to alleviate this problem, and a good example is between Cedar and Liberty streets, where the black-glass **Marine Midland Bank** (1971) features in its street-level plaza a red-and-silver Noguchi sculpture, *Cube.* One block east at Nassau and Pine streets, the plaza surrounding the 65-story **Chase Manhattan Bank Building** holds a striking black-and-white sculpture, *Group of Four Trees,* by Jean Dubuffet.

Liberty Street converges with William Street and Maiden Lane at triangular **Louise Nevelson Plaza,** which contains four black welded-steel abstract Nevelson sculptures, three middle-size pieces, and one huge 70-footer. Sit in the plaza and contemplate the **Federal Reserve Bank** directly across the street, which looks like a bank ought to look: gray, solid, imposing, absolutely impregnable—and it had better be, for its vaults reputedly contain a quarter of the world's gold reserves. *33 Liberty St., tel. 212/720-6130. 1-hr tour by advance (at least one month) reservation, weekdays at 10, 11, 1, and 2.*

Across Maiden Lane in Federal Reserve Plaza, with its huge round pillars of sandy brick, you can take an escalator downstairs to see 20th-century art at the **Whitney Museum of American Art Downtown.** *33 Maiden La., tel. 212/943-5655. Admission free. Open weekdays 11-6.*

Continue through the arcade to John Street, where on your right you'll see the **John Street Methodist Church** (44 John St.), on the site of the first Methodist Church in America. Then return to Broadway and head north to **St. Paul's Chapel** (Broadway and Fulton St.), the oldest (1766) surviving church in Manhattan and the site of the prayer service following George Washington's inauguration as president. Built of rough Manhattan stone, it was modeled after London's St. Martin-in-the-Fields. It's open throughout the day for prayer and meditation; look in the north aisle for Washington's pew.

Two blocks up Broadway is the so-called "Cathedral of Commerce," the ornate white terra-cotta **Woolworth Building** (Park Pl. and Broadway). When it opened in 1913 it was, at 792 feet, the world's tallest building; it still houses the Woolworth corporate offices. Among its extravagant Gothic-style details are gargoyles set into arches in the lobby ceiling; one of them represents old man Woolworth pinching his pennies, while another depicts the architect, Cass Gilbert, cradling in his arms a model of his creation.

Go west on Park Place and turn down Church Street to the **World Trade Center,** a 16-acre, 12 million-square-foot complex that contains New York's two tallest buildings (1,350 feet high). To reach the observation deck on the 107th floor of 2 World Trade Center, elevators glide a quarter of a mile into the sky—in only 58 seconds. The view potentially extends 55 miles, although signs at the ticket window (admission: $3.50 adults, $1.75 children) disclose how far you can see that day and whether the outdoor deck is open. You can get the same view with a meal at **Windows on the World** (*see* Chapter 8) atop 1 World Trade Center; lighter meals or drinks are available at its **Hors d'Oeuvrerie.**

Some 50,000 people work in this seven-building complex, and at street level and underground it contains more than 60 stores, services, and restaurants, as well as the adjacent Vista International Hotel (*see* Chapter 9). There's a TKTS booth selling discount tickets to Broadway and Off-Broadway shows (*see* Chapter 10) in the mezzanine of 2 World Trade Center (open Monday–Saturday 11–5:30), and on the ninth floor of 4 World Trade Center, a visitors' gallery overlooks the trading floor of the Commodities Exchange (tel. 212/938–2018; open weekdays 9:30–3).

More than a million cubic yards of rock and soil were excavated for the World Trade Center—and then moved across West Street to help beget the 100-acre **Battery Park City** development, a complete neighborhood built from scratch. Take the

16 pedestrian overpass from 1 World Trade Center to Battery Park City's centerpiece, the **World Financial Center,** a four-tower complex with some heavy-duty corporate tenants including Merrill Lynch, American Express, and Dow Jones. You'll come out into the soaring **Winter Garden Atrium,** its mauve marble cascade of steps spilling down into a plaza with 16 giant palm trees, framed by a vast arched window overlooking the Hudson. Surrounding the atrium are several upscale shops—Godiva chocolatiers, Rizzoli bookshop, clothing stores such as Ann Taylor and Barneys—plus a skylit food court.

Time Out While the courtyard also offers several full-service restaurants, for a quick bite head for **Minters** (tel. 212/945–4455)—and be sure to leave room for their ice-cream cones.

Of the few spots in Manhattan that directly overlook the rivers, Battery Park City just may be the best. The outdoor plaza right behind the atrium curls around a tidy little yacht basin; take in the view of the Statue of Liberty and read the stirring quotations worked into the iron railings. To the south, a longer riverside promenade accompanies the residential part of Battery Park City, a mix of high rises, town houses, shops, and green squares that does a surprisingly good job of duplicating the rhythms of the rest of the city, although it still lacks one vital element: crowds of people.

Tour 18: The Seaport and the Courts

Numbers in the margin correspond with points of interest on the Lower Manhattan map.

New York's role as a great seaport is easiest to understand downtown, with both the Hudson River and East River waterfronts within walking distance. While the deeper Hudson River came into its own in the steamship era, the more sheltered waters of the East River saw most of the action in the 19th century, during the age of clipper ships. This era is preserved in the South Street Seaport restoration, centered on Fulton Street between Water Street and the East River. Only a few blocks away, you can visit another seat of New York history: the City Hall neighborhood, which includes Manhattan's magisterial collection of court buildings.

Walk down Fulton Street, named after the ferry to Brooklyn that once docked at its foot (the ferry itself was named after its inventor, Robert Fulton), to Water Street, which was once the shoreline. On the 19th-century landfill across the street is the **17** 11-block **South Street Seaport Historic District,** which was created in 1967 to save this area from being overtaken by skyscrapers. The Rouse Corporation, which had already created slick so-called "festival marketplaces" in Boston (Quincy Market) and Baltimore (Harborplace), was later hired to restore and adapt the existing historic buildings.

The little white lighthouse at Water and Fulton streets is the **Titanic Memorial,** commemorating the sinking of the S.S. *Titanic* in 1912. Beyond it, Fulton Street, cobbled in blocks of Belgian granite, is a pedestrian mall that swarms with visitors, especially on fine-weather weekends; on Friday evenings during summer, young professionals from the Financial District stand shoulder-to-shoulder at cocktail hour. Immediately to your left is the **Cannon's Walk Block,** which contains 15 restored buildings.

At 211 Water Street is **Bowne & Co.,** a reconstructed working 19th-century print shop. A narrow court called Cannon's Walk, lined with shops, opens onto Fulton Street; follow it to Front Street, where you'll find the **Museum Visitors Center** at 206 Front Street.

Directly across Front Street is the **Fulton Market Building,** a new building, full of shops and restaurants, that re-creates the bustling commercial atmosphere of the old victual markets that were on this site from 1822 on. On the south side of Fulton Street is the seaport's architectural centerpiece, **Schermerhorn Row,** a redbrick terrace of Georgian- and Federal-style warehouses and countinghouses built in 1811–12. Today the ground floors are occupied by upscale shops, bars, and restaurants.

Cross South Street under an elevated stretch of the FDR Drive to **Pier 16** where the historic ships are docked, including the *Peking*, the second-largest sailing ship in existence; the full-rigged *Wavertree;* and the lightship *Ambrose.* A restored **Pilothouse** is the pierside information center. Pier 16 is also the departure point for the 90-minute **Seaport Harbor Line Cruise** (tel. 212/385–0791). The fare is $12 adults, $6 children.

To the north is **Pier 17,** a multilevel dockside shopping mall. Its weathered-wood rear decks make a splendid spot from which to sit and contemplate the river; look north to see the Brooklyn, Manhattan, and Williamsburg bridges, and look across to see Brooklyn Heights.

Tel. 212/669–9424. Admission to ships, galleries, walking tours, Maritime Crafts Center, films, and other seaport events: $6 adults, $5 senior citizens, $4 students, $3 children. Open daily 10–5, longer hours in summer.

Time Out | If you're hungry, head for the fast-food stalls on Pier 17's third-floor **Promenade Food Court.** The cuisine is nonchain eclectic: Third Avenue Deli, Pizza on the Pier, Wok & Roll, the Yorkville Packing House, the Salad Bowl, or Bergen's Beer & Wine Garden (10 brews on tap). What's really spectacular is the view from the well-spaced tables in a glass-walled atrium.

As your nose may already have surmised, the blocks along South Street north of the museum complex still house a working fish market, which has been in operation since the 1770s. Although the city has tried to relocate the hundreds of fishmongers of the **Fulton Fish Market** to the South Bronx, the area remains a beehive of activity. Get up early (or stay up late) if you want to see it: The action begins around midnight and ends by 8 AM.

Return to Fulton Street and walk away from the river to Broadway, where St. Paul's Chapel is (*see* Tour 17, above). As you turn right, forking off to your right is **Park Row,** which was known as "Newspaper Row" from the mid-19th to early 20th century, when most of the city's 20 or so daily newspapers had offices there. Today there are only four New York dailies—the *Times,* the *Daily News,* the *Post,* and *Newsday*—and Park Row is an unremarkable commercial strip. In tribute to that past, however, a statue of Benjamin Franklin (who was, after all, a printer) stands in front of Pace University at the end of Park Row.

To the left of Park Row is triangular **City Hall Park,** originally the town common. A bronze statue of patriot Nathan Hale, who was hanged as a spy by the British troops occupying New York City, stands on the Broadway side of the park. In its day this green spot has hosted hangings, riots, and demonstrations; ticker-tape parades up lower Broadway end here, with the honorees receiving keys to the city on the steps of City Hall.

18 **City Hall,** built between 1803 and 1812, is unexpectedly sedate, small-scale, and charming. Its exterior columns reflect the classical influence of Greece and Rome, and the handsome cast-iron cupola is crowned with a statue of Lady Justice. Originally its front and sides were clad in white marble while the back was faced in cheap brownstone, because the city fathers assumed New York would never grow farther north than this! (Limestone now covers all four sides.) The major interior feature is a domed rotunda from which a sweeping marble double staircase leads to the second-floor public rooms. The wood-paneled City Council Chamber in the east wing is small and clubby; the Board of Estimate chamber to the west has colonial paintings and church-pew-style seating; and the Governor's Room at the head of the stairs, used for ceremonial events, is filled with historic portraits and furniture. The mayor's office is on the ground floor. Since the spring of 1989, however, New York City has been busily redefining the roles of these governmental bodies, because the U. S. Supreme Court declared that the city's system violated the Constitution's "one man, one vote" principle.

19 Looming directly behind City Hall is the **Tweed Courthouse,** named after notorious politician "Boss" William Marcy Tweed, under whose corrupt management this building took some $12 million and nine years to build (it was finally finished in 1872, but the ensuing public outrage drove Tweed from office). Although it is imposing, with its columned classical pediment outside and seven-story rotunda inside, almost none of the boatloads of marble that Tweed had shipped from Europe made their way into this building. Today it houses municipal offices; it has also served as a location for several films, most notably *The Verdict.*

20 Across Chambers Street the **Surrogate's Court,** also called the **Hall of Records** (31 Chambers St.), is the most ornate of this City Hall trio. In true Beaux Arts fashion, sculpture and ornament seem to have been added wherever possible to the basic neoclassical structure, yet the overall effect is graceful rather than cluttered. A courtroom here was the venue for *Johnson* v. *Johnson*, where the heirs to the Johnson & Johnson fortune waged their bitter battle.

21 On the east side of Centre Street is the city government's first skyscraper, the **Municipal Building,** built in 1914 by McKim, Mead & White. The "roof" section alone is 10 stories high, bristling with towers and peaks and topped by a gilt statue of Civic Fame. This is where New Yorkers come to pay parking fines and get marriage licenses. An immense arch straddles Chambers Street (traffic used to flow through here); the vaulted plaza in front was the site of a scene in the movie *Crocodile*

Dundee, in which the Aussie hunter coolly scares off would-be muggers with his bowie knife.

㉒ Head north up Centre Street to **Foley Square,** a name that has become synonymous with the New York court system. The **U.S. Courthouse** at 40 Centre Street, designed by Cass Gilbert, has marble steps climbing to a massive columned portico; above this rises a 32-story tower topped by a gilded pyramid, not un-like that with which Gilbert crowned the New York Life build-ing uptown. This courthouse has been the site of such famous recent cases as General William Westmoreland's libel suit against CBS News, and the tax evasion trial of hotel queen Leona Helmsley.

㉓ With its stately columns, pediments, and 100-foot-wide flight of marble steps, the **New York County Courthouse,** built in 1926, set the precedent here for neoclassical grandeur. It's ac-tually more eccentric than it looks, having been built in a hex-agonal shape to fit an irregular plot of land. That quintessential courtroom drama *Twelve Angry Men* was filmed here, as was the more recent movie *Legal Eagles.*

Turn to look across Foley Square at **Federal Plaza,** which sprawls in front of the gridlike skyscraper of the **Javits Federal Building.** The black glass box to the left houses the **U.S. Court of International Trade.**

㉔ Continue up Centre Street past neoclassical civic office build-ings to 60 Centre Street, the **Criminal Court Building,** a rather grim Art Deco tower connected by a skywalk to the detention center known as The Tombs. In *The Bonfire of the Vanities,* Tom Wolfe wrote a chilling description of this court's menacing atmosphere.

In contrast, the **Civil and Municipal Courthouse** across the way at 111 Centre Street is an uninspired modern cube, although it, too, has held sensational trials, including that of subway vigi-lante Bernhard Goetz. On the east side of this small square is the slick blank granite **Family Court** (60 Lafayette St.), with its off-putting angular facade.

As you walk up Leonard Street, which runs just south of the Family Court, take a look at the ornate Victorian building that runs the length of the block on your left. This is the old New York Life Insurance Company headquarters (346 Broadway), an 1870 building that was remodeled and enlarged in 1896 by McKim, Mead & White. The ornate clocktower facing Broad-way is now occupied by the avant-garde **Clocktower Gallery.** After looking at the art on the 13th floor, the adventurous will want to climb a narrow spiral stairway inside the clocktower to see the huge clock's mechanism or step outside on the balcony for a dramatic view of New York City. *108 Leonard St., tel. 212/ 233–1096. Voluntary contribution. Open Thurs.–Sun. noon–6.*

Manhattan for Free

One of the best, and least expensive, places to be in New York is out on the streets, soaking up the city. That's where you're likely to stumble upon the many free performances—both scheduled and impromptu—given by professionals and ama-teurs year-round. Music, dance, mime, acting, magic tricks, and more are offered for free or at pass-the-hat prices in parks and plazas all around town (*see* Chapter 10).

Parks and Public Places Another free-but-fascinating New York pastime is people-watching, and one of the best places to go for that is **Central Park** (*see* Tour 7, above), where the Mall and the area around Bethesda Fountain buzz with activity on weekends and holidays from about noon to dusk. Stroll over to Wollman Rink and watch the skaters, or head up to the Great Lawn to find groups of folk dancers. In the summer, take a picnic, a blanket, and a Frisbee to the Great Lawn in the early afternoon (before noon on weekends) to stake out a spot in line for free tickets to that evening's Shakespeare performance at the Delacorte Theater. While you're waiting, settle back to watch the strollers, joggers, softball teams, and soccer players who congregate in this area. It makes for a long day—tickets aren't handed out until around 6:30 PM, and the plays begin at 8—but the experience is unforgettable.

Another lovely way to spend a day in Central Park is on a walking tour given by Urban Park Rangers, who are knowledgeable about the history, design, geology, wildlife, and botany of the park. Call the Central Park Conservancy (tel. 212/397–3165) for a calendar of free tours, events, exhibitions, family workshops, and other activity ideas.

Rockefeller Center (*see* Tour 1, above) is another good place to enjoy New York for free. In summer, there are various outdoor entertainment programs; in winter, you can watch ice skaters swirl about beneath the giant Christmas tree. **South Street Seaport** (*see* Tour 18, above) offers an assortment of fun free activities year-round: concerts on the pier during summer, a jazz festival in winter, and daily street entertainment.

Lobbies and Atriums New York City's skyscrapers can be as interesting on the inside as they are on the outside. Many of them feature beautifully landscaped atriums, art exhibits, shops, restaurants, and free entertainment (check the Convention and Visitors Bureau's "Atrium" flyer for current listings).

There's no admission charge to the special exhibits at the **IBM Gallery of Science and Art** (Madison Ave. between 56th and 57th Sts.), the **AT&T InfoQuest Center** (Madison Ave. and 56th St.), and **Nikon House** (620 5th Ave., in Rockefeller Center). You can also view art for free in the three branches of the **Whitney Museum of American Art:** in the Equitable Center (787 7th Ave. between 51st and 52nd Sts.), the Philip Morris building (42nd St. and Park Ave.), and downtown at Federal Reserve Plaza (33 Maiden La.).

Historic Sites For a free guided tour of **Grand Central Terminal,** meet under the Kodak sign (in front of the terminal's Chemical Bank branch) at 12:30 PM on Wednesdays. Admission to official meetings of the General Assembly at the **United Nations** is free (pick up tickets at the information desk in the UN lobby, at 46th St. and 1st Ave.).

The **New York Stock Exchange** on Wall Street offers free tours that include a multimedia presentation and a stop in the visitors' gallery overlooking the trading floor. In the same lower Manhattan area (*see* Tour 17, above), you can also arrange in advance for a free tour of the **Federal Reserve Bank** (33 Liberty St., tel. 212/720–6130); explore **Federal Hall** (26 Wall St.), where George Washington was inaugurated as our first president; and visit **Fraunces Tavern** (Broad and Pearl Sts.), where General Washington bade farewell to his troops.

Museums   On Tuesday evenings, the main branch of the **Whitney Museum of American Art** (945 Madison Ave. at 75th St.), the **Guggenheim Museum** (1071 5th Ave. at 89th St.), the **Cooper-Hewitt Museum** (2 E. 91st St.), the **American Craft Museum** (40 W. 53rd St.), and the **National Academy of Design** (1083 5th Ave. at 89th St.) charge no admission. The **American Museum of Natural History** (Central Park West at 79th St.) is free on Friday and Saturday evenings.

The **Metropolitan Museum of Art** (5th Ave. at 82nd St.), the **Museum of the City of New York** (1220 5th Ave. at 103rd St.), the **Cloisters** (Fort Tryon Park, at the northern tip of Manhattan), the **American Museum of Natural History** (Central Park West at 79th St.), the **New Museum of Contemporary Art** (583 Broadway), the **Pierpont Morgan Library** (33 E. 36th St.), and the **Museum of Broadcasting** (1 E. 53rd St.) all have pay-what-you-wish or suggested-donation policies. If all you can spare is a penny, they may not look too happy, but they'll still let you in. You can also pay what you wish to get into the **New-York Historical Society** (170 Central Park West) on Tuesdays and the **Museum of Modern Art** (11 W. 53rd St.) on Thursday evenings.

Television Screenings   For those who love television, free tickets to TV shows are offered on a day-to-day basis at the **New York Convention and Visitors Bureau** (2 Columbus Circle) and from network personnel buttonholing passersby along Fifth and Sixth avenues.

What to See and Do with Children

New York is as magical a place for children as it is for adults. In fact, there are very few sights or activities in the city that can't be enjoyed from a pint-size perspective. What's more, there are plenty of places to go where children come first. Look for calendars of children's events in *New York* magazine and the *Village Voice* weekly newspaper, available at newsstands. The Friday *New York Times* also has a good listing of children's activities.

Sightseeing   While you're sightseeing with your family, don't miss the **Statue of Liberty** (*see* Tour 17, above) or the **South Street Seaport** (*see* Tour 18, above), both reliable hits with children. Boat rides are also a good way to see the city with youngsters—try the **Circle Line** (Pier 83, west end of 42nd St., tel. 212/563–3200), or, for a shorter, cheaper thrill, the 25¢ ride on the **Staten Island Ferry** (terminal in Battery Park). Another fun, quick way to see the city from a fresh perspective is to ride the **Roosevelt Island Aerial Tramway** across the East River. Trams board at Second Avenue and 60th Street; the fare is the same as for subways and buses.

Museums   While just about every major museum in New York has something to interest children, certain ones hold special appeal. At the top of the list is the **American Museum of Natural History** (Central Park West at 79th St.; tel. 212/769–5100), with its giant dinosaurs, big blue hanging whale, and lifelike dioramas of stuffed beasts. Especially intriguing are the Discovery Room, which features hands-on exhibits for children, and the

Naturemax Theater, which shows amazing nature films on its gigantic screen. It's best to savor this building a few halls at a time. The **Hayden Planetarium** (attached to the museum) offers sky shows tailored to seasonal and special events; there is also a preschool show, for which you must make reservations (tel. 212/769–5901). (*See* Tour 8, above.)

The **Children's Museum of Manhattan,** designed for children ages 2–12, offers interactive exhibits organized around common childhood experiences. Children can paint, make collages, try on costumes, pet animals, and generally stay amused for hours on end. *212 W. 83rd St., tel. 212/721–1223. Admission: $4. Open Tues.–Fri. 2–5, Sat. and Sun. 10–5.*

The **Metropolitan Museum of Art** (5th Ave. at 82nd St., tel. 212/535–7710) Uris Center for Education (tel. 212/570–3932) has programs for children: workshops, gallery talks, sketching classes, films, slide talks, drawing lessons, and more, designed for children ages 5 to 12 (*see* Tour 5, above).

Another favorite of the younger generation is the ***Intrepid* Sea-Air-Space Museum.** This famous World War II aircraft carrier brings to life the history of naval aviation, the modern U.S. Navy, and attempts at space travel. On display are more than 40 aircraft, rockets, and space vehicles, as well as an impressive collection of Congressional Medals of Honor. *Pier 86 at W. 46th St., tel. 212/245–0072. Admission: $6 adults, $5 senior citizens, $3.25 children ages 6–12. Open Wed.–Sun. 10–5.*

Many of the city's skyscrapers also have ongoing exhibits that will interest youngsters. For instance, **AT&T's InfoQuest Center** (Madison Ave. at 56th St., tel. 212/605–5555) has a multilevel interactive museum where, among other activities, children can experiment with robots that respond to hand-clapping or button-pushing (*see* Tour 2, above). On the concourse of the Empire State Building you'll find the **Guinness World Records Exhibit Hall** (5th Ave. and 34th St., tel. 212/947–2335), where children can learn about the biggest, smallest, longest, or shortest world-record holders (*see* Tour 4, above).

If you're willing to venture off the beaten track, you'll find **Aunt Len's Doll and Toy Museum** a real treat. Here Lenon Holder Hoyte will show you her private collection of thousands of dolls of all types, from candy-box to character dolls, plus everything you can think of in the way of accessories. The museum is in Ms. Hoyte's town house, so you must make an appointment. *6 Hamilton Terr. at 141st St. and St. Nicholas Ave., tel. 212/926–4172. Admission $2 adults, $1 children, by appointment only.*

Zoos   Central Park's **Children's Zoo** (*see* Tour 7, above), designed with toddlers in mind, features farm animals and has some great props to climb on, around, and through: Moby Dick, Noah's Ark, a castle, and a rabbit hole, to name a few. A few steps away is the more traditional **Central Park Zoo,** which was recently refurbished. Only 100 or so species are on display, so it can be toured in a reasonable amount of time, but older children may be disappointed that it has no really big animals, as the Bronx Zoo does (*see* Chapter 4).

Parks and Playgrounds   The obvious first choice is **Central Park,** where children can ride bicycles, play tennis, row boats, go horseback riding, ice-skate, roller-skate, skateboard, jog, fly kites, feed ducks, throw Frisbees—the list goes on and on (*see* Chapter 6). Children age 12 and under will enjoy the nostalgic **Carousel** (mid-park at 65th St., tel. 212/879–0244), complete with painted horses that prance up and down to jaunty organ music; it costs only 75¢ a ride. **Belvedere Castle** offers an inviting hands-on learning center with an emphasis on natural science. *Mid-park at 79th St., tel. 212/772–0210. Admission free. Open Tues.–Thurs. and weekends 11–5, Fri. 1–5.*

There are also child-oriented activities in the **Dairy** (mid-park at 65th St., tel. 212/397–3156). Hand-puppet shows are presented at the **Heckscher Puppet House** (mid-park at 62nd St., tel. 212/397–3162 for schedule and reservations), while marionette productions appear at the **Swedish Cottage Theater** (mid-park at 79th St., tel. 212/988–9093 for schedule and reservations).

Central Park has several excellent adventure playgrounds, in which weathered-wood structures, often underlaid with soft sand, support slides, swings, bridges, ladders, monkey bars, and other devices that safely encourage active play. Playgrounds can be found along the park's western edge at 68th Street, 81st Street, 85th Street, 93rd Street, and 100th Street; along the eastern edge at 67th Street, 71st Street, 77th Street, 85th Street, and 95th Street; and at the large Heckscher playground mid-park at 62nd Street.

Other good public playgrounds can be found at **Battery Park City** (West St. south of Vesey St.), **Washington Square** (at the foot of 5th Ave., between Waverly Pl. and W. 4th St.), **Abingdon Square** (at the triangular junction of Hudson, Bleecker, and Bank Sts. in the West Village), **John Jay Park** (east of 1st Ave. between 76th and 78th Sts.), and **Riverside Park** (west of Riverside Drive; playgrounds at 82nd and 89th Sts.).

Entertainment Madison Square Garden (7th Ave. between 31st and 33rd Sts., tel. 212/563–8300) offers, besides sports events (*see* Chapter 6), some extravaganzas that especially appeal to children. There are major **ice shows** in winter, and each spring brings the **Ringling Bros. Barnum & Bailey Circus.** (Check local newspapers for dates, times, and ticket information.) Another favorite New York spectacle is the **Big Apple Circus** (tel. 212/268–3030), which performs in Lincoln Center November through January.

For theater groups catering to children, *see* Chapter 10.

Storytelling **Eeyore's Books for Children** (2212 Broadway at 79th St., tel. 212/362–0634, or 25 E. 83rd St., tel. 212/988–3404), a wonderful children's bookstore, has storytelling on Sundays (11 AM on the West Side, 12:30 on the East Side, except July–Aug.). **Storyland** (1369 3rd Ave., tel. 212/517–6951) has a weekly story hour on Sundays at 1:30. In summer, the **Hans Christian Andersen Statue** in Central Park (at 74th St.) is the site for storytelling on Saturdays from 11 AM to noon. Pick up the monthly "Events for Children" brochure at branches of the **New York Public Library** to find out about library story hours, as well as child-oriented film programs. Branch libraries with particularly good children's rooms include the Donnell (20 W. 53rd St.), the Jefferson Market (425 6th Ave. at 10th St.), and the St. Agnes (444 Amsterdam Ave. at 82nd St.).

Shopping   Besides toy stores (*see* Chapter 7), children—especially older ones—may want to investigate the following shops. **Village Comics** (163 Bleecker St., 2nd fl., and 227 Sullivan St., tel. 212/777–2770) and **Funny Business Comics** (656 Amsterdam Ave., tel. 212/799–9477) carry a delightful, esoteric stock of old and new comic books. **Forbidden Planet** (821 Broadway at 12th St., tel. 212/473–1576) has everything the science-fiction or fantasy fanatic could ever want, including stuffed animals, coloring books, comic books, and collectibles.

Restaurants   At the East Village's **Two Boots** (37 Ave. A, between 2nd and 3rd Sts., tel. 212/505–2276), young customers are provided with crayons and coloring books. TV monitors and crayons make the waiting easier at the East Side and West Side locations of **Border Cafe** (244 E. 79th St., tel. 212/535–4347, and 2637 Broadway at 100th St., tel. 212/749–8888). Good hamburgers are served in a casual, fun atmosphere at **Hamburger Harry's** in TriBeCa (157 Chambers St. between Hudson and Greenwich Sts., tel. 212/267–4446) and in midtown (145 W. 45th St., tel. 212/840–2756). At South Street Seaport, Pier 17's **Promenade Food Court** offers a wide variety of quick foods to eat in a wide-open space.

Swensen's Ice Cream of Mercer Square (14 W. 4th St., tel. 212/674–7664) has simple, good food priced from $1.75–$7, and some of the richest ice cream in the city. **Peppermint Park Cafe and Bakery** (1225 1st Ave. at 66th St., tel. 212/288–5054) is a delight for the eyes and palate—huge green peppermints adorn the walls and sweets, treats, and main-course fare are served. **Serendipity** (225 E. 60th St. between 2nd and 3rd Aves., tel. 212/838–3531) is perfect for an ice-cream break, lunch, tea, or dinner (it gets pretty jammed on Saturdays, though). **Pappa's Place** (510 6th Ave. and 13th St., tel. 212/924–3799) is pink and perfect for homemade ice cream, cakes, candies, and frozen yogurt, as well as meals. **Eclair** (141 W. 72nd St. between Broadway and Columbus Ave., tel. 212/873–7700) has a long-standing reputation for clean surroundings and scrumptious food.

Off the Beaten Track

Public Spaces   Under the city's zoning laws, new office buildings can receive a variance—to add extra stories, for example—by designing and maintaining a portion of interior or exterior space for public use. Such spaces are a boon for city dwellers and visitors: They provide clean, safe, attractive areas where you can sit, relax, read a newspaper, and people-watch. Most are planted with greenery, from potted plants to towering trees, or have some form of falling water to muffle the sounds of the city. Many have snack bars, working telephones, and—what can be very difficult to find elsewhere in Manhattan—clean public rest rooms. The following public spaces are listed from lower Manhattan up.

In the modernistic atrium of the **Continental Insurance Building** (180 Maiden La. at Front St.) just two blocks south of the South Street Seaport Museum, benches surround copious foliage amid an ultramodern structure that looks as if it's made out of Tinker Toys. *Near Tours 17 and 18.*

ChemCourt (272 Park Ave. between 47th and 48th Sts.) in the Chemical Bank Building provides benches around plantings of exotic shrubs, all informatively labeled in English and Latin. A glass roof lets the sunshine into the ground floor of the 50-story silver-gray tower. *Near Tour 2.*

On the mezzanine and basement floors of 875 **Third Avenue** (between 52nd and 53rd Sts.), tables and chairs are set in a lobby surrounded by an array of fast-food establishments selling pizza, bagels, muffins, Chinese food, sandwiches, and salads. The basement also connects with the 53rd Street subway station (E, F lines). *Near Tour 2.*

Beside the Museum of Broadcasting, **Paley Park** (3 E. 53rd St.) was the first of New York's "pocket parks" to be inserted among the high-rise behemoths, placed on the site of the former society night spot the Stork Club. A waterfall blocks out traffic noise, and feathery honey-locust trees provide shade. There's a snack bar that opens when weather permits. *Near Tour 1.*

Another pocket park, **McGraw-Hill Park** (6th Ave. between 48th and 49th Sts.) behind the McGraw-Hill Building, has a stunning walk-through wall of water. *Near Tour 1.*

Nice Places to Live Many of the loveliest residential areas of the city remain so precisely because they *are* off the beaten track, and hence out of the commercial flow. New Yorkers all eventually find their own dream blocks, where they intend to move as soon as they hit the lottery. Here, from south to north, is an utterly subjective sampling, uptown and down.

The city's longest stretch of redbrick town houses preserved from the 1820s and 1830s runs along the north side of **Charlton Street** (west of 6th Ave.), with high stoops, paneled front doors, leaded-glass windows, and narrow dormer windows all intact. While you're here, stroll along parallel King and Vandam streets for more fine Federal houses. This quiet enclave was once an estate called Richmond Hill, whose various residents included George Washington, John and Abigail Adams, and Aaron Burr. *Near Tours 12 and 14.*

Sniffen Court (off 36th St. between Lexington and 3rd Aves.) is an easily overlooked cul-de-sac of 19th-century brick stables converted into town houses, with an atmosphere that's equal parts old London and New Orleans. Sniffen Court was for many years the home of sculptor Malvina Hoffman. *Near Tour 4.*

In the exclusive East Side neighborhood known as Turtle Bay, the secluded two-block-long **Beekman Place** (east of 1st Ave. between 49th and 51st Sts.) has an aura of unperturbably elegant calm. Residents of its refined town houses have included the Rockefellers, Alfred Lunt and Lynn Fontanne, Ethel Barrymore, and Irving Berlin. Go down the steps at 51st Street to reach a walkway along the East River. *Near Tour 2.*

Roosevelt Island (East River, 50th to 86th Sts.) is a 2½-mile-long East River island that was taken over by a residential complex in the 1970s, although only half of the high-rise buildings originally planned have been built. Some fragments remain of the asylums and hospitals once clustered here, when it was known as Welfare Island. Walkways along the edge of the island provide fine river views, and it's surprisingly quiet, compared with the city so near. The real treat, however, is the 3½-

minute ride over on an aerial tram that looks like an oversize Fisher-Price toy. The one-way fare is the same as for city subways or buses. *Near Tour 6.*

Pomander Walk (94th to 95th Sts., between Broadway and West End Ave.) is a surprising hidden slice of Merry Olde England, inspired by the stage sets for an American version of a 1911 British play, *Pomander Walk*. Peep through the gate—it's generally locked—to see Tudor-style houses, window boxes, and neatly trimmed hedges. *Near Tours 8 and 9.*

Built at the turn of the century, the white Beaux Arts town houses lining **West 105th Street** (between West End Ave. and Riverside Dr.) are like a vision of Paris. The apartment building at the northeast corner of Riverside Drive now belongs to the American Buddhist Academy; go around the corner to see its immense bronze Buddha. Marion Davies, mistress of William Randolph Hearst, once lived in the house at 331 Riverside Drive. *Near Tours 8 and 9.*

Commercial Districts The tendency in New York is for merchants in similar trades to cluster together in certain neighborhoods, where their customers can hop from one office to another. As you walk about the streets, you'll come upon sudden thickets of fur dealers, hat makers, button sellers, or flower suppliers, to name just a few. These three districts are particularly large and vibrant:

Gansevoort Market (around Gansevoort and Greenwich Sts.) features otherwise undistinguished warehouse buildings that each morning become the meat market for the city's retailers and restaurants. Racks of carcasses make a fascinating if not very pretty sight. Action peaks on weekdays from 5 to 9 AM. *Near Tours 11 and 12.*

The **Garment District** (7th Ave. between 31st and 41st Sts., also called "Fashion Avenue") teems with warehouses, workshops, and showrooms that manufacture and finish mostly women's and children's clothing. On weekdays the streets are crowded with trucks and the sidewalks swarm with daredevil deliverymen wheeling garment racks between factories and specialized subcontractors. *Near Tour 3.*

The relatively unglitzy jewelry shops at street level in the **Diamond District** (47th St. between 5th and 6th Aves.) are just the tip of the iceberg; upstairs, millions of dollars' worth of gems are traded, and skilled craftsmen cut precious stones. Wheeling and dealing goes on at fever pitch, all rendered strangely exotic by the presence of a host of Hasidic Jews in severe black dress, beards, and curled sidelocks. *Near Tour 1.*

4 Exploring the Other Boroughs

Many visitors to Manhattan notice the four outer boroughs—Brooklyn, Queens, the Bronx, and Staten Island—only from a Circle Line cruise, leaving those areas to remain ciphers, part of the city yet not. *Don't fall asleep on the subway*, the unschooled tourist tells himself, *or you may end up in the Bronx!*

Manhattanites themselves, many driven over the river by astronomical rents, have only recently begun to discover the outer boroughs. They've found sky, trees, and living space among the 19th-century brownstones, converted industrial lofts, art deco apartment palaces, and tidy bungalows. They've also found fascinating ethnic enclaves and a host of museums, parks, and gardens.

The reality is that Manhattan is only a small part of New York City. Its population of nearly 1.5 million is smaller than that of either Brooklyn (2.31 million) or Queens (1.92 million), and only slightly larger than that of the Bronx (1.214 million). Staten Island may be less populous (380,000), but it's 2½ times the size of Manhattan.

There are things to see and do in the outer boroughs that you simply won't find in Manhattan and most are just a subway ride away from midtown.

Manhattanites may try to put you off such a journey, but don't be daunted. After a couple of beers, those same people may rave about their favorite place for cheesecake (Junior's on Flatbush Avenue in Brooklyn), or a great outdoor barbecue they had at their sister-in-law's suburban-style house (in Forest Hills Gardens, Queens); you may even have to listen to a story about their life's peak experience—found in the bleachers of Yankee Stadium in . . . the Bronx!

Brooklyn

Tour 19: Brooklyn Heights

Numbers in the margin correspond with points of interest on the Brooklyn Heights map.

"All the advantages of the country, with most of the conveniences of the city." So ran the ads for a real-estate development that sprang up in the 1820s just across the East River from downtown Manhattan. Brooklyn Heights—named for its enviable hilltop position—was New York's first suburb, linked to the city first by ferry and later by the Brooklyn Bridge. Feverish construction quickly transformed the airy heights into a fashionable upper-middle-class community. Happily, some 600 buildings more than 100 years old remain intact today, making Brooklyn Heights a kind of picture book of 19th-century American architecture.

This walking tour actually begins in lower Manhattan near City Hall (take the Lexington Avenue line to City Hall or the Broadway IRT to Park Place). From there you'll approach the Heights in grand fashion, via the pedestrian walkway over the

❶ Brooklyn Bridge. The Great Bridge promenade takes little more than an hour to walk and is a New York experience on a par with the Statue of Liberty trip or the Empire State Building ascent. Even if you haven't the time to poke around the Brooklyn side, take the unforgettable walk across the bridge.

The Five Boroughs

ATLANTIC OCEAN

Jacob Riis
Park

Jamaica Bay
Wildlife Refuge

J.F.K.
International
Airport

SPRINGFIELD
GARDENS

JAMAICA

Southern Pkwy.

Van Wyck Expwy.

OZONE
PARK

SOUTH
OZONE PARK

Floyd
Bennett
Field

Rockaway Inlet

BROOKLYN

CANARSIE

EAST
NEW YORK

Marine
Park

Inlet Boro Pkwy.

495

MASPETH

GREENPOINT

WILLIAMSBURG

EAST

Atlantic Ave.

Eastern Pkwy.

Brooklyn Museum
and Botanic Gardens

Linden Blvd.

Ocean Pkwy.

BENSONHURST

Bay Pkwy.

CONEY ISLAND

Queens
Midtown
Tunnel

East River

Williamsburg
Bridge

Manhattan
Bridge

BROOKLYN
HEIGHTS

PARK
SLOPE

Prospect
Park

Brooklyn
Battery
Tunnel

Brooklyn

Queens Expwy.

Belt Pkwy.

BAY
RIDGE

Verrazano
Bridge

Lower
Bay

N

A

Lincoln
Tunnel

WEEHAWKEN

UNION
CITY

HOBOKEN

Holland
Tunnel

Battery
Park

Ellis I.

Liberty
State
Park

Statue of
Liberty

Liberty I.

Governors I.

Upper
Bay

The
Narrows

STATEN
ISLAND

SECAUCUS

HUDSON

LYNDHURST

17

KEARNY

280

NEWARK

ESSEX

1
9

Pulaski Skway.

JERSEY
CITY

Newark Bay

BAYONNE

Kill Van Kull

78

Newark
International
Airport

ELIZABETH

UNION

(You can catch a ride back to Manhattan on the No. 2 or 3 subway at the Clark street station, just a few blocks southwest of the walkway terminus.)

Before this bridge was built, Brooklynites had to rely on a ferry that connected Manhattan's Fulton Street to Brooklyn—a charming way to travel, surely, but unreliable in the fog and ice of winter. (Today there is talk of reinstating ferry service, though the armies of Wall Street nine-to-fivers commuting from Brooklyn manage just fine riding the subway or taking an invigorating morning constitutional over the bridge.)

After some 50 years of talk about a bridge, John Augustus Roebling, a respected engineer, was handed a bridge construction assignment in 1867. As the project slowly took shape over the next 15 years, it captured the imagination of the city; on its completion in 1883, it was called the Eighth Wonder of the World. Its twin Gothic-arched towers rise 268 feet from the river below. The roadway is supported by a web of steel cables, hung from the towers and attached to block-long anchorages on either shore. It is hardly the longest suspension bridge in the world anymore; the George Washington Bridge over the Hudson River has twice its span. But it remains a symbol of what man can accomplish and is a beautiful monument as well—in Walt Whitman's words, "the strong, light work of engineers."

In 1884 P. T. Barnum took 21 elephants across the bridge, just to prove it was sound, and motion picture directors have capitalized on it for photo opportunities: Gene Kelly danced across it in *On the Town;* Meryl Streep quaffed champagne there in *Sophie's Choice;* and in *Tarzan's New York Adventure*, Johnny Weismuller used it as a diving board.

As you look south from the walkway, the pinnacles of downtown Manhattan loom on your right, Brooklyn Heights stands sentinel on your left, and before you yawns the harbor, with Lady Liberty showing herself in profile. Turn about for a fine view up the East River, spanned within sight by the Manhattan and Williamsburg bridges. You don't need binoculars to enjoy the vistas, but you'd do well to bring a hat or scarf, because the wind whips through the cables like a dervish.

The bridge spills you out into Breukelen—as the founding Dutch first called this part of Long Island—at Cadman Plaza West, where a not-too-inviting park surrounds a conglomeration of government buildings, including the **New York Supreme Court** (former domain of fighting U.S. Attorney Rudolph Giuliani) and Brooklyn's **Borough Hall.** There's little reason to linger here, particularly as it's less safe than the residential Heights area, so turn right on Cadman Plaza West and descend toward the riverbank.

❷ As you approach the **Fulton Ferry Landing,** you'll pass the solid-looking expanse of the bridge's eastern Anchorage (tel. 718/802–1215), which is the setting for occasional performance-art extravaganzas and art exhibitions. Along this route you'll also cross under a noisy ramp of the Brooklyn–Queens Expressway. The pavement frequently gives way to cobblestone, a reminder of the past century, and Cadman Plaza takes on another name, Old Fulton Street.

At first glance the Old Fulton Street area will seem dark and depressing, shadowed by ancient warehouses whose contents

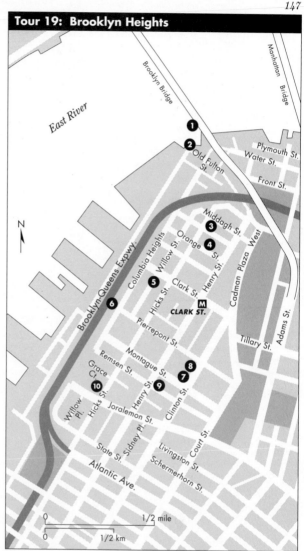

one can only speculate on. But look up and around. Several blocks north you'll notice the **Walentas Building** (1 Main St.), a handsomely be-towered and -clocked, post–Civil War structure erected by a corrugated-box magnate. On the south side of Fulton Street is the **Eagle Warehouse** (28 Old Fulton St.), with its striking round-arched Romanesque Revival entryway, enhanced by bronze lettering and fancy ironwork. The first office of the *Brooklyn Eagle* newspaper, it is now a residential co-op.

Continue toward the river to Front Street, where, a few blocks down, there are two newcomers to the neighborhood: **Gleason's Boxing Arena** (29 Front St.) and **Gym** (75 Front St.), which moved here from Manhattan's West Side. For 50 years, boxing greats such as Muhammad Ali, Roberto Duran, and Jake LaMotta put up their dukes and trained at Gleason's.

At the foot of Old Fulton Street is the **Fulton Ferry Terminal,** a self-possessed yellow-shingled tower that lists slightly. Walk out onto the **Ferry Pier** for a surprisingly pleasant whiff of the river and a worm's-eye view of the bridge. A plaque by the rail will help you identify the buildings of the downtown Manhattan skyline you'll see. Nearby, a former Erie Lackawanna coffee barge is moored to the pier. Dubbed *Bargemusic* (tel. 718/624–4061) by its operators, it is the setting for a regular series of chamber-music concerts.

At 1 Water Street you'll find the **River Café** *(see* Chapter 8), which looks like a mobile home beached beside the river, though clusters of festive white Christmas lights liven up this excellent restaurant.

The Ferry Landing is a much-neglected place, although plans exist for full-scale reclamation—for instance, turning the tobacco warehouse next to the River Café into a museum and mall. For those who venture there now, the place is genuinely atmospheric, with none of the finished corners of South Street Seaport.

Turn your feet south along Columbia Heights and climb toward Brooklyn Heights. On your way you'll pass the world headquarters of **Jehovah's Witnesses,** located in the Heights since 1909. The church published more than 43 million Bibles between 1926 and 1980.

❸ Bear left onto Middagh Street (pronounced *mid*-awe) and continue on until you arrive at **No. 24,** the oldest home in the neighborhood—a Federal-style wood residence with a mansard roof. If you're tall enough, peer over the wall for a glimpse of the cottage garden and carriage house in the rear.

❹ Carry on along Middagh, turning right at Henry Street, a happy commercial avenue of restaurants and greengrocers, then turn again onto Orange Street. On the north side of the block between Henry and Hicks streets is a formidable institution: the **Plymouth Church of the Pilgrims,** which was the vortex of abolitionist sentiment in the years before the Civil War, thanks to the stirring oratory of Brooklyn's most eminent theologian, Henry Ward Beecher. In the Underground Railroad that smuggled slaves to freedom, Plymouth Church was more or less Grand Central Station. Beside the church is a courtyard (locked, alas) with a statue of Beecher. His house, a prim Greek Revival brownstone, lies around the corner at 22 **Willow Street.**

❺ Turn left off Orange onto Willow Street, crossing Pineapple and Clark. (Street names in the Heights are an eccentric collection, reportedly created by a certain Miss Middagh, who despised the practice of naming streets for the town fathers and preferred instead various fruits.) **Willow Street,** between Clark and Pierrepont, is one of the prettiest and most architecturally varied blocks in the Heights. Note Nos. 108–112, built in the blend of terra-cotta reliefs, bay windows, and towers known as the Shingle or Queen Anne style. Farther down the block, on the west side, stand three distinguished brick Federal row houses allegedly part of the Underground Railroad.

As you turn right onto Pierrepont Street, heading toward the river, glance down Columbia Heights to your right, where Nos.

210–220 compose a brownstone grouping often cited as the most graceful in New York. Norman Mailer lives on this street —lucky Mr. Mailer—and from a rear window in No. 111, John Roebling's reclusive son Washington (who in 1869 succeeded his father as chief engineer for the Brooklyn Bridge) used to sit and watch the titan take shape.

⑥ Pierrepont Street ends at the **Brooklyn Heights Promenade,** a sliver of park one-third of a mile long, hanging over the ferry district like one of Babylon's fabled gardens. Cantilevered over two lanes of the Brooklyn–Queens Expressway and a service road, this quiet esplanade area is lined with benches offering front-row seats for the Manhattan skyline show. Circling gulls squawk, tugboats honk, and the city seems like a vision from another planet.

As you leave the Promenade (via Montague Street), look left to see Nos. **2** and **3 Pierrepont Place,** two brownstone palaces built in the 1850s by a China trader and philanthropist, and recently used as a location for John Huston's film *Prizzi's Honor* (the frightful Mafia chieftain Don Corrado lived here). On your right lies **Montague Terrace,** where Thomas Wolfe lived when he finished *You Can't Go Home Again.* In the 1940s and 1950s, the neighborhood was said to be home to the city's largest number of writers outside Greenwich Village, among them Carson McCullers, W. H. Auden, Arthur Miller, and Truman Capote.

As you head east, Montague Street turns into a commercial district often disparaged for its homogeneous Yuppie character. Still, restaurants here feature everything from Hungarian to Japanese food, and window shopping can be fun. On the last block before Cadman Plaza West (north side), note an interesting row of banks: the art deco **National Title Guarantee Building** (No. 185); a **Citibank** (No. 183) that looks like a latter-day Roman temple; and **Manufacturer's Hanover Trust Company** (No. 177), a copy of the Palazzo della Gran Guardia in Verona, Italy.

⑦ The **Church of St. Ann and the Holy Trinity** lies at the northwest corner of Montague and Clinton streets. Its historic stained-glass windows—the first made in the United States— are currently being restored. In recent years, the church has become a performing arts and film series center frequented by downtown Manhattan types. *157 Montague St., tel. 718/858– 2424. Box office open Tues.–Sat. noon–6.*

A block north, at the corner of Clinton and Pierrepont, is the
⑧ **Brooklyn Historical Society,** with its new Shellens Gallery. The collection includes Brooklyn Dodgers' bats and balls, trick mirrors from Coney Island, and a 300-pound cast-zinc eagle saved from the offices of the *Brooklyn Eagle.* The society's library on the second floor—with its rich carved-wood bookcases and lustrous stained-glass windows—is a showcase for late 19th-century interior design; it also holds 10,000 rare photographs and 100,000 books. *128 Pierrepont St., tel. 718/624–0890. Library admission: $2.50. Open Tues.–Sat. 10–4:45. Shellens Gallery admission: $2.50 adults, $1 children. Open Tues.– Sun. noon–5.*

Return south along Clinton Street, then turn right onto Remsen Street. At the corner of Remsen and Henry streets, stop to
⑨ take in the Romanesque Revival **Our Lady of Lebanon Roman Catholic Church** (113 Remsen St.), designed by prolific church

architect Richard Upjohn. It features the Shrine of St. Sharbel Marklouf and doors salvaged from the 1943 wreck of the ocean liner *Normandie*. Turn left onto Hicks Street to visit another Upjohn creation, **Grace Church** (254 Hicks St.). Built in Gothic Revival style, it is shaded by an 80-foot elm tree. Across Hicks Street is **Grace Alley,** a traditional mews with a score of restored carriage houses.

The extreme southwest corner of Brooklyn Heights, encompassing the west ends of Joralemon Street and Willow and Columbia places, is a quiet, leafy, untrammeled area, rich in architectural pleasures. Along the north side of Joralemon, 25 **Greek Revival brownstones** (Nos. 29–75) delicately sidestep their way down the hill toward the river and the piers. Peek into Columbia Place to see an early attempt at humane, low-cost housing, the **Riverside tenements** (4–30 Columbia Pl.), dating from the 1870s. Then follow **Willow Place** south along the peaceful block between Joralemon and State streets; in late afternoon, the houses take on the colors of a faded quilt. Shrinking back from the street is an old chapel (26 Willow Pl.), now home to an amateur theater group.

Time Out Camille's (311 Henry St.) is a cozy and inexpensive spot, with antique counters and no more than 10 tables. The muffins, challah bread, and cakes are homemade, as are the soups. Imagine Berkeley come to Brooklyn and you've got the picture.

To return to Manhattan from here, find your way back to Court Street and go north to the Borough Hall subway station. To explore more of nearby Brooklyn, however, you may want to head up **Atlantic Avenue,** with its exotic Syrian and Lebanese shops and, farther east, a string of antiques stores crammed with relatively reasonable buys. Or go south along Court Street to **Carroll Gardens,** the Italian brownstone neighborhood pictured in the 1987 film *Moonstruck*. The **Cammareri Brothers Bakery** (502 Henry St.) is where Nicholas Cage worked in that film; in real life, the bakery turns out staff-of-life-like Italian loaves and dense cheesecake. The food stores in the neighborhood are in general an Italian cook's dream.

Tour 20: Park Slope

Numbers in the margin correspond with points of interest on the Park Slope map.

This neighborhood, which grew up in the late 1800s on the west side of Prospect Park, is today one of Brooklyn's most sought-after sections. Many families have moved in to renovate the handsome brownstones that line its blocks—beware the heavy traffic in baby strollers!

Begin on **Seventh Avenue,** the area's main commercial street, accessible by the D, Q, 2, or 3 subway trains. Here, among other interesting shops, you'll find a wine store of real distinction, **Leon Paley Ltd.** (88 7th Ave.), as well as three diet-defying bakeries: **Cousin John's** (70 7th Ave.); **Faith's** (around the corner on 169 Lincoln Pl.); and the **New Prospect Gourmet** (52 7th Ave.). The corner of Seventh Avenue and Sterling Place was the site of a horrendous plane crash in 1960, which leveled several buildings around the intersection; down the street, the

Brownstone Gallery (76 7th Ave.) displays in its window a photograph of the grounded plane.

❶ Turn east on Lincoln Place to find the Slope's most venerable edifice, the **Montauk Club** (25 8th Ave.), an 1891 mansion modeled on Venice's Ca' d'Oro. Notice the friezes of Montauk Indians and the private side entrance, built especially for members' wives in the 19th century.

❷ Make your way south along Eighth Avenue, sampling the brownstones on various streets along the way (President and Carroll streets are especially handsome), until you reach **Montgomery Place,** a block-long street between Eighth Avenue and Prospect Park West. This is considered by many to be the neighborhood's finest block, lined by a picturesque variety of town houses designed by the Romanesque Revival genius C.P.H. Gilbert.

❸ Return along Prospect Park West to **Grand Army Plaza,** a geographic star from which radiate Prospect Park West, Eastern Parkway, and Flatbush and Vanderbilt avenues. At its center stands the **Soldiers' and Sailors' Memorial Arch,** patterned on the Arc de Triomphe in Paris. Three heroic sculptural groupings adorn the arch: atop, a four-horsed chariot by Frederick MacMonnies, so dynamic that it almost seems on the verge of catapulting off the arch; to the sides, the victorious Union Army and Navy of the Civil War. Inside are bas-reliefs of Presidents Abraham Lincoln and Ulysses S. Grant, sculpted by Thomas Eakins and William O'Donovan, respectively. A secret doorway leads to a spiral staircase and, ultimately, the arch's top (it's open April 29–June 17, weekends 11–4:30). To the northwest, Neptune and a passel of debauched tritons leer over the edges of the **Bailey Fountain,** where tulle-drenched brides and grooms in technicolor tuxes come to pose after exchanging vows.

To the southeast of the plaza is the main entrance to **Prospect Park,** a 536-acre urban playground designed by Frederick Law Olmsted and Calvert Vaux, who considered it superior to their earlier creation, Central Park, because no streets divided it and no bordering skyscrapers would break its rural illusion. Woods, water, and meadows remain the park's three basic thematic elements. Inside the entrance is the 90-acre **Long Meadow,** full of picnickers and kite-fliers on weekends. Follow the circular drive to the right, and at the entrance at Prospect Park ❹ West and 4th Street you'll see the **Litchfield Villa,** an Italianate mansion built in 1857. It now holds the park's administrative offices, but visitors are welcome to step inside and view the interior. Across the main drive is the **Picnic House** (tel. 718/788–0055), stage for a year-round schedule of drama, dance, music, storytelling, and puppetry.

❺ If you follow the drive to the left of the main entrance, you'll come to the **zoo,** currently closed for renovation into a children's zoo. Just beyond the zoo is a restored 1912 **carousel** ❻ (50¢ a ride) and the **Lefferts Homestead,** a gambrel-roofed Dutch colonial farmhouse (1783) that holds a museum of period home furnishings and changing exhibits. *Tel. 718/965–6505. Admission free. Open May–Sept., Wed.–Sat. noon–4, Sun. noon– 5; Oct.–Dec. and Apr., Wed.–Sun. noon–4; Jan.–Mar., weekends noon–4.*

Tour 20: Park Slope

7 The middle of the park is a forested ravine, cut by a stream and dotted with bridges. Follow the central drive, which bisects the park here, to the **Quaker Cemetery,** where you will find Montgomery Clift's quiet grave. If you stay on the circular drive,

8 you'll soon pass the terra-cotta **Boathouse** (tel. 718/287–3474), styled after the Library of St. Marks in Venice; today it houses a visitor center and art exhibits. A few yards down the path is the giant, gnarled **Camperdown Elm,** which Marianne Moore immortalized in a poem in the 1960s. Moore became one of the park's chief advocates, a labor she termed "my only mortal en-

9 tanglement." South of here is a formal **garden terrace,** near the shore of a 60-acre **lake** inhabited by a fleet of ducks and swans.

If you return to Grand Army Plaza, to the east of the park's

10 main entrance, you will find the main branch of the **Brooklyn Public Library.** Built in 1941, it applies art deco streamlining to the grand neoclassical look of Beaux Arts public buildings. Notice the bas-relief carvings and the inscription picked out in gold above the entrance. Step inside to admire the murals in the lobby. *Tel. 718/780–7700. Open Mon.–Thurs. 9–8, Fri. and Sat. 10–6, Sun. 1–5.*

Eastern Parkway, which runs from Grand Army Plaza past the library, mimicks the grand sweep of the boulevards of Paris and Vienna. Every Labor Day weekend the parkway hosts the biggest and liveliest carnival outside the Caribbean—a cacophony of calypso, steel band, and reggae music, with plenty of conch curry, spice bread, and meat patties to go around.

A couple of hundred yards along the parkway is an entrance to **⓫** the **Brooklyn Botanic Garden,** which occupies 52 acres across Flatbush Avenue from Prospect Park. The garden exudes a beguiling Oriental atmosphere, due to the presence of a **Japanese Garden,** complete with a blazing red torii gate and a pond laid out in the shape of the Chinese character for "heart." The Japanese cherry arbor turns into a heart-stopping cloud of pink every May. Wander through the **Cranford Rose Garden** (5,000 bushes, 900 varieties); the **Fragrance Garden,** designed especially for the blind; the **Shakespeare Garden,** featuring plants immortalized by the bard; and **Celebrity Path,** Brooklyn's answer to Hollywood's famous sidewalk, with the names of homegrown stars—including Mel Brooks, Woody Allen, Zero Mostel, Barbara Stanwyck, and Mae West—inscribed on stepping-stones. In May 1988, the garden gained a complex of handsome greenhouses called the **Steinhardt Conservatory,** which holds thriving desert, tropical, temperate, and aquatic vegetation, as well as a display charting the evolution of plants over the past 140 million years. The **C.V. Starr Bonsai Museum** in the Conservatory grows about 75 miniature Japanese plants. The Botanic Garden Shop is a fine place to stop, particularly if you're a gardener yourself. *1000 Washington Ave., tel. 718/ 622–4433. Admission to garden free. Admission to Steinhardt Conservatory Nov.–Mar. free; Apr.– Oct., $2 adults, $1 senior citizens and children 3–12. Garden open Apr.–Sept., Tues.– Fri. 8–6, weekends and holidays 10–6; Oct.–Mar., Tues.–Fri. 8–4:30, weekends and holidays 10–4:30. Conservatory open Apr.–Sept., Tues.–Sun. 10–5; Oct.–Mar., Tues.–Sun. 10–4.*

⓬ The **Brooklyn Museum,** designed by the McKim, Mead & White team in 1897, sports huge Daniel Chester French statues of Brooklyn and Manhattan (as classical ladies) on its Eastern Parkway front. With over 2 million objects, the Brooklyn collection is the seventh largest in the country. Look especially for its **Egyptian Art** collection (third floor), considered the best of its kind anywhere outside London or Cairo, or the African and Pre-Columbian Art (first floor), another collection recognized worldwide. In the gallery of **American painting and sculpture** (fifth floor) you'll find *Brooklyn Bridge* by Georgia O'Keeffe, as well as striking works by Winslow Homer, John Singer Sargent, and Gilbert Stuart. The **Period Rooms** (fourth floor) include the complete interior of the Jan Martense Schenck House, built in the Brooklyn Flatlands section in 1675, as well as a suite of rooms decorated in Moorish style from the 54th Street mansion of John D. Rockefeller. Outdoors, the **Frieda Schiff Warburg Memorial Sculpture Garden** features relics from "lost New York," such as a lion's head from Coney Island's Steeplechase Park. The museum also offers excellent special exhibits, a treasure chest of a gift shop, and dramatic views of Manhattan from its Eastern Parkway-Washington Avenue corner. *200 Eastern Pkwy., tel. 718/638–5000. Suggested contribution: $3 adults, $1 senior citizens, $1.50 students with valid ID, children under 12 free. Open Wed.–Mon. 10–5.*

Queens

Tour 21: Long Island City and Astoria

Numbers in the margin correspond with points of interest on the Long Island City and Astoria map.

In the 1800s, along the East River in Queens, a string of neighborhoods thrived due to their ferry links with Manhattan. One of the busiest ferries connected a finger of land called Hunters Point with East 34th Street, Manhattan. Here, a business district known as Long Island City burgeoned. (Queens is, after all, on the western end of Long Island, as is Brooklyn.) Factories, boardinghouses, municipal buildings, and restaurants clustered around the intersection of Vernon Boulevard and Jackson Avenue, while north along Vernon Boulevard tycoons built summer homes, with boathouses and lawns that reached gracefully to the banks of the river. Today the community has found new life as a mecca for artists, who've migrated with their paint pots and welding tools to airy, low-rent studios.

A 10-minute ride on the No. 7 subway from Times Square or Grand Central Station will take you to the 45th Avenue Court House Square station. This noisy intersection is a fine introduction to this part of Queens, where the dark, clanking hulk of the El keeps the sunlight from penetrating to the street.

Long Island City's streets puzzle cartographers and visitors alike; you'll find numbered streets running north and south, and numbered avenues, roads, and drives going east–west. Consider 45th Avenue: To its south lies 45th Road, and to its north is 44th Road, 44th Avenue, and 44th Drive. But bear with this confusion and turn east onto 45th Avenue, where you'll

❶ find the **Hunters Point Historic District,** full of immaculate row houses with their original stoops and cornices. Their fine condition is due partly to their having been faced in resilient Westchester stone. At 21st Street, a small park offers benches (for pigeons and people) and a setting for a large metal sculpture called *Bigger Bird* by Daniel Sinclair. The warehouses surrounding the park are a warren of artists' studios; above their low roofs there's an unimpeded view of Manhattan.

❷ On 21st Street, between 46th Road and 46th Avenue, is **P.S.1,** a contemporary art museum housed in what was originally a Ward 1 school. The founders of P.S.1 were the first of the art-conscious to take up residence in the area; a little more than 11 years ago they turned the old school into lecture rooms, studio space for artists, and wide white galleries. On display are special exhibits and a number of permanent works, including James Turrell's sky piece *Meeting* and Alan Saret's *Fifth Colar Chthonic Wall Temple* (1976). *46–01 21st St., tel. 718/784–2084. Admission: $2. Open Wed.–Sun. noon–6.*

❸ The **Kenneth Bernstein Gallery** opened six years ago as **Studio K,** the first private gallery to come to Hunters Point. Its setting is the skylit second floor of the old Queens Borough Hall (the new one is in Kew Gardens). The gallery features the work of Queens artists, whose styles range from abstract to traditional. *10–63 Jackson Ave., tel. 718/784–0591. Call in advance to arrange a viewing, or buzz from street level.*

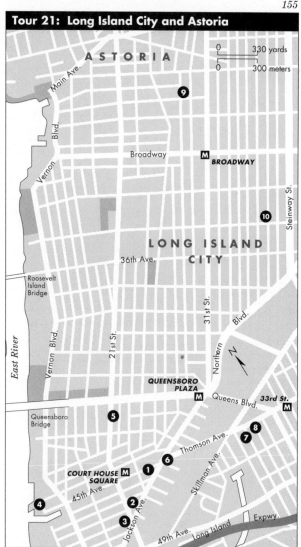

Tour 21: Long Island City and Astoria

The intersection of **Jackson Avenue and Vernon Boulevard** is still the commercial center of the neighborhood, as it was when the ferry operated from the foot of Borden Avenue. Modest shingled homes, butcher shops, diners, and the Vernon–Jackson subway stop crowd together beneath the huge, four-barreled stacks of the old Pennsylvania Railroad generating plant. (Schwartz Chemicals, as the structure is identified on its eastern face, was a later occupant; today the behemoth contains an assortment of smaller manufacturing firms and some indoor tennis courts.) At 49th Avenue and Vernon Boulevard, the steeple of **St. Mary's Roman Catholic Church** rises more spiritually into the sky than the stacks of old Schwartz.

Vernon Boulevard, originally called the Williamsburg Turnpike Road, was Queens's first true highway, leading to the mansions along the river, all now demolished. The area to the west of Vernon is slated to change dramatically once again, when the Hunters Point Development plan turns 70 acres of riverfront and 20 acres of landfill between the Midtown Tunnel and Queensboro Bridge into a sprawling apartment complex and commercial mall.

Time Out Only locals know about **The Partenope** (46–18 Vernon Blvd., tel. 718/784–8518), a tiny, unassuming Italian restaurant at Vernon Boulevard and 46th Road. Don't let its modesty fool you, though, because it offers splendid, filling repasts of Italian sandwiches, soups, and pastas. Lasagne is the house specialty. Prices are low; the atmosphere is homey.

A gray concrete block of a building rises at the foot of 44th Drive. Another warehouse? Hardly. This is the **Water's Edge Restaurant and East River Yacht Club,** where in summertime gay umbrellas sprout up on the dock, and boaters check in for quick vodka tonics. Inside is an elegant restaurant that charges Manhattan prices, bringing in its sophisticated clientele via a complimentary ferry service from the city's 23rd Street Marina between April and November. From the pier outside you can survey the **Queensboro Bridge,** which extends 7,000 feet, from Manhattan's East 60th Street to Crescent Street, Queens. Finished in 1909, its construction claimed the lives of 50 workers. A detour north on Vernon Boulevard will take you to the bridge's base at Queens Plaza, where there's a riverfront park and a lonely remnant of the past century, the old **New York Architectural Terra Cotta Company,** complete with Tudor Revival adornments and chimney pots.

It's ironically appropriate that the sometimes tatty eastern section of Queens should have become an outpost for America's glitziest industry, the motion pictures. In Long Island City, filmmakers began to gather in 1983 to make movies and commercials at a 3-block-long complex, converted from a bakery into 14 soundstages. **Silvercup Studios** (42–25 21st St.) can be reached by walking west from Vernon to the intersection of 21st Street and 43rd Avenue. Here you might catch a glimpse of Billy Joel or Cyndi Lauper punching in for work on their latest music video. Such movies as *Compromising Positions*, *Broadway Danny Rose*, and *Crocodile Dundee II* were also shot within the walls of old Silvercup.

Now hike back down 21st Street to 45th Avenue, which will bring you to **Court House Square.** Notice first—you probably couldn't fail to—the brand-new green **Citicorp Building** (Jack-What's Citicorp doing in Long Island City? Currently, Manhattan office space is running at $40–$95 per square foot, while in Queens you can rent at a cool $17–$27. I. M. Pei is responsible for the building's basic design, which carries over some general themes from its sister across the river, the Citicorp Building at East 53rd Street and Lexington Avenue.

Much more modest is the 1908 Beaux Arts **New York State Supreme Courthouse** (25–10 Court House Sq.) across from Citicorp, the scene of a number of sensational trials both real and fictional—the courthouse is frequently used as a location by neighborhood movie studios.

Thomson Avenue will lead you—perilously, due to roaring traffic alongside—over the mind-boggling mesh of the Long Island Railroad tracks. Just past here, Thomson Avenue merges into **Queens Boulevard**, one of the borough's chief transverses.

To your right lie the shells of several once-thriving industries: the **Sunshine Biscuit Company** (Skillman between 29th St. and 30th Pl.), **American Eveready Building** (29–10 Thomson Ave.), **Adams Chewing Gum Factory** (30–30 Thomson Ave.), and **White Motor Company Factory** (31–10 Thomson Ave.), all built between 1914 and 1920 in a delightful mix of the practical and the ornamental. The **International Design Center** (tel. 718/937–7474), completed just two years ago, now occupies the latter three structures. This vast marketplace (1 million square feet) for the products of interior designers was built at a cost of more than $125 million. Peek inside to see the ballooning central atrium, surrounded by showrooms ad infinitum. Gigantic elevators for unloading train cars occupied those central spaces back in the days when these buildings still turned out crackers, bubble gum, and auto parts.

Next door is **LaGuardia Community College,** whose **Archives** (31–10 Thomson St., tel. 718/482–5065) contain the papers of the city's most colorful mayor, Fiorello H. LaGuardia. New York's "Little Flower," as LaGuardia came to be called, presided over the metropolis during the Depression.

Walk three blocks west to the 33rd Street station of the No. 7 subway—which *could* take you back into Manhattan, or, better still, a bit farther into Queens. Travel two stops to Queensboro Plaza, then change for the R train, getting off at Broadway to visit **Astoria,** one of New York's most vital ethnic neighborhoods. It was originally German, then Italian, but today you're likely to hear more Greek spoken on the streets than English. Astoria's business district along Broadway bustles with curiosities. The **K & T Meat Market** (37–11 Broadway) sends 500 whole lambs to city kitchens every week. Greek pastry shops (*xaxaroplasteion*) and coffeehouses (*kaffenion*) shoot heady smells onto the avenue. The house specialty at the **Rumeli Taverna** (33–04 Broadway) is *mezadakia,* or Greek hors d'oeuvres. Late into the night the **Grecian Cave** nightclub (part of the Oyster Bay Restaurant and Crystal Palace complex at 31–01 and 31–11 Broadway) resounds with Greek crooners and bouzouki music. But Astoria's heart is the Greek Orthodox Church of **St. Demitrios** (30–11 30th Dr.), a sprawling yellow brick building with a red tile roof and the largest Orthodox congregation outside Greece.

In the 1920s, such stars as Gloria Swanson, Rudolph Valentino, and the Marx Brothers came to this neighborhood to work at "the Big House," Paramount's movie-making center in the east. Today the 13-acre **Kaufman Astoria Studios** (34–12 36th St.), with its monumentally columned entrance, remains a principal player in the movie biz. Since 1977, scores of pictures have been produced here, including *The Cotton Club, The Verdict, Arthur, The Wiz,* and *The World According to Garp.*

A visit to the **American Museum of the Moving Image** next door should satisfy almost any film fan's cravings. Opened in September 1989, the museum houses a 200-seat theater and a 70-

seat screening room where fascinating film series flicker by—among them, recently, a John Ford program and tributes to leading Hollywood cinematographers. Galleries feature exhibits such as "Behind the Screen Producing, Promoting Motion Pictures and Television," studying the technological aspects of film (and including hands-on displays that allow visitors to try their skills at editing). Commissioned artworks are on display, such as the Red Grooms and Lysiane Luong theater, *Tut's Fever*, a metaphorical recapitulation of Egyptian-style picture palaces of the 1930s (you'll find lifelike figures of Theda Bara at the ticket booth and Mae West serving up popcorn); and Korean Nam June Paik's video installation, "The Getaway Car," a commentary on movies. The museum's collection of movie memorabilia includes 60,000 items; don't miss Valentino's *Monsieur Beaucaire* costume or the set used in Paul Newman's remake of *The Glass Menagerie. 36–01 35th Ave., tel. 718/784–0077. Admission: $5 adults, $4 senior citizens, $2.50 students and children. Open Tues.–Fri. 12–5, Sat. and Sun. 11–6.*

Tour 22: Flushing

Numbers in the margin correspond with points of interest on the Flushing map.

There are two quite different reasons to visit the Flushing neighborhood of Queens: to view a historic section that played an instrumental role in the fight for religious freedom in America, and to cavort in Flushing Meadows Corona Park, with its many sports facilities. Surrounding these two focal points is a multiethnic community that is increasingly dominated by Asians; it's a bubbling melting pot rarely visited by New Yorkers themselves.

Take the No. 7 subway to its final stop, the Main Street Flushing station. Main Street and its two parallel neighbors, Prince and Union streets, serve up a banquet for Korean, Chinese, and Indian gourmands. Browse in them for exotic tastes of this "Little Asia," as it is sometimes called. At Main Street and Roosevelt Avenue you will pass a Gothic-style church built of brownstone and native Manhattan schist: this is **St. George's Episcopal Church,** built in 1854. One of the signers of the Declaration of Independence, Francis Lewis, was vestryman in the church's earlier building.

Continue to Northern Boulevard and turn right. At 137–16 Northern Boulevard is the wood-shingled, tiny-windowed **❶ Friends Meeting House,** New York City's oldest place of worship. Built in 1694, it's still used for the Quakers' Sunday-morning services; visitors are welcome the rest of the week.

Turn right on Bowne Street to see where the Quakers first met, **❷** in the **Bowne House,** one of the oldest standing residences in the city. John Bowne and his family joined the English settlers in Flushing—then called by its Dutch name, Vlissigen—in 1655; this house was built in 1661. Governor Peter Stuyvesant had banned the Quakers in 1657; they met secretly in the woods until Bowne, a Quaker convert, invited them to gather in his house. Stuyvesant imprisoned and then exiled Bowne for his defiance, but Bowne convinced the Dutch West India Company to order the colony's governor to tolerate all religious groups, a right preserved more than 100 years later in the U.S. Constitution. The Bowne House is now a museum preserving

Tour 22: Flushing

the furnishings used by nine generations of the family, who lived there until 1947. *37–01 Bowne St., tel. 718/359–0528. Admission: $2 adults, 50¢ children under 12. Open Tues., Sat., Sun. 2:30–4:30.*

Across the street is the **Fox Oaks Rock,** marking the site of an impassioned sermon delivered in 1672 by George Fox, founder of the Quaker sect. Scheduled to address the society inside Bowne's house, Fox had to move the meeting outside because of the huge turnout.

❸ Around the corner on 37th Avenue is the **Kingsland Homestead,** a gambrel-roofed wood farmhouse built in 1785. Its original owner was a Quaker farmer; his son-in-law, the dashing sea captain Joseph King, gave it its name. The house was moved to this site in 1968 to escape demolition. Now home to the Queens Historical Society, it contains several exhibits about local history. *143–35 37th Ave., tel. 718/939–0647. Admission: $2 adults, 50¢ children. Open Tues., Sat., Sun. 2:30–4:30.*

In the park beside the Kingsland Homestead is the **Weeping Beech,** a huge beech tree with trailing branches, planted from a cutting brought by Samuel Parsons from Belgium in 1847 and recently declared a historical landmark. Parsons's nursery supplied many other unusual species of trees still standing in Flushing, as well as in Central and Prospect parks. The site of the nursery is now the 219-acre **Kissena Park,** just south of Flushing.

Eight blocks south on Bowne Street is the **Hindu Temple of North America** (45–47 Bowne St.), an intricately decorated pavilioned temple erected in the 1970s by Indian artisans. Two blocks over on Burling Street is the **Won Buddhist Temple** (43–02 Burling St.).

Return to Northern Boulevard and head west to **Flushing Meadows Corona Park,** a stretch of greenery running from Flushing Bay to the Grand Central Parkway. Recreation facilities here include a marina, boats, a carousel, bicycling paths, an indoor ice-skating rink, picnic grounds, a swimming pool, and theaters and museums. Just north of the park, and linked

❹ to it by a wide wood walkway, is **Shea Stadium,** home of the New York Mets baseball team. At the other end of the

❺ walkway, at the park's northern tip, is the **U. S. Tennis Association National Tennis Center** (tel. 718/592–8000), host since 1978 to the annual U.S. Open tennis tournament. Its courts are available for play outside of tournament time (*see* Chapter 6).

The park was the site of both the 1939 and 1964 World Fairs, and several structures from those expositions remain, including the landmark **Unisphere,** a 380-ton steel globe. At the end of

❻ the fairground mall is the **Queens Museum,** housed in what was the New York Pavilion for the 1939 fair. Its most notable exhibit is the Panorama, an 18,000-square-foot architectural model of New York City's five boroughs. *Tel. 718/592–2405. Suggested donation: $2 adults, $1 senior citizens, students, and children over 5. Open Tues.–Fri. 10–5, weekends noon–5:30.*

❼ The west section of the park contains the **Queens Zoo,** currently closed for renovation.

❽ Children enjoy the park's **New York Hall of Science,** where they can interact with hands-on exhibits on such topics as color and illusion, the atom, self-sensory machines, and microorganisms. *Tel. 718/699–0005. Admission: $3.50 adults, $2.50 senior citizens and children. Open Wed.–Sun. 10–5.*

The Bronx

Tour 23: Fordham and the Zoo

Numbers in the margin correspond with points of interest on the Fordham and the Bronx Zoo map.

The only borough attached to the North American mainland, the Bronx was first settled by Dutch, French, English, and Swedish country squires, who established manorial holdings there while fighting off Indians. The Village of Fordham was founded by John Archer in the mid-1600s, although little now remains from the colonial era. But the area does dramatically illustrate another aspect of Bronx history—the influx of immigrant groups from the 1840s onward: first the Irish, then Germans, Italians, and Jews. Later waves included blacks and Hispanics, and today there are new infusions of Albanian and Cambodian immigrants.

To reach the old Village of Fordham, ride the D subway to the Kingsbridge Road station, where you'll alight alongside a fine stretch of that Bronx Champs Elysées, the **Grand Concourse.** Here you get a sense of the roadway as engineer Louis Riis envisioned it—a 4-mile-long "speedway," facilitating excursions into the country—as well as a view to the west of the **Kingsbridge Armory**, built in 1912, one of the largest such structures in the world.

Poe Park, at East Kingsbridge Road and the Grand Concourse, ❶ is so named because it contains the **Edgar Allan Poe Cottage,** whose white wood siding and green shutters recall earlier, more idyllic days. Here Poe and his wife, Virginia, sought refuge from Manhattan and from the vicissitudes of the writerly life between 1846 and 1849. He wandered the countryside on foot and listened to the tintinnabulation of the church bells at nearby St. John's College Church (now Fordham University). His rocking chair and the bed his wife died in can be seen in the cottage today. Among the works he completed during this period are the poems "Ulalume," "The Bells," "Eureka," and "Annabel Lee." *Tel. 212/881–8900. Admission: $1. Open Wed.– Fri. 9–5, Sat. 10–4, Sun. 1–5.*

One block south is the intersection of Fordham Road and the Grand Concourse, the Times Square of the Bronx. **Alexander's** department store, at the very top of the Fordham Road hill, once produced the largest number of sales per square foot of any department store in the country. Venture south on the ❷ Grand Concourse to **Loews Paradise Theater** (2417 Grand Concourse), which many claim is the best remaining 1930s-style movie house. The exterior ornamentation looks like a claymation fantasy; inside, a sloping, tiled entryway leads to a gorgeously garish Baroque lobby. Tell the ticket-taker that you're an architecture student and you may be able to get in without paying for the latest kung fu movie. John Eberson, the dean of bijou-builders, designed this gem in 1929; happily, he wasn't alive to see it converted to a quadplex in 1981.

Don't stroll farther south on the Grand Concourse from the Paradise—the neighborhood swiftly declines. Instead, turn ❸ west on East 188th Street to peek at the **Creston Avenue Baptist Church** (114 E. 188th St.), built in 1905 and looking like it belongs not among the commercial chaos of Fordham Road, but in Merry Old England.

The Bx 12 bus will take you west along Fordham Road to Arthur Avenue; if you prefer the hike, you'll pass myriad coffee shops and discount stores, the Metro North train's Fordham stop, 1 Fordham Plaza (a modern green-and-white birthday-cake-like construction), and the looming Theodore Roosevelt High School.

Belmont, the neighborhood surrounding the intersection of Arthur Avenue and East 187th Street, has come to be called "The Bronx's Little Italy"—although actually it's a bigger Little Italy than the one in Manhattan. It really lights up after the sun sets, but it's also a daytime place, where some 14,500 families socialize, shop, work, and eat fabulously. Along Arthur Avenue you'll pass **Ciccarone Park,** sporting a huge painted Italian ❹ flag. Indeed, as you study the surrounding two-story frame homes and tenements, the neighborhood begins to seem tinted exclusively in shades of white, red, and green: Italy's colors. A left turn onto East 187th Street takes you into an Italian commercial panoply; on one stellar block between Hughes and Belmont avenues you'll find **Egidio's Pastry Shop** (622 E. 187th St.), **Costanza's Wedding and Shower Favors** (624 E. 187th St.),

Danny's Pork Store (626 E. 187th St.), **Catholic Goods** (630 E. 187th St.), which sells Italian greeting cards, **Borgatti's Ravioli & Noodle Company** (632 E. 187th St.), and the **Roma Luncheonette** (636 E. 187th St.). Across the street, residents' spiritual
5 lives are tended to at **Our Lady of Mt. Carmel Roman Catholic Church** (627 E. 187th St.). Outside, some well-intentioned artist has used the sidewalk as a canvas for paintings of the Virgin and Child, plus a saint, and inside there is an indescribable smell of old religion, as well as many more saints. Drop a quarter into a slot to light a votive candle, or sit and contemplate this symbol of stability in an immigrant world.

6 A block south is the **Enrico Fermi Library and Cultural Center** (610 E. 186th St.), where the Heritage Collection contains several volumes outlining the contributions of Italians and Italian-Americans. Nearby the **Arthur Avenue Retail Market** (2344 Arthur Ave.), a skylit shopping mart, offers 70 stalls, where Italian sausages and cheeses hang from on high.

Time Out | **Dominick's** (2335 Arthur Ave., tel. 212/733–2807) enjoys a reputation as Belmont's best restaurant. Here there are no menus, no wine lists—just hearty Italian food, savored at congested common tables, and cooked by members of a family that's been at Dominick's for 30 years. Finish off your meal with an espresso laced with sambucco.

Return to Fordham Road to explore the 85-acre campus of
7 **Fordham University,** built around the site of the old Rose Hill Manor House (1838). Begun in 1841 as a Jesuit college, Ford-

ham now has an undergraduate enrollment of 7,500, and an auxiliary campus near Lincoln Center.

Enter the grounds via Bathgate Avenue and you'll find yourself in an enclave of collegiate Gothic architecture, shady trees, and green turf. Maps are posted around the campus or are available in the admissions office at Dealy Hall; use them to locate such highlights as the **Old Rose Hill Manor Dig;** the **University Church,** with its stained glass donated by King Louis Philippe of France (1773–1850); the pleasant **Edward's Parade;** and **Keating Hall,** sitting like a Gothic fortress in the center of things. After meandering through Fordham, make your way to the university's main entrance, fronting on Bronx Park.

8 Of all reasons to make a trip to The Bronx, **The New York Botanical Garden** is perhaps the best. The Fordham entrance leads into this serene but extraordinarily varied treasury, the dream of a husband-and-wife botanical team, Dr. Nathaniel Lord and Elizabeth Britton. After visiting England's Kew Gardens in 1889, they returned full of fervor to create a similar haven in New York. In 1991, the New York Botanical Garden will celebrate its centennial, which should bring even more lavish horticultural displays than usual—if that's possible.

The garden stretches for 240 acres around the dramatic gorge of the Bronx River. It holds the historic **Lorillard Snuff Mill,** built by two French Huguenot snuff manufacturers in 1840 to power the grinding of tobacco for snuff. Nearby, the Lorillards grew roses to supply fragrance for their blend. The snuff mill now houses a café, open daily 9–5. A walk along the Bronx River from the mill leads to **Hemlock Falls** and to the botanical garden's 40-acre **Forest,** the only uncut woodland in New York City. Outdoor plant collections include the **Erpf Compass Garden,** where cobblestones denoting the points of a compass are surrounded by a riotous display of flowers. Inside the luminous **Enid A. Haupt Conservatory** are displays of ferns, tropical flora, and Old and New World deserts. At the **Museum Building,** there's a gardening shop, a library, and a world-renowned herbarium holding 5 million dried plant specimens. *Bronx Park, tel. 212/220–8700. Garden admission: $1 adults, 50¢ senior citizens, 25¢ children. Open 8–6 Nov.–Mar., 8–7 Apr.–Oct. Conservatory admission free Sat. 10–12; other times $3.50 adults, $1.25 senior citizens and children. Parking: $4. Open Tues.–Sun. 10–5 (last admission at 4).*

9 Also in Bronx Park is the **Bronx Zoo,** the nation's largest urban zoo. It deserves nearly an entire day's visit on its own; if you want to return on another day, you can take the BxM11 bus that runs up Madison Avenue ($3.50).

At the Bronx Zoo you'll see two different historical methods of wild-animal keeping. The turn-of-the-century zoological garden houses monkeys, snakes, seals, and elephants (among many others) in fancy Beaux Arts–style edifices at **Astor Court.** It's being gradually replaced by the animal-in-habitat approach used in the **World of Birds,** with its capacious walk-through indoor natural habitats; in **Jungleworld,** an indoor tropical rain forest complete with five waterfalls, millipedes, flowering orchids, and pythons; and in **Wild Asia,** where large beasts can be observed from a monorail. The **Children's Zoo** features many hands-on learning activities, as well as a large petting zoo. At the Keith W. Johnson Center, visitors will find

Indian elephants and rhinos. The zoo as a whole has more than 4,000 animals representing 667 species. *Bronx Park, tel. 212/ 367– 1010. Admission: Fri.–Mon. $4.75 adults, $2 children under 12, free senior citizens and children under 2; Tues.– Thurs., voluntary contribution; open Mon.–Sat. 10–5, Sun. and holidays 10–5:30.*

Staten Island

Tour 24: Snug Harbor and Richmondtown

Numbers in the margin correspond with points of interest on the Staten Island map.

Even though Staten Island is officially a borough of New York City, many Staten Islanders refer to Manhattan as "The City." Perhaps that's because farms and vast woodlands have distinguished it from the more crowded and developed Manhattan since 1661, when Staten Island was permanently settled as a farming community by the Dutch (after several fatal battles with the Native American tribes who already inhabited the area). When oystering became a thriving industry in the early 1800s, farmers brought free blacks up from Maryland to help plant new oyster beds. The black community on the south shore became known as "Sandy Ground"; descendants of the first black oystermen still live there. Factories came later, as did shipbuilding.

Today Staten Island still feels more residential than the other boroughs. Getting around can be somewhat difficult for visitors because the various attractions are so spread out, but bus service is convenient.

❶ The greatest way to introduce yourself to Staten Island is by taking the 20-minute ride across New York Harbor on the **Staten Island Ferry,** which leaves every hour from the southern tip of Manhattan (*see* Tour 17 in Chapter 3). On the boats with outer decks, passengers can get a better look at the spectacular views of lower Manhattan's skyscrapers, Ellis Island, and the splendidly restored Statue of Liberty.

❷ From the ferry terminal, a seven-minute ride on the S40 bus will take you to the **Snug Harbor Cultural Center,** which on a warm summer afternoon might be hosting a New York Philharmonic concert, an art show, or an old-fashioned flea market. Once part of a sprawling farm, then a home for "aged and decrepit sailors," the center is based around a row of five columned Greek Revival temples, built between 1831 and 1880, facing onto the Kill Van Kull, a wide stream that flows into Upper New York Bay. The former chapel is now the 210-seat **Veterans Memorial Hall,** site of many indoor concerts and gatherings. Among several newer buildings on the 80-acre grounds is the **Newhouse Center for Contemporary Art,** which features changing exhibitions (open Wed.–Sun. noon–5; voluntary contribution). A variety of cultural events are held throughout the year in this tranquil setting. *914 Richmond Terr., tel. 718/448–2500. Admission free. Open 8 AM–dusk. Free guided tours weekends 2 PM.*

The **Staten Island Botanical Gardens,** also on the Snug Harbor grounds, feature a perennial garden, a greenhouse, 10 acres of

Tour 24: Staten Island

NEW JERSEY
Kill Van Kull
② Richmond Ter.
① Staten Island Ferry
Snug Harbor Cultural Center
Upper New York Bay
BROOKLYN
Richmond
Forest Ave.
Castleton
Broadway
Forest Ave.
Clove Rd.
Clove Lakes Park
Victory Blvd.
Bay St.
Tompkins Ave.
Hylan Blvd.
③ Alice Austen House
440
Jewett Ave.
Staten Island Expwy.
278
Verrazano Narrows Bridge
Willow Brook Park
Brielle Ave.
Rockland Ave.
Richmond Hill Rd.
Richmond Rd.
Hylan Blvd.
Father Capodanno Blvd.
Lower New York Bay
N
William T. Davis Wildlife Refuge
La Tourette Park
Richmond Rd.
④ Richmondtown Restoration
Hylan Blvd.
Arthur Kill Rd.
0   2 miles
0   3 km

natural marsh habitat, a fragrance garden for the blind, and a bonsai collection. *1000 Richmond Terr., tel. 718/273–8200. Admission free. Open 8 AM–dusk.*

The **Staten Island Children's Museum,** which moved to the complex a couple of years ago, offers four revolving hands-on exhibits to introduce children to such diverse topics as news and media, storytelling, and insects. *1000 Richmond Terr., tel. 718/273–2060. Admission: $2, children under 3 free. Open Wed.–Fri. 1–5, weekends 11–5.*

❸ Return to the ferry terminal and catch the No. 2 bus for the 2-mile ride to Hylan Boulevard and the **Alice Austen House.** Photographer Alice Austen (1866–1952) defied tradition when, as a girl of 10, she received her first camera as a gift from an uncle and promptly began taking pictures of everything and everyone around her. Austen went on to make photography her lifetime avocation, recording on film a vivid "social history" of Staten Island in the early part of the century. The cozy, ivy-covered Dutch-style cottage she lived in for almost all her life has been restored, and many of her photographs are on exhibit. *2 Hylan Blvd., tel. 718/816–4506. Suggested donation: $2 adults. Open Thurs.–Sun. noon–5.*

❹ Take the No. 113 bus from the ferry terminal to the **Richmondtown Restoration,** a unique museum village on the site of Staten Island's first permanent settlement founded in 1685. The 26 historic buildings on this 96-acre complex have been restored inside and out; some were here originally, while others were relocated from other spots on the island. Many of the buildings, such as the Greek Revival courthouse that serves as the **Visitors Center,** date from the 19th century; other architectural styles on site range from Dutch Colonial to Victorian Gothic Revival. The **Voorlezer's House,** built in 1695, is the oldest elementary schoolhouse in the United States; it looks like the mold from which all little red schoolhouses were cast.

Throughout the village, costumed interpreters demonstrate early American crafts and trades such as printing, tinsmithing, and baking. The **Staten Island Historical Society Museum,** built in 1848 as the second county clerk's and surrogate's office, now houses a collection of American china, furniture, toys, and tools, plus a gallery of Staten Island photographs, including some 7,000 works by Alice Austen.

During a summer visit, you might want to make reservations for the 19th-century dinner, cooked outdoors and served with utensils of the period. Old Home Day, in the fall, shows off craftspeople demonstrating their skills; Militia Day, a must for war buffs, is a re-creation of a Civil War battle. Richmondtown regularly hosts other fairs, flea markets, and tours of the historic buildings. *Tel. 718/351–1611. Admission: $4 adults, $2.50 senior citizens and children 6–18. Open weekdays 10–5, weekends 1–5.*

What to See and Do with Children

Museums For children who really love hands-on involvement, the place to go is the **Brooklyn Children's Museum.** Its exhibits cover everything from the environment to nature, science, and more; and its attractions include tunnels, water, bubbles, animals, steam, and neon lights. *145 Brooklyn Ave., tel. 718/735–4432. Suggested donation: $2. Open June–Aug., Wed–Mon. 10–5; Sept.–May, Mon., Wed.–Fri., and weekends 10–5.*

Hands-on exhibits are a feature of the **Staten Island Children's Museum** (*see* Tour 24, above), part of the Snug Harbor Cultural Center. Your children may also be interested in the **Staten Island Historical Society** in the **Richmondtown Restoration** (*see* Tour 24, above), which has a Museum of Childhood with displays of antique dolls, toys, and children's furnishings.

For science, the **New York City Hall of Science,** in Flushing Meadows Corona Park, Queens (*see* Tour 22, above), has touchable exhibits on—what else?—science and technology.

Queens is also the place for the movie mavens in your family. The **American Museum of the Moving Image** (*see* Tour 21), the only museum in the United States devoted to film and television, has a collection of 60,000 artifacts, a state-of-the-art theater, and an experimental video screening room.

Parks and Zoos New York is lucky enough to have the oldest and largest zoo of any city in the United States: the **Bronx Zoo** (*see* Tour 23, above). This is not a place of cramped cages and pacing beasts: Most of the animals live in replicas of their natural habitats. In the special Children's Zoo area, youngsters can wander along trails through woods and marshes and pet the animals.

Adjacent to the Bronx Zoo, the **New York Botanical Garden** (*see* Tour 23, above) is one of the world's largest botanic gardens. Its

Enid A. Haupt Conservatory is a crystal palace of ever-changing plant exhibits; there are also 12 outdoor display gardens, walking trails, and some 40 acres of New York City's original forest.

The **Staten Island Zoo** (Barrett Park, 614 Broadway, Staten Island, tel. 718/442–3100) is small but of very high quality, featuring one of the world's finest collections of reptiles, as well as a separate **Children's Zoo.**

Brooklyn's **Prospect Park Zoo** (*see* Tour 20, above) is currently closed for renovation, as is the **Queens Zoo** (*see* Tour 22, above). However, children may enjoy instead the **Queens County Farm Museum** (73–50 Little Neck Pkwy., Floral Park, Queens, tel. 718/347–3276), a restored, 200-year-old working farm. Although it's open only on weekends, the museum does offer interesting programs.

Stroll through the **Brooklyn Botanic Garden** (*see* Tour 20, above), whose 52 lush acres feature a hill-and-pond Japanese garden; gardens devoted to fragrant plants, roses, and herbs; a conservatory with tropical, desert, and temperate pavilions; and a bonsai museum.

Nearly 300 different varieties of fish are on display in Brooklyn at the **New York Aquarium** (Surf Ave. at W. 8th St., Coney Island, tel. 718/265–FISH). Children will marvel at the performance by dolphins, sea lions, and electric eels.

Off the Beaten Track

Brooklyn **Coney Island.** It's the home of the hot dog, "the king of roller coasters" (the Cyclone), the Wonder Wheel, suntan lotion, crowds, fried clams, girls and boys necking under the boardwalk, and old men staring vacantly out to sea. While it may have declined from its glory days early in this century—when visitors lunched at an ocean-side hotel built in the shape of an elephant, glided across the nation's biggest dance floor at Dreamland, or toured a replica of old Bagdad called Luna Park—Coney Island still has a boardwalk, a 2.7-mile-long beach, and a huge amusement park. The **New York Aquarium** (tel. 718/265–FISH) keeps watery beasts—sharks, black-footed penguins, octopuses, piranhas, and Beluga whales, who show off their swimming skills at feeding time—on view nearby. Two blocks away is **Brighton Beach Avenue,** the main street of a community of some 30,000 Soviet émigrés. D, Q, N, B, and F subways serve the Coney Island–Brighton Beach area.

Green-Wood Cemetery (25th St. and 5th Ave., entrance in Sunset Park). Built in the 1840s, the cemetery features a stately Gothic Revival gatehouse, designed by Richard Upjohn, that still moves visitors to a sublime pitch of melancholy. The 478 acres contain 5 lakes, 22 miles of lanes, and 209 paths named for bushes, flowers, and trees. It's open daily 8–4; call the superintendent (tel. 718/768–7300) for permission to tour.

Queens **The Isamu Noguchi Garden Museum** (32–37 Vernon Blvd., tel. 718/204–7088). East of Astoria, near riverside Rainey Park, some 30 years ago the Japanese sculptor Isamu Noguchi took studio space in a photo-engraver's factory. Part of it now holds 12 galleries that offer Noguchi devotees a concentration of the sculptor's evocative work in stone, along with videos documenting his long career. Across Vernon Boulevard lies the **Socrates Sculpture Park** (Vernon Blvd. at Broadway, tel. 718/956–1819), 4.2 acres of large, abstract artworks that first appear almost as an urban hallucination. *Saturday bus service to Noguchi Museum leaves every hour on the half hour from the Asia Society, Park Ave. and 70th St. in Manhattan. Fare: $5; Suggested contribution: $2. Museum open Apr.–Nov. Wed. and Sat. 11–6.*

Bronx   **Riverdale.** This is perhaps the Bronx's most attractive neighborhood; wide-open territory for outer-borough explorers, it's best visited by car, taking the Kappock Street exit from the Henry Hudson Parkway. Manhattan millionaires built summer homes here, with stirring views of the New Jersey Palisades across the Hudson River, in the early part of this century. A drive along Palisade Avenue, picturesque Sycamore Avenue above West 252nd Street, and Independence Avenue between West 248th and 254th streets will take you past some of Riverdale's handsomest mansions. Alas, only **Wave Hill** (675 W. 252nd St., tel. 212/549–3200) is open to the public, but a visit to this 28-acre estate will conjure up the image of Riverdale's wealthy past. Built in 1844, then lavishly added onto by J. P. Morgan's partner George Perkins, the estate offers splendid views of the Hudson, a greenhouse, a sweeping lawn with giant elm and maple trees, and old-fashioned herb and flower gardens.

City Island. At the extreme west end of the Bronx is a bona fide island measuring 230 acres wide—a little bit of Cape Cod come to the metropolis. Back in 1761, a group of the area's residents planned a port to rival New York's, but when that scheme hit the shoals, they returned to perennial maritime pursuits such as fishing and boat building. City Island-produced yachts have included a number of America's Cup contenders. Connected to Pelham Bay Park by bridge, City Island offers visitors a maritime atmosphere and good seafood restaurants with names like Sammy's Fish Box and Johnny's Reef. City Island also has the **North Wind Undersea Museum** (610 City Island Ave., tel. 212/885– 0701).

5 Sightseeing Checklists

When visiting a destination as rich and complex as New York City, it's especially important to be selective, for there's simply not enough time to see and do everything. Walking tours may help you get to know the city one neighborhood at a time, but like every visitor, you will have your own agenda to pursue as well—a love of art or architecture, perhaps, or a keen interest in colonial history.

The following checklists organize New York City's attractions by category, so you can supplement sights from the walking tours with related places of interest throughout the five boroughs. They may also help you choose walking tours by showing you which routes include sites that may be related to your own special interests. Attractions that have already been covered in Chapters 3 or 4 simply include simply a reference to the walking tour in which they appear. Attractions that appear here only are followed by a brief description and useful information.

Museums and Galleries

Abigail Adams Smith Museum. Originally the converted carriage house of the home President John Adams built for his daughter Abigail, this 18th-century treasure is now owned by the Colonial Dames of America. Nine rooms display furniture and articles of the Federal period, and an adjoining garden is designed in 18th-century style. *421 E. 61st St., tel. 212/838–6878. Admission: $2 adults, $1 senior citizens, students, and children under 12. Open weekdays 10–4, Sun. 1–5. In June and July, closed Sun., open Tues. evenings until 8. Closed Aug.*

Afro Arts Cultural Centre. Artifacts from East, West, North, and Central Africa are on exhibit. *2191 Adam Clayton Powell, Jr., Blvd. (7th Ave.), tel. 212/996–3333. Suggested contribution: $3.75 adults, $2.75 children. Open daily 9–4:30.*

American Craft Museum. *See* Tour 1 in Chapter 3.

American Museum of the Moving Image. *See* Tour 21 in Chapter 4.

American Museum of Natural History. *See* Tour 8 in Chapter 3.

American Numismatic Society. The society, founded in 1858, displays its extensive collection of coins and medals, including several that date back to ancient civilizations, in one of several museums in the Audubon Terrace complex. *Broadway at 155th St., tel. 212/234–3130. Admission free. Open Tues.–Sat. 9–4:30, Sun. 1–4.*

Americas Society. *See* Tour 6 in Chapter 3.

Asia Society Galleries. *See* Tour 6 in Chapter 3.

The AT&T InfoQuest Center. *See* Tour 2 in Chapter 3.

Black Fashion Museum. *See* Tour 10 in Chapter 3.

Brooklyn Children's Museum. *See* What to See and Do with Children in Chapter 4.

Brooklyn Historical Society. *See* Tour 19 in Chapter 4.

Brooklyn Museum. *See* Tour 20 in Chapter 4.

Bronx Museum of the Arts. Founded in 1971, this museum displays changing exhibits of contemporary and modern art. Caution is very much advised in visiting this neighborhood. *1040 Grand Concourse, Bronx, tel. 212/681–6000. Suggested donation: $2 adults, $1 children. Open Thurs.–Sat. 10–4:30, Sun. 11–4:30.*

Children's Museum of Manhattan. *See* What to See and Do with Children in Chapter 3.

China House Gallery (China Institute). *See* Tour 6 in Chapter 3.

City Gallery. Next door to the New York Convention and Visitors Bureau, the gallery shows changing exhibits by mostly local artists in all media. *2 Columbus Circle, tel. 212/974–1150. Admission free. Open weekdays 10–5:30.*

City Island Historical Nautical Museum. Tucked away on the tiny island at the end of the Bronx, this museum celebrates the area's nautical historical heritage. *190 Fordham St., City Island, Bronx. Admission: $2 adults, $1 children and senior citizens. Open Sun. 2–5.*

Clocktower Gallery (Institute for Art and Urban Resources). *See* Tour 18 in Chapter 3.

The Cloisters. Perched atop a wooded hilltop near Manhattan's northernmost tip, the Cloisters houses the Metropolitan Museum of Art's medieval collection in the style of a medieval monastery. Colonnaded walks connect authentic French and Spanish monastic cloisters, a French Romanesque chapel, a 12th-century chapter house, and a Romanesque apse. An entire room is devoted to a superb set of 16th-century tapestries depicting a unicorn hunt. The view of the Hudson River and the New Jersey Palisades (an undeveloped Rockefeller family preserve) enhance the experience. The No. 4 "Cloisters-Fort Tryon Park" bus provides a lengthy but scenic ride; catch it along Madison Avenue. You can also take the A subway to the 190th Street station. *Fort Tryon Park, tel. 212/923–3700. Suggested donation: $5 adults, $2.50 senior citizens and students, children 12 and under free. Open Tues.–Sun. 9:30–5:15. Closes at 4:45 Nov.–Mar.*

Cooper-Hewitt Museum (Smithsonian Institution's National Museum of Design). *See* Tour 5 in Chapter 3.

Dezerland's Dream Car Collection. The world's largest collection of American classic convertibles from the 1950s is displayed, alongside nostalgic exhibits. Also here are an indoor drive-in movie theater featuring seating in vintage convertibles, an automobile memorabilia store, and a gallery that sells one-of-a-kind furniture created from auto parts. *270 11th Ave., tel. 212/564–4590. Admission: $5 Tues.–Fri., $7.50 weekends. Open Tues.–Fri. 6 PM–midnight, weekends noon–midnight.*

Federal Hall National Memorial. *See* Tour 17 in Chapter 3.

Forbes Magazine Galleries. On permanent exhibit, the late publisher Malcolm Forbes's collection includes 500 toy boats, 12,000 toy soldiers, and 250 trophies, plus rotating exhibitions of paintings, presidential papers, and Fabergé Imperial Easter eggs. *62 5th Ave., tel. 212/206–5548. Admission free. Open Tues.–Wed., Fri.–Sat. 10–4. Call 212/206–5549 for group tour reservations.*

Fraunces Tavern Museum. *See* Tour 17 in Chapter 3.

Frick Collection. *See* Tour 5 in Chapter 3.

Garibaldi Meucci Museum. Housed in an altered Federal farmhouse, this museum offers letters and photographs describing the life of fiery Italian patriot Guiseppe Garibaldi; it also documents Antonio Meucci's indisputable claim to having invented the telephone before Alexander Graham Bell did. *420 Tompkins Ave., Staten Island, tel. 718/442–1608. Admission free. Open Tues.–Fri. 9–5, weekends 1–5.*

Grolier Club of New York. *See* Tour 6 in Chapter 3.

Guggenheim Museum. *See* Tour 5 in Chapter 3.

Guinness World Records Exhibit Hall. *See* Tour 4 in Chapter 3.

Harbor Defense Museum of New York City. Located at the Brooklyn end of the Verrazano-Narrows Bridge, this museum features small arms, uniforms, artillery equipment dating to the 18th century, and an array of military miniatures. *Fort Hamilton, Brooklyn, tel. 718/630–4349. Admission free. Open Mon., Thurs., and Fri. 1–4, Sat. 10–5, Sun. 1–5.*

Hayden Planetarium. *See* Tour 8 in Chapter 3.

Hispanic Society of America. An extensive collection of ancient and modern Hispanic paintings, sculpture, and decorative arts is housed in a richly appointed building. *Broadway at 155th St., tel. 212/926–2234. Admission free. Open Tues.–Sat. 10–4:30, Sun. 1–4. Closed holidays.*

IBM Gallery of Science and Art. *See* Tour 2 in Chapter 3.

ICP Mid-Town. *See* Tour 3 in Chapter 3.

International Center of Photography. *See* Tour 5 in Chapter 3.

***Intrepid* Sea-Air-Space Museum.** *See* What to See and Do with Children in Chapter 3.

Isamu Noguchi Garden Museum. *See* Off the Beaten Track in Chapter 4.

Jamaica Arts Center. An Italian Renaissance Revival building, built in 1898, showcases a variety of multiethnic arts ranging from the Yueh Lung Shadow Theatre to Olu Dara and the Natchezsippi Band. *161–04 Jamaica Ave., Queens, tel. 718/658–7400. Admission free. Open Tues.–Sat. 10–5.*

Japan Society Gallery. This wonderfully serene setting holds exhibits from well-known Japanese and American museums, as well as private collections. Also offered are movies, lectures, classes, concerts, and dramatic performances. *333 E. 47th St., tel. 212/832–1155. Suggested donation: $2.50. Open Tues.–Sun. 11–5.*

Jewish Museum. *See* Tour 5 in Chapter 3.

Library and Museum of the Performing Arts (New York Public Library at Lincoln Center). *See* Tour 8 in Chapter 3.

Lower East Side Tenement Museum. America's first urban "living-history" museum preserves and interprets the life of immigrants and migrants in New York's Lower East Side. Gallery exhibits, walking tours, and dramatic performances are offered. *97 Orchard St., tel. 212/431–0233. Tours: $12 adults, $6 students. Open Tues.–Fri. 11–4.*

Marchais Center of Tibetan Art. One of the largest private, nonprofit collections of Tibetan sculpture, scrolls, and paintings outside of Tibet is displayed in a museum resembling a Tibetan temple. *338 Lighthouse Ave., Staten Island, tel. 718/987–3478. Admission: $2.50 adults, $1 senior citizens and children. Open April–Nov., Wed.–Sun. 1–5. By appointment the remainder of the year.*

Metropolitan Museum of Art. *See* Tour 5 in Chapter 3.

Museo del Barrio. *See* Tour 5 in Chapter 3.

Museum of American Folk Art. *See* Tour 8 in Chapter 3.

Museum of the American Indian–Heye Foundation. What began as the private collection of George G. Heye has grown into the largest grouping of Native American materials in the world. Various exhibits are devoted to North, Central, and South American Indians. Soon this collection will be moved, part to the Smithsonian Institution in Washington, DC, part downtown to the U.S. Customs House (*see* Tour 17 in Chapter 3). *Broadway at 155th St., tel. 212/283–2420. Admission: $3* *adults, $2 students and senior citizens. Open Tues.–Sat. 10–5, Sun. 1–5.*

Museum of Broadcasting. *See* Tour 1 in Chapter 3.

Museum of the City of New York. *See* Tour 5 in Chapter 3.

Museum of Holography. *See* Tour 14 in Chapter 3.

Museum of Modern Art. *See* Tour 1 in Chapter 3.

National Academy of Design. *See* Tour 5 in Chapter 3.

New Museum of Contemporary Art. *See* Tour 14 in Chapter 3.

New York City Fire Museum. Hand-pulled and horse-drawn apparatus, engines, sliding poles, uniforms, and fireboat equipment are featured in this comprehensive collection of authentic fire-fighting tools from the 18th, 19th, and 20th centuries. *278 Spring St., tel. 212/691–1303. Suggested donation: $3 adults, 50¢ children. Open Tues.–Sat. 10–4. Closed Sun., Mon., and holidays.*

New York Hall of Science. *See* Tour 22 in Chapter 4.

New York City Transit Museum. A converted 1930s subway station displays 18 restored classic subway cars and has an operating signal tower. *Boerum Place at Schermerhorn, Brooklyn, tel. 718/330–3060. Admission: $1.15 adults, 55¢ children. Open weekdays 10–4, Sat. 11–4.*

New-York Historical Society. *See* Tour 8 in Chapter 3.

Nicholas Roerich Museum. Housed in an Upper West Side town house (built in 1898), this small and somewhat eccentric museum displays the work of the Russian artist who, among many other things, designed sets for Diaghilev and Stravinsky ballets. Vast paintings of the Himalayas are a focal point of the collection. *319 W. 107th St., tel. 212/864–7752. Admission free. Open Tues.–Sun. 2–5.*

North Wind Undersea Museum. Displays are devoted to marine mammal rescue and deep-sea diving. *610 City Island Ave., Bronx, tel. 212/885–0701. Admission: $3 adults, $2 children. Open weekdays 10–5, weekends noon–5.*

Pierpont Morgan Library. *See* Tour 4 in Chapter 3.

Police Academy Museum. The second floor of the city's police academy is full of law-enforcement memorabilia—uniforms, firearms, batons, badges, even counterfeit money—dating back to the time of the Dutch. *235 E. 20th St., tel. 212/477–9753. Admission free. Open weekdays 9–3.*

Queens County Farm Museum. A restored 200-year-old farm traces New York City's agricultural history. *73–50 Little Neck Pkwy., Floral Park, Queens, tel. 718/347–3276. Admission free. Open weekends noon–5.*

Queens Museum. *See* Tour 22 in Chapter 4.

Schomburg Center for Research in Black Culture (New York Public Library). *See* Tour 10 in Chapter 3.

Snug Harbor Cultural Center. *See* Tour 24 in Chapter 4.

Society of Illustrators Museum of American Illustration. A 1,000-piece collection features contemporary and historical works. Solo, group, and themed shows are exhibited. *128 E. 63rd St., tel. 212/838–2560. Admission free. Open weekdays 10–5, Tues. 10–8.*

South Street Seaport Museum. *See* Tour 18 in Chapter 3.

Staten Island Children's Museum. *See* Tour 24 in Chapter 4.

Staten Island Historical Society Museum. *See* Tour 24 in Chapter 4.

Studio Museum in Harlem. *See* Tour 10 in Chapter 3.

Ukrainian Museum. This small East Village institution celebrates the cultural heritage of the Ukraine, displaying ceramics, jewelry, hundreds of brilliantly colored Easter eggs, and an extensive collection of Ukrainian costumes and textiles. *203 2nd Ave. between 12th and 13th Sts., tel. 212/228–0110. Admission: $1 adults, 50¢ students and senior citizens, children under 6 free. Open Wed.–Sun. 1–5.*

Urban Center. Exhibits on architecture, urban design, and historic preservation are housed in the north wing of the Villard Houses, at the foot of the Helmsley Palace Hotel. *457 Madison Ave. between 50th and 51st Sts., tel. 212/935–3960. Admission free. Open Mon.–Wed., Fri. and Sat. 11–5, Sun. noon–5.*

Whitney Museum Downtown at Federal Reserve Plaza. *See* Tour 17 in Chapter 3.

Whitney Museum of American Art at Equitable Center. In this pair of galleries in the grand lobby of the new Equitable Building (itself a showcase for some fine large artworks), changing exhibitions highlight 20th-century art from the Whitney's main collection. *787 7th Ave. between 51st and 52nd Sts., tel. 212/ 554–1113. Admission free. Open Mon.–Wed. and Fri. 11–6, Thurs. 11–7:30, Sat. noon–5.*

Whitney Museum at Philip Morris. *See* Tour 3 in Chapter 3.

Whitney Museum of American Art. *See* Tour 5 in Chapter 3.

Architectural Landmarks

American Telephone & Telegraph Building (1983, Philip Johnson and Andrew Burgee). *See* Tour 2 in Chapter 3.

Bowery Savings (1923, York & Sawyer). *See* Tour 3 in Chapter 3.

Carnegie Hall (1891, William B. Tuthill). Outside it's a stout, square brown building with a few Moorish-style arches added, almost as an afterthought, to the facade. Inside, however, is a simply decorated, 2,760-seat auditorium that is considered one of the finest in the world, although some critics say the acoustics haven't been the same since a recent renovation. Tours are available on Tuesdays and Thursdays. *156 W. 57th St., tel. 212/ 247–7800.*

Chrysler Building (1929, William Van Alen). *See* Tour 3 in Chapter 3.

Citicorp Center (1977, H. Stubbins & E. Roth). *See* Tour 2 in Chapter 3.

City Hall (1812, Mangin, McComb). *See* Tour 18 in Chapter 3.

Dakota Apartments (1884, Henry J. Hardenbergh). *See* Tour 8 in Chapter 3.

Empire State Building (1931, Shreve, Lamb, Harmon). *See* Tour 4 in Chapter 3.

Flatiron Building (1902, Daniel H. Burnham). *See* Tour 4 in Chapter 3.

Ford Foundation (1967, Roche & Dinkeloo). *See* Tour 3 in Chapter 3.

Grand Central Terminal (1913, Warren & Wetmore, Reed & Stem). *See* Tour 3 in Chapter 3.

Guggenheim Museum (1959, Frank Lloyd Wright). *See* Tour 5 in Chapter 3.

Haughwout Building (1856, John P. Gaynor). *See* Tour 14 in Chapter 3.

Jacob K. Javits Convention Center (1986, I. M. Pei). The largest center of its kind in the Western Hemisphere, the center contains 1.8 million gross square feet set on a 22-acre-by-5-block site. The glassed-in entry lets in lots of sky, earning it the nickname "the Crystal Palace." *11th Ave. at 35th St.*

Lever House (1952, Skidmore, Owings & Merrill). *See* Tour 2 in Chapter 3.

Low Memorial Library (1897, McKim, Mead & White). *See* Tour 9 in Chapter 3.

New York Public Library (1911, Carrere & Hastings). *See* Tour 3 in Chapter 3.

Pan Am Building (1963, Emery Roth & Sons, Pietro Bellushi, and Walter Gropius). The waves of protest that greeted this building's construction over the north end of Grand Central Terminal were largely responsible for Grand Central's receiving protected landmark status in 1965. This 59-story monolith, with its faceted walls of precast concrete, towers over the foot of Park Avenue. *200 Park Ave. at 45th St.*

Plaza Hotel (1907, Henry J. Hardenbergh). *See* Tour 2 in Chapter 3.

RCA Building (1933, Raymond Hood). *See* Tour 1 in Chapter 3.

Seagram Building (1958, Mies van der Rohe). *See* Tour 2 in Chapter 3.

United Nations (1953, Wallace K. Harrison and international committee). *See* Tour 3 in Chapter 3.

U.S. Customs House (1907, Cass Gilbert). *See* Tour 17 in Chapter 3.

Villard Houses (1886, McKim, Mead & White). Now part of the Helmsley Palace hotel, these three brownstone mansions, conceived by newspaper publisher Henry Villard, form an early Italian Renaissance palazzo set off by elaborate ironwork. Many of the original interior spaces remain in prime condition. *Madison Ave. at 50th St.*

Woolworth Building (1913, Cass Gilbert). *See* Tour 17 in Chapter 3.

World Financial Center (1989, Cesar Pelli). *See* Tour 17 in Chapter 3.

World Trade Center (1977, Yamasaki & Roth). *See* Tour 17 in Chapter 3.

Historical Sites

Bartow-Pell Mansion. This Greek Revival restoration—with sunken gardens, period furnishings, paintings, and a 200-volume library of books on architecture, gardening, and herbs—was built in 1842. *Shore Rd. N., Pelham Bay Park, Bronx, tel. 212/885–1461. Admission: $2 adults, children under age 12 free. Open Wed., weekends, noon–4.*

Castle Clinton. *See* Tour 17 in Chapter 3.

Edgar Allan Poe Cottage. *See* Tour 23 in Chapter 4.

Ellis Island. *See* Tour 17 in Chapter 3.

Fraunces Tavern. *See* Tour 17 in Chapter 3.

Gracie Mansion. *See* Tour 6 in Chapter 3.

Morris-Jumel Mansion. George Washington spent the night at this Georgian colonial hilltop house, built in 1765. His camp bed can still be seen. *1765 Jumel Terr., tel. 212/923–8008. Admission: $3 adults, $2 senior citizens, students, and children. Open Tues.–Sun. 10–4.*

New York Stock Exchange. *See* Tour 17 in Chapter 3.

Old Merchant's House. Built in 1830, this four-story Federal-style house was home to the Tredwell family from 1835 to 1933, when the last of the elderly Tredwell sisters died. The original furnishings and architectural features remain intact, offering a rare glimpse of family life in the mid-19th century. *29 E. 4th*

St., tel. 212/777–1089. Admission: $2 adults, $1 students and senior citizens. Open Sun. 1–4. Closed Aug.

Radio City Music Hall. *See* Tour 1 in Chapter 3.

Richmondtown Restoration. *See* Tour 24 in Chapter 4.

Shrine of St. Elizabeth Ann Seton. *See* Tour 17 in Chapter 3.

South Street Seaport. *See* Tour 18 in Chapter 3.

Theodore Roosevelt Birthplace. *See* Tour 4 in Chapter 3.

Valentine-Varian House. The birthplace of Isaac L. Varian, mayor of New York City from 1839 to 1841, now houses Indian and military artifacts, natural history displays, paintings, and prints and photographs of the Bronx. *3266 Bainbridge Ave., Bronx, tel. 212/881–8900. Admission: $1. Open Sat. 10–4, Sun. 1–5, weekdays by appointment.*

Van Cortlandt Mansion. Recently renovated, this 1748 house is full of furnishings and household goods that reflect both its Dutch and British owners. It's now run by the National Society of Colonial Dames. *Broadway at 246th St., Bronx, tel. 212/543–3344. Call for admission prices and hours.*

Wave Hill. George Walbridge Perkins, an early conservationist and partner of J. P. Morgan, bought this 28-acre estate in 1903, adding greenhouses, gardens, and a second mansion (an 1844 fieldstone manor house already occupied the site). In its time, the main house's residents have included Theodore Roosevelt, Mark Twain, and conductor Arturo Toscanini; at one time it was the official residence of the United Kingdom's ambassador to the United Nations. *675 W. 252nd St., tel. 212/549–3200. Admission: $2 adults, $1 senior citizens and children; free weekdays. Open daily 10–4:30.*

Churches and Temples

Abyssinian Baptist Church (Baptist). *See* Tour 10 in Chapter 3.

Cathedral of St. John the Divine (Episcopal). *See* Tour 9 in Chapter 3.

Central Synagogue (Reform Jewish). Built in 1872, this Moorish-style temple is the oldest continually used synagogue building in the city. Note its onion-domed exterior and colorfully stenciled interior. *652 Lexington Ave., at 55th St.*

Fifth Avenue Synagogue (Orthodox Jewish). *See* Tour 6 in Chapter 3.

Friends Meeting House, now the **Brotherhood Synagogue** (Conservative Jewish). *See* Tour 4 in Chapter 3.

Grace Church (Episcopal). This fine mid-19th-century example of an English Gothic Revival church, the site of many society weddings, is set in a small green yard in Greenwich Village. Topped by a finely ornamented octagonal marble spire, it has some excellent pre-Raphaelite stained-glass windows inside. *800 Broadway, at E. 10th St.*

John Street Methodist (United Methodist). *See* Tour 17 in Chapter 3.

Little Church Around the Corner (Church of the Transfiguration) (Episcopal). *See* Tour 4 in Chapter 3.

Marble Collegiate (Reformed). *See* Tour 4 in Chapter 3.

Our Lady of Pompeii Church (Roman Catholic). *See* Tour 12 in Chapter 3.

Riverside Church (Interdenominational). *See* Tour 9 in Chapter 3.

Spanish & Portuguese Synagogue, Shearith Israel (Orthodox Jewish). *See* Tour 8 in Chapter 3.

St. Bartholomew's (Episcopal). *See* Tour 2 in Chapter 3.
St. Luke's-in-the-Fields (Episcopal). *See* Tour 12 in Chapter 3.
St. Mark's-in-the-Bowery (Episcopal). *See* Tour 13 in Chapter 3.
St. Patrick's Cathedral (Roman Catholic). *See* Tour 2 in Chapter 3.
St. Paul's Chapel (Episcopal). *See* Tour 17 in Chapter 3.
St. Paul's Chapel at Columbia University (Nondenominational). *See* Tour 9 in Chapter 3.
St. Thomas (Episcopal). *See* Tour 2 in Chapter 3.
Temple Emanu-'el (Reform Jewish). *See* Tour 6 in Chapter 3.
Trinity Church (Episcopal). *See* Tour 17 in Chapter 3.

Parks and Gardens

Battery Park. *See* Tour 17 in Chapter 3.
Brooklyn Botanic Gardens. *See* Tour 20 in Chapter 4.
Bryant Park. *See* Tour 3 in Chapter 3.
Carl Schurz Park. *See* Tour 6 in Chapter 3.
Central Park. *See* Tour 7 in Chapter 3.
Clement Clarke Moore Park. *See* Tour 11 in Chapter 3.
Columbus Park. *See* Tour 16 in Chapter 3.
Flushing Meadows Corona Park. *See* Tour 22 in Chapter 4.
Fort Tryon Park. At the northern tip of Manhattan, high over the Hudson, this park offers stunning views of the Palisades across the river, plus an attractive though somewhat wild garden. It also contains the Cloisters (*see* Museums and Galleries, above).
Gramercy Park. *See* Tour 4 in Chapter 3.
Jamaica Bay Wildlife Refuge (Crossbay Blvd., Rockaways, Queens, tel. 718/474–0613). Nearly as big as the whole of Manhattan, this refuge offers temporary accommodations for migrating birds, plus nature trails across dunes and through marshes. Open dawn to dusk.
Kissena Park (tel. 718/353–1047). Located just west of Flushing, Queens, this park protects precious acres of original Long Island forests and marshland, demonstrating to visitors what the area looked like 100,000 years ago. Visitors can enjoy the new walking trails.
Madison Square. *See* Tour 4 in Chapter 3.
Marcus Garvey Park. *See* Tour 10 in Chapter 3.
New York Botanical Gardens. *See* Tour 23 in Chapter 4.
Pelham Bay Park (tel. 212/430–1825). With more than 2,000 acres, this Bronx park is the largest in the city. Purchased by Thomas Pell from the Indians in 1654, its facilities include a mile-long beach, cycling paths, a boat basin, bridle path and riding academy, fishing, picnic grounds, and tennis courts.
Prospect Park. *See* Tour 20 in Chapter 4.
Riverside Park. *See* Tour 9 in Chapter 3.
Staten Island Botanical Gardens. *See* Tour 24.
Union Square. *See* Tour 4.
United Nations Rose Garden. *See* Tour 3 in Chapter 3.
Van Cortlandt Park (tel. 212/548–7070). Located on 2 square miles of the north-central Bronx, this park includes facilities for tennis, swimming, running, baseball, soccer, cricket, and rugby. The nation's oldest municipal golf course is here, as is Van Cortlandt Mansion (*see* Historical Sites, above).
Washington Market Park. *See* Tour 14 in Chapter 3.
Washington Square. *See* Tour 12 in Chapter 3.

Statues, Monuments, and Fountains

Alice in Wonderland, Central Park (Jose DeCreeft). *See* Tour 7 in Chapter 3.

Alma Mater, Columbia University (Daniel Chester French). *See* Tour 9 in Chapter 3.

Atlas, Rockefeller Center (Lee Lawrie). *See* Tour 1 in Chapter 3.

Bethesda Fountain, Central Park (Emma Stebbins). *See* Tour 7 in Chapter 3.

Clock Sculpture Facade, Grand Central Terminal (Jules Coutan). *See* Tour 3 in Chapter 3.

Cube, Marine Midland Bank (Isamu Noguchi). *See* Tour 17 in Chapter 3.

General Grant National Memorial, W. 122nd St. and Riverside Dr. (John Duncan). *See* Tour 9 in Chapter 3.

General Sherman, Grand Army Plaza (Augustus Saint-Gaudens). *See* Tour 2 in Chapter 3.

George Washington, Federal Hall National Memorial (John Q. Adams Ward). *See* Tour 17 in Chapter 3.

Group of Four Trees, Chase Manhattan Plaza (Jean Dubuffet). *See* Tour 17 in Chapter 3.

Hammarskjold Plaza Sculpture Garden (Don Gummer). Huge sculptures and lots of space at Second Avenue between 46th and 47th streets.

Hans Christian Andersen, Central Park (Georg Lober). *See* Tour 7 in Chapter 3.

Le Tricorne, Seagram Building (Pablo Picasso). *See* Tour 2 in Chapter 3.

Lincoln Center Fountain (Philip Johnson). *See* Tour 8 in Chapter 3.

Lions, New York Public Library's central research building (E. C. Potter). *See* Tour 3 in Chapter 3.

Louise Nevelson Sculpture Park. *See* Tour 17 in Chapter 3.

Prometheus, Rockefeller Center's lower plaza (Paul Manship). *See* Tour 1 in Chapter 3.

Pulitzer Fountain, Grand Army Plaza (Carrere & Hastings) with **Abundance** facade (Karl Bitter). *See* Tour 2 in Chapter 3.

Statue of Liberty, New York Harbor (Frederick A. Bartholdi). *See* Tour 17 in Chapter 3.

Statues on the Mall, Central Park. *See* Tour 7 in Chapter 3.

Vietnam Veterans Memorial, Water Street (William Fellows and Peter Wormser). *See* Tour 17 in Chapter 3.

Washington Square Arch, Washington Square (Stanford White). *See* Tour 12 in Chapter 3.

Zoos

Bronx Zoo & Children's Zoo. *See* Tour 23 in Chapter 4.

Central Park Zoo & Children's Zoo. *See* Tour 7 in Chapter 3.

New York Aquarium. *See* What to See and Do with Children in Chapter 4.

Prospect Park Zoo. *See* Tour 20 in Chapter 4.

Queen's Zoo and Children's Farm. *See* Tour 22 in Chapter 4.

Staten Island Zoo. *See* What to See and Do with Children in Chapter 4.

6 Sports, Fitness, Beaches

by Karen Cure

A resident of New York's Upper West Side, Karen Cure is the author of Fodor's Sunday in New York.

Never known for turning their backs on trends, New Yorkers—who were always sports-mad as spectators—have caught the fitness bug. Though surrounded by concrete, they have discovered that the out-of-doors is a wonderful place, and they are stopped by nothing in their passion for their sports: You can see them jogging in the park when it's sleeting, or heading for the tennis bubble on the most blustery of Sunday winter afternoons. From boccie to croquet, no matter how esoteric the sport, there's a place to pursue it in New York. You'll find oases of greenery you'd never imagine here (13% of the city, in fact, is parkland). And if you strike up a conversation while waiting to rent a boat or a bike at the Loeb Boathouse, or while stretching before a jog around the Reservoir in Central Park, you'll discover a friendly, relaxed side of New Yorkers that you might not otherwise get the chance to see.

Just one word before you set out: Now that fitness is so popular here, weekends are very busy. If you need to rent equipment or secure specific space—for instance, a tennis court—go very early or be prepared to wait.

Spectator Sports

Many events described below take place at **Madison Square Garden** (7th Ave. between 31st & 33rd Sts.); tickets can be ordered by phone through the box office (tel. 212/563–8300) or Ticketmaster (tel. 212/307–7171). Even when events are sold out, you can often pick up a pair of tickets on the day of the game outside the venue, either from a scalper or from a fellow sports fan whose guests couldn't make it at the last minute. Ticket agencies, listed in the Manhattan yellow-pages phone directory, can be helpful—for a price.

Baseball

The **New York Mets** play at Shea Stadium (tel. 718/507–8499), at the penultimate stop on the No. 7 subway in Flushing, Queens. Watching them play to the cry of "Let's Go Mets!" is today's mania. Yankee Stadium (tel. 212/293–6000), accessible by the No. 4, D, or C subways to the 161st Street station in the Bronx, is the home of the **New York Yankees.** Baseball season runs from April to October.

Basketball

Only recently have the **New York Knickerbockers** (the "Knicks") aroused any hometown passion, but the team turnaround has made tickets for home games, played late October–April at Madison Square Garden, hard to come by. For up-to-date game roundups, phone the New York Knickerbockers Hot Line (tel. 212/751–6310).

Boxing and Wrestling

The *Daily News*'s annual Golden Gloves **boxing** bout and other major competitions are staged in Madison Square Garden. **Wrestling,** a more frequent Garden presence, is stagy and outrageous, drawing a rowdy but enthusiastic crowd.

Football

The **New York Giants** play September–December at Giants Stadium in East Rutherford, New Jersey (tel. 201/935–8111), as do the **New York Jets** (tel. 212/421–6600). All seats for Giants games and most for Jets games are sold on a season-ticket basis, and there's a waiting list for those; remaining Jets tickets for scattered singles are snapped up almost as soon as they go on sale in August.

Hockey

The **New York Rangers** play at Madison Square Garden; the **New York Islanders** at Nassau Veterans Memorial Coliseum in Uniondale, Long Island (tel. 516/794–4100); and the **New Jersey Devils** at the Brendan Byrne Arena in East Rutherford, New Jersey (tel. 201/935–6050). Tickets are usually available at game time; the season runs from October to April.

Horse Racing

Thoroughbreds Modern **Aqueduct Racetrack** (Rockaway Blvd., Ozone Park, Queens, tel. 718/641–4700), with its spate of new lawns and gardens, holds races late October–early May; the track is closed Tuesdays.

Belmont Park (Hempstead Turnpike, Elmont, Long Island, tel. 718/641–4700), the grande dame of New York racing, is home of the third jewel in horse racing's triple crown, the Belmont Stakes. Horses run here May–July and late August–October, but never on Tuesdays.

The **Meadowlands** (East Rutherford, NJ, tel. 201/935–8500), generally a trotting venue, also has a flat track season from Labor Day to December.

Standardbreds **Yonkers Raceway** (Central Ave., Yonkers, NY, tel. 212/562–9500) features harness racing daily year-round.

The **Meadowlands** (East Rutherford, NJ, tel. 201/935–8500) runs both trotters and pacers January–mid-August.

Running

The **New York City Marathon,** which has taken place annually in late October or early November since 1970, may be won by the Grete Waitzes, Bill Rodgerses, and other stars of the worldwide running circuit, but New Yorkers love to cheer on the pack of 22,000 (some 16,000 of them finish). Racewalkers, "jogglers," oldsters, youngsters, and disabled competitors help to make this what former Olympic Organizing Committee president Peter V. Ueberroth called "the best sporting event in the country." Spectators line rooftops and sidewalks, promenades, and terraces all along the route—but don't go near the finishing line in Central Park unless you relish mob scenes.

Tennis

The annual **U.S. Open,** held from late August through early September at the U.S.T.A. National Tennis Center, is one of the high points of the tennis buff's year, and tickets to watch the late rounds are some of the hottest in town. Early round matches are entertaining, too, and with a stadium court ticket you can also view matches in outlying courts—where the bleachers are so close you can almost count the sweat beads on the players' foreheads—and in the grandstand, where bleacher seating is first-come, first-served. During early rounds, ushers may help you move down to better seats in the stadium court or the grandstand (in exchange for a gratuity of $5 or $10). Wherever you sit, the attractive crowd of casual visitors, tennis groupies, and celebrities makes for terrific people-watching. The U.S. Tennis Association (Flushing Meadows-Corona Park, Flushing, NY 11368, tel. 718/271–5100) sells tickets by mail beginning in late spring; from May on, call Teletron (tel. 212/947–4840 or 800/922–2030).

Diehard tennis lovers have a special place in their hearts for the **Tournament of Champions,** which takes place in August at the West Side Tennis Club in Forest Hills, Queens, where the U.S. Open got its start. Call about tickets in March (tel. 718/268–2300).

The tennis year winds up with two tourneys in Madison Square Garden: the **Virginia Slims Tournament** in mid-November (tel. 212/563–8954), with tickets on sale beginning in September; and, in late November, the **Nabisco Masters** (write 437 Madison Ave., 17th floor, 10022, for information, or tel. 212/302–3322), with tickets on sale in October through the Madison Square Garden box office (tel. 212/563–8300) and Ticketmaster (tel. 212/307–7171).

Track and Field

The **Millrose Games** take place at Madison Square Garden every year in February.

The second annual **New York Track and Field Games** is slated for late July, to be held at Wein Stadium, Columbia University. For information, contact the New York Road Runners Club (9 E. 89th St., 10128, tel. 212/860–4455).

Participant Sports

Bicycling

Although it's a problem to keep a bicycle in most Manhattan apartments, that doesn't affect the popularity of the sport here. A sleek pack of dedicated racers zooms around Central Park at dawn and at dusk daily, and on weekends, parks swarm with recreational cyclists. **Central Park**'s circular drive is closed to traffic from 10 AM to 3 PM and 7 to 10 PM on weekdays, and from 7 PM Friday to 6 AM Monday. On holidays, it's closed from 8 PM the night before until 6 AM the day after. In **Riverside Park,** the promenade between 72nd and 110th Streets, with its Hudson River view, gets a more easygoing crowd. Other good bets: the **Wall Street** area, deserted on weekends; the Hudson-view **Battery Park Esplanade;** or the winding roads in Brooklyn's **Prospect Park,** also closed to cars.

Bike Rentals Expect to leave a deposit or a credit card at the following: **AAA Bikes in Central Park** (Loeb Boathouse, mid-park near East 74th St., tel. 212/861–4137); **Bicycles Plus** (204 E. 85th St., tel.

212/794–2201); **Gene's Bicycles** (242 E. 79th St., tel. 212/249–9218); **Metro Bicycles** (1311 Lexington Ave. at 88th St., tel. 212/427–4450); or **Pedal Pusher** (1306 2nd Ave. between 68th and 69th Sts., tel. 212/288–5592). Some rent only 3-speeds; others have 10-speeds as well.

Group Trips For organized rides with other cyclists, contact: **Central Park Cycling & Sports Association** (tel. 212/956–5920); **Hungry Pedalers Gourmet Bicycle Tours,** visiting destinations of culinary interest (771 West End Ave., tel. 212/595–5542); or the **Staten Island Bicycling Association** (Box 141016, Staten Island 10314, tel. 718/273–0805).

Billiards

It used to be that pool halls were dusty, grimy, sticky places—and there are still a few of those around. But they've been joined by a group of oh-so-chic spots with deluxe decor, high prices, and even classical music or jazz in the background.

Billiard Club (220 W. 19th St., tel. 212/206–7665).
Broadway Bay Billiards (2182 Broadway, at 77th St., tel. 212/877–0707).
Chelsea Billiards (54 W. 21st St., tel. 212/989–0096).
Julian's Billiards (138 E. 14th St., tel. 212/475–9338).
Society Billiards (10 E. 21st St., tel. 212/529–8600).
Tekk Billiards (75 Christopher St., tel. 212/463–9282).

Bird-watching

Manhattan's green parks and woodlands provide habitat for thousands of birds, everything from summer tanagers and fork-tailed flycatchers to Kentucky warblers and common nighthawks. Since the city is on the Atlantic flyway, a major migratory route, you can see birds that nest as far north as the High Arctic. May is the best season, since the songbirds are in their freshest colors—and so many are singing at once that you can hardly distinguish their songs. To find out what's been seen where, call the Rare Bird Alert (tel. 212/832–6523).

Good bets include 1,146-acre **Van Cortlandt Park** (tel. 212/548–7070) in the Bronx, with its freshwater marshes and upland woods. In Brooklyn there are 526-acre **Prospect Park** (tel. 718/287–3400) and **Green-Wood Cemetery** (tel. 718/783–8776). The Ramble in Manhattan's **Central Park** (tel. 212/397–3091) is another prime spot. In Queens, try the woodlands and wetlands of 623-acre **Alley Pond Park** (tel. 718/229–4000); and in Staten Island, head for the fairly undeveloped 317-acre **Wolfe's Pond Park** (tel. 718/984–8266), where the pond and the nearby shore can be dense with geese and ducks during the annual migrations.

Guided Walks The **New York City Audubon Society** (71 W. 23rd, tel. 212/691–7483) has occasional bird-watching outings. Also check with the **Urban Park Rangers,** a uniformed division of the Parks Department that organizes frequent outdoor walks. Each borough has its own troop: Manhattan, in Central Park (tel. 212/427–4040); the Bronx, in Van Cortlandt Park (tel. 212/548–7070); Brooklyn, in Prospect Park (tel. 718/287–3400); Queens, in Flushing Meadows (tel. 718/699–4204); and Staten Island, in High Rock Park (tel. 718/667–6042).

Boating

The boating available on New York City's ponds and lakes conjures up 19th-century images of a parasol-twirling lady being rowed by her swain. But there's a huge demand for this activity, and on weekends you'd better go early or be prepared to wait.

In **Central Park,** the boats are rowboats (plus one Venetian gondola) and the rowing terrain is the 18-acre Central Park Lake. Rent your boat at **Loeb Boathouse** (tel. 212/517–2233), near 74th Street, from spring through fall.

In **Prospect Park,** pedal-powered two- and four-seater boats scuttle across the 60-acre Prospect Lake Lullwater. Rentals are available at **Pelican Boat Rentals** (tel. 718/287–9824), near the Wollman Skating Rink.

Boccie

This Italian version of bowling thrives in New York, with 100 city courts in the five boroughs. The easiest to get to from midtown are at 96th Street and First Avenue; at East River Drive and 42nd Street; and at the Thompson Street Playground in Greenwich Village.

Bowling

The closing of several major lanes recently has left Manhattan with just one bowling alley, **Bowlmor** (110 University Pl., tel. 212/255–8188). This 44-lane operation may be funky compared to the modern layouts that you see on TV (or in your own hometown). But you can't beat the colorful Village crowd—or the intensity of the competition.

Chess and Checkers

Central Park's Chess & Checkers House is picturesquely situated atop a massive stone outcrop. Ten tables are available for indoor play on weekends, 11:30–4:30, and 24 outdoor tables are available during all daylight hours. Pick up playing pieces at the Dairy (mid-park at 64th St., tel. 212/397–3165); there is no charge, but a deposit is required.

Downtown in Greenwich Village, the **Village Chess Shop** (230 Thompson St., tel. 212/475–9580) is always an active spot. Uptown, the **Manhattan Chess Club** (154 W. 57th St., tel. 212/333–5888) sponsors tournaments and exhibitions; instruction is available on both beginning and intermediate levels.

Fishing

The smell of fish and saltwater entrances New Yorkers, and it's not far away by car or subway. No license is necessary for saltwater angling. Brooklyn's **Sheepshead Bay,** where turn-of-the-century swells like Diamond Jim Brady summered, is the main center for party boats; its fleet is among the country's largest, with some 20 boats going out every day year-round. The piers are on Emmons Avenue, and departure times are posted locally—typically 6, 7, 8, 9 and 10 AM for full-day trips, and noon and 1 PM for half-day outings. Tackle rentals and bait are provided. Call **Mike's Tackle & Bait Shop** (tel. 718/646–9261) for additional information.

On quaint City Island, a Bronx bastion of the salty life, **Jack's Bait & Tackle** (Cross St. and City Island Ave., Bronx, tel. 212/885–2042) rents small boats with 6 HP motors to go out for flounder, stripers, bluefish, porgy, eel, and blackfish.

Flounder, fluke, small blues, porgy, and bass make for good shore fishing at **Pelham Bay Park**'s Orchard Beach (tel. 212/885–2275) in the Bronx; at **Breezy Point Jetty** and **Canarsie Pier** in the Gateway National Recreation Area (tel. 718/474–4600) in Brooklyn; and at **Rockaway Beach** (tel. 718/318–4000) in Queens.

Golf

Although New York golf courses don't measure up to those in world golf meccas such as Scotland, many New Yorkers are avid golfers, and on weekends they jam the handful of verdant, well-kept city courses.

Bethpage State Park, in the Long Island town of Bethpage, about one hour and 20 minutes from Manhattan, is home to five golf courses, including its 7,065-yard par-71 Black, generally ranked among the nation's top 25 public courses. Reservations for tee times are not accepted; on weekends and Monday, the line starts forming at midnight for the Black course's tee time tickets to go on sale at 4 AM. It's not so congested on other days, or on the other four courses on the property.

Of the 13 city courses, the 6,492-yard Split Rock in **Pelham Bay Park,** the Bronx, is considered the most challenging (tel. 212/885–1258; 718/225–4653 for tee times). **Van Cortlandt Park** has the nation's first municipal golf course, established in 1895—the hilly 6,052-yard Van Cortlandt (tel. 212/543–4595). Queens has a 5,431-yard course at **Forest Park** (Park Lane S. and Forest Pkwy. in Woodhaven, tel. 718/296–0999); Staten Island has the 5,891-yard **Silver Lake** (915 Victory Blvd. near Forest Ave., tel. 718/447–5686; 718/225–4653 for tee times).

Driving Range In midtown Manhattan you can practice your swing in netted cages, with bull's-eye backdrops, at the **Richard Metz Golf Studio** (35 E. 50th St., 2nd floor, tel. 212/759–6940). In Queens, the place to go is **Pebble Beach** (near Northern Blvd. and Douglaston Pkwy., tel. 718/229–2525); in the Bronx, try **Pelham Bay Park's Turtle Cove** (north of City Island Rd., tel. 212/885–2646).

Miniature Golf Putting courses are at **Gotham Miniature Golf** (at Wollman Rink, Central Park near 64th St., tel. 212/517–4800), where putters maneuver around scale models of city landmarks, and at yuppyish **Putter's Paradise** (48 W. 21st St., tel. 212/727–7888).

Horseback Riding

A trot on the bridle path around Central Park's Reservoir, renovated in 1987, provides a pleasant look at New York. Experienced English-saddle riders can rent mounts at the carefully run **Claremont Riding Academy** (173–177 W. 89th St., tel. 212/724–5100), the city's oldest riding academy and the only riding stable left in Manhattan. Private lessons, including dressage, are available at beginner through advanced levels, for $30 per half hour; horse rentals are $27 per hour.

In Brooklyn, **Prospect Park** is a beautiful setting for riding. Hire your mount from nearby **Culmitt Stables** (51 Caton Pl., tel. 718/438–8849). Private lessons are available for $35 per hour, $17 per half hour; horse rentals for $15 per hour.

Hotel Health Clubs

Although space is tight in Manhattan hotels, most of them offer some kind of fitness facility, even if it's just an arrangement enabling guests to use a nearby health club (*see* Chapter 9). These hotels have some of the better on-premises workout centers:

Doral Park Avenue (70 Park Ave., tel. 212/687–7050), with one-on-one training and aerobic and Nautilus equipment at the Saturnia Fitness Center (also available to guests of the **Doral Court, Doral Tuscany,** and **Doral Inn**).

Le Parker Meridien (118 W. 57th St., tel. 212/245–5000), featuring a rooftop pool and a basement-level workout center.

The Peninsula (700 5th Ave., tel. 212/247–2200), with a pool on the 22nd floor, plus exercise machines and a dining terrace.

U.N. Plaza (1 United Nations Plaza, tel. 212/355–3400), combining a handsome top-floor pool with a roomful of exercise machines.

Vanderbilt YMCA (224 E. 47th St., tel. 212/755–2410), which offers guests free access to the Y's athletic facilities—pools, gym, running track, weight room, machines, and exercise classes.

Vista International (3 World Trade Ct., tel. 212/938–9100), with a pool, an exercise area, and a running track.

Ice Skating

Each of the city's rinks has its own character, but all have scheduled skating sessions, with the surfaces tended between times. Lockers, skate rentals, music, and snack bars complete the picture. Major rinks include the one in **Rockefeller Center** (50th St. at 5th Ave., lower plaza, tel. 212/757–5730), postage-stamp size and utterly romantic; **Sky Rink** (450 W. 33rd St., 16th floor, tel. 212/695–6555 or, for lessons, 212/239–8385), the city's biggest indoor skating spot and its only year-round rink, where dancer Mikhail Baryshnikov tutored Olympic skater Debi Thomas; and the beautifully situated **Wollman Memorial Rink** (Central Park near 64th St., tel. 212/517–4800). Be prepared for crowds on weekends.

Jogging and Racewalking

In New York, lawyers jog, doctors jog, investment bankers jog, antiques dealers jog, and mothers jog (sometimes pushing their toddlers ahead of them in speedy Baby Jogger strollers). Publicity notwithstanding, crime is not a problem as long as you jog when and where everybody else does.

In Manhattan, **Central Park** is the busiest spot, specifically along the 1.58-mile track circling the **Reservoir,** New York Road Runners' Club President Fred Lebow's favorite running ground. A runners' lane has been designated along the park roads, which are closed to traffic weekdays 10–3 and 7–10, and from 7 PM Fridays to 6 AM Mondays. A good 1.72-mile route starts at Tavern on the Green along the West Drive, heads south around the bottom of the park to the East Drive, and circles back west on the 72nd Street park road to your starting point. **Riverside Park,** along the Hudson River bank in Manhattan, is glorious at sunset. You can cover 4½ miles by running from 72nd to 116th streets and back. There are eight laps to a mile on the park's outdoor track near 74th Street.

Other favorite Manhattan circuits are around **Gramercy Park** (⅕ mile), **City Hall Park** (½ mile), **Washington Square Park** (½ mile), the **Battery Park Esplanade** (about 2 miles), and **Roosevelt Island** (3.6 miles). In Brooklyn, try the **Brooklyn Heights Esplanade,** facing the Manhattan skyline, or the roads in **Prospect Park.**

Races and Group Runs A full, year-round schedule is organized by the **New York Road Runners Club** (9 E. 89th St., tel. 212/860–4455), including group runs at 6:30 PM and 7:30 PM Monday through Friday, starting at the club headquarters, and at 10 AM Saturdays at 90th Street and Fifth Avenue in Central Park.

Roller Skating

While roller skating is no longer the mania it once was, there are certain New Yorkers who ignore that; wearing headphones, they whirl and twirl to music that they alone can hear. A prime spot, particularly on weekends, is in **Central Park** between the Mall and Bethesda Fountain. **Wollman Rink** (mid-park at 63rd St., tel. 212/517–4800) converts to a roller rink during warm months, and rentals are available.

Swimming

Municipal pools, such as the **Carmine Street Pool** (7th Ave. S and Clarkson St., tel. 212/397–3107), are great places to mix with a real cross-section of native New Yorkers. The **U.N. Plaza, Parker Meridien,** and **Vista International** hotels (*see* Chapter 9) all have good swimming pools for use by their guests (*see* also Beaches, below).

Tennis

The New York City Parks Department maintains scores of tennis courts. The most scenic are the 30 in **Central Park** (mid-park near 94th St., tel. 212/397–3194), set in a thicket of trees with the skyline beyond. Modestly priced, same-day, single-play admissions are available at the Tennis House adjoining the courts. Lessons are given on four hard courts (tel. 212/289–3133).

You can also play where John McEnroe and Ivan Lendl do: at the **U.S.T.A. National Tennis Center** (tel. 718/592–8000) in Flushing Meadows-Corona Park, Queens, site of the U.S. Open tournament. The center has 23 outdoor and 9 indoor courts, all Deco Turf II. Reservations are accepted up to two days in advance.

Local clubs and private courts include:

Boulevard Gardens Tennis Club (51–26 Broadway, Woodside, Queens, tel. 718/545–7774), whose six good red-clay courts, bubble-covered in winter, are very easy to get to by car from Manhattan.

Columbus Racquet Club (795 Columbus Ave. near 99th St., tel. 212/663–6900), where Margaux Hemingway, Robert Redford, Dustin Hoffman, and various other New Yorkers have served and volleyed on its 9 courts.

Crosstown Tennis (14 W. 31st St., tel. 212/947–5780), with four indoor hard courts that are air-conditioned in summer.

HRC Tennis (Piers 13 & 14, East River at Wall St., tel. 212/422–9300), with eight Har-Tru courts under two bubbles, which are air-conditioned in summer.

Manhattan Plaza Racquet Club (450 W. 43rd St., tel. 212/594–0554), on whose five courts Virginia Slims and U.S. Open players have been known to practice.

Beaches

Fine weather brings sun-worshiping New Yorkers out in force. Early in the season, the nearest park or even a rooftop is just fine for catching rays, but later on everyone heads for New York City beaches. Call before you go to check on swimming conditions.

Long Island

New Yorkers' favorite strand may be **Jones Beach** (tel. 516/785–1600), one of the great man-made beaches of the world, built during the era of the famous parks commissioner Robert Moses. The Long Island Railroad (tel. 718/454–5477) runs regular transportation in the summer from Penn Station to Jones Beach. Up the shore is another good beach at **Robert Moses State Park** on Fire Island (tel. 516/669–0449).

City Beaches

The most popular spots are just a subway ride away: the 7½-mile Atlantic strand in Queens's **Rockaways** (tel. 718/318–4000), site of some of the city's best surf: the 3½-miler, also on the Atlantic, at Brooklyn's **Coney Island** (tel. 718/946–1350); and Coney Island's extension, 3 miles down the boardwalk, **Brighton Beach.**

Jacob Riis Park (tel. 718/474–4600), part of the Gateway National Recreation Area in Brooklyn, has a boardwalk stretching a full mile along the surfy Atlantic. On Staten Island, there are terrific Atlantic-surf beaches at **Wolfe's Pond Park** (tel. 718/984–8266) and along the 7,500-foot **Franklin D. Roosevelt Boardwalk,** from Miller Field in the Gateway National Recreation Area (tel. 718/351–8700) to Fort Wadsworth.

7 Shopping

by Karen Cure

For New Yorkers, shopping is a way to get over a defunct romance, to relieve tension at lunchtime, to stave off boredom, to get together with friends, or to get out of tiny apartments and onto the streets, where it's crowded and lively and there's lots to see. For a visitor, shopping in New York can be one of the most satisfying sightseeing experiences: It's theater, architecture, and people-watching all rolled into one.

With this kind of market, New York supports a thriving retail community. Big stores and small ones, one-of-a-kinds and chains, all together present an overwhelming array of "Things." While the big department stores are fabulous generalists, with something for everyone, they aren't the main attraction—what makes shopping here most interesting is the number of stores with a sharply defined specialty. You can find a whole store full of balloons in all sizes, shapes, thicknesses, and materials (**Toy Balloon,** 204 E. 38th St., tel. 212/682–3803), or another with every conceivable object made of rubber (**Canal Rubber Supply,** 329 Canal St., tel. 212/226–7339). There are stores specializing in Japanese-style screens (**Tonee Corp.,** 108 Wooster St., tel. 212/966–4213), personal security equipment (**Counter Spy Shop,** 675 3rd Ave., tel. 212/557–3040; by appointment only), and kayaks and folding boats (**Hans Klepper Corp.,** 35 Union Sq. W., tel. 212/243–3428).

Another important lure of Manhattan shopping is the bargain. Major intersections become instant markets as street peddlers hawk fake Gucci and Cartier watches at $15–$25 each. (These may just possibly last a year or two.) There are thrift shops and resale shops where, it's whispered, Jackie O sends her castoffs and Catherine Deneuve snaps up antique lace. At off-price and discount stores, the mark-offs are, as locals say, "to die for," and the sales are even better. Designers' showroom sales allow you to buy cheap at the source; auctions promise good prices as well.

To make the most of your shopping time in New York, visit one of the prime retail neighborhoods described below, or follow one of our "blitz tours," designed to hit the high spots within certain special-interest categories.

Shopping Hours Stores are generally open Monday–Saturday from 10 AM to 5 or 6 PM, but neighborhood peculiarities do exist. In midtown and lower Manhattan, shops are often closed all weekend. Most stores on the Lower East Side close on Friday afternoon and all day Saturday for the Jewish Sabbath, while keeping normal hours on Sunday. On the Upper East Side, Sunday closing is the rule, but it's the exception on the West Side and in the Village.

Sales Sales take place in August (for summer merchandise) and in December and January (for winter wares); these sales are announced in the papers. Sales of special merit may end up in *New York* magazine's "Sales and Bargains" column. These often include sales in manufacturers' showrooms that are otherwise never promoted to the public. If your visit is planned for April or October, when most of these showroom sales take place, you might phone your favorite designer and ask whether one is in the offing. Find out before you go whether the seller requires cash or accepts credit card or checks (whether local or out-of-state).

A & S Plaza, **14**
Alexander's, **2**
575 Fifth Avenue, **10**
Barneys New York, **15**
Bergdorf Goodman, **4**
Bloomingdale's, **1**
Henri Bendel, **5**
Herald Center, **13**
Lord & Taylor, **11**
Lower East Side
(Orchard Street), **16**
Macy's, **12**
Manhattan Art and
Antiques Center, **7**
Place des
Antiquaires, **3**
Rockefeller Center, **8**
Saks Fifth Avenue, **9**
South Street
Seaport, **19**
Trump Tower, **6**
World Financial
Center, **17**
World Trade
Center, **18**

Manhattan Shopping Highlights

Shopping Neighborhoods

New York shops are collected in neighborhoods rather than in malls, so there's nothing more pleasant than shop-crawling when the weather is fine. Locations, if not included here, can be found in store listings below.

South Street Seaport The Seaport's shops are located along the cobbled, pedestrians-only extension to Fulton Street; in the Fulton Market building, the original home of the city's fish market; and on the three levels of Pier 17. You'll find some of the best of the country's upscale retailers: **Ann Taylor** and **Laura Ashley** for women's clothing, **Brookstone** for fancy gadgets and hardware, **Coach** for handbags, **Caswell-Massey** for fragrances, and **Sharper Image** for high-tech gimmickry. The big catalogue house **J. Crew** chose the Seaport as the location for its first retail outlet. There are also few-of-a-kind shops, notably the **Strand** bookstore, where second-hand volumes overflow into sidewalk bins; **Mariposa** for butterflies; and **Hats in the Belfry** for every kind of inexpensive hat. Business is brisk, especially on fine summer days and even more so on weekends.

World Financial Center Although the World Trade Center across the street bills its concourse as the city's busiest shopping center, the World Financial Center in Battery Park City is shaping up as a shopping destination to reckon with, thanks to stores such as **Barneys New York** for clothing, **Godiva Chocolatier** for chocolates, **Mark Cross** for leather goods, **Ann Taylor**, and **Caswell-Massey**. The **Gallery of History** sells original historical documents as works of art. **State of the Art** has home and office accessories, **Il Papiro** offers hand-marbled Italian paper products, and **CD Street** strives to be the ultimate compact disc store. Most are open on Sundays.

Lower East Side Once home to millions of Jewish immigrants from Russia and Eastern Europe, this area is New Yorkers' bargain beat. The center of it all is narrow, unprepossessing Orchard Street, which is crammed with tiny, no-nonsense clothing and shoe stores where the merchandise ranges from kitschy to elegant. An influx of Israeli merchants has made things perhaps not quite as friendly as they used to be, but then Orchard Street was never for schmoozing, especially not on Sunday, the busiest day of the week. Start at Houston Street, walk down one side as far as Canal Street, then walk back up. Essential stops include **Fine & Klein** for handbags and leather goods; **Forman's** for women's clothing; and **Lace-Up Shoes.** Grand Street (off Orchard St., south of Delancey St.) is chockablock with linens, towels, and other items for the home.

SoHo On West Broadway, SoHo's main drag, and on Wooster, Greene, Mercer, Prince, Spring, Broome, and Grand streets, major art galleries keep company with chic clothing stores such as **La Rue des Rêves** and **Victoria Falls.** Well-known stops include decorative-items specialist **Wolfman-Gold & Good Company** and Southwest-themed **Zona;** gourmet food emporium **Dean & DeLuca;** and **D.F. Sanders,** where gifts and tabletop items are sleekly, stunningly contemporary. Many stores in SoHo close on Mondays.

Herald Square The huge **Macy's** department store at 34th Street and Sixth Avenue anchors this intersection; across 34th Street, the for-

SoHo Shopping

mer E. J. Korvette—the original Saks & Company—has been renovated into the multilevel **Herald Center,** whose 32 shops include **Ann Taylor** and **Toys R Us,** as well as several discount apparel and jewelry stores. Business has been less than brisk here. But that didn't deter Brooklyn's **A&S** department store, which anchors a newer atrium-mall, **A&S Plaza,** just to the south on Sixth Avenue, with nine floors of more than 60 shops.

Midtown Near Grand Central The biggest men's clothiers are here in the stretch of Madison Avenue nicknamed "Trad Avenue": **J. Press; Brooks Brothers; Paul Stuart; F. R. Tripler;** and **Wallachs.** Most also handle women's clothing in dress-for-success styles.

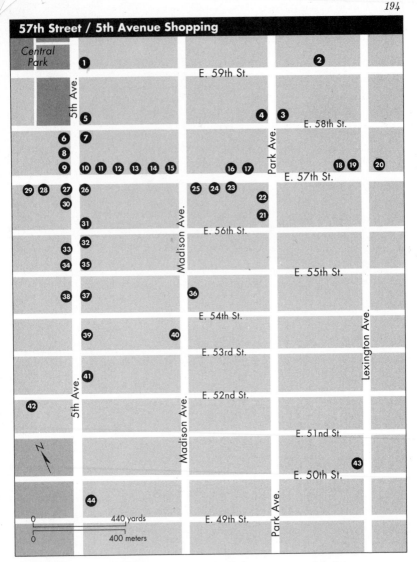

57th Street / 5th Avenue Shopping

A La Vieille Russie, **1**
André Emmerich
Gallery, **16**
Beltrami, **34**
Bergdorf
Goodman, **6, 7**
Bijan, **37**
Buccellati, **31**
Bulgari, **27**
Burberry, **11**
Cartier, **41**
Chanel, **10**
Charivari 57, **28**
Charles Jourdan, **31**

Ciro, **35**
Dempsey & Carroll, **23**
Doris Leslie Blau, **12**
Doubleday
Bookshop, **8**
F.A.O. Schwarz, **5**
Fiorucci, **2**
Fortunoff, **39**
Godiva
Chocolatier, **36, 43**
Hammacher
Schlemmer, **20**
Harry Winston, **33**
Hermès, **13**
Hoya Crystal
Gallery, **22**

Israel Sack, **12**
J.N. Bartfield
Books, **29**
James Robinson, **12**
Kenneth Jay Lane, **31**
Laura Ashley, **15**
Louis, Boston, **19**
Martha, **3, 31**
Maud Frizon, **17**
Morrell &
Company, **36**
Pace Gallery, **25**
Place des
Antiquaires, **18**
Saks Fifth Avenue, **44**

Salvatore
Ferragamo, **30**
Steuben, **32**
Susan Bennis Warren
Edwards, **21**
T. Anthony, **4**
Tiffany & Co., **26**
To Boot, **40**
Traveller's
Bookstore, **42**
Van Cleef & Arpels, **9**
Victoria's Secret, **24**
Wally Findlay
Gallery, **14**

Fifth Avenue The boulevard that was once home to some of the biggest names in New York retailing is not what it once was, that role having been usurped by Madison Avenue north of 57th Street. But Fifth Avenue from Central Park South to Rockefeller Center still shines with **F.A.O. Schwarz** and **Bergdorf Goodman** (at 58th St.), **Tiffany** and **Bulgari** jewelers (at 57th St.), the various luxury stores in **Trump Tower** (at 56th St.), **Steuben** glassware and **Ferragamo** shoes (at 55th St.), **Cartier** jewelers (at 52nd St.), and so on down to **Saks Fifth Avenue** (at 50th St.). **Rockefeller Center** itself provides a plethora of shops ranging from moderately priced to chichi. South of there is **575,** a bright-and-shiny atrium shopping area named for its Fifth Avenue address (at 47th St.).

57th Street The thoroughfare that runs past Carnegie Hall, the Russian Tea Room, and the Hard Rock Café supports stores that sell everything from remaindered books to $50,000 diamond-and-platinum bracelets. Begin at the **Compleat Strategist** game store (between 8th and 9th Aves.) and head eastward, via the **Pottery Barn, Coliseum Books,** and **Jerry Brown** and **Paron** fabric stores. As you approach Fifth Avenue, you're in the creamiest New York retail territory, with the exclusive specialty stores, **Henri Bendel** and **Bergdorf Goodman.** East of Fifth you'll find such exclusive stores as **Chanel; Burberrys; Louis, Boston;** and the **Place des Antiquaires** antiques mall. Above and alongside these stores are some of the city's top art galleries, including **André Emmerich** and **Wally Findlay.**

Columbus Avenue Between 66th and 86th streets, this former tenement district is now home to some of the city's hottest retail real estate. Shops are mostly modern in design, upscale but not top-of-the-line. Clothing runs the gamut from preppy for men and women **Frank Stella Ltd.** to high funk (**Betsey Johnson**), high style (**Charivari**), and high-tech Euro-Jap (**Parachute**). It's a good source for fine costume jewelry (**Ylang Ylang**). Children will enjoy stops at **The Last Wound-Up, Mythology,** and **Penny Whistle Toys.**

Upper East Side Along Madison and Lexington avenues, roughly between 57th and 72nd streets, New York branches of world-renowned designer emporiums are joined by a group of spirited retailers who fill their stores with the unique and the stylish. Items for the home, fine antiques, and wonderful clothing predominate —and the prices aren't always sky-high. The best course is to walk up Madison, walk over two blocks, then stroll down Lexington Avenue with a finale at **Bloomingdale's.**

Blitz Tours

Get a handful of subway tokens ready, and save enough cash for cab fare to lug all your packages back with you. Here are citywide shopping itineraries arranged by special interest; addresses, if not included here, can be found in the store listings below.

Antiques Spend two hours at the **Manhattan Art & Antiques Center** (1050 2nd Ave. at 55th St.), then swing over to 57th Street to the **Place des Antiquaires** and spend two hours there. Stroll westward across 57th Street, stopping at **James Robinson** and **Israel Sack.** Then head up Madison to **America Hurrah** (at 65th St.), **Didier Aaron** (on 67th St.), **Thomas K. Woodard** (near 69th St.), **Hirschl & Adler Folk** (at 70th St.), **Leigh Keno** (on

Acker Merrall &
Condit, **29**
Ann Taylor, **33**
Aris Mixon &
Company, **16**
The Ballet Shop, **35**
Betsey Johnson, **31**
Charivari, **5,
10, 14, 32**
Conran's, **13**
Ecco, **22**
Eeyore's Books for
Children, **17**
Endicott
Booksellers, **6**
Frank Stella Ltd., **7**
Greenstones and Cie, **8**
Gryphon Record
Shop, **27**
The Last
Wound-Up, **25**
Laura Ashley, **15**
Morris Brothers, **3**
Murder Ink, **2**
Mythology, **19**
P.S. 44 Market, **20**
Parachute, **24**
Penny Whistle
Toys, **9**
Peter Fox, **18**
Pottery Barn, **26**
Putumayo, **21**
Shakespeare &
Company, **11**
Star Magic, **28**
To Boot, **30**
Tower Records, **34**
Toy Park, **1**
West Side Kids, **4**
Ylang Ylang, **23**
Zabar's, **12**

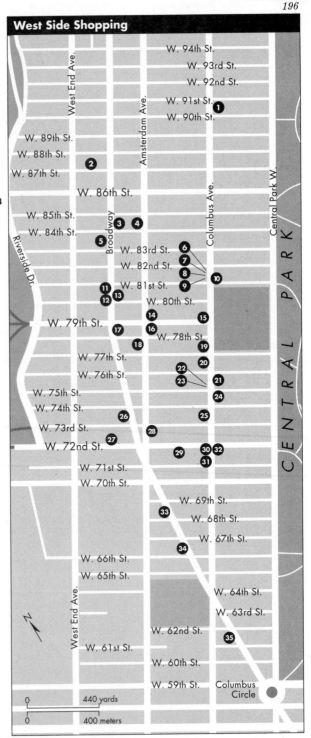

West Side Shopping

74th St.), **Stair & Company** (near 74th St.), **DeLorenzo** and **Leo Kaplan** (near 75th St.), **David A. Schorsch** (on 76th St.), **Florian Papp** (at 76th St.), and **Barry Friedman** (at 83rd St.).

Bargains Start out at 8 AM, downtown on Park Place, as the doors open at **Syms** (its motto: "an educated consumer is our best customer"). Take a cab to Hester and Orchard streets and shop along Orchard to Delancey Street. (Prowl along Grand Street if you're more interested in soft goods for your home than in clothing.) Leave at 2:30 and take a cab to **S&W** in Chelsea; then take the subway uptown to **Loehmann's,** which is open until 9. Pick up snacks at street vendors and nosh as you whiz from one spot to the next. But remember: On Saturdays, things are closed on the Lower East Side.

Children If your kids have stamina, start with **Louis Tannen's,** the magic store, which opens at 9, or **Forbidden Planet,** which opens at 10 —whichever is of greater interest to your youngster. Then take a cab uptown and do Columbus Avenue, beginning with **Penny Whistle Toys** (at 81st St.), and on to **Mythology** (at 77th St.), **The Last Wound-Up** (at 73rd St.), and **Star Magic** (Amsterdam Ave. at 73rd St.). Stop at **Steve's Ice Cream** (Columbus Ave. at 73rd St.) for an ice-cream cone with mix-ins, then go visit the dinosaurs at the American Museum of Natural History (Central Park West at 77th St.).

Cook's Tour Browse in **Zabar's** for a couple of hours beginning at 8 AM; then go across town to **Kitchen Arts & Letters** bookstore (1435 Lexington Ave., between 93rd & 94th Sts., tel. 212/876–5550) and proceed down to **Bridge Kitchenware** (214 E. 52nd St., tel. 212/ 688–4220). Head downtown to hit **Balducci's** in the Village, **Dean & DeLuca** in SoHo, and, if there's time before 6, **Kam-Man** in Chinatown. If not, head up to **Macy's,** where the Cellar's gourmet food hall is open Monday, Thursday, and Friday till 8:30, Tuesday, Wednesday, and Saturday till 6:45, and Sunday till 6. If you live in an inland state, make your last stop in New York **Citarella** (2135 Broadway at 75th St., tel. 212/874–0383), and have some great fish packed in ice to go.

Luxury Spend 90 minutes at **Saks Fifth Avenue,** then stroll up Fifth. Leave **Trump Tower** by 2:30. Visit **Tiffany** and **Bergdorf Goodman** before closing time. On Monday or Thursday, windowshop your way across 57th Street and north on Lexington Avenue to **Bloomingdale's,** which doesn't close until 9 PM. On other nights, take a cab downtown to **Barneys New York** for a finale. (It's open until 9 Monday through Thursday, until 8 on Friday.)

Home Furnishings Start at **Barneys New York,** which opens at 10, and visit its Chelsea Passage. Then take a cab to SoHo and stroll around, making sure not to miss **D. F. Sanders, Wolfman-Gold & Good Company,** and **Zona.** When things there close—at 6 or 7—take the No. 6 subway to **Bloomingdale's,** if it's Monday or Thursday, or the Q or R train to **Macy's,** which is open late Mondays, Thursdays, and Fridays.

Department Stores

Most of these stores keep regular hours on weekdays and are open until 8 at least one night a week. Many have personal shoppers who can walk you through the store at no charge.

Aberbach Fine Art, **8**
America Hurrah, **35**
Baccarat, **43**
Barry Friedman, **3**
Bottega Veneta, **42**
Caviarteria, **40**
Cerutti, **27**
Christie's, **41**
Coe Kerr, **4**
D.F. Sanders, **9**
David Schorsch, **14**
DeLorenzo, **10**
Didier Aaron, **34**
Eeyore's Books for Children, **2**
Emanuel Ungaro, **28**
Encore, **1**
Erica Wilson, **36**
Ffolio 72, **26**
Florian Papp, **11**
Floris, **37**
Giorgio Armani, **25**
Givenchy, **12**
Hirschl & Adler Folk, **19**
Isselbacher, **7**
Koos van den Akker, **29**
Lederer, **44**
Leigh Keno American Furniture, **16**
Leo Kaplan Ltd., **13**
Madison Avenue Bookshop, **21**
Michael's Resale, **5**
Mishon, Mishon, **17**
Missoni, **23**
Montenapoleone, **33**
North Beach Leather, **32**
Polo/Ralph Lauren, **18**
Second Act Children's Wear, **6**
Sherry Lehman, **38**
Sonia Rykiel, **30**
Stair & Company, **15**
T. Anthony, **45**
Teuscher Chocolates, **39**
Thomas K. Woodard, **22**
Valentino, **24**
Ylang Ylang, **31**
Yves St. Laurent Rive Gauche, **20**

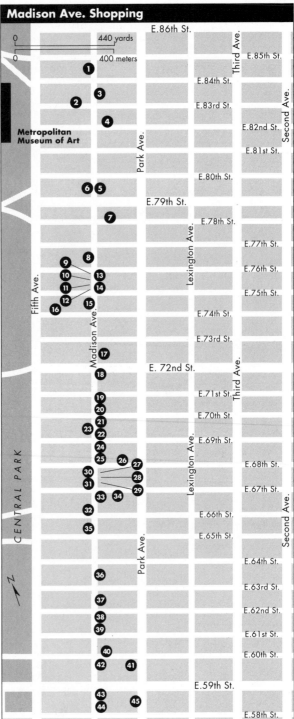

Madison Ave. Shopping

Alexander's (Lexington Ave. between 58th and 59th Sts., tel. 212/593–0880). This store has a dual personality: half polyester paradise, half bastion of high style at a discount.

A&S (33rd St. and 6th Ave., tel. 212/594–8500). The old Gimbel's, a block south of Macy's, lives again as home to A&S Plaza, whose nine floors are anchored by Abraham & Straus, well established in the outer boroughs.

Barneys New York (106 7th Ave. at 17th St., tel. 212/929–9000). Founded by Barney Pressman as a discount outlet for men's clothing some 60 years ago, Barneys is now the place to see what's hot. The still-extensive selection of menswear ranges from made-to-measure and European and American couture to mass-market natural-shouldered suits; the women's store, in an adjacent group of brownstones, is a showcase of current women's fashion. The Chelsea Passage area can be counted on for handmade and antique linens, cachepots, and distinctive accessories for the home.

Bergdorf Goodman (754 5th Ave. at 57th St., tel. 212/753–7300). Good taste reigns in an elegant and understated setting. The Home Department is room after exquisite room of wonderful linens, tabletop items, and gifts. The expanding men's store is soon to move across the street to the premises once occupied by the giant F.A.O. Schwarz toy store.

Bloomingdale's (1000 3rd Ave. at 59th St., tel. 212/355–5900). Its main floor is a stupefying maze of mirrors, black walls, and low ceilings; in the rest of the store, the layout is chaotic, the racks are overfull, the help is overworked, and the departments are constantly being moved around. Still, selections are dazzling at all but the lowest end of the price spectrum, and the markdowns on top-of-the-line designer goods are extremely rewarding. Exotic special promotions regularly fill the store with the manufactured items and handicrafts of a single country or region.

Henri Bendel (10 W. 57th St., tel. 212/247–1100). Though under new ownership, Bendel's is still known for its savvy buying, stylish displays, and sophisticated first floor full of little boutiques—most notably the Street of Shops and the Gilded Cage.

Lord & Taylor (424 5th Ave., between 38th and 39th Sts., tel. 212/391–3344). This store can be relied upon for the wearable, the fashionable, and the classic in clothes and accessories for women. It's refined, well-stocked, never overwhelming—and a favorite among many busy New York women.

Macy's (Herald Sq., Broadway at 34th St., tel. 212/695–4400). No less than a miracle on 34th Street, Macy's main store is the largest retail store in America and the biggest on earth. Over the past 15 years, it has grown chic enough to rival Bloomingdale's in the style department, but its main floor is reassuringly traditional, with beige travertine columns and escalators with wide oak grooves. The latest trends are represented in almost every area the store covers. The several shoe departments, for instance, offer everything from your basic fake suede Life Stride–brand pumps to Joan & David and Ralph Lauren. Estate Jewelry, on the mezzanine, offers an excellent selection of fine antique pieces. And for cooking gear and housewares, the Cellar nearly outdoes Zabar's, with which it has an annual year-end caviar price war.

Saks Fifth Avenue (611 5th Ave., between 50th and 51st Sts., tel. 212/753–4000). This wonderful store still embodies the spirit of service and style with which it opened in 1926. Saks believes in good manners, the ceremonies of life, and dressing for the part; the selection for men, women, and children—now doubled by recent expansion—reflects this quality.

Specialty Shops

Antiques Antiquing is fine sport in Manhattan, and goods run the gamut from rarefied museum-quality to wacky, way-out, and eminently affordable. Premier shopping areas are on Madison Avenue north of 57th Street, and on 57th Street east of Fifth Avenue. Around 11th and 12th streets, between University Place and Broadway, a tantalizing array of settees and tables, bedsteads and rocking chairs, overflow onto the sidewalks in front of wholesalers with "To The Trade" signs on their doors; however, a card from your hometown architect or decorator may be all you need to get inside. Saturdays are the best time to find most dealers open.

Many small dealers cluster in two antiques "malls":

Manhattan Art & Antiques Center (1050 2nd Ave., between 55th and 56th Sts., tel. 212/355–4400). More than 100 dealers stocking everything from paisley and Judaica to satsuma, scientifica, and samovars jumble the three floors here. The level of quality is not, as a rule, up to that of Madison Avenue, but then neither are the prices.
Place des Antiquaires (125 E. 57th St., tel. 212/758–2900). From its 30-foot-high marble-paved entrance to its glittering glass-walled shops, this is a lavish place. Its dealers offer such high-end goods as 17th-century tapestries, export porcelain, European works of art, American folk art, and opulent Chinese textiles.

American and **America Hurrah** (766 Madison Ave., between 65th and 66th
English Sts., 3rd floor, tel. 212/535–1930). Superb American patchwork quilts and other Americana can be found here.
David A. Schorsch (30 E. 76th St., No. 11A, tel. 212/439–6100). New York's Shaker specialist, Schorsch sees customers by appointment only.
Florian Papp (962 Madison Ave., between 75th and 76th Sts. tel. 212/288–6770). This store has an unassailed reputation among knowledgeable collectors.
Hirschl & Adler Folk (851 Madison Ave., between 70th and 71st Sts., tel. 212/988–3655). This relatively new branch of the well-known Hirschl & Adler Modern gallery, at the same address, is devoted to the best in Americana.
Hyde Park Antiques (836 Broadway, between 12th and 13th Sts., tel. 212/477–0033). This store features English furniture and accessories, particularly William and Mary through Regency periods.
Israel Sack (15 E. 57th St., tel. 212/753–6562). This is widely considered one of the very best places in the country for 18th-century American furniture.
Leigh Keno American Furniture (19 E. 74th St., 1st floor, tel. 212/734–2381). Before he was 30, Leigh Keno set a new auction record in the American antiques field by paying $2.75 million

for a hairy-paw-foot Philadelphia wing chair. He has a good eye and an interesting inventory, including some more-affordable pieces.

Steve Miller American Folk Art (17 E. 96th St., tel. 212/348–5219). This gallery is run by one of the country's premier folk art dealers, the author of *The Art of the Weathervane.*

Thomas K. Woodard (835 Madison Ave., between 69th and 70th Sts., 2nd floor, tel. 212/794–9404). Americana and antique quilts are among the specialties of this prestigious dealer.

Eclectic **Elliott Galleries** (155 E. 79th St., tel. 212/861–2222). Furniture and large accessories are upstairs; reproduction furniture—at lesser prices—below.

Newel Art Galleries (425 E. 53rd St., tel. 212/758–1970). Located in the heart of the East Side's interior design district, this gallery has a huge collection from all periods.

European **Artisan Antiques** (81 University Pl. at 11th St., tel. 212/751–5214). Art Deco chandeliers, lamps, sconces, and other lighting fixtures from France are featured in merry profusion.

Barry Friedman (1117 Madison Ave., between 83rd and 84th Sts., tel. 212/794–8950). Wiener Werkstatte, Baujaus, De Stijl, Russian Constructivist, and European avant-gardists are the specialties here.

DeLorenzo (958 Madison Ave., between 75th and 76th Sts., tel. 212/249–7575). Come here to explore the sinuous curves, strongly articulated shapes, and highly polished surfaces of French Art Deco furniture and accessories at their best.

Didier Aaron (32 E. 67th St., tel. 212/988–5248). This highly esteemed gallery specializes in superb 18th- and 19th-century furniture and paintings.

Leo Kaplan Ltd. (967 Madison Ave., between 75th and 76th Sts., tel. 212/249–6766). The impeccable items here include Art Nouveau glass, pottery, and porcelain from 18th-century England, stunning antique and modern paperweights, and Russian artworks, including creations by Fabergé.

Pierre Deux Antiques (367 Bleecker St., tel. 212/243–7740). The company that brought French provincial to America still offers an excellent selection.

Malmaison Antiques (253 E. 74th St., tel. 212/288–7569). This gallery has the country's largest selection of Empire furniture and decorative arts.

Stair & Company (942 Madison Ave., between 74th and 75th Sts., tel. 212/517–4400). Fine 18th- and 19th-century English mahogany is displayed in handsome period rooms.

Fun Stuff **Back Pages Antiques** (125 Greene St., tel. 212/460–5998). Here's the spot to visit if you want an antique juke box or slot machine.

Darrow's Fun Antiques (309 E. 61st St., tel. 212/838–0730). The first of the city's nostalgia shops, the store is full of whimsy.

Apothecary and Fragrance Shops **Caswell-Massey** (48th St. and Lexington Ave., tel. 212/755–2254). The original store displays its fragrant toiletries in polished old cases; branches are in the World Financial Center and South Street Seaport.

Essential Products Company (90 Water St., tel. 212/344–4288). This company, established in 1895, sells knock-offs of famous fragrances at a fraction of the original price tags.

Floris (703 Madison Ave., between 62nd and 63rd Sts., tel. 212/935–9100). Floral English toiletries beloved of such beauties as

Cher, Sophia Loren, and Catherine Deneuve fill this re-creation of the cozy London original.

Art Galleries Long a capital of the American art world, New York has profited from the presence of many rich collectors, and its galleries form a rank of minimuseums well worth visiting (*see* also Auctions, below).

Aberbach Fine Art (980 Madison Ave., between 76th and 77th Sts., tel. 212/988–1100). Exhibits here include paintings and sculptures by various modern and contemporary artists.

André Emmerich Gallery (41 E. 57th St., tel. 212/752–0124). Located in the art deco Fuller Building, this gallery displays major works by major modern artists.

Art in General (79 Walker St., tel. 212/219–0473). This gallery offers art in a wide variety of mediums (including painting, sculpture, and photography), by emerging and contemporary artists.

A Clean, Well-Lighted Place (363 Bleecker St., tel. 212/255–3656). Prints by well-known artists, including Sean Scully, Susan Rothenberg, Robert Motherwell, and David Hockney, are displayed here.

Coe Kerr (49 E. 82nd St., tel. 212/628–1340). The collection here spans 19th- and 20th-century American paintings.

Fred Dorfman, Inc. (123 Watts St., tel. 212/966–4611). This gallery has a reputation for being a place where dealers and collectors go to discover new pieces. You'll find paintings and graphics by Keith Haring, Roy Lichtenstein, Andy Warhol, and Mark Kostabi.

Gagosian (980 Madison Ave., tel. 212/744–2313). Works on display are by such artists as Richard Serra, Willem DeKooning, Jasper Johns, Frank Stella, and Andy Warhol.

Gallery 121 (121 Spring St., tel. 212/925–4331). Featured are paintings, graphics, and sculptures by such artists as Erté, Marc Chagall, Salvador Dali, Keith Haring, Joan Miró, Robert Motherwell, and Andy Warhol.

Isselbacher (41 E. 78th St., tel. 212/472–1766). This gallery offers prints by late-19th- and 20th-century masters such as Lautrec, Matisse, Chagall, Miró, Picasso, and Munch.

Multiple Impressions (128 Spring St., tel. 212/925–1313). Twentieth-century American, European, and South American paintings and prints are offered here at reasonable prices.

O. K. Harris (383 W. Broadway, tel. 212/431–3600). The oldest gallery in SoHo, opened in 1969, O. K. Harris showcases paintings, sculpture, and photography by contemporary artists.

Pace Gallery (32 E. 57th St., tel. 212/421–3292). This gallery features such well-known modern and contemporary artists as Picasso, Calder, and Schnabel.

Paula Cooper (155 Wooster St., tel. 212/674–0766). Exhibits include contemporary paintings and sculpture.

SoHo Photo (15 White St., tel. 212/226–8571). In the heart of TriBeCa, this gallery features exhibitions of various photographers' work.

Wally Findlay Gallery (17 E. 57th St., tel. 212/421–5390). The specialty here is 20th-century art.

Books With so many of the country's publishing houses, magazines, and writers based here, there is an abundance of book shops, small and large. You can still find books in New York that you can't buy in many smaller cities, where big chains dictate what is read.

Barnes & Noble (105 5th Ave. at 18th St., tel. 212/807–0099). This local chain's main store is the world's largest bookstore, with some 3 million books in stock.

Biography Bookshop (400 Bleecker St., tel. 212/807–8655). Diaries, letters, and other biographical and autobiographical material from small and large publishers worldwide fill this tidy, well-organized store.

Books & Company (939 Madison Ave., between 74th and 75th Sts., tel. 212/737–1450). A comfy leather sofa invites lingering here.

Coliseum Books (1775 Broadway at 57th St., tel. 212/757–8381). This supermarket of a bookstore has a huge, quirky selection of remainders, best-sellers, and scholarly works. Its late hours are a plus.

Doubleday Book Shop (724 5th Ave. between 56th and 57th Sts., tel. 212/397–0550, and other locations). Kids will like the glass elevator at the main branch.

Endicott Booksellers (450 Columbus Ave., between 81st and 82nd Sts., tel. 212/787–6300). This intelligent, wood-paneled bookstore features evening readings.

Gotham Book Mart (41 W. 47th St., tel. 212/719–4448). The late Frances Steloff opened this store years ago with just $200 in her pocket, half of it on loan. But she helped launch D. H. Lawrence and Henry Miller and is now legendary among bibliophiles all over the English-speaking world, as is her bookstore, an oasis for those who truly love to read. Solid fiction and nonfiction are emphasized in the collection of nearly a quarter of a million books and 50,000 magazines. Though organization may seem haphazard, the knowledgeable staff can help you find what you want.

Irish Books & Graphics (90 West Broadway, tel. 212/962–4237). Here you'll find the country's widest selection of books about Ireland, both current and out-of-print titles.

Librairie de France/Libraria Hispanica (610 5th Ave., in Rockefeller Ct., tel. 212/581–8810; 115 5th Ave. at 19th St., tel. 212/673–7400). These huge collections of foreign-language books, periodicals, and records are among the country's largest.

Madison Avenue Bookshop (833 Madison Ave., between 69th and 70th Sts., tel. 212/535–6130). Serious stuff is sold here in pleasant surroundings.

Rizzoli (31 W. 57th St., tel. 212/759–2424; 454 West Broadway, tel. 212/674–1616; World Financial Center, tel. 212/385–1400). An elegant marble entrance, oak paneling, chandeliers, and classical music accompany a stock of records and books on art, architecture, dance, design, foreign language, and travel uptown; the selection downtown, which compares favorably, comes without the fin-de-siècle frills.

Shakespeare & Company (2259 Broadway at 81st St., tel. 212/580–7800). The stock here represents what's happening in publishing today in just about every field. Late hours are a plus.

Children's Books **Books of Wonder** (464 Hudson St., tel. 212/645–8006; 132 7th Ave. at 18th St., tel. 212/989–3270). This store offers an excellent stock of children's books for all reading levels. Oziana is a specialty, and the 18th Street branch offers antique books as well as new publications.

Eeyore's Books for Children (2212 Broadway, between 78th and 79th Sts., tel. 212/362–0634; 25 E. 83rd St., tel. 212/988–3404). The large, shrewd selection here should delight any young reader.

Maps **Hagstrom Map and Travel Center** (57 W. 43rd St., tel. 212/398–1222). This may be the ultimate map store.
Rand McNally Map & Travel (150 E. 52nd St., tel. 212/758–7488). The excellent selection covers countries and major cities around the world.

Music **Joseph Patelson Music House** (160 W. 56th St., tel. 212/582–5840). A huge collection of scores has long made this the heart of the music lover's New York.

Mystery and Suspense Whodunits are the specialty at: **Foul Play** (108th Ave., between 12th and Bleecker Sts., tel. 212/675–5115; 1465 2nd Ave., between 76th and 77th Sts., tel. 212/517–3222); **Murder Ink** (271 W. 87th St., tel. 212/362–8905); and **Mysterious Bookshop** (129 W. 56th St., tel. 212/765–0900).

Rare and Used Books **Argosy Bookstore** (116 E. 59th St., tel. 212/753–4455). This sedate nook keeps a scholarly stock of books and autographs.
J. N. Bartfield Books (30 W. 57th St., tel. 212/245–8890). This legend in the field offers old and antiquarian books distinguished by binding, author, edition, or content.
Pageant Print and Book Shop (109 E. 9th St., tel. 212/674–5296). Michael Caine browsed in this relic of old New York in Woody Allen's *Hannah and Her Sisters*.
Strand (828 Broadway at 12th St., tel. 212/473–1452). Eight miles of shelves house more than two million books at this biggest of Manhattan's used-book stores. Among them are antiquarian books, fiction, nonfiction, how-to, history, and all kinds of other books—remainders and reviewer's copies, as well as secondhand titles.

Travel Books **Complete Traveller Bookstore** (199 Madison Ave. at 35th St., tel. 212/685–9007). Old and new titles are sold here.
Traveller's Bookstore (22 W. 52nd St., tel. 212/664–0995). The stock includes essays and novels, as well as maps and guides.

Children's Clothing **Bébé Thompson** (98 Thompson St., tel. 212/925–1122). Downtown style is evident here: plenty of black and white, batiks, and jungle prints among the embroidered treasures.
Cerutti (807 Madison Ave., between 67th and 68th Sts., tel. 212/737–7540). This is where Nanny takes her Little Princess, and Yoko Ono shopped for her son Sean Lennon.
Citykids (130 7th Ave., between 17th and 18th Sts., tel. 212/620–0120). This busy store carries colorful, fun clothing and accessories. Don't miss the hand-painted T-shirts and sweatshirts with New York themes.
Greenstones & Cie (442 Columbus Ave., between 81st and 82nd Sts., tel. 212/580–4322). Catering to junior Yuppies, this store offers some handsome clothes, particularly sweaters.
Morris Brothers (2322 Broadway, between 84th and 85th Sts., tel. 212/724–9000). Here is one children's clothing store that takes into account the reality of life with kids.
Once Upon A Time (171 E. 92nd St., tel. 212/831–7619). This resale shop deals in quality kids' clothes.
Second Act Children's Wear (1046 Madison Ave. at 80th St., tel. 212/988–2440). Top-quality clothes are resold here, along with games, toys, and books.
Wicker Garden and Wicker Garden's Baby (1318 and 1327 Madison Ave., near 93rd St., tel. 212/410–7000). Top-of-the-line pretties for boys, girls, babies, and their rooms are sold here.

Crystal Three of the greatest sources are: **Baccarat** (625 Madison Ave., between 58th and 59th Sts., tel. 212/826–4100); **Hoya Crystal**

Gallery (450 Park Ave., between 56th and 57th Sts., tel. 212/223–6335); and **Steuben** (715 5th Ave. at 56th St., tel. 212/752–1441).

Food For food lovers visiting New York, there are two major pastimes: eating in the restaurants, and prowling the scores of food specialty shops. The latter are a feast for all five senses—and a good deal of the food can travel home with you.

Chocolate and Candy **Elk Candy Company** (240 E. 86th St., tel. 212/650–1177). This is a marzipan fantasy and a chocoholic's sweet dream.

Godiva Chocolatier (701 5th Ave., between 54th and 55th Sts., tel. 212/593–2845; 560 Lexington Ave. at 50th St., tel. 212/980–9810; 85 Broad St., tel. 212/514–6240). This famous maker features cleverly molded chocolates—and oh, those embossed gold boxes!

Li-Lac Chocolates (120 Christopher St., tel. 212/242–7374). This wonderful, unpretentious sliver of a store feeds the Village's sweet tooth.

Neuchatel Chocolates (2 W. 59th St., in the Plaza Hotel, tel. 212/751–7742; 55 E. 52nd St., in Park Avenue Plaza between Park and Madison, tel. 212/759–1388). Velvety chocolates come in five dozen varieties here—all made in New York to approximate the Swiss chocolates.

Teuscher Chocolates (620 5th Ave., in Rockefeller Ct., tel. 212/246–4416; 25 E. 61st St., tel. 212/751–8482). Fabulous chocolates made in Switzerland are flown in weekly for sale in these jewel-box shops, newly decorated each season.

Caviar **Macy's** and **Zabar's** (*see* below) feature good deals on a variety of caviars; specialty stores include **Caviarteria** (29 E. 60th St., tel. 212/759–7410) and **Petrossian** (182 W. 58th St., tel. 212/245–2217).

Coffee **Empire Coffee and Tea Company** (592 9th Ave., between 42nd and 43rd Sts., tel. 212/586–1717). The selection here includes 75 different beans.

McNulty's Tea & Coffee Company (109 Christopher St., tel. 212/242–5351). Antique wood paneling says "Old New York"; the barrels of beans say "Timor," "Java," or "New Guinea."

Porto Rico Importing Company (201 Bleecker St., tel. 212/477–5421). This dark, old-fashioned, and highly aromatic store has been a local coffee source since 1907.

Gourmet Markets **Balducci's** (424 6th Ave. at 9th St., tel. 212/673–2600). In this former mom-and-pop food shop, now one of the city's finest food stores, the displays are like art: mounds of baby carrots nudging scallions alongside frilly lettuce leaves and feathery dill. You'll also find some of the city's best meats, fish, cheeses, chocolates, imported cookies, exotic pastas, vinegars, oils, crackers, and prepared foods.

Dean & DeLuca (560 Broadway at Prince St., tel. 212/431–1691). This huge SoHo trendsetter, newly renovated to bright-white splendor, has an encyclopedic selection, from the austere cheese counter to the shelves of crackers and the display cases of prepared foods.

Kam-Man (200 Canal St., tel. 212/571–0330). The city's premier Chinese market, Kam-Man is stuffed with bizarre exotic foods. The staccato sound of Chinese and the mysterious smells make a stop here like an instant trip to Asia.

Zabar's (2245 Broadway at 80th St., tel. 212/787–2000). Visit here not so much to snap up everything in sight—Zabar's now sells by mail order, too—as to enjoy the atmosphere of one of New York's favorite feeding troughs. As you're exploring the possibilities among the jams and jellies from a dozen makers and several countries, or checking out the barrels of coffees or the wonderful array of teas, keep an eye peeled for celebrities —perhaps the first violinist with the New York Philharmonic or the villainess on a long-running soap opera. Dried herbs and spices, dried fruits, chocolates, and assorted bottled foods are downstairs, along with a fragrant jumble of fresh breads and the cheese, meat, and smoked-fish counters. Upstairs is one of New York's largest selections of kitchenware.

Wine   **Acker Merrall & Condit** (160 W. 72nd St., tel. 212/787–1700). Known for its selection of red burgundies, this store has knowledgeable, helpful personnel.

Garnet Liquors (929 Lexington Ave., between 68th and 69th Sts., tel. 212/772–3211). The excellent selection here includes champagne at prices that one wine writer called "almost charitable."

Morrell & Company (535 Madison Ave., near 54th St., tel. 212/688–9370). Peter Morrell is a well-regarded and very colorful figure in the wine business.

Sherry Lehmann (679 Madison Ave., between 61st and 62nd Sts., tel. 212/838–7500). This large dealer is a New York institution.

Sokolin (178 Madison Ave., between 33rd and 34th Sts., tel. 212/532–5893). Knowledgeable oenophiles shop here.

Goldstar (103–05 Queens Blvd., Forest Hills, Queens, tel. 718/459–0200). This may be the best spot in the country for Italian wine.

Fun and Fantasy   These are stores that adults and kids can enjoy together— stores by adults, for adults, but with a sense of humor and whimsy.

Compleat Strategist (11 E. 33rd St., tel. 212/685–3880; 320 W. 57th St., tel. 212/582–1272). All kinds of strategy games are supplied for the serious enthusiast.

Game Show (474 6th Ave., between 11th and 12th Sts., tel. 212/633–6328). The mix here includes board games, box games, card games, and computer games.

Louis Tannen's (6 W. 32nd St., 4th floor, tel. 212/239–8383). You'll find sword chests, dove-a-matics, magic wands, and crystal balls, not to mention the all-important top hats with rabbits, at this six-decades-old magicians' supply house.

Mythology (370 Columbus Ave., between 77th and 78th Sts., tel. 212/874–0774). This store stocks nearly everything with a sense of the fanciful, from robots to antique toys.

Star Magic (743 Broadway, between 8th St. and Astor Pl., tel. 212/228–7770; 275 Amsterdam Ave. at 73rd St., tel. 212/769–2020). Astronomy meets the New Age in a clutter of crystals, star charts, and planet mobiles.

Think Big! (390 West Broadway, between Broome and Spring Sts., tel. 212/925–7300). Huge replicas of various ordinary objects stock this amusing store.

The Last Wound-Up (290 Columbus Ave., between 73rd and 74th Sts., tel. 212/787–3388; 889 Broadway at 19th St., tel. 212/529–4197). "If it winds up, it winds up here" is one motto of this store. The other is "Don't postpone joy."

Gizmos   The high-end gadgets sold at these stores are often more fascinating than practical, but they make for fun gifts.

Hammacher Schlemmer (147 E. 57th St., tel. 212/421–9000). The store that offered America the first pop-up toaster, the first automatic steam iron, and the first telephone answering machine and microwave oven still ferrets out the outrageous, the unusual, and the best-of-kind.

Sharper Image (Pier 17, South Street Seaport, tel. 212/693–0477; 4 W. 57th St., tel. 212/265–2550). This retail outlet of the catalogue company stocks gifts for the pampered executive who has everything.

Home Decor   **Aris Mixon & Company** (381 Amsterdam Ave., between 78th and 79th Sts., tel. 212/724–6904). The intrigue here is in the mix of newly manufactured, handmade, and antique decorative objects.

Charlotte Moss & Company (1027 Lexington Ave., between 73rd and 74th Sts., tel. 212/772–3320). Within what looks like a vine-wrapped, chintz-cozy English country house, you'll find country-house-style treasures.

Clodagh, The Center for American Design (122 St. Marks Pl., tel. 212/505–1774). Come here for a glove-shaped vase of rubber and steel, or some other whatnot on the cutting edge.

Conran's (2–8 Astor Pl., tel. 212/505–1515; 160 E. 54th St., tel. 212/371–2225; 2248 Broadway at 81st St., tel. 212/873–9250). This outpost of the British Habitat store features components of a stylish yet not-too-expensive life.

D. F. Sanders (386 West Broadway, tel. 212/925–9040; 952 Madison Ave., between 75th and 76th Sts., tel. 212/879–6161). Here's the place to buy trendy postmoderns destined to be classics.

Jenny B. Goode (1194 Lexington Ave., between 80th and 81st Sts., tel. 212/794–2492; 11 E. 10th St., tel. 212/505–7666). These upscale gift shops highlight a charming collection of French china.

Pottery Barn (117 E. 59th St., tel. 212/753–5424; 2109 Broadway, between 73rd and 74th Sts., tel. 212/595–5573; 250 W. 57th St., tel. 212/315–1855; 231 10th Ave., between 23rd and 24th Sts., tel. 212/206–8118; and other locations). The emphasis here is on setting the oh-so-chic table. Overstocks are discounted at Tenth Avenue.

Wolfman-Gold & Good Company (116 Greene St., tel. 212/431–1888). This is a major New York trendsetter—and really wonderful.

Zona (97 Greene St., tel. 212/925–6750). SoHo's bastion of the Southwestern look offers solieri bells, earth-toned textiles, and terra cottas.

Jewelry, Watches,   Most of the world's premier jewelers have retail outlets in New
and Silver   York, and the nation's jewelry wholesale center is on 47th Street.

A La Vieille Russie (781 5th Ave., between 59th and 60th Sts., tel. 212/752–1727). Stop here to behold, up close, bibelots by Fabergé and others, encrusted with jewels or exquisitely enameled.

Buccellati (725 5th Ave., between 56th and 57th Sts., tel. 212/308–5533). The oversize Italian jewelry here makes a statement.

Bulgari (730 5th Ave. at 57th St., and 2 E. 61st St., in the Pierre Hotel, tel. 212/486–0086). The expertly crafted jewelry here has an understated, tailored look.

Cartier (2 E. 52nd St., tel. 212/753–0111). Simple but superb pieces are displayed in the former mansion of the late yachtsman and society king Morton F. Plant.

Fortunoff (681 5th Ave., between 53rd and 54th Sts., tel. 212/758–6660). Good prices on gold and silver jewelry, flatware, and hollowware draw crowds to this large store.

Jean's Silversmiths (16 W. 45th St., tel. 212/575–0723). Where to replace the butter knife missing from your great-aunt's set? Try this dusty, crowded shop.

James Robinson (15 E. 57th St., tel. 212/752–6166). This family-owned business features wonderful new and antique silver, fine estate jewelry, and table accessories.

Tiffany & Co. (727 5th Ave., at 57th St., tel. 212/755–8000). A shiny turquoise box from this venerable New York jeweler announces the contents as something very special. Along with the $50,000 platinum-and-diamond bracelets, there is a great deal that's affordable on a whim.

Van Cleef & Arpels (744 5th Ave. at 57th St., tel. 212/644–9500). The jewelry here is sheer perfection.

Harry Winston (718 5th Ave. at 56th St., tel. 212/245–2000). The moneyed clientele here appreciates this store's oversized stones and impeccable quality.

Costume Jewelry Fabulously faux wares can be found at **Ciro** (711 5th Ave. at 56th St., tel. 212/752–0441, and other locations); **Kenneth Jay Lane** (725 5th Ave., in Trump Tower, tel. 212/751–6166); **Mishon Mishon** (899 Madison Ave., between 72nd and 73rd Sts., tel. 212/288–7599); and **Ylang Ylang** (806 Madison Ave., between 67th and 68th Sts., tel. 212/879–7028; 324 Columbus Ave., between 75th and 76th Sts., tel. 212/496–0319; and 4 W. 57th St., tel. 212/247–3598).

Luggage and **Beltrami** (711 5th Ave., between 55th and 56th Sts., tel. 212/
Leather Goods 838–4101). Italian leathers are this store's stock in trade.

Bottega Veneta (635 Madison Ave., between 59th and 60th Sts., tel. 212/319–0303). The superb goods here are for people who know real quality.

Crouch & Fitzgerald (400 Madison Ave. at 48th St., tel. 212/755–5888). Since 1839, this store has offered a terrific selection in hard- and soft-sided luggage, plus handbags.

Fine & Klein (119 Orchard St., tel. 212/674–6720). Fabulous handbags are discounted here.

Lederer (613 Madison Ave. at 58th St., tel. 212/355–5515). The excellent selection here includes exotic skins.

North Beach Leather (772 Madison Ave. at 66th St., tel. 212/772–0707). The specialty here is high-fashion leather clothing in many colors.

T. Anthony (480 Park Ave. at 58th St., tel. 212/750–9797). This store's hard- and soft-sided luggage of coated fabric with leather trim has brass fasteners that look like precision machines.

Menswear Because New York is home to investment bankers, corporate lawyers, international businessmen, movie moguls, architects, and writers, its menswear purveyors have to offer a number of looks. In addition to the big stores—**Barneys, Saks, Bloomingdale's, Macy's,** and **Bergdorf's**—a number of specialists are important stops.

Bijan (699 5th Ave., between 54th and 55th Sts., tel. 212/758–7500). The many-paned front window is one of the landmarks of Fifth Avenue; the by-appointment-only policy appeals to a rarefied clientele.

Brooks Brothers (346 Madison Ave. at 44th St., tel. 212/682–

8800). The bare travertine underfoot, high ceilings overhead, and undecorated showcases on the ground floor suggest a New England spareness at this institution in American menswear. Styles are conservative, and tailoring standards are extremely high—as they have always been.

Frank Stella Ltd. (440 Columbus Ave. at 81st St., tel. 212/877–5566; 1382 6th Ave., between 56th and 57th Sts., tel. 212/757–2295). Classic clothing with subtle variations is offered here.

F. R. Tripler (366 Madison Ave. at 46th St., tel. 212/922–1090). Oxxford, Hickey Freeman, and other top-notch manufacturers are represented here. The styles are a bit less conservative than at Brooks Brothers.

J. Press (17 E. 44th St., tel. 212/687–7642). This store emphasizes the oxford-cloth shirt, the natural-shoulder suit, the madras-patch Bermuda shorts, and the amusing club tie.

Louis, Boston (131 E. 57th St., tel. 212/308–6100). Luxurious conservative fashions from this estimable New England clothier have garbed four generations of Harvard men.

Mano à Mano (580 Broadway, between Houston and Prince Sts., tel. 212/219–9602). The keynote here is SoHo chic.

Paul Smith (108 5th Ave. at 16th St., tel. 212/627–9770). Dark mahogany Victorian cases display downtown styles.

Paul Stuart (Madison Ave. at 45th St., tel. 212/682–0320). In this celebrated if pricey New York menswear store, the fabrics are subtle and interesting, the tailoring is superb, and the look is traditional but not stodgy.

Saint Laurie, Ltd. (897 Broadway, between 19th and 20th Sts., tel. 212/473–0100). This family-owned business sells suits manufactured on the premises in styles ranging from the oxy to the Italianate in lovely fabrics. Prices are lower than for comparable garments elsewhere, but still not cheap.

Wallachs (555 5th Ave. at 46th St., tel. 212/687–0106). Here you'll find good service and a sound collection of reasonably priced classics.

Discounts New York men looking for bargains rely on **BFO** (149 5th Ave. at 21st St., 6th floor, tel. 212/254–0059); **Eisenberg and Eisenberg** (85 5th Ave. at 16th St., tel. 212/627–1290); **Harry Rothman** (200 Park Ave. S at 17th St., tel. 212/777–7400); **Moe Ginsburg** (162 5th Ave. at 21st St., tel. 212/242–3482); and **Syms** (42 Trinity Pl., tel. 212/797–1199), which doesn't accept credit cards.

Men's Shoes **Church English Shoes** (428 Madison Ave. at 49th St., tel. 212/755–4313). This store has been selling beautifully made English shoes since 1873; the fitters are especially knowledgeable.

To Boot (520 Madison Ave., between 53rd and 54th Sts., tel. 212/644–5661; 256 Columbus Ave., between 71st and 72nd Sts., tel. 212/724–8249). Here you'll find stylish shoes and boots for a more fashionable business look.

Needlecraft **Erica Wilson** (717 Madison Ave., between 63rd and 64th Sts., 2nd floor, tel. 212/832–7290). The eponymous British-born needlepoint authority is a top resource.

New York Yarn Center (29 W. 35th St., 2nd floor, tel. 212/594–9770). There's a huge selection of yarns here to suit many purposes.

Pamela Duval (833 Lexington Ave., between 63rd and 64th Sts., tel. 212/751–2126). Look for the needlepoint canvases with funny quotations ("Toto, this can't be Kansas!").

Paper, Greeting Cards, Stationery

Dempsey & Carroll (110 E. 57th St., tel. 212/486–7508). Supplying New York's high society for a century, this firm is always correct, but seldom straitlaced.

Ffolio 72 (33 E. 68th St., tel. 212/628–0897). Bold colors and striking graphic designs are this store's hallmark.

Kate's Paperie (8 W. 13th St., tel. 212/633–0570). This wonderful spot features fabulous wrapping papers, some handmade; bound blank books; and more.

Untitled (159 Prince St., tel. 212/982–2088). The stock here includes thousands of tasteful greeting cards and postcards.

Performing Arts Memorabilia

Programs, books, posters, videos, and autographs are terrific New York souvenirs. Try:

The Ballet Shop (1887 Broadway, between 62nd and 63rd Sts., tel. 212/581–7990). This balletomane's delight near Lincoln Center showcases dance ephemera and artifacts.

Drama Book Shop (723 7th Ave., between 48th and 49th Sts., tel. 212/944–0595). The comprehensive stock here includes scripts, scores, and libretti.

Memory Shop (109 E. 12th St., tel. 212/473–2404). Movie stills and posters by the million are on sale here.

Motion Picture Arts Gallery (133 E. 58th St., 10th floor, tel. 212/223–1009). Vintage posters enchant collectors here.

Movie Star News (134 W. 18th St., tel. 212/620–8160). The film memorabilia emphasizes Hollywood glamour.

One Shubert Alley (Shubert Alley, between 44th and 45th Sts. west of Broadway, tel. 212/944–4133). Show-biz souvenirs reign at this Theater District shop.

Richard Stoddard (18 E. 16th St., Room 202, tel. 212/645–9576). This veteran dealer offers out-of-print books, back issues of magazines, old programs, and other printed matter.

Theatrebooks (1600 Broadway, between 48th and 49th Sts., Room 1009, tel. 212/757–2834). This is a good place to schmooze and browse. Twofers are usually available, too.

Triton Gallery (323 W. 45th, between 8th and 9th Aves., tel. 212/765–2472). Theatricals!

Posters

Posteramerica (138 W. 18th St., tel. 212/206–0499). Victorian to 20th-century posters are displayed in this renovated carriage house, the country's oldest store of its type.

Records

The city's best record stores match its music scene: diversified, esoteric, and very in-the-know. They also provide browsers with a window to New York's hipper subcultures.

Bleecker Bob's Golden Oldies (118 W. 3rd St., tel. 212/475–9677). The staff sells punk, new wave, progressive rock, reggae, and R&B until the wee hours.

Footlight Records (113 E. 12th St., tel. 212/533–1572). Stop here to browse through New York's largest selection of old musicals and movie soundtracks.

Gryphon Record Shop (251 W. 72nd St., 2nd floor, tel. 212/874–1588). *New York* magazine called this the city's best rare-record store, citing its 40,000 out-of-print and rare LPs.

House of Oldies (35 Carmine St., tel. 212/243–0500). The specialty here is records made between 1950 and the present—45s and 78s, as well as LPs; there are more than a million titles.

Jazz Record Center (135 W. 29th St., 12th floor, tel. 212/594–9880). Here is the city's only jazz-record specialist.

J&R Music World (23 Park Row, tel. 212/732–8600). This store offers a huge selection with good prices on major releases.

Midnight Records (263 W. 23rd St., tel. 212/675–2768). This rare rock specialist stocks obscure artists from the '50s on.

Tower Records (692 Broadway at 4th St., tel. 212/505–1500; 1965 Broadway at 66th St., tel. 212/799–2500). The founder's objective here—to offer every record in the world—has been complicated by the onslaught of CDs and tapes, but it does suggest the broad scope of selection in all three media. The scene is pure New York; at the Village branch, the black leather usually goes with pink, green, or tiger-striped hair in bizarre cuts; the Upper West Side outlet has good selection but less local color.

Souvenirs of New York City Ordinary Big Apple souvenirs can be found in and around all major established tourist attractions. More unusual items can be found at:

Accent New York (489 5th Ave., between 41st and 42nd Sts., tel. 212/599–3661). This store features every possible variation of the New York souvenir T-shirt, mug, key chain, etc.

Citybooks (61 Chambers St., tel. 212/669–8245). Come here for photo calendars, maps, books, seals, subway token tietacks and letter openers, traffic signs ("Don't Even Think of Parking Here"), Sanitation Department T-shirts, and even teddy bears wearing miniature versions of the above.

New York Bound Bookshop (50 Rockefeller Plaza, tel. 212/245–8503). Old or rare New York books and prints are the specialty in this delightfully knowledgeable store.

Think New York (875 7th Ave., between 55th and 56th Sts., tel. 212/957–8511). New York City stars on mugs, aprons, and even battery-powered LCD (liquid crystal display) lapel pins.

Toys Many toy companies are headquartered here, and the windows of the Toy Center at 23rd Street and Fifth Avenue display the latest thing, especially during February's Toy Week, when all the out-of-town buyers come to place orders for the Christmas season (*see also* Fun and Fantasy, above).

Enchanted Forest (85 Mercer St., tel. 212/925–6677). This fanciful shop has unique handmade toys, stuffed animals, and books.

F.A.O. Schwarz (767 5th Ave. at 58th St., tel. 212/644–9400). You will be hooked on this sprawling two-level children's store from the minute you walk through the door and one of the costumed staff members—a donkey, a clown, a cave woman, or a mad scientist—extends a welcome. In front of you is a wonderful mechanical clock with many dials and dingbats; beyond are all the stuffed animals in the world, dolls large and small, things to build with (including blocks by the pound), things to play dress-up with, computer things, games, toy cars (including a multi-thousand-dollar Ferrari), and much more.

Penny Whistle Toys (132 Spring St., tel. 212/925–2088; 448 Columbus Ave., between 81st and 82nd Sts., tel. 212/873–9090; 1283 Madison Ave., between 91st and 92nd Sts., tel. 212/369–3868). Meredith Brokaw, wife of newscaster Tom Brokaw, has developed an intriguing selection of quality toys here.

Toy Park (626 Columbus Ave., between 90th and 91st Sts., tel. 212/769–3880, 112 E. 86th St., tel. 212/427–6611). The store is large, the selection is right, and there are plenty of toys set out for kids to play with while you shop.

West Side Kids (498 Amsterdam Ave., at 84th St., tel. 212/496–7282). The shrewd selection here mixes educational toys with a grab bag of fun little playthings.

Dolls and Miniatures **Dollhouse Antics** (1343 Madison Ave. at 94th St., tel. 212/876–2288). This is a miniaturist's paradise, with infinitesimal accessories such as a small *New York Times*.

Trains and Models Railroad aficionados will be dazzled by the vast selections at: **America's Hobby Center** (146 W. 22nd St., tel. 212/675–8922); **Polk Hobby** (314 5th Ave., tel. 212/279–9034); **Red Caboose** (16 W. 45th St., 4th floor, tel. 212/575–0155); and **Train Shop** (23 W. 45th St., basement level, tel. 212/730–0409).

Umbrellas and Canes **Novak Stanley** (115 W. 30th St., Room 400, tel. 212/947–8466). The cane's the thing, and there are hundreds here.
Uncle Sam Umbrella (161 W. 57th St., tel. 212/247–7163). This is the city's best-known umbrella dealer, great for both basics and oddball stuff.

Women's Clothing The department stores' collections are always good: **Saks** for its designers; **Macy's** for its breadth; **Bloomingdale's** for its extremes; **Barneys** for its trendy chic; and **Lord & Taylor** for its classicism. The stores below, however, add another important dimension.

Trendsetters **Charivari** (2315 Broadway, between 83rd and 84th Sts., tel. 212/873–1424). Since Selma Weiser founded this store on the Upper West Side, she has made a name for herself internationally for her eagle eye on the up-and-coming and avant-garde. The branches, too, take a high-style, if pricey, approach: **Charivari Sport** (201 W. 79th St., tel. 212/799–8650); **Charivari Workshop** (441 Columbus Ave. at 81st St., tel. 212/496–8700); **Charivari 72** (257 Columbus Ave. at 72nd St., tel. 212/787–7272); and **Charivari 57** (18 W. 57th St., tel. 212/333–4040).
Parachute (121 Wooster St., tel. 212/925–8630; 309 Columbus Ave., between 74th and 75th Sts., tel. 212/799–1444). The SoHo styles here are what you need for your next club date.
Patricia Field (10 E. 8th St., tel. 212/254–1699). This store collects the essence of the downtown look.
La Rue des Rêves (139 Spring St., tel. 212/226–6736). Stylish clothing for stylish women who like either an elegant, understated look or Tina Turner styles.

Salons At these salons, members of New York's charity-ball set drop more on a single dress than most of us spend on a whole wardrobe for a year: **Martha** (475 Park Ave. at 58th St., tel. 212/753–1511; 725 5th Ave., in Trump Tower, tel. 212/826–8855); and **Sara Fredericks** (508 Park Ave., between 59th and 60th Sts., tel. 212/759–1254).

Designer Showcases **Betsey Johnson** (130 Thompson St., tel. 212/420–0169; 248 Columbus Ave., between 71st and 72nd Sts., tel. 212/362–3364). The look here is still hip.
Chanel (5 E. 57th St., tel. 212/355–5050). The classic designs here never go out of style.
Comme des Garçons (116 Wooster St., tel. 212/219–0660). A SoHo shop showcases this Japanese designer.
Emanuel Ungaro (803 Madison Ave., between 67th and 68th Sts., tel. 212/249–4090). The style here is body-conscious but it's never flashy.
Emporio Armani (110 5th Ave., between 16th and 17th Sts., tel. 212/727–3240). The Italian designer's casual line is featured.
Giorgio Armani (815 Madison Ave., between 68th and 69th Sts., tel. 212/988–9191). In this lofty blond-and-beige space with grand, arched windows and doors, Armani's high-end line looks oh-so-chic.

Givenchy (954 Madison Ave. at 75th St., tel. 212/772–1040). This designer is famous for timeless elegance.

Hermès (11 E. 57th St., tel. 212/751–3181). The hallmarks here are patterned scarves, the Grace Kelly bag, and horse-leg wraps.

Koos van den Akker (795 Madison Ave., between 67th and 68th Sts., tel. 212/249–5432). Collage meets couture in the home of the Dutch-born former Dior designer once known as the Rembrandt of ready-to-wear.

Missoni (836 Madison Ave. at 69th St., tel. 212/517–9339). This is a source for wonderfully textured knits, plus suits and sportswear.

Norma Kamali O.M.O. (11 W. 56th St., tel. 212/957–9797). The look here ranges from sweatshirts to evening gowns.

Polo/Ralph Lauren (867 Madison Ave. at 72nd St., tel. 212/606–2100). Lauren's flagship store is not only the ultimate expression of the Ralph Lauren way of life, but it's also one of New York's most distinctive shopping experiences, in a grand, carefully renovated turn-of-the-century town house.

Sonia Rykiel (792 Madison Ave., at 67th St., tel. 212/744–0880). Signature knits for day and evening pack the racks.

Valentino (825 Madison Ave., between 68th and 69th Sts., tel. 212/744–0200). The mix here is at once audacious and beautifully cut, with the best of France and Italy on its racks.

Yves St. Laurent Rive Gauche (855 Madison Ave., between 70th and 71st Sts., tel. 212/988–3821). The looks range from chic to classic for day and evening.

Classicists **Ann Taylor** (1293 Broadway at 34th St., in Herald Center, tel. 212/695–4474; 2017 Broadway, near 69th St., tel. 212/873–7344; 25 Fulton St., tel. 212/608–5600; 805 3rd Ave. at 50th St., tel. 212/308–5333; 3 E. 57th St., tel. 212/832–2010). These stores provide what the elegant young woman with a sense of style needs for work and play.

Burberry's (9 E. 57th St., tel. 212/371–5010). The look is classic, British, and conservative—and nobody does a better trench coat.

Romantics **Laura Ashley** (21 E. 57th St., tel. 212/752–7300; 398 Columbus Ave. at 79th St., tel. 212/496–5110; 4 Fulton St., tel. 212/809–3556). Old-fashioned English frocks abound at these appealing shops.

Victoria Falls (451 West Broadway, tel. 212/254–2433). The romantic clothes here are antique or made just yesterday.

Ethnic Looks **Putumayo** (857 Lexington Ave., between 64th and 65th Sts., tel. 212/734–3111; 339 Columbus Ave., between 76th and 77th Sts., tel. 212/595–3441; and 147 Spring St., tel. 212/966–4458). There's cool cotton clothing here, much of it crinkly and easy to pack.

Young and Hip **Canal Jean** (504 Broadway, between Spring and Broome Sts., tel. 212/226–1130). The look in this cavernous store is casual funk.

Fiorucci (125 E. 59th St., tel. 212/751–5638). This wild and whimsical Italian fashion house, high-tech by design, is the place to buy your rubber shoes, rhinestoned sneakers, and plastic dresses.

Reminiscence (74 5th Ave., between 13th and 14th Sts., tel. 212/243–2292). The theme is strictly '50s and '60s, in vintage and new clothing.

Trash and Vaudeville (4 St. Mark's Pl., tel. 212/777–1727). Black, white, and electric colors are the focus here.

Vintage **Harriet Love** (412 West Broadway, tel. 212/966–2280). This is the doyenne of the city's vintage clothing scene.
Screaming Mimi's (22 E. 4th St., tel. 212/677–6464). Old clothes go avant-garde here.

Lingerie Exquisite little things in silk and lace, both naughty and nice, are found at **Joovay** (436 West Broadway, tel. 212/431–6386); **Montenapoleone** (789 Madison Ave. at 67th St., tel. 212/535–2660); and **Victoria's Secret** (34 E. 57th St., tel. 212/758–5592).

Discount **Aaron's** (627 5th Ave., between 17th and 18th Sts., Brooklyn, tel. 718/768–5400). A half hour on the R train and a one-block walk access high-end clothing at a savings.
Bolton's (225 E. 57th St., tel. 212/755–2527; other locations). The styles won't stop traffic, but the basics are here at moderate prices.
Daffy's (111 5th Ave. at 18th St., tel. 212/529–4477). Cheap stuff is priced cheaper, and pricey stuff is marked way down.
Forman's (82 Orchard St., tel. 212/228–2500). This is an unexpectedly attractive longtime mainstay of the Lower East Side.
Loehmann's (236th St. and Broadway, tel. 212/543–6420). The flagship store of this premier off-price outlet is an institution among shopaholics.
Ms., Miss or Mrs. (462 7th Ave., between 35th and 36th Sts., 3rd fl., tel. 212/736–0557). This Garment Center fixture is known to canny shoppers for 30% to 60% discounts.
S&W (165 W. 26th St., tel. 212/924–6656). This complex of stores has good to great prices on coats, furs, lingerie, handbags, and accessories.

Women's Shoes
Designer Shoes **Charles Jourdan** (725 5th Ave., in Trump Tower, tel. 212/644–3830; 769 Madison Ave. at 66th St., tel. 212/628–0133). Distinctive shoes feature quirky heels and extravagant colors or patterns.
Maud Frizon (49 E. 57th St., tel. 212/980–1460). These extravagant styles come in outrageous shapes and sizzling colors.
Peter Fox (105 Thompson St., tel. 212/431–7426 and 431–6359; 378 Amsterdam Ave. at 77th St., tel. 212/874–6399). Here are looks that are outside the fashion mainstream; really fun.
Salvatore Ferragamo (717 5th Ave. at 56th St., tel. 212/759–3822). No stylistic gimmicks here, just beautiful shoemaking.
Susan Bennis Warren Edwards (440 Park Ave. at 56th St., tel. 212/755–4197). Here you'll find alligator, silk, satin, suede, canvas, and buttery-soft leather exquisitely worked.

Moderate Styles The shoes at these stores tend toward the classic, in a good range of colors and styles: **Ecco** (324 Columbus Ave., between 75th and 76th Sts., tel. 212/799–5229; 94 7th Ave., between 15th and 16th Sts., tel. 212/675–5180; 111 Thompson St., tel. 212/925–8010); **Galo** (825 Lexington Ave. at 63rd St., tel. 212/832–3922; 692 Madison Ave., between 62nd and 63rd Sts., tel. 212/688–6276); **Joan & David** (805 3rd Ave., between 49th and 50th Sts., tel. 212/486–6740); and **Maraolo** (782 Lexington Ave., between 60th and 61st Sts., tel. 212/832–8182).

Discount and Lower-Priced Shoes Discounters dot Reade Street between Church and West Broadway, including **Anbar** (93 Reade St., tel. 212/227–0253). Several Orchard Street stores discount uptown shoe styles; try **Lace-Up Shoes** (110 Orchard St., tel. 212/475–8040) for moderate discounts on very highly styled shoes.

Secondhand Shops

Thrift Shops   The affluent particle of New York donates castoffs to support charities funded by a dozen thrift shops. And oh, such castoffs! Often they're supplemented by closeouts from major New York department and specialty stores. Hours are limited, so call ahead.

Arthritis Foundation Thrift Shop (121 E. 77th St., tel. 212/772–8816).

Council Thrift Shop (767 9th Ave., between 51st and 52nd Sts., tel. 212/757–6132).

Dalton Vintage Emporium (156 E. 86th St., tel. 212/831–4908).

Everybody's Thrift Shop (261 Park Ave. S, between 20th and 21st Sts., tel. 212/355–9263).

Four Charities Thrift Shop (380 2nd Ave., between 21st and 22nd Sts., tel. 212/674–1444).

Girls Club of New York Thrift Shop (202 E. 77th St., tel. 212/535–8570).

Irvington Institute for Medical Research Thrift Shop (1534 2nd Ave. at 80th St., tel. 212/879–4555).

Memorial Sloan-Kettering Cancer Center Thrift Shop (1440 3rd Ave., between 81st and 82nd Sts., tel. 212/535–1250).

New York Hospital Auxiliary Thrift Shop (439 E. 71st St., tel. 212/535–0965).

Spence-Chapin Corner Shop (1430 3rd Ave., between 80th and 81st Sts., tel. 212/737–8448).

Thrift Shop East (336 E. 86th St., tel. 212/772–6868).

Resale Shops   When the oh-so-social women of New York have clothing too good to give away, they consign it to their local resale shop. To find top-of-the-line designs at secondhand prices, try: **Encore** (1132 Madison Ave., between 84th and 85th Sts., upstairs, tel. 212/879–2850); **Exchange Unlimited** (563 2nd Ave. at 31st St., tel. 212/889–3229); **Michael's Resale** (1041 Madison Ave., between 79th and 80th Sts., tel. 212/737–7273); and **Renate's** (218 E. 83rd St., tel. 212/472–1698).

Auctions

New York's lively auction scene means regular sales from internationally known houses. Fine art has been selling at record prices in the millions, but for almost everything else, prices are often a steal. Sales are regularly advertised in *The New York Times*, particularly in Friday's "Weekend" and Sunday's "Arts & Leisure" sections. If you note a sale of interest, attend the exhibition or viewing to inspect the wares close up and to peruse the catalogue. If something strikes your fancy, discuss possible payment methods at that time; find out whether you'll need a paddle for bidding.

Christie's (502 Park Ave. at 59th St., tel. 212/371–5438). This 200-year-old London firm is the oldest of its kind in the world; it's had an American presence for a decade. The annex is **Christie's East** (219 E. 67th St., tel. 212/606–0400).

Sotheby's (1334 York Ave. at 72nd St., tel. 212/606–7245). This is Christie's chief rival, also originally from London. On the premises is the **Arcade,** where interesting and well-priced also-rans go on the block.

William Doyle Galleries (175 E. 87th St., tel. 212/427–2730).

The charismatic and amazingly energetic William Doyle has turned his instinct for accumulation into a booming business that's now considered a major force on the New York auction scene. Sales here are always entertaining.

Smaller houses include: **Gotham Galleries** (80 4th Ave., between 10th and 11th Sts., tel. 212/677–3303); **Greenwich Auction Room** (110 E. 13th St., tel. 212/533–5930); **Guernsey's Auction** (136 E. 73rd St., tel. 212/794–2280); **Lubin Galleries** (30 W. 26th St., tel. 212/627–9213); **Swann Galleries** (104 E. 25th St., tel. 212/254–4710); and **Tepper Galleries** (110 E. 25th St., tel. 212/677–5300).

Flea Markets

There's no telling what you'll find at markets held in black-topped school playgrounds and grungy parking lots. The season runs from March or April to November or December.

Annex Antiques Fair and Flea Market (6th Ave., between 25th and 26th Sts., tel. 212/243–5343), Saturdays and Sundays.

Canal Market (370 Canal St., tel. 718/693–8142), Saturdays and Sundays.

Tower Market (Broadway, between W. 4th and Great Jones Sts., tel. 718/273–8702), Saturdays and Sundays.

P.S. 183 Market (67th St., between York and 1st Aves., tel. 212/737–8888), Saturdays.

P.S. 44 Market (Columbus Ave., between 76th and 77th Sts., tel. 212/947–6302 evenings), Sundays.

P.S. 41 (Greenwich Ave. at Charles St., tel. 212/752–8475), Saturdays.

8 Dining

*by John F.
Mariani and Peter
D. Meltzer*

*John F. Mariani
is food and travel
correspondent for*
Esquire, *food
writer for* USA
Today, *and host of
the PBS television
series "Crazy for
Food." Peter D.
Meltzer is
editor-at-large for*
Food Arts, *wine
columnist for*
Ultra, *and author
of* The Wine
Spectator's *"Grand
Award" restaurant
wine listing.*

In much the same way that New York has long been considered America's financial and artistic capital, it has also become the nation's—some might even say the world's—gastronomic epicenter. The sheer quantity of New York restaurants is staggering: There are some 16,000 establishments in all if you count corner coffee shops and diners.

More important are the variety and the quality. Within its few square miles, the island of Manhattan contains dozens of culinary cultures—including Brazilian, Cuban, Greek, Hungarian, Mexican, and Japanese, to mention a few—all enriched by a pragmatic American style and a very hip gloss. The city also offers the finest French food outside of Paris, the most authentic Italian specialties outside of Bologna, the most varied styles of Chinese cuisine outside of Hong Kong, and the spiciest Thai dishes outside of Bangkok. This is the place that gave the world lox, fettuccine primavera, negimaki, Delmonico steak, and a number of other dishes one might have thought originated in Europe or Asia. And when it comes to steak houses, New York created and defines the genre.

Yet from the down-to-earth hot dog pushcarts in Central Park to the elegant skyscraper heights of Windows on the World and the Rainbow Room, New York's restaurants are not so different from one another as their ethnic models might suggest. They all have a particular New York swagger about them; most aim for a sparkle and conviviality that reflect the city's own vitality. A New York delicatessen like Katz's is every bit as lively and boisterous as the street outside its doors, while the bar at the "21" Club has that ring of raucousness that is an extension of the corporate pressure cooker. Go to 150 Wooster or Florent, and you'll get an instant sense of what a hip Manhattan scene is all about. Even deluxe restaurants such as Le Cirque and The Four Seasons possess an exuberance and spontaneity you'd miss in Paris, for example, at the celebrated Maxim's.

As Los Angeles chefs strive to come up with yet another portmanteau cuisine, and chefs in Texas and Arizona struggle with new species of chili pepper, New York chefs and restaurateurs simply do a better and better job of refining the New York gastronomic experience. To meet their standards—which are challenged and reformed almost every night—is to be at the top of the form. Take, for example, chef Anne Rosenzweig at Arcadia, who'll make a club sandwich with lobster meat, or chef Debra Ponzek at Montrachet, who will take your breath away with her sautéed New York State foie gras or her salmon in red wine sauce with lentils. If you're lucky enough to snare a reservation at Lutèce, you'll be in the hands of New York's most dedicated and driven chef—André Soltner, who after all these years seems much more a New York City phenomenon than the Alsatian he is by birth.

Dining out in Manhattan has become as much an exercise in one-upmanship as it is a reflection of one's worldliness. New Yorkers follow restaurant news—ratings, openings, changes of chefs—with avid interest; they take pride in unearthing a hitherto unknown bistro in the depths of SoHo or in addressing a stellar chef on a first-name basis. For some, the restaurant has

All restaurant reviews in this chapter have been adapted from
Passport to New York Restaurants *(Passport Press, Ltd.), a
pocket guide by John F. Mariani and Peter D. Meltzer.*

become an extension of the living room, a place in which to not only eat but to entertain, romance, and impress.

With so much to pick from, choosing where to dine in New York may be exasperating. Probably the best strategy is to select your restaurant on the basis of your budget and the neighborhood you're visiting; after that, you can decide which type of cuisine and what atmosphere you prefer. We've set this chapter up first by region and then by cost, giving choices for every price range within each neighborhood.

Prices New York may not be the most expensive city in the world when it comes to dining out (Tokyo probably takes that honor), but by and large, New York restaurants are quite a bit more expensive than those in most American cities. It has become increasingly difficult to find a good meal for under $20 a head. And while you might spend $100 per person in Boston, Los Angeles, or Washington, DC, you can easily spend that much in New York, even at lesser restaurants where all too often you're paying for a false sense of chic, a panorama, or a valued table. We've skirted such restaurants in favor of places we think represent true value, even for those for whom money is no object. Highly recommended restaurants in each category are indicated by a star ★.

Category	Cost*
Very Expensive	over $60
Expensive	$30–$60
Moderate	$20–$30
Inexpensive	under $20

per person, excluding drinks, service, and sales tax (8¼%)

The following credit card abbreviations are used: AE, American Express; CB, Carte Blanche; DC, Diners Club; MC, MasterCard; and V, Visa.

It's worth noting that lunch prices tend to be much lower than dinner prices at the better spots; you can dine regally at the most deluxe restaurants in town for less than $40 per person at lunch, eating the same meal that would cost you $75–$100 at dinner. New York restaurants thrive on the expense account crowd, and lunch is a much more elaborate affair here than in most other cities, where noontime menus bear little resemblance to what's offered at night. Lunch is a good time to sample the best the city has to offer without spending a fortune. Be aware, however, that most of the top-flight restaurants are not open for lunch on Saturday.

Many haute cuisine restaurants offer three-course, fixed-price menus, which usually cost a bit less than meals ordered à la carte, but be wary of the ubiquitous supplements and surcharges on such menus. Some fixed-price meals are called "tasting menus" or, in French, *menus dégustation*. These offer a sampling of anywhere from five to 10 dishes—usually at quite a high price—and give you a very good indication of a kitchen's strengths, since they include the best the chef is making that night.

Even with fixed-price meals, coffee and after-dinner beverages are almost never included, so if a waiter suggests an item, ask whether it is complimentary or additional. A waiter who asks, "Would you like a soufflé for dessert?" does not necessarily mean that it's a giveaway—it may cost you plenty on top of your bill. If a waiter says, "The owner would like to buy you a drink," however, you should not have to pay for that drink. Check your bill accordingly.

In many restaurants, your waiter may come to your table to recite a long list of the evening's specials, often without quoting prices. If you're tempted, don't be bashful about asking a dish's price—you don't want to discover when the bill arrives that you've paid for the ingredients' airfare from Alaska!

Wine Some of the best wine cellars in the country are to be found here at grand restaurants such as Le Cirque, Lutèce, The Four Seasons, and Laurent. You'll find equally great wines at Felidia, Spark's, Smith & Wollensky, and the Grand Central Oyster Bar. While it's possible to spend upwards of $100 per bottle at these places, good value often lurks at the lower end of the list. As a general rule, plan on spending at least the equivalent of a dinner entrée on your bottle. Unless budget requires, however, don't go for the cheapest listing you find because it's probably no bargain: An $18 bottle usually bears a much higher markup than a $28 one.

Dress Codes For men, a jacket and tie (and very often a suit) are never out of place and always welcome at New York restaurants; many specifically require them. For women, it's always safe to be "dressy." There are, however, a large number of restaurants where "casual" dress is acceptable—as long as it's neat and carries a certain amount of taste. Blue jeans might be all right in Chinatown or a pizza parlor, but slacks and a sweater or tweed jacket will put you in better stead elsewhere. Cutoffs and shorts are worn only in the heat of summer, and then only at very casual restaurants.

New Yorkers use dining spots to show off their finery, so have some fun and show off yours.

Reservations Because of the popularity of dining out in New York, even a mediocre restaurant may be jammed every night of the week, and the really hot and trendy spots may have people waiting at the bar for hours. Reservations are always a good idea, and more often than not are essential. At places such as Lutèce, Le Bernardin, and the Rainbow Room, reservations should be made weeks, not days, in advance, although weekdays and lunches are easier to reserve. You'd be surprised, however, at how many times no-shows open up tables, even on a Saturday night, so it's worth a last-minute call to find out. Another way to snare an otherwise booked table is to make a very early (say, 6 PM) or quite late (9:30 PM) reservation. Even the best restaurants often have tables at those hours. Concierges at hotels can help sometimes, but it is not always a great idea to trust their critical judgment, since it may be clouded by "honorariums" from restaurants.

New York City law now stipulates that restaurants with more than 50 seats must set aside nonsmoking sections. Make your preference known when you reserve.

Dining Hours Most New Yorkers dine out at approximately 8 PM. Pretheater dining can be a lot of fun, but expect it to be rushed: You'll want to be out by 7:45, and restaurants that cater to the theater crowd will make sure you are. If you prefer to wait until after the show to eat, you'll find that New York restaurants take good care of hungry night owls who want something more than diner food.

Seating Many people worry about the "seating game"—who gets the best tables and how to avoid being placed in what's known as "Siberia"—in deluxe or trendy restaurants. The best tables are customarily doled out to regulars or high-powered celebrities. Don't assume that not getting an *A* table is a deliberate slight. If you are seated at a table you find truly awful—next to the rest room, the kitchen, or service station, for instance—politely request another. If space allows, the maître d' will happily place you elsewhere—perhaps not at the window table, but at a better one. Whatever you do, DO NOT "grease the palm" of the maître d': It may work, but it'll mark you as a patsy, ready to be gouged by the rest of the staff.

Tipping If you have received good service and liked where the maître d' seated you, on the way out you may want to give him a tip (anywhere from a few dollars to $10 or more if you wish to be remembered), but it is in no way mandatory. As for tipping others, remember that most service staffs pool their tips at the end of each evening (busboys and bartenders are given a share), so it is not necessary to provide a separate tip for everyone who serves you. If you do want to separate your tip in a deluxe restaurant, give 15% to the waiter and 5% to the captain. Otherwise, just leave behind 15%–20% in one lump sum.

Wine stewards are tipped only when they perform special services, such as decanting rare wines or advising you throughout a multicourse meal, in which case a tip of a few dollars is in order. Coat-check attendants usually get $1 per coat; parking valets get about the same per car. If you're just ordering drinks, a tip of $1 on a $5–$10 order is just fine.

A quick way to figure your tip is to double the tax you've been charged: that would equal 16½%, a perfectly adequate amount.

Lower Manhattan

Expensive **Fraunces Tavern.** A good, evocative American restaurant inside a historic structure (where Washington bade farewell to his troops in 1783), Fraunces Tavern is one of the last bits of Colonial New York remaining, and the museum upstairs is delightful. Downstairs there's a barroom that fills up at midday and after 5 PM with the bulls and bears of Wall Street. The main dining room is a cheery spot in antique style where you can enjoy everything from a hearty breakfast of oatmeal and eggs to lunches and dinners that focus on such classic American dishes as steak, chops, and seafood. The pies and cakes are fitting endings. *54 Pearl St. (at Broad St.), tel. 212/269–0144. Reservations required at lunch, advised at dinner. Jacket and tie advised. AE, CB, DC, MC, V. Closed Sat. and Sun.*

★ **Windows on the World.** Perched on the 107th floor of the World Trade Center, with a spectacular view of the city unfolding beneath, this restaurant is one of the country's most awesome. Remember, however, that window tables are hard to get, and you may feel disappointed if you go on a rainy or foggy night. The simpler food items—such as paillard of chicken or veal, rack of lamb, and American chocolate cake—are often the best choices. The wine list at Windows is one of the most extensive

Manhattan Dining (Uptown)

Al Amir, **19**	Da Gianvito, **21**	Mocca Hungarian	Sidewalkers, **11**
Alcala, **8**	Dieci, **17**	Restaurant, **16**	Sign of the Dove, **27**
Amerigo's, **1**	Docks, **5**	Parioli	Sylvia's, **2**
Amsterdam's Bar and	The Ginger Man, **32**	Romanissimo, **12**	Table d'Hote, **3**
Rotisserie, **6**	Gallagher's, **42**	Petrossian, **36**	Tavern on the
Anatolia, **15**	Hard Rock Café, **37**	Pig Heaven, **18**	Green, **30**
Arizona 206, **28**	J.G. Melon, **9, 23**	Poiret, **7**	The Terrace, **4**
Bangkok Cuisine, **41**	Joe Allen, **43**	Post House, **29**	Vasata, **20**
Cabana Carioca, **42**	La Cité, **39**	Punsch, **33**	Vico Ristorante, **13**
Café des Artistes, **41**	La Metairie, **14**	Russian Tea Room, **37**	
Café Luxembourg, **10**	Le Bernardin, **38**	San Domenico, **34**	
Chez Josephine, **44**	Le Cirque, **26**	Sette Mezzo, **24**	
Café des Artistes, **41**	Le Regence, **25**		
	Mezzaluna, **22**		

Manhattan Dining (Downtown)

Acme Bar & Grill, **22**
Alison on Dominick Street, **30**
America, **9**
An American Place, **3**
Angelo's, **39**
Benito's II, **38**
Bouley, **32**
Cafe Iguana, **11**
Capsouto Freres, **31**
Chanterelle, **34**
The Coach House, **21**
El Teddy's, **36**
Florent, **16**

Fraunces Tavern, **46**
Gage & Tollner, **45**
Giorgio, **10**
Gotham Bar & Grill, **17**
Il Cortile, **41**
Indochine, **20**
Jerry's, **28**
Katz's Delicatessen, **23**
La Colombe D'Or, **4**
La Tulipe, **15**
Le Madri, **8**
Lola, **6**
Montrachet, **37**

Noodle Town, **40**
The Odeon, **35**
Omen Restaurant, **26**
Park Bistro, **5**
Periyali, **13**
Provence, **25**
Quatorze, **14**
The River Café (Brooklyn), **48**
Rojas-Lombardi Ballroom, **2**
Rose Cafe, **18**
Silver Palace, **42**
Siracusa Gourmet Café, **19**

Soho Kitchen and Bar, **29**
South Street Seaport, **47**
Tommy Tang , **33**
Union Square Café, **12**
Villa Mosconi, **24**
Windows on the World, **44**
Wong Kee, **43**
150 Wooster, **27**
World Yacht Cruises, **1**
Zig Zag Bar & Grill, **7**

in the country, with tremendous breadth of choice and very fair prices. In fact, Windows is so committed to wine that it actually offers a special dining experience for oenophiles at **Cellar in the Sky,** a compact, enclosed dining room in which a seven-course menu is served with carefully matched wines at a fixed price of $80. *1 World Trade Center, tel. 212/938–1111. Reservations required. Jacket and tie required. AE, CB, DC, MC, V. Closed to public weekday lunch.*

Moderate **South Street Seaport.** This is not a restaurant but an impeccably restored 19th-century historic district (*see* Tour 18) stretching from Water Street to John Street. Its attractions include many restaurants that make pleasant places for lunch or dinner. A host of better-than-average fast-food restaurants serve every imaginable type of ethnic cooking. One good bet is **Sloppy Louie's,** a very old place specializing in seafood and antique charm, though it's a bit touristy. *92 South St., tel. 212/509–9694. Reservations advised. Dress: casual. AE, DC, MC, V.*

SoHo and TriBeCa

Very Expensive
★
Bouley. This is a modern restaurant whose truly genteel roots are reflected in every piece of furniture, as well as in the arched ceilings, the impressionistic landscapes on the walls, and the sedate lighting. David Bouley, a very sensible cook who never strays from good taste, offers a bargain ($65 for dinner, $32 for lunch) tasting menu of many courses, along with a regular à la carte menu. The food is exciting without ever being trendy. Bouley does beautiful grilled lobster with artichokes, monkfish with tomato-coriander sauce, and sturgeon with summer squash, and he is justly famous for his hot dessert soufflés. His staff has good and bad nights, however, and waits between courses may turn into lapses. *165 Duane St. (near Hudson St.), tel. 212/608–3852. Reservations required. Jacket and tie required. AE, CB, DC, MC, V. Closed Sat. lunch and Sun.*

Chanterelle. Despite a much-touted move from Grand Street to its present location, Chanterelle looks basically the same—the food is quite up to par. Such is its ongoing popularity that tables are generally booked up to a month in advance. The place is intentionally very stark, with bare walls and one massive floral arrangement. Chef-owner David Waltuck's menus, limited and ever-changing, offer a few meals each night at a prix fixe of $68. Recommended dishes include cold lobster consommé, sweetbreads and morrels, and beef filet in red wine sauce. Desserts are somewhat disappointing. An extensive but expensive wine list is available. *2 Harrison St. (near W. Broadway), tel. 212/966–6960. Reservations advised. Jacket and tie advised. AE, DC, MC, V. Closed Sat. lunch, Sun., and Mon.*

Expensive
★
Alison on Dominick Street. This small and intimate neighborhood restaurant is one of the best of the new breed; owner Alison Price really enjoys making her customers feel right at home. The low-key dining rooms featuring white walls, blue banquettes, and entertaining black-and-white photographs help make this a congenial spot. Chef Thomas Valenti's excellent Provençal-inspired menu includes braised beef with white beans, vegetable tart, skate with cabbage and bacon, and fig tart with crème fraîche. *38 Dominick St. (near Hudson St.), tel. 212/727–1188. Reservations advised. Jacket advised. AE, DC, MC, V.*

★ **Montrachet.** Set in a quaint TriBeCa location and presided over by the dedicated Drew Nieporent, Montrachet has proved to be one of the most consistently satisfying restaurants in New York City. Its current chef, Debra Ponzek, is serious about the essential flavors of her ingredients, and care is shown in the preparation of every dish. The wines are very carefully chosen, too, so rely on sommelier Daniel Johnnes's advice. Montrachet is priced somewhat below comparable establishments. Signature dishes include sautéed foie gras, red snapper with red peppers and lemon, rib eye steak with wild mushrooms and garlic potatoes, salmon with lentils, pheasant with olives, and apricot tart. *239 W. Broadway (near White St.), tel. 212/219–2777. Reservations advised. Dress: casual. AE. Closed Sun., and Mon.–Thurs. and Sat. lunch.*

Moderate **Capsouto Freres.** Its setting in a glorious old landmark build-
★ ing, its view of the Hudson, and its own soaring architectural design make this a stand-out restaurant in TriBeCa. The brothers Capsouto were among the first in the city to offer Mediterranean and Provençal cuisine, and they do it very well indeed. The soft-shell crabs *à la meunière* are superb, and the Provençal dishes—especially terrine Provençale, roasted lotte and lobster in sauternes, and steak with mixed peppercorns—are terrific, as is the blueberry crumble cake. The Sunday brunch is very popular. *451 Washington St. (near Canal St.), tel. 212/966–4900. Reservations advised. Jacket required on Sat. night and Sun. brunch; otherwise casual. AE, DC. Closed Mon. lunch.*

El Teddy's. Lots of glitter and tile—the legacy of restaurants past—provide one of the city's more offbeat interiors. This is also one of the few spots in New York where margaritas are made to measure with your choice of several different tequilas. The promising menu includes updated Mexican specialties, such as masa tarts with chicken and chile, cactus salad with jicama, portobello mushrooms with salsa verde, shrimp marinated in lime and tequila, and charred tuna steak with salsa fresca. *219 W. Broadway (between Franklin and White Sts.), tel. 212/941–7070. Reservations advised. Dress: casual. AE, MC, V.*

★ **The Odeon.** Housed in a 1930s art deco cafeteria, this was the first notable restaurant in the TriBeCa neighborhood. Popularized by the SoHo art set, who still make it one of their chief stomping grounds after midnight, it's a great place to plug into the "scene" in this very artsy district. Everybody seems to wear black, look slightly world-weary, and recognize each other. The food is high-quality bistro/brasserie fare with changing specials. The crab cakes are moist and meaty; the roast lamb with beans is juicy; and the sorbet is very good. *145 W. Broadway (at Thomas St.), tel. 212/233–0507. Reservations advised. Dress: casual. AE, DC, MC, V. Closed Sat. lunch.*

150 Wooster. Who knows? By the time you read this 150 Wooster may be passé, but for the moment this red-hot spot attracts an astounding number of celebrities from both coasts—artists, models, publishing people, and all those who want to be where the most current action is. The dining room can be rather cold, the service is lazy, and the French-influenced American cuisine is little more than good, but because the prices aren't too steep, you may want to drop in anyway to see what all the fuss is about. Stargazers won't be disappointed. *150 Wooster St. (near*

Prince St.), tel. 212/995–1010. Reservations advised. Dress: casual chic. AE, MC, V.

Provence. An authentic bistro, of the kind that dot the Riviera, this spot has become very popular for its unprepossessing decor, its decent prices, and its commendable Provencal food. The seafood dishes are especially good, from the *pissaladiere* (a kind of French pizza) to the bourride. The early crowd at dinner are locals; the later crowd, artists and gallery owners from the area. The restaurant attracts a very artsy-literary bunch, as shown in the scene filmed here for the movie *Crossing Delancey*. The front room on the street is charming, but the rear is rather plain. *38 MacDougal St. (near Prince St.), tel. 212/475–7500. Reservations advised. Dress: casual. AE. Closed Mon.*

★ **Tommy Tang.** This Hollywood transplant to TriBeCa has traveled well. Still going very strong, it attracts home-bound Wall Streeters in the early evening and a mixed bag of area residents and fans of Thai cuisine later on. Its high-ceilinged, geometric design and attractive young staff create a lively backdrop for some serious eating. You might want to share a variety of appetizers to sample a wide array of the kitchen's output: Start with chicken saté, "naked" shrimp, or spicy chicken-and-pork wontons. For a main course, try ginger beef with black beans, blackened whole chili fish, grilled breast of chicken, Original Tommy Duck, or any of a number of spicy Thai pasta dishes. For dessert, a homemade sorbet serves as a refreshing finale. *323 Greenwich St. (near Reade St.), tel. 212/334–9190. Reservations advised. Dress: casual chic. AE, CB, DC, MC, V. Closed Sat. lunch and Sun.*

Inexpensive **Jerry's.** The decor at this lively spot might be described as updated diner. Although the ambience is relaxed, the kitchen is far from laid back in its diligent preparation of American specialties. You can expect an eclectic repertoire, including duck breast and duck sausage salad, spinach salad with Swedish bacon, grilled swordfish with cucumber tomato raita, and wholesome sandwiches. Don't miss the superb french fries. *101 Prince St. (between Mercer and Greene Sts.), tel. 212/966–9464. Dinner reservations advised. Dress: casual. AE, MC, V. Closed Sun. dinner.*

Katz's Delicatessen. This is a long-standing favorite of New Yorkers who like to shop for bargains on Orchard Street, then repair to Katz's for big, fat pastrami or corned beef sandwiches, knishes, briskets, garlicky franks, dripping pickles, terrific french fries, and cream soda. This is an original Jewish deli (you can still buy wonderful salami and cold cuts to go) with a 1950s atmosphere that includes lots of schmoozing and yelling. Food is served cafeteria style: You move along the line, shout your order, and then sit down. You've got to know what you want because the counter men can make sandwiches faster than you can say "pastrami-on-rye." *205 E. Houston St. (near Orchard St.), tel. 212/254–2246. Reservations unnecessary. Dress: casual. AE ($50 minimum).*

Soho Kitchen and Bar. This characteristic and special SoHo eatery has a great deal of spaciousness, good music, a casual-but-well-groomed crowd, plenty of laughter, and good, basic fare at decent prices. Soaring ceilings are a fit halo for the giant artwork here, and one of the main draws is the oversize bar offering at least 100 wines by the glass on any given night. The wines are often served in sequences of eight selections at a time. Try the crisp-edged pizzas and any of the pasta dishes. *103 Greene St. (near Prince St.), tel. 212/925–1866. Reservations advised. Dress: casual. AE, DC, MC, V.*

Chinatown and Little Italy

Moderate

Angelo's. A very old-fashioned Italian-American spot, smack in the middle of Little Italy, this is certainly better than most of the tourist traps that surround it. Angelo's has a homey feel, with its simple decor and black-and-white tile floors. The pasta is very good, especially the perciatelli with vegetable sauce, and the chicken with garlic is as fine as you'll find in the neighborhood. Go with the whole family—this place welcomes kids. *146 Mulberry St., tel. 212/966–1277. Reservations advised weekends. Dress: casual. AE, CB, DC, MC, V. Closed Mon.*

★ **Il Cortile.** Easily the best restaurant in Little Italy, Il Cortile is a tad more refined than some of the other storefront operations in the neighborhood, and its menu is far more interesting. The garden room in back is lovely, and there are a couple of coveted window tables up front. The management really cares about every customer here, and they take reservations and credit cards—not everyone in this area does. The waiters gladly help you with the menu (it's all in Italian), and if you ask for the wine list, your waiter will say, "I'm the wine list." Trust him, but ask the price. Then tuck into a greaseless *spiedino alla romana* (fried mozzarella and bread with anchovy sauce), a plate of potato *gnocchi* dumplings with rosemary and fresh *porcini* mushrooms, or a beautifully cooked San Pietro fish with wine and oil. *125 Mulberry St. (near Hester St.), tel. 212/226–6060. Reservations advised. Dress: casual. AE, CB, DC, MC, V.*

Inexpensive

Benito's II. There are so many restaurants in Little Italy that pack 'em in and turn 'em out, it's nice to be able to make a reservation at Benito's II, where you can relax and enjoy the fresh tomato sauce on the pasta, the garlicky chicken, and the strolling guitarist (he's not all that good but he does enliven the place). The premises have brick walls, tile murals, and very funny waiters, so this is a good, if undistinguished, spot in which to soak up the Little Italy atmosphere. There is a Benito's I across the street, but for reasons known only to the Benitos, there is no association between the two. *163 Mulberry St. (near Grand St.), tel. 212/226–9012. Reservations advised. Dress: casual. No credit cards.*

Noodle Town. Despite the ridiculous name and premises that might charitably be called "quaint," this Chinatown noodle parlor in the Hong Kong tradition of "sit-'em-serve-'em-move-'em" offers absolutely scrumptious food at very low prices. The half duck for $8.50 is the most expensive item here. Don't miss the Hong Kong noodles, the luscious, brimming soups, the pan-fried noodles with black beans, or just about anything else you can point to on the enormous menu. *28½ Bowery (near Canal St.), tel. 212/349–0923. Dress: casual. No credit cards.*

Silver Palace. A vast hall in which waiters rush about with trays full of dim-sum dumplings, this is a great place to go for weekend lunch. Food is served all day and the crowds are a fun-loving bunch. You pay by the plate—just point to what you want and be adventurous. Although the service can be quite rude, the dumplings are irresistible—everyone orders too much, but you'll find it difficult to spend more than $15 per person. There is entertainment on Sundays featuring Chinese performers. *52 Bowery (near Canal St.), tel. 212/964–1204. No reservations. Dress: casual. AE.*

Wong Kee. Here is a clean, bright, and completely uncluttered Chinese restaurant that has the added virtue—rare in Chinatown—of being consistent and dependable. It's a cliché to say you should order what the Orientals are ordering, but here it is true: Look around you and ask for whatever everybody else seems to be eating that day—duck with star anise, perhaps, or beef with sour cabbage. The bare-bones decor and fast service are part of the fun. If you don't make a reservation, be prepared for a wait on weekends. *113 Mott St. (near Canal St.), tel. 212/226–9018. Reservations advised. Dress: casual. No credit cards.*

Greenwich Village

Expensive **The Coach House.** Owner Leon Lianides opened The Coach House in the late 1940s, and American cooking has never had higher standards to meet than those he's set here for generations of diners. The premises are exquisitely set, with antiques and fine paintings on old, wood-panelled walls. A lovely passage about The Coach House in Pat Conroy's novel *Prince of Tides* points out that a restaurant such as this one puts you in touch with New York's unique greatness. You can't go wrong with anything on the menu, from the corn sticks to the famous black-bean soup. The rack of lamb is superlative, as is the fish cooked in bouillon, and the desserts are nonpareil, especially the quince tart and the pecan pie. The place is traditionally popular on Sunday evenings. *110 Waverly Pl. (near Ave. of the Americas), tel. 212/777–0303. Reservations required weekends. Jacket required. AE, CB, DC, MC, V. Closed Mon.*

★ **Gotham Bar & Grill.** Chef Alfred Portale, with the support of owner Jerry Kretchmer, has brought the Gotham into the front ranks of New York City restaurants. It was always beautiful, with high ceilings, a long bar, muted tones of butter yellow and sea green, and a crowd of attractive diners, but the food is now up to par with the decor. Portale, a careful chef, draws out flavors and combines tastes with true panache, making this a major stop on the gourmet circuit. He's at his best with Italian and Provençal-style items, such as quail salad with shiitake mushrooms, ravioli stuffed with rabbit, and warm raspberry gratin. *12 E. 12th St. (near 5th Ave.), tel. 212/620–4020. Reservations advised. Dress: casual. AE, CB, DC, MC, V. Closed lunch weekends.*

★ **La Tulipe.** This is probably the most romantic and charming Greenwich Village family restaurant. It is owned by Sally and John Darr, whose dedication to good food has been unflagging over the years. Although the menu has not changed much, it is still a bellwether of good taste. The staff is attentive; Mr. Darr is an affable host; and Mrs. Darr's cooking has never been anything less than delicious. The wine list is carefully chosen for the restaurant's kind of food, which has all the flavors of Provençe in perfect order. The rich duck confit is highly recommended, as are the pigeon timbale with Chartreuse of cabbage and the apricot soufflé. *104 W. 13th St., tel. 212/691–8860. Reservations required. Jacket advised. AE, CB, DC, MC, V. Closed Mon.*

Moderate **Florent.** This is absolutely, positively one of the hippest restaurants in lower Manhattan, not for its food—which is only passable French bistro fare (grilled flank steak, sausages, onion soup and vegetable gratinés)—but for the retro neighborhood it's in (the meat market district), its decor (barely converted diner), and the late-night crowd that comes here (Madonna, the Talking Heads, and a lot of other musicians). The waiters are friendly enough, however, so if you can get a table after 9 PM, just inhale the atmosphere and have a good time. It won't cost you much. Do take a taxi (and have one waiting outside when you exit). *69 Gansevoort St. (between Greenwich and Washington Sts.), tel. 212/989–5779. Reservations advised. Dress: casual. No credit cards. Open 24 hrs.*

Indochine. Tucked away opposite the Public Theater is this exotic Vietnamese restaurant, complete with a banana-leaf motif on its walls. Convenient as it is for theater goers, Indochine has developed a certain cachet and draws an interesting crowd from all over town. The menu features good shrimp beignets, marinated beef salad, and chicken wings. *430 Lafayette St. (near Astor Pl.), tel. 212/505–5111. Reservations advised. Dress: casual. AE, DC, MC, V. Dinner only.*

Omen Restaurant. This casual and inviting country-style Japanese restaurant boasts an original and well-executed menu. An effective use of wood paneling creates a serene and vaguely oriental atmosphere. You'll find traditional dishes, such as tuna sashimi and seafood tempura, along with more innovative preparations, such as scallops with peanut cream and grilled seaweed. Try the house sake. *113 Thompson St. (near Houston St.), tel. 212/925–8923. Reservations suggested. Dress: casual. AE, DC. Closed Mon.*

★ **Quatorze.** Although the location of this attractive French bistro, loosely modeled on Paris's celebrated Brasserie Lipp, lacks the elan of the Boulevard St. Germain, staples—such as *saucisson chaud* (garlic sausage), *salade aux lardons* (chicory lettuce with bacon), creamy paté, *coq au vin* (chicken in red wine sauce), calf's liver, and *choucroute garni* (sausages and ham on a bed of sauerkraut)—are worthy of the real thing. You'll also find here one of the best apple tarts in the city, as well as a very good wine list. *240 W. 14th St. (off 7th Ave.), tel. 212/206–7006. AE. Reservations advised. Dress: casual. Closed for lunch Sat. and Sun.*

Rose Cafe. Chef-owner Richard Krause, who formerly owned the pricey restaurant, Melrose, offers a menu of some enticing, moderately priced dishes that seems a judicious balance of the old and the new. Right on Fifth Avenue, the premises are open, relaxed, and unpretentious; the service is quite the same. Ask for a window table and watch the passing parade of Greenwich Village nightlife. Krause is at his best with full-flavored meats (such as rabbit with basil-tomato cream), wild mushrooms in a salad, and candy-sweet desserts. His Peking duck Chinois with scallion pancakes is particularly delightful. *24 5th Ave. (at 9th St.), tel. 212/260–4118. Reservations advised. Dress: casual. AE, DC, MC, V.*

Siracusa Gourmet Café. Although the ambience is friendly and ultrasimple, there is nothing unassuming about the cuisine at this popular little Village haunt. Ignore the nondescript decor and focus instead on the menu: an enticing array of antipasti—fried vegetables, superb charcuterie—and excellent pastas, such as ravioli stuffed with eggplant and pignoli nuts, and tagliarini with sausage and tomato. There is a take-out counter up front featuring many of the menu highlights, plus wonderful *biscotti* (Italian cookies) to go. *65 4th Ave. (near 10th St.),*

*tel. 212/254–1940. Reservations advised. Dress: casual. AE.
Closed Sat. lunch and Sun.*

Villa Mosconi. Here's a pleasant, old-fashioned Greenwich Village trattoria, the kind they don't often make any more. You come here to eat heartily at a fair price and to be treated like an old friend by owner Peter Mosconi; you'll get a good feeling of the way the Village used to be a decade or so ago. The warm, comfortable premises have the requisite Italian landscapes and still lifes on the walls. Among the good and gutsy food, the tagliatelle (flat-ribboned egg pasta) al pesto, the seafood stew, and the veal alla giardiniera (with vegetables) are especially recommended. *69 MacDougal St. (near Houston St.), tel. 212/ 673–0390. Reservations advised. Dress: casual. AE, DC, MC, V.*

Inexpensive **Acme Bar and Grill.** Here's an authentic, down-home Cajun
★ joint, complete with corrugated tin ceilings, exposed beams, and every conceivable type of hot sauce ever produced, lined up along an enormous interior wall. Deep-fried oyster po' boys, Cajun shrimp, and brown rice and greens are just a few of the regional specialties offered at this casual and ever-lively Louisiana transplant. *9 Great Jones St. (near Broadway), tel. 212/ 420–1934. No reservations. Dress: casual. No credit cards.*

Chelsea, Gramercy, Murray Hill

Expensive **An American Place.** Located in stunning art deco quarters
★ (nearly three times as large as its former Lexington Avenue space), An American Place continues to maintain the very high standards that won it so many accolades in the past. Although he has abandoned a fixed-price menu in favor of à la carte, chef Larry Forgione has preserved several signature dishes, such as terrine of American three-smoked fish and warm duck sausage with scallion spoonbread griddlecakes. Pleasing additions to his roster of appetizers include peanut barbecued gulf shrimp and lobster-and-wild-mushroom croquettes with spicy red-pepper sauce. A trio of winning main courses worth considering include sautéed breast of free-range chicken, roast fillet of salmon coated with cracked wheat, and roast loin of lamb crusted with goat cheese and herbs. For dessert, be sure to try the banana betty or the apple pandowdy. *2 Park Ave. (entrance on 32nd St.), tel. 212/684–2122. Reservations advised. Dress: casual. AE, DC, MC, V. Closed Sun.*

★ **Le Madri.** Certainly one of the most highly publicized new Italian restaurants to recently hit New York, this establishment has succeeded not due to the hype but because of its good food. A very beautiful crowd of regulars from the fashion and publishing world may be seen here. Owner Pino Luongo brings in talented, regional Italian women chefs on a rotating basis, while executive chef Alan Tardi maintains the day-to-day consistency. The pizzas can be terrific, the pastas remain true to the best in Italy, and the steak alla fiorentina is nonpareil. Don't miss the tempting desserts, either. Expect a crush, wobbly service, and too often a wait, but this is a great spot to go for lunch after shopping at Barneys across the street. *168 W. 18th St. (on 7th Ave.), tel. 212/727–8022. Reservations advised. Jacket advised. AE. Closed for lunch Sat. and Sun.*

★ **World Yacht Cruises.** A three-hour yacht cruise around Manhattan gives you more spectacle than Windows on the World, the Rainbow Room, and The River Café combined. Add to this some above-average Continental cuisine, dancing to a good band, and gratuities (but not drinks)—and you'll still pay only $59–$64.50 per person ($24.75 for lunch; $37.50 for brunch). You can experience the thrill of the stars, the water, and the lights of New York over lunch, dinner, or Sunday brunch. *Pier 62, W. 23rd St. (on the Hudson River), tel. 212/929–7090. Reservations required. Jacket required. AE, MC, V.*

Moderate   **Cafe Iguana.** As fast-paced as a road runner, this big, sprawling bar-restaurant, often packed tight with singles and vibrating with music, is a gregarious Mexican eatery. Its fans are legion; witness the number who purchase the T-shirts and other Iguana memorabilia in the upstairs gift shop. The wild decor features lots of variations on its lizard namesake. The fajitas and chicken Tijuana are excellent, and a good Sunday brunch and children's special meals are also available. This can be a good spot to take the family early in the evening. *235 Park Ave. S (at 19th St.), tel. 212/529–4770. Reservations advised. Dress: casual. AE, DC, MC, V. Closed Sat. lunch.*

★ **La Colombe D'Or.** For years this has been a paragon of French bistros, serving up good Provençal food under the supervision of the Studley family. It's very cozy, both downstairs and upstairs (though the bar gets smoky), thanks to printed fabrics, brick walls, and the ring of laughter from people enjoying a night out. The food is pure Provençal—excellent bouillabaisse, rich cassoulet, and luscious walnut tort, for example—and the well-priced wine list has chosen bottlings to complement the food. *134 E. 26th St. (near Lexington Ave.), tel. 212/689–0666. Reservations advised. Dress: casual. AE, DC, MC, V. Closed Sat. lunch and Sun.*

Lola. Boisterous, seductive, and very "hot," Lola is one of the most convivial restaurants in this area. The food, a blend of Southern, Caribbean, and French cooking, is overseen by Lola herself, a sexy woman whose style is mirrored in the glow of the lighting, the beautiful bar up front, and the flowers that deck the large, open room. The noise level can be a bit deafening, though. This is a great spot for brunch on Sunday, when live music is performed. Lola's "100 spice" chicken is renowned, and the onion crisps are simply terrific. *30 W. 22nd St. (near 6th Ave.), tel. 212/675–6700. Reservations advised. Dress: casual. AE. Closed Sun. dinner.*

★ **Park Bistro.** In look and feel, this is one of Manhattan's best approximations of a French bistro. Leather banquettes, posters, and photographs create the right ambience, and a trio of Frenchmen at the helm assure that everything will be *comme il faut.* Chef Jean-Michel Diot's Provence-inspired cooking is a delight. Be sure to sample a signature appetizer consisting of slices of potato smothered in grilled goat cheese, radicchio, and an olive vinaigrette dressing. The shellfish and mussel soup are both worthwhile. For a main course, consider the medaillons of beef in red wine sauce, rabbit with salsify, or lamb with eggplant. *414 Park Ave. S (near 28th St.), tel. 212/689–1360. Reservations advised. Jacket advised. AE, DC.*

Periyali. This enticing Greek restaurant does some out-of-the-ordinary cooking that clearly appeals to its regular crowd. The food is nicely seasoned and amply portioned. If you're in the mood for Greek cooking—albeit not of the classic variety—Periyali (which means seashore) is the place to go. Specialties include grilled lamb chops, grilled shrimp with herbs, and charcoal-grilled octopus. Don't overlook the cinnamon ice cream. *35 W. 20th St. (near 6th Ave.), tel. 212/463–7890. Reservations advised. Dress: casual. AE, MC, V. Closed Sun.*

Rojas-Lombardi Ballroom. This popular cabaret also has the city's first tapas restaurant—serving plates and platters of Spanish "snacks" that range from anchovies in grape leaves to squid, pork, chorizo, seviche, and everything else in between. Chef-owner Felipe Rojas-Lombardi is also a master of main courses, though there is some inconsistency in his presentations. This is a charming spot for unusual food and entertainment, not too far from Madison Square Garden. *253 W. 28th St. (near 8th Ave.), tel. 212/244–3005. Reservations advised. Dress: casual. AE, CB, DC, MC, V. Closed Sun. dinner, and Mon.*

★ **Union Square Café.** Owner Danny Meyer and chef Michael Romano have created an unusual and attractive scene for animated dining. Oysters Union Square are a signature appetizer; mousse of chicken liver is another sure bet. You can count on good beef, lamb, roast loin of rabbit, and grilled marinated tuna. Don't overlook the nightly pasta specials, such as penne with sausage. The wine list is one of the city's most innovative. Desserts are irresistibly rich; try the warm banana tart or the old-fashioned blueberry shortcake. *21 E. 16th St. (near Broadway), tel. 212/243–4020. Reservations advised. Jacket advised. AE, DC, MC, V. Closed Sun.*

Inexpensive **America.** This cavernous and lively spot tends to attract a youngish crowd, many of whom are content to hang out at the enormous and inviting bar and simply watch the scene. Noise levels can be problematic. Not surprisingly, America serves up an ambitious but often inconsistent array of American favorites and specials, from po' boy sandwiches to burgers and fajitas. *9 E. 18th St. (near 5th Ave.), tel. 212/505–2110. Reservations advised. Dress: casual. AE, MC, V.*

Giorgio. This pleasant trattoria bristles by day with a smattering of publishing and advertising types and takes on a more relaxed, neighborhood feeling by night. Regardless of the hour, its kitchen churns out good *pappa al pomodoro* (tomato and bread soup), excellent brick oven pizzas, pasta specials, and tasty sandwiches, such as smoked salmon and mozzarella. *245 Park Ave. S (between 19th and 20th Sts.), tel. 212/460–9100. Reservations advised. Dress: casual. AE, DC, MC, V. Closed for lunch Sat. and Sun.*

Zig Zag Bar & Grill. More a bar than a grill and more a hangout than a fine restaurant, this popular Chelsea establishment hosts a cross-section of New York City's artists, photographers, stylists, and other nightcrawlers who come here all dressed in black to meet their friends and to gossip about each other. You'll easily enter into the spirit of it all, for the long bar is a friendly one, and the food is actually much more than you might expect—big sandwiches of red peppers and salami, juicy hamburgers, and good, gloppy desserts. Skip the barbecued ribs. *206 W. 23rd St. (near 7th Ave.), tel. 212/645–5060. Reservations advised for 5 or more. Dress: casual. AE.*

Midtown East

Very Expensive **The Four Seasons.** One of the city's most important and beautifully designed restaurants, this place never rests on its laurels, thanks to co-owners Paul Kovi and Tom Margittai and the outstanding team they have assembled. The food is simple and elegant in the Pool Room, where you can dine on shrimp in three-fruit-and-mustard sauce, fresh pheasant or venison in season, or on offerings of the highly popular Spa Cuisine. The Grill Room is a powerhouse at lunch; at dinner, a menu with imaginative borrowings from Oriental cuisine takes over. There's a stellar wine list and the service is superb. *99 E. 52nd St. (near Park Ave.), tel. 212/754–9494. Reservations required. Jacket required. AE, CB, DC, MC, V. Closed Sat. lunch and Sun.*

La Côte Basque. Here's a restaurant with a history of revival: It was opened some decades ago by the legendary Henri Soulé, foundered when he died, and was restored to eminence by current owner Jean-Jacques Rachou. The place still looks very glamorous—with butter-colored walls, sprightly murals, dark beams, and a glittering bar—but the greeting at the door may be ice-cold if you're not known, and service may be little more than adequate. This is an institution, however, and the food, which comes out of the kitchen lickety-split, is hearty, classic, elaborate, and satisfying, though no longer anything to crow about. The extensive and inordinately expensive wine lists can be irritating, since there are no vintages given for many white wines. Still, you can't go wrong with the veal chop and mushrooms or the sky-high soufflés. *5 E. 55th St. (near 5th Ave.), tel. 212/688–6525. Reservations required. Jacket and tie required. AE, CB, DC, MC, V. Closed Sun.*

★ **Lutèce.** Lutèce is widely considered the finest restaurant in New York City, a fact attested to by an up-to-three-week wait for a reservation. Spruced up by design maven Sam Lopata, this East Side town house looks better than ever. But regulars come here not for dazzle but for perfection. Chef-owner André Soltner is a brilliant and highly dedicated cook who frets over every dish; ask him to choose your meal and you will never forget the experience. The repertoire ranges from terrine of cod in aspic, crêpes filled with home-smoked salmon and crabmeat, and red snapper *goujonettes* (slender strips) in red pepper sauce, to caramelized rack of lamb, roast guinea hen, foie gras en brioche, and gratin of chestnuts with *crême anglaise*. The wine list is extensive and expensive. *249 E. 50th St. (near 2nd Ave.), tel. 212/752–2225. Reservations required. Jacket and tie required. AE, CB, DC, MC, V. Closed Sat. lunch, Sun., Mon., and Aug.*

The Quilted Giraffe. Owners Barry and Susan Wine brought fresh ideas to modern cuisine some 10 years ago in the original Quilted Giraffe on Second Avenue, then moved into this stunningly designed new space in the AT&T building. There is continuous evolution in the food, which may range from a box of beautifully composed sushi to a "chocolate delirium" for dessert. The food can be either breathtaking or so quirky that you wonder whether it's worth the astronomical price, especially since portions are on the small side. (This may well be the most expensive restaurant in the country.) Mr. Wine is going through an Oriental phase just now, creating such dishes as wasabi tuna pizza, but you may also sup with delight on confit of duck, sweetbreads with caramel sauce, or duck breast with ratatouille. *550 Madison Ave. (off 55th St.), tel. 212/593–1221. Reservations advised. Jacket required. AE, CB, DC, MC, V. Closed Sat. lunch, Sun., and Mon.*

★ **The Rainbow Room.** This is still the most talked-about rehab on the Manhattan restaurant beat. Together, restaurateur-cum-impresario Joe Baum and architect Hugh Hardy marshaled a $25 million budget to renovate and revitalize one of the city's

Midtown East Dining

Alfredo's the Original
of Rome, **20**
American Festival
Café, **24**
Aquavit, **5**
Billy's, **36, 40**
Brasserie, **21**
Bukhara, **31**
Chez Louis, **35**
Chin Chin, **30**

China Grill, **6**
Dawat, **15**
Docks, **43**
The Edwardian
Room, **2**
Extra! Extra!, **42**
Felidia, **16**
The Four Seasons, **22**
Grand Central Oyster
Bar & Restaurant, **41**
Hatsuhana, **28**
Il Nido, **19**
La Caravelle, **3**
La Côte Basque, **4**

La Reserve, **25**
Laurent, **11**
Le Cygne, **8**
Le Perigord, **37**
Lutèce, **33**
Mickey Mantle's, **1**
Nippon, **29**
Palm, **38**
The Quilted Giraffe, **9**
Raga, **27**
The Rainbow
Room, **26**
Restaurant Lafayette
New York, **10**

Rosa Mexicano, **18**
Sandro's, **17**
Scarlatti, **23**
Serendipity, **14**
Shun Lee Palace, **12**
Smith & Wollensky, **32**
Sparks Steak
House, **39**
The "21" Club, **7**
Yellowfingers, **13**
Zarela's, **34**

greatest institutions. The result is a dramatic setting towering over midtown and serving up an unusual array of dishes. Some, such as tournedos Rossini and baked Alaska, are redolent of a bygone era; others, such as sautéed foie gras, are very contemporary. An extensive wine list, full of vintage treasures, enables you to order anything from a '28 claret to an '82 cabernet sauvignon. The musical entertainment changes regularly. Go with a group, dress festively, and don't forget your dancing shoes. *30 Rockefeller Plaza (at 50th St.), tel. 212/632–5000. Reservations required (6 wks. in advance). Jacket and tie required. Closed Mon.*

★ **Restaurant Lafayette New York.** Located in the Drake Hotel, this sumptuous dining room is one of the most exciting in the city. The menu is overseen by France's famous Louis Outhier, who gives long rein to chef Jean-Georges Vongerichten, a young man of real brilliance. He has a tendency toward exotic and Oriental seasonings, which sometimes don't click, but when they do—as in the ravioli with celery, the lobster in Thai curry sauce, and the gratin of malibu pineapple—the results are nothing short of sublime. This is a chef other French chefs in New York keep a close eye on. The staff is well trained and the place sedately furnished without being particularly modish. The wine list is excellent and well balanced. *65 E. 56th St. (near Park Ave.), tel. 212/832–1565. Reservations required. Jacket and tie required. AE, CB, DC, MC, V. Closed Sat. lunch, Sun., and Mon.*

The "21" Club. One of the most famous restaurants in the world, the "21" Club originally opened as a speakeasy during Prohibition and flourished well into the 1980s, when it started to seem both stuffy and scruffy to many. Since its renovation in 1987, "21" has improved its food 100%. However, it has gone through several changes in the kitchen, and the main dining room is still not as crowded as it once was. The greeting at the door by Ken Aretsky is friendlier than it used to be, and *éminence gris* Gerry Berns is as energetic as ever. Moreover, the place looks just great with its period paintings, Remington bronzes, and eclectic array of bric-a-brac ranging from beer steins and football helmets to vintage toys suspended from the ceiling. The club's challenge will be to attract some of its old-guard clientele, or at least their sons and daughters, and establish a new breed of regulars. If you go, try the "21 burger" or the crab cakes and, in the spirit of Hemingway and Bogart, have a drink at that great downstairs bar. *21 W. 52nd St. (near 5th Ave.), tel. 212/582–7200. Reservations advised. Jacket and tie required. AE, CB, DC, MC, V. Closed Sun.*

Expensive **Aquavit.** This is a splendid-looking Scandinavian restaurant (it's about time!) set on three levels in Nelson Rockefeller's former town house, where soaring walls, a waterfall, a smorgasbord bar, a wonderful selection of iced aquavits, and delicious food set the mood. At night the lighting is particularly dramatic, turning the main room into a unique dining spot. By day cool gray tones dominate, making this a good place for a business lunch. The menu is weighted towards seafood specialties: assorted smoked fish, graavlax, and salmon. Don't overlook the arctic venison in juniper-and-apple sauce, or the Swedish pancakes. The fixed-price menu is $60; an à la carte menu upstairs is good for a fast bite. *13 W. 54th St. (near 5th Ave.), tel. 212/ 307–7311. Reservations required downstairs. Jacket required. AE, DC, MC, V. Closed Sun.*

The Edwardian Room. The splendor of this dining room in the Plaza Hotel is unmatched by any other restaurant in New York, thanks to Ivana Trump's restoration of this dowager dining room to its former grandeur. Executive chef Kerry Simon is slowly developing the menu to balance standard Continental dishes with some new ones that are lighter and more modern, such as salmon tartare with curry oil or roast duck with lentils and mint. A dessert of banana slices with coconut ice cream is spectacular. This is a wonderful spot for a romant c twilight dinner or a quiet, uninterrupted business lunch. *59th St. and 5th Ave., tel. 212/759–3000. Reservations advised. Jackets required (jacket and tie at dinner). AE, DC, MC, V. Closed for Mon. dinner.*

★ **Grand Central Oyster Bar & Restaurant.** Opened in 1912, this granddaddy of American seafood restaurants is renowned for its extraordinary offerings of oysters and every kind of fish that swims into the Fulton Fish Market downtown. Located underneath Grand Central terminal's Great Hall, it's an astounding space to eat in; it's always crowded at lunchtime (less so for dinner), but there's a quieter rear room, as well as that famous oyster bar. Don't try coming late for your reservation or you'll lose it. The range of offerings here—chowders, grilled and poached fish, smoked salmon—is the best you'll ever see, and everything is prepared with great integrity. The white wine list is one of the most interesting in the United States. *Grand Central Terminal, tel. 212/490–6650. Lunch reservations required, dinner reservations advised. Dress: casual. AE, CB, DC, MC, V. Closed weekends.*

★ **Il Nido.** This is a major player in Northern Italian (specifically, Tuscan) cuisine, and it's constantly jammed with expense-accounters who'll pay a hefty tab for some of the best food in New York. The dining room is sophisticated without being studied: a mix of dark wood beams, white walls, plaid carpet, and a sea of white tablecloths. The regulars know what they like—a sampling of three pastas on one plate, massive veal chops with wild mushrooms, and the delicious *tiramisu*, the classic Italian dessert—but ask owner Adi Giovanetti what he'd suggest and you should be very happy. The wine list is long and impressive. *251 E. 53rd St. (near 2nd Ave.), tel. 212/753–8450. Reservations required. Jacket and tie required. AE, CB, DC, MC, V. Closed Sun.*

★ **Felidia.** Lidia and Felix Bastianich have long led the movement for authentic *cucina Italiana* in New York City, and have had tremendous influence across the country thanks to their unbridled enthusiasm, their attentiveness to detail, and their spectacular wine list. The food is usually great, refined but homey, full of delicacy and flavor, and always cooked with fervor. The only flaw is the crush at the bar from people waiting for reserved tables. The brick and blanched-wood decor is very cozy. Choose from a wide array of daily specials, or go with such standbys as cold antipasti, ziti with lamb sauce, *pappardelle* (wide noodles) with broccoli di rape, salmon with mustard sauce, or pineapple and strawberries with balsamic vinegar. Felidia's wine cellar is one of the country's finest, and Lidia herself will be happy to instruct you on the latest estate bottlings from Italy. *243 E. 58th St. (near 2nd. Ave.), tel. 212/758–1479. Reservations required. Jacket and tie advised. AE, CB, DC, MC, V. Closed Sun.*

★ **La Caravelle.** Owner André Jammet has restored this great classic restaurant to eminence, bringing the Jean Pages murals of Paris back to pristine condition, keeping the atmosphere both bright and genteel, and appointing a talented young chef—a move that ensures La Caravelle's position as one of the most consistently rewarding dining experiences in New York City. Many of the classic dishes remain, but the chef has been encouraged to innovate, and every week he changes his menu dégustation (priced at $70) which is offered on request. Go for his specials: Enjoy the fresh foie gras, the light crab ravioli, and, for dessert, the tour de force coconut soufflé. The wine list is very fine; the service staff is affable; and there is a lovely pretheater dinner available. *33 W. 55th St. (near 5th Ave.), tel. 212/586–4252. Reservations required. Jacket and tie required. AE, CB, DC, MC, V. Closed Sat. lunch and Sun.*

La Reserve. Catty-corner to Rockefeller Center is this airy, stylish restaurant, which serves a good balance of classic, nouvelle, and regional French cuisine. The large front dining room is decorated with rural murals, the lighting is cheerful, and the staff, under owner Jean-Louis Missud, is admirably professional. The large rear room, however, lacks personality. The menu changes to suit the seasons; specialties include terrine of lobster with sweetbreads, scallops of duck liver with peppercorns, and extravagant desserts filled with berries and pastry. This is a very fine place—and far more friendly than many of the French deluxe establishments. The wine list is solid. *4 W. 49th St. (near 5th Ave.), tel. 212/247–2993. Reservations advised. Jacket and tie required. AE, CB, DC, MC, V. Closed Sat. lunch and Sun.*

★ **Laurent.** This is one of the most gratifying dining experiences in town. The setting is stately and the staff most attentive, and owner Laurent Losa has assembled one of the finest wine cellars in America. All this is complemented by a highly skilled kitchen that turns out such eclectic Continental fare as *saucisson chaud* (warm sausage), gazpacho, salade Laurent, deviled roast beef bones (a popular Thursday lunch special), soft-shell crabs, and an unbelievably good throwback: beef Wellington. *111 E. 56th St. (near Park Ave.), tel. 212/753–2729. Reservations advised. Jacket required. AE, CB, DC, MC, V. Closed Sat. lunch and Sun.*

Le Cygne. After a few years of relative decline, Le Cygne has bounced back to stardom thanks to the arrival of chef Jean Michel Bergognoux. More changes are still in the works at this charming French restaurant. The beautiful pastel interior and conscientious service are appropriate complements to such notable dishes as timbale of poached egg and lobster roe, fresh marinated salmon, duck confit, breast of chicken with leek and truffle, and fettuccine with wild mushrooms. Leave room for such luscious desserts as cassis delight. *55 E. 54th St. (near Madison Ave.), tel. 212/759–5941. Reservations required. Jacket and tie required. AE, CB, DC, MC, V. Closed Sat. lunch and Sun.*

★ **Le Perigord.** This deluxe French restaurant is a perfect example of how classicism can be renewed successfully and maintain its vibrancy year after year. Le Perigord, under owner Georges Briguet, has long been one of Manhattan's finest dining spots, but with the addition of chef Antoine Bouterin a few years ago, its kitchen has become truly inspired. With its soft lighting, pretty flowered accents, and superb staff, this is a very romantic place, and there is no better host than Mr. Briguet for making a newcomer feel right at home. Your best bet is to put yourself in Bouterin's hands or go with his specials—items such as beef with truffles on a potato galette (a bed of thinly sliced potatoes) and passion fruit mousse. His halibut in court bouillon is great. *405 E. 52nd St. (near 1st Ave.), tel. 212/755–6244. Reservations required. Jacket and tie required. AE, CB, DC, MC, V. Closed Sun.*

★ **Palm.** Since the 1920s, Palm has been known as the New York steak house par excellence—though hardly for its decor: The floors are covered with sawdust; the walls with the discolored murals of favorite customers. You'll probably have to wait in the much-too-smoky, cramped bar if your reservation is anytime after 6 PM. The waiters don't hold much truck with amenities, but they're not really brusque, just robotic. You come here for 16-ounce aged steaks, gargantuan lobsters, great cheesecake, and anything else on the menu (well, the spaghetti's not so good). The wine list is a joke. Palm Too, right across the street, is just as good though not as antique. *837 2nd Ave. (near 45th St.), tel. 212/687–2953. Lunch reservations required, dinner reservations for 4 or more. Dress: casual. AE, CB, DC, MC, V. Closed Sat. lunch and Sun.*

Scarlatti. Owner Lello Arpaia has made this peach-colored dining room with its formal accents into one of the best Italian restaurants in midtown. The best specialties are in the Southern Italian mode, but this is not your "red sauce" kind of place: It offers authentic Italian cookery of a very high order. The staff can sometimes be too mannered (as in, "Let me suggest a nice veal chop for the young lady"), but Lello is a dedicated restaurateur who really wants you to have a great meal and some good wine. Try the malfatti pasta with artichokes, the sea bass roasted with herbs, or the mezzaluna ravioli with cream and saffron sauce. *34 E. 52nd St. (near Madison Ave.), tel. 212/753–2444. Reservations required. Jacket required. AE, CB, DC, MC, V. Closed Sun.*

★ **Smith & Wollensky.** Here is a very large, handsome, oak-floored steak-and-seafood house; it may not have Palm's historic dowdiness, but its food can be just as good. The steaks are unassailably among the best anywhere; the breads, veal chops, lobsters, stone crabs, and apple brown betty are all recommended; and the wine list is quite extraordinary, especially for cabernet sauvignon and vintage claret. Service is brisk and adequate to the job, although the place is jammed with businessmen day and night, before theater and after work. This is a smooth operation, very much a "New York joint." *201 E. 49th St. (at 3rd Ave.), tel. 212/753–1530. Reservations advised. Jacket advised. AE, CB, DC, MC, V.*

★ **Sparks Steak House.** This mock colonial dining room is paradise for the oenophile—or even the amateur wine buff—who's curious about sampling mature vintages of French, Italian, Spanish, or California wine. Indeed, owner Pat Cetta can lay claim to the biggest collection of fine and rare wines in the city. What's more, his markups are reasonable. Opt for Sparks's signature steak au fromage, accompanied by a magnum of '73 Mayacamus cabernet sauvignon. (Beef is hardly de rigueur; you can choose from a wide array of fish, fowl, lamb, and veal dishes.) Cap off the evening with a late-harvest Riesling or a Château d'Yquem '81 with luscious cheesecake. *210 E. 46th St. (near 3rd Ave.), tel. 212/687–4855. Reservations required. Jacket and tie advised. AE, CB, DC, MC, V. Closed Sun.*

Moderate **Alfredo's the Original of Rome.** Despite the hoopla about its links to the glamorous Alfredo's of Rome, and despite its tucked-away location in the Citicorp building, this popular place happens to serve Italian food of a very high order. Owner Guido Bellanca and his sons work hard to maintain an authentic level of cooking, as do the chefs regularly imported from Italy. You won't go wrong with any of the pastas, especially the famous fettuccine Alfredo, the risotto with mascarpone and spinach, or the panzotti with walnuts and herbs. Recommended for dessert are the tiramisu and the gelati. There's a bargain lunch on Sunday with good jazz. *153 E. 53rd St. (near 3rd Ave.), tel. 212/371-3367. Reservations required. Dress: casual. AE, CB, DC, MC, V.*

American Festival Café. If you have time for just one dining stop in New York with your family, this should be it. Set right next to the Rockefeller Center skating rink, the restaurant offers a view of the Prometheus statue, the row of flags from all nations, and majestic skyscrapers. The dining room is decorated with fine folk art in a casual, amiable way, and the food sticks to American classics, with a few modern touches. You won't go wrong with prime rib, crab cakes with cole slaw, or Sedutto's ice cream. This is a great place for pretheater dining; at Christmastime, when the plaza's giant tree is lighted, it's the most festive spot in the city. *20 W. 50th St. (in Rockefeller Center), tel. 212/246-6699. Reservations required. Dress: casual. AE, CB, DC, MC, V.*

Brasserie. At any hour, 24 hours a day, you can find something warm and good to eat at the Brasserie, which can come in handy after a long evening at the opera or a brisk early morning walk. The subterranean dining room is bright and cheerful, and it serves a good rendering of French bistro classics. There's a rectangular counter where you can sit for a quick or solitary meal, and the place always draws a friendly crowd. Try such items as the cassoulet or the roast chicken. Desserts are homey and good, too. *100 E. 53rd St. (near Park Ave.), tel. 212/751-4840. Reservations unnecessary. Dress: casual. AE, CB, DC, MC, V.*

Bukhara. Bukhara stands out for specializing in Uzbekistan cooking, especially for its savory barbecued meats and luscious tandoori specials. You'll eat this food with your fingers amid a sedate dining room full of glistening copper pots and colorful Bukhara rugs. Don't miss the pork spareribs, the Seekh kebab, or the Sikandari raan. You won't find this kind of food in too many other cities. The prices here are fair, and the service is courteous. A good Sunday brunch is also available. *148 E. 48th St. (near Lexington Ave.), tel. 212/838-1811. Reservations advised. Dress: casual. AE, CB, DC, MC, V.*

★ **Chez Louis.** Period posters are juxtaposed with a contemporary setting and garden view at this midtown bistro loosely modeled on Paris's famed L'Ami Louis. Large portions and hearty fare are the rule here. House specialties include roasted wild mushrooms with roast garlic, grilled fennel and leeks, roast *poussin* (young chicken) with foie gras butter, and confit of duck with marinated cucumbers; don't miss the potato pie. Rich desserts, including samples of owner David Lieberman's famous cookies (also sold at David's Cookies shops all around town) round out the meals here. *1016 2nd Ave. (near 54th St.), tel. 212/752-1400. Reservations advised. Dress: casual. AE, CB, DC, MC, V. Closed lunch weekends.*

China Grill. This is a vast and handsome, kite-festooned dining room that fills the ground floor of the CBS building (known to locals as "Black Rock"). In concept, the China Grill is essentially a California transplant à la Wolfgang Puck's Chinois on Main in Los Angeles (though he has no connection with China Grill). The menu features a variety of grilled fare with Oriental flavorings and leans toward seafood dishes. All are beautifully presented. It's a very popular place, and can be quite noisy, but the standards have been kept up. It's great for lunch and pre- or post-theater dinners. *52 W. 53rd St. (off 6th Ave.), tel. 212/ 333-7788. Reservations advised. Jacket advised. AE, CB, DC, MC, V. Closed lunch Sat. and Sun.*

Chin Chin. Vintage photographs snapped in the Far East at the turn of the century, combined with bleached walls, plush banquettes, and dramatic lighting, create a sleek, stark look at this beguiling but noisy Chinese café. Happily, the kitchen's output equals the drama of the decor, making this an excellent midtown outpost for Chinese fare. It serves good pork dumplings, fried squid, three-glass chicken (a glass each of water, soy sauce, and wine are added to the sauce), orange beef, sesame noodles, and scallion pancakes. *216 E. 49th St. (near 3rd Ave.), tel. 212/888-4555. Reservations advised. Jacket and tie advised. AE, CB, DC, MC, V. Closed lunch weekends.*

★ **Dawat.** Unquestionably the city's most attractive Indian restaurant, Dawat specializes in authentic and unusual regional dishes. Veteran Indian-food-lovers make this their second home. Whether you fancy chicken tikka, fish or goat stew, or such vegetable preparations as baked eggplant, green beans in coconut, baghari jhinga, or kheer, you will not be disappointed. Try the Taj Mahal beer. *210 E. 58th St. (near 3rd Ave.), tel. 212/355-7555. Reservations advised. Dress: casual. AE, CB, DC, MC, V. Closed Sun. lunch.*

★ **Hatsuhana.** This is considered New York City's best sushi restaurant. There are two locations: The original on 48th Street is pleasant enough, but the newer Park Avenue branch (actually wedged off the avenue between the streets) is prettier, with a greenhouse dining room. At both you'll find Japanese businesspeople at the sushi bar or the tables, challenging the *itamae* (master sushi chef) to come up with something interesting. He always does—from mackerel and pickled ginger to broiled squid feet! The sashimi is perfectly fresh; the service, fast-paced. *237 Park Ave. (on 46th St.), tel. 212/661-3400; 17 E. 48th St. (near Madison Ave.), tel. 212/355-3345. Reservations required. Jacket and tie advised. AE, MC, V. Closed Sat. and Sun.*

Mickey Mantle's. You can practically conjure up the whole scenario before setting foot in this fun midtown restaurant: Oversize television screens throughout are tuned to (what else?) baseball games past and present; ball club paraphernalia— bats, gloves, antique uniforms—abound. The food is hearty and the portions, whether of burgers, fries, or salads, are very large. What's more, Mickey Mantle himself actually drops in from time to time. This place is great for kids, both little and big. *42 Central Park S (near 6th Ave.), tel. 212/688-7777. Reservations advised. Dress: casual. AE, CB, DC, MC, V.*

★ **Nippon.** One of the first modern Japanese restaurants in the United States, Nippon has long been a pioneer in everything from fine decor and tatami rooms to bringing sushi and sashimi to the attention of the American public. At this large and bright place, the negimaki roll was created to satisfy Americans' taste for beef with a Japanese accent. The staff has remained cordial to all its customers. It's best to allow the chef to prepare a special dinner for you, featuring everything from imaginative sushi to exotic main courses; your meal will be unforgettable. The tatami rooms are for parties. *155 E. 52nd St. (near Lexington Ave.), tel. 212/355–9020. Reservations advised. Jacket advised. AE, CB, DC, MC, V. Closed Sun., and Sat. lunch.*

Raga. This sensuous dining place was the first in the city to prove that Indian restaurants can be every bit as elegant and refined as French or Italian ones. From the ornate door to the seductive lighting, this is a beautifully designed room, but the service can be impersonal. Indian music establishes a mood for the luscious Mogul cooking that issues forth sizzling from the kitchen. Highly recommended are the hot vindaloo dishes and the wonderful breads; the seafood is not quite as successful. *57 W. 48th St. (in Rockefeller Center), tel. 212/757–3450. Reservations required. Dress: casual. AE, CB, DC, MC, V. Closed lunch weekends.*

Rosa Mexicano. This is a good choice for classic regional Mexican fare, served up in attractive stucco-and-wood surroundings. Marvelous margaritas and excellent guacamole are prepared tableside, to your taste; spicy sausage, beef, and chicken are cooked on an open grill. Other specialties include stuffed peppers, *carnitas* (morsels of meat), and *helados* (ice creams). *1063 1st Ave. (near 58th St.), tel. 212/753–7407. Reservations advised. Dress: casual. AE, CB, DC, MC, V.*

★ **Sandro's.** Nowhere will you find a more ebullient chef than Sandro Fioriti, who bounds *ex culina* and slaps down whatever it is that strikes his fancy that night—roast pork *alla romana* (Roman style) with fennel and rosemary, roast chicken, luscious *bruschetta* (toast) with tomato, or fresh-from-the-oven lemon cookies. There is a menu, but go with Sandro's suggestions and you'll have hearty food, full of flavor. The gelati are among the best in the city. The staff is getting better, and everything is on the upswing here. The premises are effectively modern and simple, ideal for large parties or groups. *420 E. 59th St. (near 1st Ave.), tel. 212/355–5150. Reservations advised. Jacket required. AE, CB, DC, MC, V.*

★ **Shun Lee Palace.** One of the problems with most Chinese restaurants is their lack of consistency from month to month and year to year. Shun Lee's owner Michael Tong, however, shows what can be done when restaurateur and customer have the same standards. The result is the most reliably satisfying Chinese food in New York City, from the Peking duck and the beautifully orchestrated banquet dishes to the pork wontons and the mussels in black bean sauce. The premises, though cramped, are visually exciting; the staff can be either helpful or not, depending on your captain. *155 E. 55th St. (off Lexington Ave.), tel. 212/371–8844. Reservations advised. Jacket advised. AE, DC.*

Zarela's. This is one of the city's best spots for sophisticated Mexican cuisine served in comfortable surroundings. Owner Zarela Martinez (formerly of Café Marimba) continues to innovate and change her menu according to the seasonal availability of ingredients. Her trademark dishes include chicken Chilaquiles (chicken prepared with layers of fried tortillas), *calamar a la Veracruzana* (fried squid in a spicy tomato, onion, green olive, and jalapeño sauce), fajitas, whole grilled trout, and tuna with mole sauce. Sample the fried plantains, and try to leave room for the luscious desserts, especially the maple walnut pumpkin cheesecake. *953 2nd Ave. (near 50th St.), tel.*

212/644-6740. Reservations advised. Dress: casual. AE, DC. Closed lunch weekends.

Inexpensive **Billy's.** Charging a fair price for a fair meal, this neighborhood pub has been serving up seafood, steaks, chops, burgers, and corned beef hash—a house specialty—for the better part of the century, and numbers many a devoted regular. The old New York decor is completely apt for a pleasant lunch or early dinner. *948 1st Ave. (near 52nd St.), tel. 212/355-8920. Reservations advised for 3 or more. Dress: casual. AE, CB, DC, MC, V.*

Extra! Extra! Located in the *Daily News* building, this restaurant has an interior that really is black and white and red all over. The menu sports such eclectic offerings as Indian onion fritters with banana-tamarind chutney, the Dagwood Sandwich With Everything (breast of chicken, ham, salami, cheese, etc.), and fried calamari with *chipolte* (chili) sauce. It's a friendly and lively spot, for lunch in particular. *767 2nd Ave. (at 41st St.), tel. 212/490-2900. Reservations advised. Dress: casual. AE, CB, DC, MC, V. Closed weekends in summer only.*

Theater District

Very Expensive **Le Bernardin.** This commodious and elegant dining room has
★ dazzled the most demanding gourmets since its opening. With his light, flavorful sauces and tasteful creativity, Gilbert LeCoze is a true master of form and substance, and his sister Maguy greets customers with a French chic found nowhere else in New York. The service is usually impeccable, though there can sometimes be a wait for a confirmed table. The wine list is very good, but quite expensive. Creative appetizers include black bass tartar with caviar, marinated cod with ginger, and shrimp beignets. Among the entrées, the poached halibut with rosemary and onion confit vies in excellence with another version prepared with capers and a warm vinaigrette. The fish carpaccios are excellent, and the trademark roast monkfish with cabbage is a must. *155 W. 51st St. (near 7th Ave.), tel. 212/489-1515. Reservations required. Jacket and tie required. AE, CB, DC, MC, V. Closed Sun.*

Expensive **La Cité.** Owner Alan Stillman's (of Smith & Wollensky, The Post House, and Manhattan Ocean Club) latest creation evokes the image of a grand Franco-American restaurant; close attention has been paid to interior design. Chef Frederic Perier does wonderful Alsatian brasserie classics like *choucroute garnie* (sausages and ham over a bed of sauerkraut), *frise aux lardons* (chicory lettuce with bacon), and *confit de canard* (preserved duck), with nightly specials that are equally appealing. You'll also find good grilled mustard coated chicken and excellent frites. The interesting wine list includes several French country wines. Prices are generally higher, however, than you'd expect for such relatively simple fare, and service can sometimes be agonizingly slow. *120 W. 51st St. (near 6th Ave.), tel. 212/956-7100. Reservations advised. Dress: casual. AE, DC, MC, V.*

Gallagher's. The best of the West Side steak houses, this spot has a lot of tradition and Broadway razzle-dazzle about it. The place has always been a big hangout for sports figures, and there are photos of all the great ones on the walls. The meat—unquestionably fine aged prime—hangs in the window, and the whole place buzzes with masculine guffaws. If you like that kind of environment, this is an enticing place, especially before or after the theater. Stay with the steaks, lobster, onion rings, and cheesecake, and you'll be happy as a clam. *228 W. 52nd St. (off Broadway), tel. 212/245-5336. Reservations advised. Dress: casual. AE, CB, DC, MC, V.*

Petrossian. Here's a special spot for fanciers of fine caviar and smoked fish in every manifestation imaginable. At the New York outpost of his famed Parisian emporium, Christian Petrossian has imposed a highly stylized, updated-deco interior to set the stage for a unique evening, exotic lunch, or unusual theater outing. The fixed-price menus include tastings of most delicacies and, at today's prices, actually represent very good value. Indulge yourself in a trio of sevruga, osetra, and beluga caviar, or sample the superb smoked salmon ravioli. There's also a good champagne list. *182 W. 58th St. (near 7th Ave.), tel. 212/245-2214. Reservations advised. Jacket and tie advised. AE, CB, DC, MC, V. Closed Sun.*

★ **Russian Tea Room.** Justly famous for its longevity, its polished Imperial Palace decor, and its endless parade of celebrities (a scene from the movie *Tootsie* was filmed here), the RTR is legendary—and well it should be. Of course, if you're not Dustin Hoffman or Luciano Pavarotti, you probably won't get an "A" table downstairs, but upstairs is just as bright and shining, especially at holiday time. The food has improved measurably over the past year or two, since noted chef Jacques Pepin began consulting here. Enjoy the blini with caviar, the chicken Kiev full of butter, and the delicious borscht soup. *150 W. 57th St. (near 7th Ave), tel. 212/265-0947. Reservations advised. Jacket required at dinner. AE, CB, DC, MC, V.*

Moderate **Chez Josephine.** Quintessential French bistro fare—quail,
★ roast chicken, *pommes frites*—is served in a setting designed to pay homage to the late nightclub singer Josephine Baker (the owner is her adopted son). The place is decked out with paintings and posters from the period when Baker was all the rage in Paris. Even the famed piano on which she used to practice has been restored; it is now occupied by a modern-day chanteuse who evokes a bygone era. This place is great fun. *414 W. 42nd St. (near 9th Ave.), tel. 212/594-1925. Reservations advised. Dress: casual. AE, MC, V. Closed Sun. and lunchtime.*

Inexpensive **Bangkok Cuisine.** New York doesn't have the number of good Thai restaurants many smaller cities have, but Bangkok Cuisine is one of the oldest and best. It doesn't look like much—rather dark and bare-bones with a fish tank in the dining room—but the food is delicious and (on request) as hot as you can stand it. The pad Thai noodles and shrimp is a great dish here, as are the crispy mee krob noodles and the whole fried fish. *885 8th Ave. (near 53rd St.), tel. 212/581-6370. Reservations advised. Dress: casual. AE, CB, MC, V. Closed Sun. lunch.*

Cabana Carioca. It may seem dingy—you follow the music up a flight of stairs to a thickly varnished, rather weird-looking dining room—but Cabana Carioca serves the best Brazilian food in New York: great platters and pots steaming with black beans, manioc flour, *feijoada* (the Brazilian national stew), and seafood. All of it is lusty and filling, and nothing is particularly expensive. *123 W. 45th St. (near 7th Ave.), tel. 212/581-8088. Reservations advised. Dress: casual. AE, DC, MC, V.*

Hard Rock Café. People come here not so much for dinner or lunch as for a lift. Music blares from noon until the wee hours. The decor aptly consists of a collection of guitars belonging to celebrated musicians. You can count on decent hamburgers, sandwiches, and french fries. There is *always* a line to get in, even at 11:30 in the morning; they don't take reservations, so be prepared for a wait. *221 W. 57th St. (near Broadway), tel. 212/ 459–9320. No reservations. Dress: casual. AE, DC, MC, V.*

Joe Allen. A longtime hangout for theater goers and actors, Joe Allen (there's a Los Angeles and a Paris branch) has no pretensions and serves decent, simple food. The ribs and burgers are dependable, the service is affable (often by actors between jobs), and the place buzzes with a certain theatrical history. It's a good spot for before or after the show. *326 W. 46th St. (near 8th Ave.), tel. 212/581–6464. Reservations required. Dress: casual. MC, V.*

Upper East Side

Very Expensive **Le Regence.** Located in the glorious Plaza Athenée Hotel, this very formal restaurant is an elaborate exercise in *ancien regime* decor. It's ideal for business entertaining, with tables spaced widely apart. The fabulous food is overseen by France's noted Rostang family (Jo, Philippe, and Michel), who cook here on rotation while a superlative chef mans the kitchens day to day. This place is for serious eating: pompano with black olive crust, salmon rillettes with sour cream, lobster ravioli, figs with coulis of fruit, and several other delicacies you won't find elsewhere in this country. There's a good wine list, too. *37 E. 64th St. (near Madison Ave.), tel. 212/606–4647. Reservations required. Jacket and tie required. AE, CB, DC, MC, V.*

★ **Parioli Romanissimo.** The reserved beauty of Parioli, set in a town house off Fifth Avenue, makes this a very romantic spot, but it is the food that draws well-heeled customers here year after year. Owner Rubrio Rossi serves up exquisite Northern Italian cooking. You may feast on *cotechino* (fresh pork sausage) with white truffles, risotto with wild mushrooms, or an enormous rack of lamb with rosemary. Leave room for a selection from the finest cheese cart in the city. Prices are very, very high, but you do get value—except on the wine list, which is not particularly extensive but is exorbitantly priced. *24 E. 81st St. (off 5th Ave.), tel. 212/288–2391. Reservations required. Jacket and tie required. AE, CB, DC. Closed Sun. and Mon.*

Expensive **Arizona 206.** Despite its casual atmosphere and potentially piercing noise level, this remains a dynamic restaurant. Chef Marilyn Frobuccino maintains a very high level of Southwestern cuisine. At lunchtime be sure to sample the superb corn pizza with red onion raja and andouille (large enough for two), the wonderfully seasoned fresh-rock shrimp posole, or the Southwestern chef salad. At dinner, try the barbecued foie gras and cactus pear salad, blue-corn oysters with cabernet shallots, pistachio-encrusted tenderloin of beef with mole poblano, or rib eye of lamb with tomato chili. For a refreshing finale, treat yourself to the white-chocolate ice cream. (The adjacent Arizona Café, a no-reservation, less-expensive sibling, features innovative grilled specials and can be a lively alternative.) *206 E. 60th St. (near 3rd Ave.), tel. 212/838–0440. Reservations advised. Dress: casual. AE, CB, DC, MC, V. Closed Sun. lunch.*

★ **Dieci.** Of the string of Italian restaurants that line the Upper East Side, this is clearly one of the best and most consistent. Owner Joe Franco cares about everything, especially his customers, whom he wants to see well fed and happy. The atmosphere is low-key, with a few Hollywood portraits on the walls for decoration. Ask Franco for his suggestions, such as penne with vodka, grilled goat, and zabaglione. He knows his wines, too. *1568 1st Ave. (near 81st St.), tel. 212/628–6565. Reservations advised. Dinner only. Jacket required. AE, DC, MC, V.*

La Metairie. Here you'll find an attractive interior replete with a roaring fire in winter and charming oversize stuffed sheep. The menu is full of scrumptious Provençal items with real flavor. From the homemade bread rolls to the tarte tatin, the food here is completely satisfying. You might want to consider sardines Provençal, bouillabaisse, osso buco, or any number of grilled game or beef specials. Cap off the meal with a chocolate terrine with raspberry sauce. *1442 3rd Ave. (near 83rd St.), tel. 212/988–1800. Reservations advised. Dress: casual. AE, MC, V.*

★ **Le Cirque.** Here is the international restaurant par excellence. Glamorous, extravagant, studded nightly with famous names from every walk of life, Le Cirque glitters under the ownership of Sirio Maccioni, and Daniel Boulud is one French chef every other chef in town watches for his never-ending array of great dishes, which may be sea scallops with black truffles, a homey pot-au-feu, or a grandiose baby lamb of unsurpassed succulence. A multitude of signature dishes, including pasta primavera, is available on request. Desserts are always a delight, from the famous crème brûlée to the spun-sugar fantasies. The ever-expanding, ever-innovative wine list remains one of the city's very best and most moderately priced. *58 E. 65th St. (near Park Ave.), tel. 212/794–9292. Reservations required. Jacket and tie required. AE, CB, DC. Closed Sun.*

Post House. Here's a lively and engaging spot for both lunch and dinner, with a sleek checkerboard interior complemented by an eclectic array of Americana artifacts. Such standbys as Caesar salad, crab cakes, grilled sirloin, and addictive cottage fries vie with such creative new additions as venison chili, lobster pot pie, and Cajun beef. All can be paired with selections from a stellar wine list. *28 E. 63rd St. (near Madison Ave.), tel. 212/935–2888. Reservations required. Jacket and tie advised. AE, CB, DC, MC, V. Closed lunch Sat. and Sun.*

★ **Sette Mezzo.** In the space of a year, this restaurant has become the Upper East Side's trattoria of record, attracting a very posh uptown crowd. The menu is similar to Vico, its older sibling (*see* below), with such signature dishes as homemade stuffed mozzarella, fried zucchini, red snapper with balsamic vinegar, and penne with sausage and broccoli rappe (bitter Italian broccoli). The flattened breaded veal chop is another must; alternatively, try the paillard of veal with olives and tomatoes. For dessert, sample the excellent *tiramisu* (custard and sponge cake) or *tartufo* ice cream. *969 Lexington Ave. (near 70th St.), tel. 212/472–0400. Reservations advised. Dress: casual. No credit cards.*

Sign of the Dove. For years this place was the quintessential celebration restaurant, known for its lavish decor, its outrageous prices, and the lineup of limos outside its door. Today the decor is somewhat toned down but still luxurious, and the prices are still high—but the food is better than ever. Clearly owner Joe Santo has brought this old bird back to life, so there's good reason for romance to take hold again. Go with the bright young chef's Muscovy duck confit, the perfect rack of lamb, and the lemon creamcake. *1110 3rd Ave. (at 65th St.), tel. 212/861–8080. Reservations required. Jacket required. AE, CB, DC, MC, V. Closed Mon. lunch.*

Moderate **Al Amir.** This comfortable and cheerful spot specializes in Mid-
★ dle Eastern cuisine. Because such a tantalizing array of cold and hot appetizers are available, you might consider dispensing with a main course altogether. The starters include excellent *hummos* (mashed chick peas and sesame paste), *baba ghannouj* (broiled eggplant with sesame cream), *makanek* (spicy lamb meat sausage), and *falafel* (crushed fava beans and chick peas). Charcoal broiled *chich taouk* (marinated chicken), *kafta* (grilled ground lamb meat), or *gambari* (grilled jumbo shrimps) make worthwhile entrées. Leave room for the excellent homemade pastries. You might also try a bottle of Château Musar, a superb red wine from Lebanon. *1431 2nd Ave. (near 74th St.), tel. 212/737–1800. Reservations advised. Jacket advised. AE, CB, DC, MC, V. Closed for lunch Mon.–Sat.*

Anatolia. Faux marble columns, striking abstract light fixtures, and a trace of traditional Turkey (an antique samovar and tray) make for an unusual, effective setting. Go with an appetite because you'll want to eat at least three full courses. Superb appetizers include zucchini "pancakes" stuffed with feta cheese, dill, and scallions; baked vine leaves stuffed with pilaf; and Turkish meat and arugula pie. For the main course, try the skewers of grilled quail in grape leaves or "Sultan's Bliss"—lamb in a tomato sauce, served on a bed of roasted eggplant. For dessert, you can choose from an irresistible selection of baklava (both traditional and contemporary) and custards; there's also a delectable rendering of apricots in light cream. *1422 3rd Ave. (between 80th and 81st Sts.), tel. 212/517–6262. Reservations advised. Dress: casual. AE, CB, DC, MC, V. Closed Sun. lunch (and dinner in summer).*

★ **Da Gianvito.** Come here for well-prepared, honest Italian fare at reasonable prices. Ask for some *focaccia* (puffy pizza-like bread) with tomato and oregano—which usually comes gratis to the table. Specials, such as grilled portabello and shitaake mushrooms vie with standbys, such as antipasto dal Carello (assorted appetizers) or beef carpaccio. Equally good are the special pastas, such as coquille, shell-shaped pasta with meatballs and tomato sauce, or grilled sea bass in a basil and herb sauce. Under the heading scaloppine a piacere (veal as you please), diners have numerous options for preparation, including marsala, picatta, pizzaiola, or gorgonzola. *1373 1st Ave. (near 74th St.), tel. 212/472–4272. Reservations advised. Dress: casual. AE, DC, MC, V.*

Mezzaluna. The walls are decked out with dozens of artful interpretations of the two-handled chopping device for which the restaurant is named. This bristling trattoria is alive until the wee hours and is still populated by a trendy European crowd. The menu's highlights include carpaccio, insalata Mezzaluna, fresh tortellini (filling varies seasonally), pasta specials, and superb brick-oven pizzas. *1295 3rd Ave. (near 74th St.), tel. 212/535–9600. Reservations for 4 or more. Dress: casual. No credit cards.*

Mocca Hungarian Restaurant. If you're feeling low, head straight for Mocca Hungarian, where you'll find some well-made, though not particularly refined, Hungarian specialties such as *gulyas* (a classic stew), chicken paprikas, and dessert crêpes. Drink the robust red Hungarian wine, Egri Bikaver, and you'll soon feel very happy. This is a real neighborhood restaurant, with very little in the way of decor but a great deal of warmth. *1588 2nd Ave. (near 83rd St.), tel. 212/734-6470. Reservations advised. Dress: casual. No credit cards.*

Pig Heaven. This place is great fun for its piggy decor— dancing pigs, ceramic pigs, all kinds of porcine jokes. But it's also one of the neighborhood's most interesting Chinese restaurants, specializing in barbecued pork and other dishes that will make you wonder what you ever saw in egg rolls. The place is always crowded and boisterous, but no one seems to mind. Begin with the light dumplings, sample the Cantonese suckling pig, and try the special three-glass chicken. It's open late on weekends. *1540 2nd Ave. (near 80th St.), tel. 212/744-4887. Reservations advised. Dress: casual. AE, DC.*

★ **Table d'Hôte.** With a total of only nine tables, this tiny, antique-festooned restaurant qualifies as one of the smallest eateries in New York. Yet it is an ideal spot to retreat to after an evening exhibit at one of the Upper East Side museums or when your travels take you to the neighborhood. Here you can count on very well-prepared American/Continental fare, with first courses such as snails in puff pastry, black bean soup with jalapeno cream, or goat cheese croquettes. Entrées include grilled chicken breast with wild rice, carrots and cabbage; lamb; and salmon. End your meal with good tarte tartin. Nine wines are offered by the glass. *44 E. 92nd St. (near Madison Ave.), tel. 212/348-8125. Reservations required. Jacket and tie advised. AE.*

Vasata. This is one of the few remaining Czech restaurants in a neighborhood that was once full of Eastern European places. Vasata is still a solid and very friendly little spot where you get good value for the dollar and you'll never leave hungry. Sample the menu—roast goose, dumplings, apricot crêpes— everything is wonderful and filling. The atmosphere is very Old World, and the owners are delighted you paid them a visit. *339 E. 75th St. (near 1st Ave.), tel. 212/988-7166. Reservations advised. Dress: casual. AE, CB, DC, MC, V. Closed Mon.*

★ **Vico Ristorante.** This intimate, white-walled sliver of a space has become a hit. Bordering on boisterous, this neighborhood trattoria more than offsets the noise level with wonderful homespun pastas and innovative creations such as wilted radicchio with grilled smoked mozzarella, expertly fried zucchini and baby artichokes, country sausage with broccoli, flattened breaded veal chop, and delicious tiramisu. *1603 2nd Ave. (near 83rd St.), tel. 212/772-7441. Reservations advised. Dress: casual. No credit cards. Closed lunch.*

Inexpensive **J. G. Melon.** This popular neighborhood pub bristles with activ-
★ ity well past midnight. The casual decor is enlivened by paintings and prints of—what else?—the melon in myriad manifestations. Melon attracts a diverse uptown crowd and gives the first-time visitor an instant slice of neighborhood life. (There's also a West Side branch at 74th and Amsterdam Avenue.) Both serve excellent bacon cheeseburgers, club sandwiches, and cottage fries, and have great bars. *1291 3rd Ave. (at 74th St.), tel. 212/744-0585. No reservations. Dress: casual. No credit cards.*

Serendipity. Looking as bright as when it opened in the 1960s, Serendipity is as good as its name—a swell little place where you'll find all sorts of surprises, from campy gifts, postcards, and paraphernalia to some very tasty food: chili, burgers, and scrumptious desserts like frozen hot chocolate. The people who eat here range from Brooke Shields to prom queens; from East Side artists to Scarsdale matrons and children of all ages. *225 E. 60th St. (near 2nd Ave.), tel. 212/838–3531. Reservations advised. Dress: casual. AE, DC, MC, V.*

Yellowfingers. This bright, lively corner restaurant is especially convenient to Bloomingdale's and perfect for a light bite after a movie (several cinemas are located nearby). You'll find quality food here, including a good Caesar salad and onion rings that are offered as a first course. An enticing array of entrées ranges from sandwiches, such as grilled tuna steak with parsley and red onion on *foccacia* (puffy pizza bread), to homemade herbed sausages. You'll also have a nice selection of wines by the glass. *1009 3rd Ave. (at 60th St.), tel. 212/751–8615. No reservations. Dress: casual. AE, DC, MC, V.*

Lincoln Center

Expensive **Café des Artistes.** The history surrounding Café des Artistes
★ goes back to just after World War I, when the apartment building it's in was home to many of the finest artists and musicians of the day—including Howard Chandler Christy, who painted the restaurant's celebrated murals of young girls romping in a primeval forest that looks a little like Central Park. The paintings give this beautiful dining room a romance few other restaurants possess, but owner George Lang also demands high standards in the food, from the fine bistro fare, the pâtés, and the terrines to the chocolate Ilona torte. After a Lincoln Center performance, expect to see some of the city's most notable notables dining here. *1 W. 67th St. (near Central Park W), tel. 212/877–3500. Reservations required. Jacket required at dinner. AE, CB, DC, MC, V.*

★ **San Domenico.** This bellwether restaurant replicates its famed namesake in Imola, Italy. Owner Tony May and Chef Paul Bartolotta show that Italian food can be as good here as over there. The premises are deluxe but not overly formal, jarred only by orange tablecloths. The wine list is extraordinary in its Italian offerings, and the service staff is most attentive. This is one of the most talked-about restaurants of the year. Have the signature ravioli with egg and truffles, the lusty *pappa al pomodoro* (a broth of tomato, onion, garlic, and bread), the lobster fricasee with artichokes, and finish off with mascarpone cream with espresso sauce. *240 Central Park S (off Columbus Circle), tel. 212/265–5959. Reservations required. Jacket and tie required. AE, CB, DC, MC, V. Closed Sat. lunch. and Sun.*

Tavern on the Green. Just about every tourist has heard of this fanciful restaurant, and most come here to stare at its flamboyant architecture. But New Yorkers come too, because Tavern is undeniably lively and fun. Warner LeRoy's fantasy of lights and antiques in this sumptuous Central Park setting works brilliantly; he does more banquet business here than anyone in the city. You may feast on such dishes as foie gras on greens, but it's safer to go with the rack of lamb. The wine list is quite good. *Central Park W (at 67th St.), tel. 212/873–3200. Reservations advised. Jacket advised. AE, CB, DC, MC, V.*

Moderate **Café Luxembourg.** Still stylish, but now a lot less boisterous
★ than it was, Café Luxembourg remains one of the West Side's

better bistros—and is priced accordingly. Though its original chef has departed, you can still expect a solid menu and satisfying specials. Go for the seafood appetizers, baby lamb, steak au poivre, and crème brûlée. *200 W. 70th St. (near Amsterdam Ave.), tel. 212/873-7411. Reservations advised. Dress: casual chic. AE, CB, DC, MC, V. Lunch Sun. only.*

Punsch. The latest hit in the Lincoln Center area is hardly a knockout. A Scandinavian menu and reasonable prices are the drawing card, enlivened by the nightly inundation of dancers and theater people from the neighborhood, especially after the ballet and opera let out. (Indeed, several members of the New York City Ballet are backers here.) However, this instant popularity can also lead to overcrowding, excessive noise, and a lengthy wait for a confirmed dinner reservation. The lunch menu features tasty Danish open-faced sandwiches, as well as hefty pea soup, pastas studded with duck confit, and good graavlax; at dinner, more Scandinavian specialties, such as "Janson's Temptation" (a potato-cream-anchovy casserole), are featured. Skip the more traditional fare, such as rack of lamb or grilled beef. Desserts are also disappointing. *11 W. 60th St. (near Broadway), tel. 212/767-0606. Reservations advised. Dress: casual. AE, DC, MC, V. No lunch Sat. and Sun.*

Inexpensive **The Ginger Man.** There's little to recommend the food at The Ginger Man, which serves up rather humdrum burgers, french fries, and other staples, but its proximity to Lincoln Center makes this an ideal spot to grab a bite before or after the ballet or opera. And you never know who might be coming through the door next—quite possibly a celebrity or a whole corps de ballet. *51 W. 64th St. (off Broadway), tel. 212/399-2358. Reservations required. Dress: casual. AE, CB, DC, MC, V.*

Upper West Side

Expensive **The Terrace.** Perched atop a Columbia University dorm (though
★ not associated with the school), this elegant dining room, with its panoramic view of Manhattan and the Hudson River, is packed most nights but remains unknown to most people. It should be better known: The food is every bit the equal of the view, with prices slightly below those of comparable downtown menus. There is a new chef here, but you may expect expertly conceived French and Continental classics executed with considerable flourish. *400 W. 119th St. (near Amsterdam Ave.), tel. 212/666-9490. Reservations required. Jacket and tie required. AE, CB, DC, MC, V. Closed Sat. lunch, Sun., and Mon.*

Moderate **Alcala.** An innovative Spanish restaurant-cum-tapas-bar, this place is designed for conservative uptown tastes. The decor is unassuming (the ubiquitous brick-and-brass look) and at times the food can be equally restrained. Good tapas include empanadas and wild mushrooms with chorizo; the seafood paella can be garlicky, and the grilled tuna can be bland. *349 Amsterdam Ave. (near 76th St.), tel. 212/769-9600. Reservations advised. Dress: casual. AE, CB, DC, MC, V. Dinner and Sun. brunch only.*

Amsterdam's Bar and Rotisserie. This modest eatery and bar lacks all pretension, yet it is an important watering hole for Westsiders, who flock here to eat and drink with their good-looking friends. It's high-ceilinged and decorated with minimal effort, throwing the burden of showmanship on the customers, who dress up in the latest styles and wait at the bar for tables. The food is good, substantial, and low in price. You can't go wrong with the burgers or the well-regarded roast chicken and french fries. Desserts are gooey and worth every calorie. *428 Amsterdam Ave. (near 80th St.), tel. 212/874-1377. No reservations. Dress: casual. AE, CB, DC, MC, V.*

Docks. This highly popular spot for seafood is contemporary in look but has the charm of an old-time seafood house. You dine on two separate levels separated by stairs and a gleaming brass rail. A blackboard lists the daily oyster specials and the catch of the day (which will also be rhymed off by your waiter). Such staples as grilled scallops or salmon can be found on the regular menu along with grilled halibut. *2427 Broadway (near 89th St.), tel. 212/724-5588; also at 633 3rd Ave. (near 40th St.), tel. 212/986-8080. Reservations advised. Dress: casual. AE, CB, DC, MC, V.*

★ **Poiret.** White walls with a floral motif, candlelit tables, and a handsome flower-festooned vitrine create an airy ambience at this popular French spot. The only flaw in the design is the soundproofing: but the first-rate bistro fare more than compensates, even when you have to raise your voice a tad to be heard over the beautifully seasoned and flavorful Mediterranean soup. Try the chicken-liver mousse and frisé salad. Whether you order the steak au poivre or steak bearnaise, be sure to request a side dish of pommes frites. For dessert, Poiret makes an admirable crème brûlée. *474 Columbus Ave. (between 82nd and 83rd Sts.), tel. 212/724-6880. Reservations advised. Dress: casual. AE, DC, MC, V. Dinner and Sun. brunch only.*

Sidewalkers. This is one of New York's few Maryland crab houses, where you drink beer while you pound and pick away at spiced blue crabs. The huge dining room, which appears once to have been a lobby, is jammed with casually dressed Westsiders. The Creole gumbo is excellent, but the rest of the dishes just aren't up to those crabs. *12 W. 72nd St. (near Central Park W), tel. 212/799-6070. Reservations advised. Dress: casual. AE, CB, DC, MC, V. Dinner only.*

Worth a Special Trip

Brooklyn
Very Expensive
★
The River Café. The beauty of the water, the Brooklyn Bridge, and the Manhattan cityscape make this a must-go for a unique sense of New York City's majesty. A new chef, David Burke, has real talent and creates some innovative cuisine, although he sometimes tries a bit too hard and comes up with assemblages that are eccentric at best: curried noodle-and-oyster cake with squid and red wine butter, or salad of foie gras and tongue confit with pickled peaches and almond wafers. If he calms down, he should be a real contender. The dining room has no bad tables, but those smack on the window do not come cheap—expect a wait even with a reservation. *1 Water St., tel. 718/522-5200. Reservations required. Jacket required. AE, CB, DC, MC, V.*

Moderate **Gage & Tollner.** On looks alone, this 110-year-old landmark warrants a visit. Authentic gas lamps (among the last remaining examples in the city), a tin-lined ceiling, and roomy banquettes create a charming, old-fashioned New York feel. Now that Edna Lewis presides over the menu, the kitchen has been given new life (although service can sometimes be lethargic). Some of her signature appetizers include Charleston she-crab soup, crab cakes, and lobster bisque. As an alternative, you can choose among dozens of clam and oyster appetizers, such as soft clam belly fritters. For the main event, try the shrimp and crab gumbo, crabcakes Freetown, or braised brisket of beef. Don't forget a side order of corn fritters, and leave room for the double chocolate cake. *372 Fulton St. (on Fulton Mall), tel. 718/875-5181. Reservations advised. Dress: casual. AE, DC, MC, V. Closed weekends in summer.*

Harlem
Moderate
★

Sylvia's. If you're craving great barbecue, down-home soul food, and something uniquely New York, catch a cab to Harlem (and have one waiting outside when you exit) and stop in at Sylvia's, a marvelous and justly famous restaurant serving up huge portions of great ribs, pork chops, candied sweet potatoes, and pecan pies. Bring an appetite and expect to take something home. It's good for Sunday lunch. *328 Lenox Ave. (near 126th St.), tel. 212/996-0660. Reservations required. Dress: casual. No credit cards.*

The Bronx
Moderate
★

Amerigo's. In the safe Bronx neighborhood of Throgs Neck, this has been an institution for half a century; under owners Tony and Anna Cortese, it gets better every year. There are two dining rooms: one casual, the other a bit more refined, with low lighting, sculpture, and a spacious bar. The Italian-American menu offers everything from rich, lusty *spiedino* (mozzarella fried in bread-crumb batter, with anchovy sauce) and gnocchi with a verdant pesto to terrific prime steaks, chops, and fresh lobsters. The osso buco is among the best in New York City. The Italian wine list is comprehensive in all regions, and prices for enormous portions are fair indeed. *3587 E. Tremont Ave., tel. 212/792-3600. Reservations required weekends. Jacket suggested in main dining room. AE, CB, DC, MC, V. Closed Mon.*

9 Lodging

by Jane Hershey

A New York–based freelance writer whose work has appeared in Good Housekeeping, US, *and* Elle, *Jane Hershey is a long-time contributor to various Fodor's guides.*

If any single element of your trip to New York City is going to cost you a lot of money, it'll be your hotel bill. European cities may offer plenty of low-priced—albeit undistinguished—lodgings, but New York doesn't. Real estate is at a premium here, and labor costs are high, so hoteliers start out with a lot of expenses to cover. And there are enough well-heeled visitors to support competition at the premium end of the spectrum, which is where the profits are. Considering the healthy occupancy rate, market forces are not likely to drive current prices down. Fleabags and flophouses aside, there's precious little here for under $100 a night. We have noted a few budget properties, but on the sliding scale of Manhattan prices even our "Inexpensive" category includes hotels that run as high as $160 for one night's stay in a double room.

Once you've accepted that you must pay the going price, though, you'll have plenty of choices. In general, Manhattan hotels don't measure up to those in other U.S. cities in terms of room size, parking, or outside landscaping. But, this being a sophisticated city, New York hotels usually compensate with fastidious service, sprucely maintained properties, and restaurants that hold their own in a city of very knowledgeable diners. Besides, where else can you sleep in Frank Lloyd Wright's former apartment, swim with a view of the Empire State Building, or eat breakfast in bed while watching sea lions at play?

Price is by no means the perfect indicator of impeccable service, pleasant surroundings, or delicious cuisine, so we've tried to indicate the shortcomings of various properties, as well as their strong points. Common sense should tell you not to anticipate the same kind of personal service from even a top-flight convention hotel, such as the New York Hilton, as you would from a smaller, sedate property like the Doral Tuscany, even though both have rooms in the same price range. Know your own taste and choose accordingly. If you like bright lights, a lively lobby, and a central location, a residential-style hotel could disappoint you, no matter how elegant it is.

Basic rules of decorum and dress are observed at the better hotels. With few exceptions, jackets (and frequently ties) are required in formal dining and bar areas after 5 or 6 PM. Bare feet or beach sandals are not allowed, and an overall sloppy appearance won't encourage good service.

Women on their own, even at upscale hotels like the Waldorf-Astoria or the Helmsley Palace, should be aware that they may be accosted in public areas, either by male guests trying to find companions or by hotel staff trying to chase away the hookers who transact business in hotel lobbies. Because these "working girls" often look quite respectable, any single woman may be suspect. You might want to ask the concierge to point out places where you'll feel comfortable relaxing or waiting on your own. Many female travelers find VIP floors, with their concierge-controlled lounges and complimentary beverages and snacks, a boon for avoiding such situations.

Most Manhattan hotels are in the midtown area, so we have categorized them by price range rather than location. Exact prices could be misleading: Properties change their so-called "rack rates" seasonally, and most hotels offer weekend packages that include such tempting extras as complimentary meals, drinks, or tickets to events. Your travel agent may have brochures about such packages; also look for advertisements in travel magazines or the Sunday travel sections of major newspapers such as the *New York Times*, the *Washington Post*, or the *Los Angeles Times*.

Visitors can also take advantage of reputable discount booking services such as **Express Hotel Reservations.** This Boulder, Colorado, company offers savings of 20–30% on superior rooms at a variety of New York hotels, along with travel advice and other information. There is no charge for any of the company's services (it is used frequently by major companies, such as Hallmark and The Limited). Participating hotels include the New York Hilton, Le Parker Meridien, and several of the Doral properties. Call 800/356–1123 for further information.

Highly recommended lodgings in each price category are indicated by a star ★. Though not *every* acceptable hotel has been included, enough ground has been covered to help you find a good match.

Category	Cost*
Very Expensive	over $260
Expensive	$200–$260
Moderate	$160–$200
Inexpensive	under $160

All prices are for an above-standard double room, excluding 13¼% city and state sales tax and $2 occupancy tax.

The following credit card abbreviations are used: AE, American Express; CB, Carte Blanche; DC, Diners Club; MC, MasterCard; V, Visa.

Reservations New York is constantly full of vacationers, conventioneers, and business travelers, all requiring hotel space. Try to book your room as far in advance as possible, using a major credit card to guarantee the reservation; you might even want to work through a travel agent. Because this is a tight market, overbooking can be a problem, and "lost" reservations are not unheard of. Most properties, especially those that are part of national or worldwide chains or associations (i.e., Marriott or Leading Hotels of the World), are cooperative and generous when a reservation is lost, but guaranteed reservations usually prevent any problems. When signing in, take a pleasant but firm attitude; if there is a mix-up, chances are the outcome will be an upgrade or a free night.

Hotels with famous restaurants appreciate it when guests who want to use those facilities book tables when they make their room reservations.

Services Unless otherwise noted in the individual descriptions, all the hotels listed have the following features and services: private baths, central heating, air-conditioning, private telephones, on-premises dining, valet and room service (though not necessarily 24-hour or short notice), TV (including cable and pay-per-view films), and a routine concierge staff. Larger hotels will generally have video or high-speed checkout capability.

New York City has finally allowed liquor minibars to be installed in rooms. Most hotels have added this much-anticipated amenity—at least in their more expensive units.

Pools are a rarity, but most properties have fitness centers; we note only those that are on the premises, but other hotels usually have arrangements for guests at nearby facilities.

We've already warned you against bringing a car to Manhattan, but here's another reason: the lack of hotel parking. Many properties in all price ranges *do* offer parking facilities, but they are often at independent garages that charge up to $20 or more per day.

Very Expensive

★ **The Carlyle.** Located in one of the city's finest residential areas, this beautifully appointed traditional hotel is considered one of New York's finest. The mood is English manor house; larger rooms and suites, many of them decorated by the famous interior designer Mark Hampton, have terraces, pantries, and antique furnishings. Baths, though more subdued than others in town, are marbled and chock-full of de rigueur amenities such as hair dryers, fine toiletries, and makeup mirrors. Most visitors have heard about the famous Café Carlyle, where performers such as Bobby Short and George Shearing entertain throughout the year. But the hotel also contains the charming Bemelman's Bar, with whimsical animal murals on the walls and live piano music at night, and the formal Carlyle Restaurant, with French cuisine and old-fashioned courtly service. This is one of the few grand hotels where European elegance and American friendliness really mix; you don't have to be Nancy Reagan to get a smile or good treatment. The concierge service is especially excellent. *35 E. 76th St. (at Madison Ave.), 10021, tel. 212/744–1600, fax 212/717–4682. 185 rooms. Facilities: restaurant, café, bar, lounge, VCRs and stereos, kitchenettes and pantries in larger units, fitness center, meeting rooms. AE, CB, DC, MC, V.*

The Lowell. Think how nice it would be to arrive in New York and find that a rich uncle had offered you the run of his elegant pied-à-terre—that's the feeling you'll get at The Lowell. There's no lobby in the true sense, just a regal front-desk area with a few chairs and newspapers. Upstairs, on the second floor, is a picture-perfect tea-and-lunch-room in the English-country-house style; adjacent is a first-rate steak restaurant, the Post House (*see* Chapter 8). The guest rooms, mostly suites, are at once fashionable and homey: Furnishings are an eclectic mix of traditional pieces with surprisingly modern accents. Bathrooms have good lighting and generous amenities. Some rooms have wood-burning fireplaces, a relative rarity in the city. This is not a hotel for hunting down celebrities, although it has become a favorite of many, such as George Michael and Mick Jagger, who prize its amiable but utterly discreet service. *28 E. 63rd St., 10021, tel. 212/838–1400 or 800/345–3457, fax 212/319–4230. 60 rooms. Facilities: restaurant, small meeting room, some kitchenettes. AE, CB, DC, MC, V.*

★ **The Mayfair Regent.** General manager Dario Mariotti adds a cheery Italian influence to this low-key, gracious hotel. Locals know it for its traditional tea lounge and its always-white-hot restaurant, Le Cirque (*see* Chapter 8). Even the smallest of the guest rooms have marble baths and traditional-style, peach-

Algonquin, **45**
Beekman Tower, **35**
Carlyle, **4**
Days Inn, **27**
Doral Court, **49**
Doral Inn, **34**
Doral Park Ave., **50**
Doral Tuscany, **49**
Drake, **17**
Dumont Plaza, **52**
Grand Hyatt, **48**
Helmsley
Middletowne, **37**
Helmsley Palace, **32**
Holiday Inn Crowne
Plaza, **28**
Hotel Edison, **41**
Hotel Empire, **11**
Hotel Elysee, **23**
Hotel Wentworth, **43**
Inter-Continental, **38**
Le Parker
Meridien, **19**
Lowell, **9**
The Mark, **3**
Marriott Marquis, **42**
Mayfair Regent, **8**
Milford Plaza, **47**
N.Y. Hilton, **22**
N.Y. Int'l Youth
Hostel, **1**
Novotel, **26**
Omni Berkshire, **24**
Omni Park Central, **21**
Peninsula, **18**
Pickwick Arms, **29**
Pierre, **13**
The Plaza, **15**
Plaza Athenée, **7**
Ramada Inn, **40**
The Regency, **12**
Ritz-Carlton, **14**
Roger Smith
Winthrop, **39**
Royalton, **46**
San Carlos, **31**
Shelburne, **51**
Sheraton Centre, **25**
Sloane YMCA, **53**
Southgate Tower, **54**
Stanhope, **2**
Summit, **30**
Surrey Hotel, **5**
U.N. Plaza, **44**
Vanderbilt YMCA, **36**
Vista Int'l, **55**
Waldorf-Astoria, **33**
Wellington, **20**
Westbury, **6**
West Side YMCA, **10**
Wyndham, **16**

Manhattan Lodging

tone decor with up-to-date extras such as dual-line telephones and outlets to accommodate portable computers and facsimile machines. Service is super-efficient; guests are offered umbrellas, room humidifiers, and the ingenuity of longtime concierge Bruno Brunelli, who can usually conjure up impossible tickets or reservations. While its overall appearance isn't quite as glitzy as that of some other hotels in this price category, The Mayfair Regent more than makes up for its slightly lived-in feel (which many guests, incidentally, prefer) with friendliness and an always-lively atmosphere. *610 Park Ave. (at 65th St.), 10021, tel. 212/288-0800 or 800/545-4000, fax 201/737-0538. 150 rooms. Facilities: restaurant, lounge, meeting rooms, unlimited local phone calls. AE, CB, DC, MC, V.*

The Peninsula. The former Gotham Hotel on Fifth Avenue has gone through more changes in the past five years than the plot of a TV soap opera. After being magnificently renovated as the Hotel Maxim, it is now owned and operated by the respected Peninsula Group of Hong Kong. The new owners have wisely left the Maxim's furnishings intact, including the sumptuous (by New York or any standards) marble baths. Even the smaller rooms have graceful sculpted art-nouveau headboards, desks, and armoires; some also have the same sweeping views down Fifth Avenue as the more expensive suites. Many bathrooms feature Jacuzzi tubs; all have bidets and Lanvin toiletries. The total effect is stylishly French without frippery. The acclaimed (and very pricey) Adrienne restaurant, under the direction of the outstanding Swiss chef, Gray Kunz, and its less lofty café and bar serve high-style French cuisine. The new rooftop health club, with state-of-the-art exercise machines, a decent-size pool, massage and facial services, and a dining area with a terrace, is a knockout. Time will tell whether the hotel's service, which was sometimes less than perfect under the former management, will live up to worldwide Peninsula standards. *700 5th Ave., 10019, tel. 212/247-2200 or 800/262-9467, fax 212/903-3949. 250 rooms. Facilities: restaurant, café, lounge, meeting rooms, pool, fitness center. AE, DC, MC, V.*

★ **The Pierre.** The Four Seasons, a Canadian hotel group, has made a specialty of "freshening up" classic properties, and the Pierre is one of their notable successes. Ever since its opening at the height of the Depression, the Pierre has symbolized dignified elegance. One might expect haughtiness along with the creamy, oriental-carpeted halls and bright chandeliers, but you won't find that here: The staff has a sense of fun about working in these posh surroundings. Rooms, most of which have been recently refurbished, are traditionally decorated in soft floral patterns, with quilted bedspreads and fine wood furniture. Bathrooms have recently been upgraded and are generously stocked with Four Seasons' amenities. The Boudoir suites, overlooking the Central Park Zoo and Wollman Ice Rink, are worth the extra price. Café Pierre, under the direction of executive chef Franz Klampfer, can hold its own against many of the city's best spots; the Bar features low-key jazz piano in the evenings, and formal afternoon tea is served under the blue cherubim-filled dome of the Rotunda. There are no gimmicks here—just good old-fashioned style and service. *5th Ave. at 61st St., 10021, tel. 212/838-8000 or 800/332-3442, fax 212/940-8109. 204 rooms. Facilities: restaurant, bar, tearoom, meeting rooms, manned elevators, packing service upon request, hand-laundry service. AE, CB, DC, MC, V.*

The Plaza. When real-estate developer and casino operator

Donald Trump purchased this National Historic Landmark in 1988, locals shuddered a bit, but there is actually much to applaud. Although this former haunt of F. Scott Fitzgerald, George M. Cohan, Frank Lloyd Wright, and the Beatles is going through growing pains, it's ready to receive a relatively demanding public. Prices have edged up, but so has the quality of even the least expensive rooms. New color schemes are in burgundy or teal blue; fresh, floral-patterned quilted spreads grace the large beds. Furnishings, though still "hotel-like" in most units, are of high quality. Bathrooms, even those not yet fully redone, have fluffy new towels and Chanel toiletries. One real advantage here is the size of guest rooms—only a handful of other classic properties can offer similar spaciousness in nearly all accommodations. Food-and-beverage service has made major strides throughout the property. Current executive chef Kerry Simon (formerly of Lafayette and Lutèce) will certainly earn plaudits here. The Edwardian Room and the Oak Room, always known for elegant atmosphere, now offer food to match; Stanley Kramer, formerly of the Grand Central Oyster Bar, has taken over the Plaza's Oyster Bar and should upgrade matters there. Even the scones at the Palm Court, that gracious, classic lobby lounge, seem fresher. The last word was that Trader Vic's bar—renowned for its elaborate exotic drinks—will stay open, although the space formerly occupied by its restaurant will possibly be turned into a health club. *5th Ave. at 59th St., 10019, tel. 212/759–3000 or 800/228–3000, fax 212/753–1468. 807 rooms. Facilities: 2 restaurants, 2 bars, café, art gallery, handicapped-guest rooms, meeting rooms, packing service upon request, large concierge staff. AE, CB, DC, MC, V.*

The Plaza Athenée. This Trusthouse Forte property on Madison Avenue is currently New York's priciest hotel, but it's not really worth the money, except for the baroque blue Le Regence restaurant. Rooms here are rather small, though elegant and stylish. Service—unless one happens to be Elizabeth Taylor or Princess Diana—can be snooty and lax. A better bet would be to go with its sister hotel, The Westbury (*see* Expensive, below). *37 E. 64th St., 10021, tel. 212/734–9100 or 800/225–5843, fax 212/772–0958. 160 rooms. Facilities: restaurant. AE, CB, DC, MC, V.*

The Ritz-Carlton. This property—once hot, then lukewarm—has recently been brought under genuine Ritz-Carlton management, and overall service should soon be raised to the company's high standards. Guest rooms, which will be refurbished during this year, are, even in their current state, superior. The rooms with Central Park views are definitely preferable, but all accommodations are identical in decor and amenities. The style is English country house with modern accents, designed by American decorator Mrs. Henry "Sister" Parish II. The relatively understated atmosphere manages not to be stuffy. The hotel's most notable guests of late include rock group U2 and *Dallas* star Linda Gray. In fact, bartender Norman Bukofzer in the Jockey Club draws a coterie of convivial celebrities. *112 Central Park S, 10019, tel. 212/757–1900 or 800/241–3333, fax 212/757–9620. 210 rooms. Facilities: restaurant, bar, meeting rooms, complimentary limousine service to Wall Street. AE, CB, DC, MC, V.*

The Stanhope. This formal and slightly intimidating hotel across the street from the Metropolitan Museum of Art has recently been purchased by a low-profile Japanese construction company that plans, thus far, to keep it just the way it is. The lobby's Louis XVI grandeur is carried through to the small, though expensively furnished, guest rooms and suites. Bathrooms, though not opulent, are nicely appointed. Public dining and bar areas can be prim, with a decor that smacks of Liberty's of London and Mayfair clubs; this is the only hotel in Manhattan where ties and jackets are required at all times (even celebrities have been sent upstairs for the proper neckwear). Still, regular customers are unswervingly loyal, so the staff must be more relaxed and friendly than they first appear to be. *995 5th Ave. (at 81st St.), 10028, tel. 212/288–5800 or 800/ 828–1123, fax 212/517–0088. 118 rooms. Facilities: restaurant, outdoor café in season, tearoom, lounge, meeting rooms, complimentary limousine service weekday mornings to midtown and evenings to the theater district. AE, CB, DC, MC, V.*

Expensive

Doral Court, Doral Park Avenue, and **Doral Tuscany.** Doral has created a cozy enclave of three hotels in the East 30s Murray Hill district. Guests at any one property can sign for meals and drinks at all three; they also have complimentary access to the Doral Saturnia Fitness Center at 90 Park Avenue. The Doral Tuscany and its adjacent neighbor, the Doral Court (which has slightly lower prices that actually put it in the "Moderate" category), have attractive, traditionally furnished guest rooms and suites; the Tuscany's baths and bedrooms are more formal and elegant, though both properties are well maintained. The Doral Park Avenue has recently been refurbished with the business traveler firmly in mind, so this is where one finds more high-tech amenities, such as in-room computer outlets. All three have good restaurants, the best and most acclaimed being the Tuscany's Time and Again, which features a changing menu of American nouvelle specialties. The Park Avenue's new restaurant, Saturnia, has spa cuisine, while the Doral Court's Courtyard Café offers one of the city's nicer outdoor dining spaces. *Doral Court, 130 E. 39th St., 10016, tel. 212/685–1100 or 800/624–0607, fax 212/889–0287. 248 rooms. Facilities: café, meeting rooms, complimentary parking on all weekend packages. AE, CB, DC, MC, V. Doral Park Avenue, 70 Park Ave. (at 38th St.), 10016, tel. 212/687–7050 or 800/847–4135, fax 212/ 808–9029. 220 rooms. Facilities: 2 restaurants, bar, café, meeting rooms, fitness center, complimentary parking on all weekend packages. AE, CB, DC, MC, V. Doral Tuscany, 120 E. 39th St., 10016, tel. 212/686–1600 or 800/847–4078, fax 212/ 779–7822. 119 rooms. Facilities: restaurant, lounge, meeting rooms, complimentary parking on all weekend packages. AE, CB, DC, MC, V.*

The Drake. Swissôtel took over this former Loews property in 1981; it is favored by many business travelers from here and abroad for its solid service and highly desirable location, just off Park Avenue at 56th Street. The hotel is in the process of remodeling its public areas. Guest rooms have been refreshed with improved furnishings and a more contemporary look; the same goes for the well-stocked bathrooms. The advantage here is room size: The prewar building was originally designed as an apartment house, so the rooms have enough space for refrigerators and other homey touches. Where this lodging truly shines is in its dining services—this is the home of the Lafayette (*see* Chapter 8), with the inspired cuisine of Jean-Georges

Vongerichten. Reservations are difficult to get, but the agreeable hotel staff will do their utmost to get hotel guests in. For a good deal less money, the Café Suisse is a pleasant surprise—many locals enjoy its Swiss specialties and hard-to-find Swiss wines, and its desserts are made by the Lafayette pastry chef. There's more comfort here than spit and polish, but the prices and the quality of the food-and-beverage service more than make up for any lapses. *440 Park Ave., 10022, tel. 212/421–0900 or 800/63–SWISS, fax 212/371–4190. 600 rooms. Facilities: restaurant, café, bar, meeting rooms, complimentary limousine service to Wall Street, luggage check-in for Swissair passengers. AE, CB, DC, MC, V.*

Grand Hyatt New York. What was formerly the Commodore is now a glittering marble-and-chrome edifice co-owned by Hyatt and Donald Trump. Sports fans will enjoy gawking at their favorite athletes in the lobby—almost all the pro teams stay here when in town. Like other towering midtown hotels, this one's designed primarily for business travelers. Guests have remarked at the odd shapes of certain rooms, but the savvy staff tries to avoid using these when the hotel is not full. Color schemes are blessedly soft, running to teal blue, gray, and rose. Regency Club rooms on the 31st and 32nd floors are worth the extra money if you require extra pampering and service; otherwise, they are nearly identical with regular units. The lounge is truly gracious, and the free treats taste as good as they look. The hotel's food in general is superior to that of many other Hyatt properties. Trumpet's, the formal dining room, serves better-than-average nouvelle cuisine and has a truly impressive wine list for a commercial hotel. Service throughout the hotel is pleasant, if not as polished as that of smaller New York properties. As with many other chains, it's quite easy to book a room or even a suite here at reduced rates. *Park Ave. at Grand Central Terminal (at 42nd St.), 10017, tel. 212/883–1234 or 800/228–9000, fax 212/697–3772. 1,400 rooms. Facilities: restaurant, café, lounge, ballroom, meeting rooms, VIP floor. AE, CB, DC, MC, V.*

The Helmsley Palace. This glass monolith with a landmark palazzo at its feet is many visitors' vision of the ideal New York hotel: big, slightly overwrought, and always busy. Palace rooms are generous by Manhattan standards, and those on the higher floors have views of St. Patrick's Cathedral and the East Side. Furnishings are cookie-cutter plush: padded and gilded headboards, reproduction chairs and tables, and pseudo-brocade bedcovers. Smaller suites are cramped and not worth the extra money. Public rooms, many of them located in the original 100-year-old Villard Houses, contain valuable pieces of art and lovely architectural details. The hotel has a variety of bars and eating spots; the cuisine is Continental and overpriced. The staff is friendly and the location can't be beat for those who want to shop on Fifth Avenue or have business in midtown. *455 Madison Ave., 10022, tel. 212/888–7000 or 800/221–4982, fax 212/355–0820. 963 rooms. Facilities: restaurant, 2 lounges, tearoom, meeting rooms, kitchenettes in suites. AE, CB, DC, MC, V.*

Holiday Inn Crowne Plaza. The new deluxe flagship of the famous commercial hotel chain, a towering roseate stone edifice, has been built on the exact site of the original music publishing company of Irving Berlin—he wrote the music for the show "Holiday Inn," from which the chain took its name. At the entranceway, you'll find the "Broadway Walk of Stars," six bronze plaques commemorating the first winners of the Tony Awards, including Helen Hayes, Ingrid Bergman, and José Ferrer. Public areas with a rose and beige color scheme are softer and more opulent than those of its neighboring competitor, The Marriott Marquis. Upstairs, the decent-sized rooms continue the rose color scheme, this time with a touch of teal blue. Guest rooms start at the 16th floor so that everyone gets an eyeful from the panoramic windows. Bathrooms are beyond basic, though the amenities found within could be more lavish. Another minor drawback is the serious lack of closet space, even in the suites. An attractive, surprisingly sophisticated lobby restaurant, Samplings, features appetizer- and full-size dishes, salads, and desserts, and there's also a larger restaurant, The Broadway Grill, run by David Liederman, of David's Cookies fame. The health club includes a shallow (3½ feet deep throughout) lap pool, run by the same company that built the Vista's well-regarded facility. At press time, future plans include a complete business center. New Yorkers are divided on the hotel's Vegas-style neon nighttime facade, though it may just be what's needed to restore one's confidence in the wild West Side. *1605 Broadway (at 49th St.), 10019, tel. 212/977–4000, fax 212/333–7393. 770 rooms. Facilities: 2 restaurants, café, lounge, fitness center, pool, ballroom, meeting rooms, business center. AE, CB, DC, MC, V.*

The Inter-Continental New York. The stately old Barclay was bought by this reputable worldwide company a few years ago but, happily, not much has changed. The warmly lit traditional lobby, with its faded Persian carpets and aviary, still stands, as does the rather old-fashioned American restaurant. Rooms, alas, could use some updating, as could the charmless bathrooms. Some suites have been nicely refurnished, but even these have somewhat less panache than those of other hotels in this price category. Some businesspeople swear by the hotel's service, though a few recent reports have not been as favorable. The new on-premises workout and massage facility is attractive and well-designed, as are the redecorated banquet and meeting rooms on the same level. One can only hope that the Inter-Continental's new owners, the Japanese Saison Group and SAS airlines, will get busy and spruce this place up—it has the potential to shine. *111 48th St. (E. of Park Ave.), 10017, tel. 212/755–5900 or 800/327–0200, fax 212/644–0079. 680 rooms. Facilities: restaurant, bar, meeting rooms, fitness center, complimentary parking on weekends. AE, CB, DC, MC, V.*

Le Parker Meridien. This dramatic, modern French hotel, whose soaring blond-wood lobby links 56th and 57th streets, is within a short stroll of some of the city's finest stores and cultural spots. This is one of the best luxury bets for fitness-minded visitors: It has an airy rooftop swimming pool and a state-of-the-art basement-level workout center—both complimentary to guests. Its main drawback is that its guest rooms lack the stylish touches one might anticipate from a French-managed property. Rooms are a bit small, though comfortable in standard hotel fashion. Fortunately, a complete room redecorating plan should be well underway by this year, along with a modernization of the pool area. Baths are on a par with the rooms, though there are luscious Hermes soaps. The hotel's service is anything but snooty. If only someone would make those guest rooms a little more eye-popping . . . *118 W. 57th St., 10019, tel. 212/245–5000 or 800/543–4300, fax 212/307–1776. 700 rooms. Facilities: restaurant, café, bar, meeting*

rooms, voice mail, fitness center, pool, accompanied jogging.
AE, CB, DC, MC, V.

★ **The Mark.** Just one block north of the Carlyle (*see* Very Expensive, above), the former Madison Avenue Hotel has recently been completely redone by its new owner, Rafael Hotels; it could provide its neighbor with some healthy competition in terms of price and amenities. Even the least expensive rooms have high-quality TVs and VCRs, and its bathrooms feature art deco tiles or marble, deep tubs, *and* separate stall showers. Most rooms have pantries, too. Color schemes are warm to reflect the neoclassical Italian motif. Women will feel comfortable in the discreet public areas. Mark's, a cozy and elegant restaurant and lounge, features the unique French-American cuisine of chef Philippe Boulot. The staff seems committed and professional. Mr. Rafael came from Regent Hotels International, and the current manager came from the Mayfair Regent—two highly promising omens for ensuring the hotel's future success. *25 E. 77th St., 10021, tel. 212/744–4300 or 800/THE–MARK, fax 212/744–2749. 185 rooms. Facilities: restaurant, café, lounge, meeting rooms, VIP suites with terraces. AE, CB, DC, MC, V.*

The Marriott Marquis. This five-year-old giant is one of the places New Yorkers love to hate: It's obvious, brash, bright, and definitely geared to conventions and groups. Still, anything that brings new life and light to the Times Square area is welcome. As at other Marriotts, the help is ultrafriendly and informative, if not terribly polished. Rooms (though Marriott claims otherwise) are *not* the largest in town, but they're large enough; their color schemes are restful and their bathrooms perfectly adequate and modern. Some rooms have dramatic urban views. Good news for those with a fear of heights: The glass-walled atrium elevators have been slowed down considerably. There's a revolving restaurant, The View, on the 46th floor, and a second revolving lounge on the 8th-floor lobby level. Most patrons have booked here on some sort of reduced or group rate. This place is a logical choice for those seeking a stay in the heart of theaterland. *1535 Broadway, 10036, tel. 212/398–1900 or 800/228–9290, fax 212/704–8930. 1,877 rooms. Facilities: 3 restaurants, café, 3 lounges, several meeting rooms, theater, VIP floor, business center. AE, CB, DC, MC, V.*

The New York Hilton. In a sense, this is the city's premier hotel for professional meetings, large and small. It has a special conference center, a business center run by the *Wall Street Journal*, and loads of multilingual help. Hilton spends vast sums on keeping it trim, and it shows: There's a distinctive landscaped driveway, and the modern lobby, with its new fountain, sparkles with well-kept furnishings. Considering the size of this property (more than 2,000 rooms), guest areas are surprisingly well maintained, if not always spacious or terribly fashionable. Even the smaller rooms are tastefully arranged and have many modern touches, such as alarm clock/radios and remote-control TVs. Guests who pay extra for recently refurbished Tower Level accommodations get slightly larger rooms and use of a stylish lounge with a separate boardroom and complimentary drinks and snacks throughout the day. The new Grill 53 restaurant, featuring live jazz nightly, has better-than-average hotel fare. If you don't expect high levels of personal attention or unfaltering elegance, this well-run machine will usually satisfy. *1335 6th Ave. (at 53rd St.), 10019, tel. 212/586–7000 or 800/HILTONS, fax 212/315–1374. 2,034 rooms. Facilities: restau-*

rant, nightclub, 2 cafés, bar, several meeting rooms, multilingual desk, VIP floor, fitness center, business center, American Express desk. AE, CB, DC, MC, V.

The Omni Berkshire Place. This is the Omni chain's luxury property; the public area—with its soft colors, sunken tea lounge, art nouveau dining room, and two of the tidiest public rest rooms in town—certainly lives up to that role. The guest rooms and baths are undergoing a complete upgrading. The new look is more traditionally Continental, with elegant headboards and desks and high-quality fabrications in subtle patterns. Relatively small rooms have been cleverly redesigned with "rotunda" ceilings. The quality and variety of the cuisine in the hotel's two main restaurants has also improved. All of this is indeed good news for this extremely well-situated hotel. *21 E. 52nd St., 10022, tel. 212/753–5800 or 800/THE–OMNI, fax 212/308–9473. 435 rooms. Facilities: 2 restaurants, lounge, butler service for unpacking, complimentary limousine service to Wall Street. AE, CB, DC, MC, V.*

★ **The Regency.** Loews' upper-echelon property is a favorite for power breakfasts and fancy press events (the working rich-and-famous enjoy its discreet and surprisingly relaxed atmosphere). The stately, chandeliered lobby is reminiscent of the kind of private apartment house that comes with a personal staff to help with every need. Guest rooms and suites feature high-quality dark-wood furniture and brocade bedspreads. Bathrooms are of marble, and some have tiny TVs. Service is paramount at this property, where the King—Loews Hotel's president Jonathan Tisch—really does stand guard (and eats breakfast every day). *540 Park Ave., 10021, tel. 212/759–4100 or 800/223–2356, fax 212/826–5674. 400 rooms. Facilities: restaurant, lounge, meeting rooms, fitness center. AE, CB, DC, MC, V.*

The Royalton. Former Studio 54 disco kings Ian Schrager and the late Steve Rubell, in their quest for a second career as New York hotel moguls, completely rehabilitated this once-shabby property directly across from the Algonquin (*see* Moderate, below) on West 44th Street off Fifth Avenue. The Royalton, with its witty "art moderne" design by French decorator Philippe Starck, has a plush but slightly spooky atmosphere: The halls are narrow and dark, as are some of the strangely shaped rooms. Still, the beds and other furnishings are quite comfy, and the bathrooms are decidedly fun—they all have either oversize slate shower stalls or giant circular tubs (a few have both). Toiletries are elegant, and so is the service. The on-premises Restaurant 44 has excellent cuisine and a full liquor license (Note: guests cannot purchase alcoholic beverages anywhere else on the property, including through room service). However, at press time, 44's chef and senior staff had just departed, so catch up with current reviews before dining. This could be a delightful spot for a romantic theater weekend for two people with a sense of the absurd. *44 W. 44th St., 10036, tel. 212/869–4400 or 800/635–9013, fax 212/869–8965. 205 rooms. Facilities: restaurant with bar, meeting rooms, game and library areas, VCRs, stereos. AE, CB, DC, MC, V.*

★ **U.N. Plaza.** It's easy to miss the entrance to this favorite among the business and diplomatic set—it's on a quiet side street near (naturally) the United Nations. The small but striking lobby gives the illusion of endless space, thanks to clever designs in dark marble and mirrors; Japanese floral arrangements add warmth and drama. What makes this place really special, though, are the guest rooms, all with breathtaking views of Manhattan's East Side, and the delightful rooftop pool, where one can do laps while watching jets bank along the skyline. This is also the only hotel in New York that boasts its own on-premises tennis court. The decor is modern but not overpoweringly sterile, and the color schemes are soothing. The burgundy-hued Ambassador Grill, which offers one of the best complete-dinner buys (under $30) in midtown, has a Gascon chef who lavishes his menu with rich game and foie gras. Service throughout the hotel is first-rate. Families with young children will especially appreciate the nearby U.N. park and the hotel's safe location. Recently, this property became a member of the distinctive Park Hyatt group of hotels, which can only mean that high standards will be continued. *1 United Nations Plaza, 10017, tel. 212/355-3400 or 800/223-1234, fax 212/702-5051. 444 rooms. Facilities: restaurant, 2 lounges, meeting rooms, pool, fitness center, tennis court, complimentary limousine service to Wall Street and theater district. AE, CB, DC, MC, V.*

The Vista International. Managed by Hilton International, this striking downtown property has been the only significant hotel below 34th Street since it opened nine years ago. Soon, however, there will be a new Marriott on West Street, and other competitors to follow. This new competition should eventually force the Vista up to par. Until then, try to book a redecorated room. Guest rooms have nice views of nearby Battery Park City and the new World Financial Center on the Hudson River, but they are otherwise undistinguished. However, the hotel has a dramatic health club, with a swimming pool that sits in the center of a multifunction exercise area, under a running track. In addition, the hotel's dining rooms offer above-average American cuisine. The best-known is The American Harvest, which features a seasonally changing menu of domestic meats, seafood, and produce. *3 World Trade Center, 10048, tel. 212/938-9100, fax 212/321-2107. 829 rooms. Facilities: 2 restaurants, 2 lounges, meeting rooms, pool, fitness center, VIP floor, free parking with weekend packages. AE, CB, DC, MC, V.*

The Waldorf-Astoria. Along with the Plaza (*see* Very Expensive, above), this art deco masterpiece personifies New York at its most lavish and powerful. Hilton, its owner, has spent a fortune on refurbishing both public areas and guest rooms. Original murals and mosaics, elaborate plaster ornamentation, fine old-wood walls and doors—all look fresh and new. In the guest rooms, some of which start at the low end of this category, there are new bedspreads, carpets, and other signs of upgrading. Bathrooms throughout are old but beautifully kept up and rather spacious by today's standards. Everyone from the Duchess of York to the honeymoon couple from Miami or the salesman from Omaha gets the same amenities; of course, in the very private Tower section, everything becomes just that much grander. There has been a move to modernize the menu at Peacock Alley, where Waldorf salad first made news. Famous guest chefs are adding innovative touches, some of which fortunately stick. Service in the dining areas, however, can be pokey and rude, especially outside of regular meal times. The hotel's richly tinted, hushed lobby serves as an interior centerpoint of city life; it's nice to see the rest of the place looking proud, too. This year marks the hotel's 60th anniversary, so anticipate some special events. *301 Park Ave., 10022, tel. 212/355-3000 or 800/HILTONS, fax 212/421-8103. 1,692 rooms. Facilities: 3* *restaurants, coffee shop, tearoom, lounge, ballroom, meeting rooms. AE, CB, DC, MC, V.*

The Westbury. There's an English Channel's worth of differences between this Trusthouse Forte hotel and its French sister, the Plaza Athenée (*see* Very Expensive, above). The Westbury is run more like the company's London flagship property, the Hyde Park Hotel. Sedate and comfortable, it delivers friendly and efficient service. Rooms have recently been redone, either with Laura Ashley or Ralph Lauren fabrics. Bathrooms, though small, are nonetheless pleasant. There is an elegant new workout area. The Polo restaurant, under sous-chef Joseph Guarra, has recently changed over from a traditional to an American nouvelle menu with excellent results. Many celebrities, such as Omar Sharif, enjoy this hotel, as do dignified business travelers. *69th St. at Madison Ave., 10021, tel. 212/535–2000 or 800/321–1569, fax 212/535–5058. 235 rooms. Facilities: restaurant, meeting rooms, fitness center. AE, CB, DC, MC, V.*

Moderate

★ **The Algonquin.** While this landmark property's English-drawing-room atmosphere and burnished-wood lobby are being kept intact, its working parts (the plumbing, for instance) are being improved under new Japanese owners. Management is also redecorating, restoring the old mahogany doors and trim, improving the telephone service, and creating a conference and business area. This much-beloved hotel, where the Round Table group of writers and wits once met for lunch, still shelters many a celebrity, particularly literary types visiting nearby publishing houses or the *New Yorker* magazine offices across the street. Late-night performances go on as usual at the Oak Room, with singers such as Steve Ross and Andrea Marcovicci. Bathrooms and sleeping quarters retain Victorian-style fixtures and furnishings, only now there are larger, firmer beds, modern TVs, VCRs (upon request), computerized phones, and Caswell-Massey toiletries. Tubs, tiles, and sinks are being relined as needed. Personal service, especially for repeat customers, continues to be excellent. Even if you choose another hotel to sleep in, stop by the Algonquin for afternoon tea or a drink in its cozy, clubby lobby. *59 W. 44th St., 10036, tel. 212/840–6800 or 800/548–0345, fax 212/944–1419. 165 rooms. Facilities: restaurant, 2 lounges, meeting rooms, complimentary parking on weekends, business center. AE, CB, DC, MC, V.*

The Doral Inn. While this Doral is far more modest in decor and commercial in feeling than the others discussed above, it is nonetheless a good value among the many hotels along Lexington Avenue. Rooms are average in size and cheerful, if not inventive, in decor; there are some surprisingly impressive terrace suites. A small workout area is connected to a squash club, and guests can also use the Doral Park Avenue's Saturnia Fitness Center. *541 Lexington Ave. (at 50th St.), 10022, tel. 212/755–1200 or 800/223–5823, fax 212/319–8344. 700 rooms. Facilities: 2 restaurants, meeting rooms, fitness center, squash club, self-service laundry. AE, CB, DC, MC, V.*

★ **Empire Hotel.** This old hotel recently changed ownership, so it's a matter of time before one knows what's what, but since the new owner is media mogul John Kluge, the Empire should only gain in luster. The lobby is warm and inviting; halls are decorated in soft gray with elegant lamps. Rooms and suites are a bit like small boxes, but nicely furnished; special room features include high-tech electronics, and the small but immaculate baths have heated towel racks. Although this hotel's prices have gone up, it's still one of the city's better buys in terms of quality and location, right across the street from Lincoln Center. At press time there was no room service, but no matter: The neighborhood is loaded with all-hours dining options. *Broadway (at 63rd St.), 10023, tel. 212/265–7400, 800/221–6509, or 800/223–9868, fax 212/315–0349. 368 rooms. Facilities: restaurant, voice mail. AE, CB, DC, MC, V.*

The Helmsley Middletowne. It may be hard to believe that this low-key residential-style retreat is managed by the same flamboyant folks who run the Helmsley Palace (*see* Expensive, above). Tucked away on East 48th Street near Lexington Avenue, the Helmsley Middletowne is a more than serviceable money-saver for those who can take care of their own business and social needs: There's no lobby, no restaurant, and no room service, but the area is packed with dining options. Most units are suites or oversize doubles, and many are large enough for families. The decor is homey traditional; most units have been redone, though there are still some signs of wear-and-tear in the bathrooms. Most rooms have pantries and dual-line telephones. *148 E. 48th St., 10017, tel. 212/755–3000 or 800/221–4982, fax 212/832–0261. 192 rooms. AE, CB, DC, MC, V.*

Hotel Elysée. This relatively small hotel, on a prime block between Madison and Park avenues, has a rather offbeat atmosphere with a 1950s feel. Rooms have a slightly lived-in charm; all of them have names instead of numbers. Bathrooms are currently being modernized. Among the surprising amenities for the price are VCRs. The friendly desk staff is happy to help with standard requests. *60 E. 54th St., 10022, tel. 212/753–1066, fax 212/980–9278. 110 rooms. Facilities: restaurant, lounge, art gallery, concierge. AE, CB, DC, MC, V.*

Loews Summit, *see* the Summit, below.

★ **Manhattan Suites East.** Here's a group of good-value properties for the traveler who likes to combine full hotel service with independent pied-à-terre living. These nine midtown hotels have different characters and varying prices, though all fall within the Moderate category. The four best are the **Beekman Tower** (3 Mitchell Pl.), near the United Nations and on the edge of a trendy East Side residential area; the **Dumont Plaza** (150 E. 34th St.), especially convenient for convention goers with its location on a direct bus line to the Javits Center; the **Surrey Hotel** (20 E. 76th St.), in the neighborhood of Madison Avenue art galleries and designer boutiques; and the **Southgate Tower** (371 7th Ave.), the most attractive and secure place to sleep within close range of Madison Square Garden and Penn Station. Except for the modern style at the Dumont, all have traditional guest-room decor; the Surrey's rooms border on the truly elegant. Most accommodations have pantries, and larger units have dining areas with full-size tables. Other hotels in this group tend to be more residential, except for the full-service **Shelburne** (303 Lexington Ave.); many top corporations use them as interim lodgings for newly relocated executives. The Beekman, Surrey, Shelburne and Dumont Plaza have restaurants (Harold's at the Dumont Plaza is a well-priced winner) which can also be used for room service. The Dumont, Southgate, and the Shelburne have on-premises fitness centers. The older hotels in the group do have some disappointing rooms, but overall these properties are outstanding for the price, considering their convenience, location, and space. Their weekend package rates are hard to beat. *Sales office, 505 E. 75th St., 10001, tel. 212/772–2900 or 800/ME–SUITE. AE, CB, DC, MC, V.*

Novotel. At the northern boundary of the theater district stands an uninspiring red tower. You check in at street level, then take the elevator up to a seventh-floor lobby with full registration desk, a sundries shop, a ticket agent, and a café. The atmosphere is surprisingly warm and pleasant; rooms are small but well thought out, with Euro-style touches. The Café Skylight, also a nice surprise, serves better-than-adequate French bistro fare at moderate prices in a glass-walled room that gives diners a busy Broadway eyeful. This hotel has nothing to make the pulse quicken with delight, but it's a much better buy in terms of quality and safety than other hotels in the same price range and location. *226 W. 52nd St., 10019, tel. 212/315–0100 or 800/221–3185, fax 212/765–5369. 485 rooms. Facilities: restaurant, café, lounge, wine bar, meeting rooms. AE, CB, DC, MC, V.*

The Omni Park Central. Practically across the street from Carnegie Hall, this large hotel, very popular with groups, has a somewhat split personality. While the guest rooms are of standard quality and design, the outrageous lobby resembles a combination of an Egyptian tomb and a futuristic set from *Star Wars.* Throwing another style into the overall picture is the street-level French brasserie, which offers wine by the glass and impressive food preparation. While each of this hotel's parts is less than perfection, their sum creates what may be a wise choice over other chain properties in this neighborhood. Omni offers several seasonal packages, including some geared specifically at travelers with children in tow. Note: In an earlier incarnation, this hotel was Jackie Gleason's New York home. *870 7th Ave., 10019, tel. 212/247–8000 or 800/THE–OMNI, fax 212/484–3374. 1,450 rooms. Facilities: restaurant, café, bar, meeting rooms, children's concierge. AE, CB, DC, MC, V.*

★ **The Roger Smith Winthrop.** Don't be put off by the dusty, faded lobby—the hotel is in the process of a gradual redecoration. At press time, the lobby and public areas of this sleeper were being completely overhauled. The guest rooms upstairs are clean, well decorated, and spacious, and special units on the ninth floor have small but luxurious marble baths with Jacuzzis. All rooms have pantries, and there's a complimentary Continental breakfast on weekends. Guests also receive free passes (one per person) to the Museum of Modern Art. A tea lounge and a new full-service restaurant are in the works. This is a homey, attractive place to return to at the end of a busy day in midtown. *501 Lexington Ave., 10017, tel. 212/755–1400 or 800/241–3848, fax 212/319–9130. 200 rooms. Facilities: restaurant, meeting room. AE, CB, DC, MC, V.*

The San Carlos. This small, residential-style property offers basic hotel service, clean modern rooms, and a neighborly atmosphere. Larger suites come with kitchenettes, making them a good choice for families. The small wood-paneled lobby is gracious and well lit; women travelers can feel quite secure here. *150 E. 50th St., 10022, tel. 212/755–1800 or 800/722–2012. 140 rooms. Facilities: restaurant. AE, CB, DC, MC, V.*

The Sheraton Centre & Towers. Although the Sheraton chain's slogan asserts that its hotels have taste, don't look for any at this run-down, overworked, and frequently overbooked property. Used mainly by convention and tour groups, the hotel's guest rooms, even those in the VIP Tower zone, are in dire need of renovation, especially the carpets and wood furnishings. Cleanliness, however, does seem to have improved. The luncheon buffet in the lobby restaurant isn't a bad bet for pre-matinee dining. The lobby looks relatively bright, but it was fixed up specially to appear in a Disney film; other parts of the hotels are marred by soiled upholstery and peeling wall coverings. Things aren't much better at the sister property across the street, the **Sheraton City Squire,** which is where Sheraton Centre guests whose reservations got "lost" often are shunted. The City Squire does have an indoor pool which, though far from luxurious, is surprisingly large. With all the new competition in town, this property's prices won't be that appealing for long if the owners don't start upgrading with a vengeance. *811 7th Ave., 10019, tel. 212/581–1000 or 800/325–3535, fax 262–4410. 1,835 rooms. Facilities: restaurant, café, coffee shop, disco, ballroom, several meeting rooms. AE, CB, DC, MC, V.*

The Summit. Loews' moderate-price New York property has an impersonal style, but most of its regulars—business travelers —don't mind because the hotel generally runs quite well. Rooms, most of them recently refurbished, are comfortable and well-designed. Deluxe units (only slightly higher in price than standard) come with goodies, such as Godiva chocolates and complimentary liquor miniatures. At press time, there were plans to change Maude's to a more contemporary restaurant. Loews takes care of its properties, so the Summit can more than hold its own with some of its neighbors. *Lexington Ave. (at 51st St.), 10022, tel. 212/752–7000, fax 212/758–6311. 766 rooms. Facilities: restaurant, lounge, meeting rooms, fitness center. AE, CB, DC, MC, V.*

Inexpensive

★ **Chatwal Inns.** This latest welcome group addition to the Big Apple hotel scene features six properties, located mostly in the Broadway-midtown area, that provide clean, attractively designed rooms at relatively unpainful prices. All guests receive a complimentary continental breakfast. Some of the larger properties, like the **Days Inn** affiliate (234 W. 48th St.) have on-premises full-service restaurants as well. Rooms, though relatively small throughout all six hotels, are immaculate and have all the basic amenities travelers have come to expect, including bathroom toiletries, modern telephones, and TVs. Since many of the buildings were, until recently, rather dilapidated, don't be put off by the dingy facades of Chatwal properties like **The Quality Inn Midtown** (157 W. 47th St.) or **The Chatwal Inn** (132 W. 45th St.); their interiors are among the chain's nicest. Sant S. Chatwal, owner of Bombay Palace restaurants, is to be applauded for his restoration and pricing efforts. Right now, this is a budget-minded New York visitor's best bet, especially if Broadway shows are part of the plan. *Tel. 800/826–4667; in Canada: 800/621–4667. Facilities: restaurants, small meeting rooms, lounges, depending on the property. AE, CB, DC, MC, V.*

Hotel Edison. A popular budget stop for tour groups from here and abroad, this offbeat old hotel has a sense of weatherbeaten style in its art deco lobby. A gruesome murder scene for *The Godfather* was shot in what is now Sophia's restaurant, and the pink plaster coffee shop has become a hot place to eavesdrop on show-business gossip thanks to such celebrity regulars as Jackie Mason. Guest rooms are brighter and fresher than the dark corridors seem to hint. There's no room service, but this part of the theater district has so many restaurants and delis that it doesn't matter much. The crowd here is perfectly wholesome, so save money on your room and spend the big bucks on better theater seats. *228 W. 47th St., 10036, tel. 212/840–5000. 1,000 rooms. Facilities: restaurant, coffee shop, bar. AE, CB, DC, MC, V.*

Hotel Wentworth. This relatively small prewar hotel is on a midtown street that's usually pulsating with South American atmosphere—some of the city's best-known Brazilian restaurants are right outside the door. Don't be put off by the grim lobby; upstairs you'll find perfectly acceptable bedrooms and modern bathrooms. The atmosphere is similar to that of many second-class European hotels. This is a popular stop for South Americans, although one frequently sees well-dressed U.S. businessmen, too. Single women might find the area a bit eerie at night. *59 W. 46th St., 10036, tel. 212/719–2300 or 800/223–1900. 250 rooms. No facilities. AE, CB, DC, MC, V.*

The Milford Plaza. A Best Western affiliate, this old hotel has modernized its entire interior, but the gray decor doesn't help alleviate the gloomy atmosphere, and the guest rooms are still closet-size. In the bright public areas, security appears to be tight, as well it should be in this somewhat seedy section of Eighth Avenue. Restaurants include Mamma Leone's Italian restaurant, a popular spot with tourists. The theater-district location is this hotel's main draw, but be forewarned: Many guest rooms are truly claustrophobic, though new wall coverings offer some relief. *270 W. 45th St., 10036, tel. 212/869–3600, 800/221–2690 or, in NY, 800/522–6449; fax 212/819–1433. 1,300 rooms. Facilities: 3 restaurants, meeting rooms. AE, CB, DC, MC, V.*

New York International Youth Hostel. American Youth Hostels recently opened this ambitious facility on Manhattan's Upper West Side. Here, in a renovated 19th-century Gothic-style building, you'll find dormitory accommodations at rock-bottom prices. In addition, the hostel will eventually provide conference areas, kitchens, dining rooms, a retail travel store, a public restaurant, and an Off-Off Broadway theater. There are no private baths, except in a few large "family" units; rooms hold up to six beds; and guests must bring their own sheets. All ages are welcome, but there is a limit of one week per stay. Each guest is responsible for minor housekeeping chores, as well as other services that in other properties would be performed by hotel employees. Although the immediate neighborhood is still a bit rough, the location is convenient to Columbia University, Harlem, and new stores and eating spots on upper Broadway and Columbus and Amsterdam avenues. This is a welcome alternative for the self-sufficient traveler. At press time, the hostel was going through an early shakedown period, so call in advance about exact prices and available amenities. *891 Amsterdam Ave., 10025, tel. 212/932–2300. 90 rooms. Planned facilities: dining area, patio, kitchen, self-service laundry, travel service desk, theater, public restaurant, conference rooms for nonprofit groups. AE, CB, DC, MC, V.*

Pickwick Arms Hotel. This convenient East Side establishment charges $75 a night for standard renovated doubles but has older singles with shared baths for as little as $37. The marble-clad lobby is small but brightly lit, and the staff is friendly. Guest rooms have been comfortably furnished in white bamboo. Guests have access to a roof garden; although there is no restaurant, the neighborhood is loaded with places to eat, and a deli on the ground floor sells sandwiches, soft drinks, beer, and snacks. This is an acceptable budget alternative in a good area. *230 E. 51st St., 10022, tel. 212/355–0300 or 800/PICKWIK, fax 212/755–5729. 400 rooms. No facilities. AE, CB, MC, V.*

Ramada Hotel. Another of Loews' budget properties, this motel-style building has an outdoor rooftop swimming pool and lounge area with snack bar. Rooms and suites were recently upgraded. Daily garage rates are reasonable. This is a good bet for theater-bound families during the summer months. *48th St. and 8th Ave., 10019, tel. 212/581–7000 or 800/2–RAMADA, fax 212/974–0291. 366 rooms. Facilities: restaurant, lounge, pool, meeting room. AE, CB, DC, MC, V.*

Vanderbilt YMCA. Of the various Manhattan Ys offering accommodations, this is the best as far as location and facilities are concerned. Although rooms hold up to four people, they are little more than dormitory-style cells—even with only one or two beds to a room, you may feel crowded. Each room does have a late-model TV, however. There are no private baths; communal showers and toilets are worn but clean. Guests are provided with basics such as towels and soap. Besides the low price, this Y offers instant free membership to its on-premises pool, gym, running track, exercise rooms, and sauna. An informal cafeteria and a friendly hospitality desk encourage travelers to mix with one another. The Turtle Bay neighborhood is safe, convenient, and interesting (the United Nations is a few short blocks away). Other YMCAs in town include the 561-room **West Side Y** (5 W. 63rd St., 10023, tel. 212/787–4400), which may be hard to get into but is in the desirable Lincoln Center area; and the 1,490-room **Sloane House YMCA** (356 W. 34th St., 10001, tel. 212/760–5860), which is in a gritty and somewhat unsafe neighborhood. *224 E. 47th St., 10017, tel. 212/755–2410. 430 rooms. Facilities: cafeteria, meeting rooms, self-service laundry, gift shop, luggage storage, pool, fitness center. No credit cards.*

Wellington Hotel. A large, old-fashioned property whose main advantages are reasonable prices and a midtown location, the Wellington attracts many budget-conscious Europeans. Rooms are small but clean and reasonably cheery; baths are serviceable. Standard hotel services are available upon request. The brightly lit lobby provides a reassuring welcome for late-night returns. *871 7th Ave. (at 55th St.), 10019, tel. 212/247–3900 or 800/652–1212, fax 212/768–3477. 700 rooms. Facilities: restaurant. AE, CB, DC, MC, V.*

★ **The Wyndham.** This genteel treasure sits across from The Plaza and adjacent to the Helmsley Park Lane. The savvy, independent traveler who cares more about gracious rooms and a friendly atmosphere than about imposing lobbies and hand-to-mouth service might well choose this spot over its neighbors. Owner and general manager John Mados keeps prices down by not offering room service or fancy amenities; what he does provide is some of the prettiest and most spacious accommodations in Manhattan. Even the least expensive double room has fresh floral-print bedspreads, comfortable chairs, and decorator wall coverings. A slight drawback is the old-fashioned, white-tile bathrooms. Suites (all of which come with pantries) start as low as $160 per night; they are painted in sunny shades and fitted with antique furniture, tasteful Chinese rugs, and an eclectic mix of everything else. The small lobby is unusually secure—a doorman controls the "in" buzzer 24 hours a day. The limited staff is pleasant, and they can be extra attentive once they get to know you. This hotel is a favorite of stars such as Carol Burnett and media personalities Leonard Maltin and Barbara Walters. However, some of our readers have reported less-than-perfect service and hospitality. *42 W. 58th St., 10019, tel. 212/753-3500, fax 212/754-5638. 201 rooms. Facilities: restaurant. AE, CB, DC, MC, V.*

Bed-and-Breakfasts

Hundreds of rooms are available on a bed-and-breakfast basis in Manhattan and the outer boroughs, principally Brooklyn. B&Bs almost always cost well below $100 a night; some singles are available for under $50.

New York B&Bs, however, are not the quaint old mansions you find in other localities. They fall into two categories: (1) *Hosted apartments*, a bedroom in an apartment where the host is present; (2) *unhosted apartments*, entire apartments that are temporarily vacant. The unhosted option is scarcer and somewhat more expensive.

Along with saving money, B&Bs permit you to mingle with New Yorkers and stay in "real" neighborhoods rather than in tourist enclaves. The disadvantages are that accommodations, amenities, service, and privacy fall far short of what you get in hotels. Sometimes you really do get breakfast and sometimes you don't. And you usually can't pay by credit card.

Here are a few reservation agencies that book B&B accommodations in and near Manhattan. There is no fee for the service, but they advise you to make reservations as far in advance as possible. It's a good idea to find out something about the city before you contact them, and then to request accommodations in a neighborhood that you prefer.

Bed and Breakfast Network of New York (134 W. 32nd St., Suite 602, 10001, tel. 212/645-8134).

City Lights Bed and Breakfast, Ltd. (Box 20355, Cherokee Station, 10028, tel. 212/737-7049).

New World Bed and Breakfast (150 5th Ave., Suite 711, 10011, tel. 212/675-5600 or 800/443-3800).

Urban Ventures (306 W. 38th St., 10018, tel. 212/594-5650).

10 The Arts

by Susan Spano Wells

Brooklyn resident Susan Spano Wells writes about travel for The New York Times, Ladies' Home Journal, and Woman's Day. She is the author of a young adult novel and a frequent contributor to the book review pages of Newsday.

On a bad day in New York—when it's raining and a cab can't be engaged for blood or money, the subways are flooded, and the line at the cash machine stretches to Poughkeepsie—many New Yorkers may feel as if they'd sell the city back to the Indians for two bits. But in the end, they put up with the urban hassles for at least one obvious reason: New York's unrivaled artistic life. Despite the immense competition, artists from all disciplines continue to come to the city to find their compatriots, produce their work, thrive, persist, or crash. Audiences can only benefit.

There are somewhere between 250 and 300 legitimate theaters in New York, and many more ad hoc venues—parks, churches, universities, museums, lofts, galleries, streets, and rooftops—where performances ranging from Shakespeare to sword-dancing take place. The city is, as well, a revolving door of festivals and special events: Summer jazz, one-act play marathons, international film series, and celebrations of music from the classical to the avant-garde are just a few. One of the most extensive events is the Second International Festival of the Arts, planned for June 1991. With a budget of approximately $6.5 million, it will draw a worldwide roster of performers to Manhattan.

In New York, the arts routinely make the headlines. Pick up a week's worth of newspapers and you'll learn of casting disputes at the Metropolitan Opera, prima ballerinas with bruised knees, big Broadway musicals whose directors are replaced hours before opening, and the constant entertaining haggles between backers, artists, and critics. It's chaos. What a town!

New York's most renowned centers for the arts are tourist attractions in themselves:

Lincoln Center (W. 62nd to 66th Sts., Columbus to Amsterdam Aves., tel. 212/877–2011) is a 14-acre complex that houses the Metropolitan Opera, the New York Philharmonic, the Juilliard School, the New York City Ballet, the American Ballet Theatre, the New York City Opera, the Film Society of Lincoln Center, the Chamber Music Society of Lincoln Center, the Lincoln Center Theater, the School of American Ballet, and the New York Public Library's Center for the Performing Arts. Tours of Lincoln Center are available (tel. 212/877–1800; *see* Tour 8 in Chapter 3).

Carnegie Hall (154 W. 57th St., tel. 212/247–7800) is a premier hall for musical concerts. An old joke says it all: A tourist asks an old guy with a violin case, "How do you get to Carnegie Hall?" His reply: "Practice, practice." Such music masters as Rudolph Serkin, Leonard Bernstein, Judy Collins, Isaac Stern, and Frank Sinatra, along with great orchestras and debuting talents, compose the Carnegie bill. Performances are held in both its main auditorium (opened in 1891 with a concert conducted by Tchaikovsky) and in Weill Recital Hall. Recent restorations brought a face-lift to the building's facade, an enlarged lobby at street level, and a modernized backstage. However, critics still dispute whether the restoration altered the main auditorium's famed acoustics. From August 1990 to May 1991, Carnegie will pull out all stops to celebrate its centennial. Scheduled are appearances by opera stars Placido Domingo and Kathleen Battle; a performance of the complete Bach suites for unaccompanied cello, by Yo-Yo Ma; concerts by the

New York and Leningrad philharmonics; and the farewell stint of Sir Georg Solti conducting the Chicago Philharmonic.

Radio City Music Hall (1260 6th Ave., tel. 212/632–4000), an Art Deco gem, opened in 1932 with 6,000 seats, a 60-foot-high foyer, two-ton chandeliers, and a powerful Wurlitzer organ. Here you'll find everything from Grateful Dead concerts to Christmas and Easter extravaganzas (featuring the perennial Rockettes kickline), restored movie classics, and star-studded TV specials. Tours (tel. 212/632–4041) are conducted daily, departing from the main lobby (*see* Tour 1 in Chapter 3).

City Center (131 W. 55th St., tel. 212/581–7907), under its eccentric, tiled Spanish dome (built in 1923 by the Ancient and Accepted Order of the Mystic Shrine and saved from demolition in 1943 by Mayor Fiorello LaGuardia) hosts dance troupes, such as the Joffrey Ballet and Martha Graham, and occasional operettas. Recently, the Manhattan Theatre Club also took up residence there, bringing along its highly touted bill of innovative modernist drama.

Madison Square Garden (W. 31st to W. 33rd Sts. on 7th Ave., tel. 212/563–8300), camped atop Penn Station, includes a 20,000-seat Arena, and the 1,000-seat Felt Forum, which will be in the final stages of a $200 million renovation by 1991. Sports events such as ice hockey and boxing, plus big-draw pop music concerts, keep it rocking. There's even room for the Knicks and the Rangers to call it home. Should your favorite rock band not be appearing at the Garden, check out its suburban sister halls: the **Nassau Coliseum** (Long Island, tel. 516/794–9300 or 212/307–7171) and the **Meadowlands Arena** (New Jersey, tel. 201/935–3900).

Brooklyn Academy of Music (BAM; 30 Lafayette Ave., Brooklyn, tel. 718/636–4100) is America's oldest performing arts center (begun in 1859), but its reputation is decidedly contemporary thanks to feistily innovative dance, music, opera, and theater productions. The present building, a white Renaissance Revival palace, was built in 1908. In 1987 BAM opened its **Majestic Theatre,** a partly restored vaudeville house, around the corner; The Helen Owen Carey Playhouse and the Lepercq Space are also part of BAM.

Other important arts centers include **Town Hall** (123 W. 43rd St., tel. 212/840–2824) for, among other things, concert versions of lost Broadway musicals; **Symphony Space** (Broadway at 95th St., tel. 212/864–5400), a cavernous converted movie theater with an eclectic offering that ranges from Chinese opera to short stories read by stars; the **92nd Street Y** (1395 Lexington Ave., tel. 212/996–1100), known for its classical music concerts, readings by famous writers, the Lyrics and Lyricists series; and **The Kitchen** (512 W. 19th St., tel. 212/ 255–5793), a showcase for "downtown," avant-garde videos, music, performance art, dance, and films.

Getting Tickets

Much has been made of the ballooning cost of tickets, especially for Broadway shows—though major concerts and recitals don't come cheap in New York, either. *Jerome Robbins' Broadway* nudged top Broadway ticket prices up from $50 to $60. Members of the League of American Theaters and Producers would be quick to remind frustrated play goers that the rise in ticket prices hasn't been out of line with the rise in the cost of everything else. But that's cold comfort when you're faced with an expenditure of more than $100 for one night's entertainment for two people.

On the positive side, tickets for New York City's arts events aren't hard to come by—unless, of course, you're dead set on seeing the season's hottest, sold-out show. Generally, a theater or concert hall's box office is the best place to buy tickets, since in-house ticket sellers make it their business to know about their theaters and shows and don't mind pointing out (on a chart) where you'll be seated. For advance purchase, send the theater or hall a certified check or money order, several alternate dates, and a self-addressed stamped envelope.

You can also pull out a credit card and call **Tele-Charge** (tel. 212/239–6200), **Ticketron** (tel. 212/246–0102), **HIT–TIX** (tel. 212/564–8038), or **Ticketmaster** (tel. 212/307–7171) to reserve tickets—newspaper ads generally will specify which you should use for any given event. A small surcharge ($1–$3) will be added to the total, and your tickets will be waiting for you at the theater.

For those willing to pay top dollar to see that show or concert everyone's talking about but no one can get tickets for, try a ticket broker. Last year tickets to the long-sold-out *Phantom of the Opera* began at $75 plus commission through brokers; had the same seat been available at the box office, it would have sold for $50. A few brokers to try are **Union Tickets** (tel. 800/234–TIXS), **N.Y. Theatre Tickets** (tel. 201/392–0999), **Golden/Leblang Ticket Service** (tel. 212/944–8910). Also, check the lobbies of major hotels for ticket broker outlets.

You may be tempted to buy from the ticket scalpers who frequently haunt the lobbies of hit shows. But beware: Last year they were reportedly selling tickets to *Les Misérables* for $100–$150, when seats were still available at the box office for a fraction of that price.

Off- and Off-Off-Broadway theaters have their own joint box office called **Ticket Central** (416 W. 42nd St., tel. 212/279–4200). While there are no discounts here, tickets to performances in these theaters are less expensive than Broadway tickets—Ticket Central prices average $8–$75 per person—and they cover an array of events, including legitimate theater, performance art, and dance. Because Ticket Central is located on Theatre Row (42nd St. between 9th and 10th Aves.), the emphasis is on selling nearby Off-Broadway theaters, such as Playwrights' Horizons or The Harold Clurman Theatre, which send their most successful offerings on to Broadway.

Discount Tickets The best-known discount source may be the **TKTS booth** in Duffy Square (47th St. and Broadway, tel. 212/354–5800), a venerable institution operated by the Theatre Development Fund that sells tickets for Broadway and some Off-Broadway plays at half price (plus a $1.50 surcharge per ticket; $2.00 for tickets originally over $50.00) on the same day of the performance. The names of shows available on that day are posted on boards in front of the booth. If you're interested in a Wednesday or Saturday matinee, go to the booth between 10 and 2, check out what's offered, and then wait in line. For evening performances, the booth is open 3–8; for Sunday matinee and evening performances, noon–8. One caution: TKTS accepts only cash or traveler's checks—no credit cards. The wait is generally pleasant (weather permitting), as the bright lights and babble of Broadway surround you. You're likely to meet friendly theater lovers eager to review shows they've recently seen; often you'll even meet struggling actors who can give you the inside scoop. By the time you get to the booth, you may be willing to take a gamble on a show you would otherwise never have picked, and it just might be more memorable than one of the long-running hits.

So successful has TKTS proved (last year it sold 2.3 million seats), that auxiliary booths have opened in the Wall Street area (2 World Trade Center) and in Brooklyn Heights (near the intersection of Court and Montague Sts.). The World Trade Center branch is open Monday–Friday 11–5:30, Saturday 11:30–3:30; for matinees and Sundays, 11–5:30 the day before the performance; for Off-Broadway evening performances, 11–1. In Brooklyn, evening-performance tickets are on sale weekdays 11–5:30, Saturday 11–3:30; tickets for matinees and Sundays are sold a day ahead; Off-Broadway tickets are sold until 1. The lines at these TKTS out-stations are shorter than those at Duffy Square, though occasionally the offerings are somewhat limited.

A setup similar to TKTS has arisen in the **Bryant Park Music and Dance Discount Ticket Booth,** located in Bryant Park, just west of the New York Public Library. This booth sells discounted tickets for music and dance events (including performances at Lincoln Center, City Center, Carnegie Hall, and even a few nightclubs). It's open Tuesday, Thursday, and Friday noon–2 and 3–7; Wednesday and Saturday 11–2 and 3–7; Sunday noon–6. Unlike TKTS, the Bryant Park booth has a telephone information line (tel. 212/382–2323).

Discounts on big-name, long-running shows (such as *Cats* and *Les Misérables*) are often available if you can lay your hands on a couple of "twofers"—discount ticket coupons found on various cash registers around town, in line at TKTS, at the New York Visitors and Convention Bureau (at 2 Columbus Circle), and at the office of their producer, the **Hit Show Club** (630 9th Ave., 8th floor, tel. 212/581–4211; open weekdays 9:15–3:45).

The Public Theater (425 Lafayette St., tel. 212/598–7150) regularly sets aside tickets for sale at a discount through its **Quiktix.** If you're interested in sampling Joe Papp's current offerings *(see* Theater, Beyond Broadway, below), join the Quiktix line anytime before 6 PM for evening performances, and before 1 PM for matinees. Tickets are sold on a first-come, first-served basis.

A slew of ticket clubs exist to serve repeat theater goers, so if you plan to be in the city for a long time, they may be worth investigating. The newest is **Advance Entertainment New York** (tel. 212/239–2570), essentially a telemarketing firm whose phones are manned by "resting" actors and actresses. For $85 a year, members receive constant updates on what's hot and free ticket procurement—sometimes at a discount and with special attention paid to getting good seats. AENY can be used on a one-time, no obligation-to-join basis. Other ticket groups include **Stubs Preview Club** (tel. 212/398–8370), $35 a year, specializing in preview showings; and the **Theatre Development Fund** (1501

Broadway, tel. 212/221–0885), whose TDF vouchers are available for $3 to students, union members, teachers, performing arts professionals, and members of volunteer groups, among others. When redeemed at the box office, the vouchers are worth $5 off the cost of a ticket for dance, theater, and musical events at Off-Off-Broadway theaters.

Finding Out What's On

To find out who or what's playing where, your first stop should be the newsstand. The *New York Times* isn't a prerequisite for finding out what's going on around town, but it comes in pretty handy, especially on Fridays with its "Weekend" section. On Sundays, the *Times*'s "Arts and Leisure" section features longer "think pieces" on everything from opera to TV—and lots more ads.

If your tastes are more adventurous, try the weekly paper *The Village Voice*—at this point hardly iconoclastic, but its club listings are unrivaled, its "Choices" section reliable. When its club-tattler-cum-critic Michael Musto talks (in a column called "La Dolce Musto"), night prowlers and club pixies listen. The *Voice* is published on Wednesdays.

Some of the most entertaining listings are to be found in *New Yorker* magazine. "Goings On About Town" heads off each weekly issue with ruthlessly succinct reviews ("a crass actor who seems to dote on the sound of his own voice"; "a long, rambling bar and restaurant with a white-trash-chicken-shack theme") of theater, art, music, film, and nightlife. *New York* magazine's "Cue Listings" and "Hot Line" section are useful, too. The late Malcolm Forbes's pet project **Egg** magazine is another helpful reference. *New York Native* covers the gay scene.

The League of New York Theatres and Producers publishes a weekly *Broadway Theatre Guide,* available in hotels and at the Visitors and Convention Bureau offices. For information on the lower Manhattan cultural scene, write for a *Downtown Arts Activities Calendar* (Lower Manhattan Cultural Council, 42 Broadway, 10004).

You can also get updated information by phone from the New York Department of Cultural Affairs hotline (tel. 212/956–2787), open weekdays 10–5; NYC/ON STAGE, the Theatre Development Fund's 24-hour information service (tel. 212/587–1111 or 800/STAGE–NY); or the New York Visitors and Convention Bureau (tel. 212/397–8222).

Theater

Almost everyone who visits New York ends up spending several hours in a theater seat. The theater—not the Statue of Liberty or South Street Seaport—is the city's number-one tourist attraction; though pundits would have you believe it's a doomed beast, if it is it's putting on a surprisingly lively, not to mention prolonged, death scene. Theater folk continue to make their rounds, combining business and art to produce their crazy stew. Delicate little ladies tottering about in their pillbox hats are really theatrical grande dames, with fast answers to the flashers on Eighth Avenue; shifty-looking guys toting battered briefcases turn out to be famous directors; and the girls and boys scuttling through stage doors are chorus members rushing to exchange their Reeboks for tap shoes.

Broadway Theater District To most people, New York theater means Broadway, that region bounded by 42nd and 53rd streets, between Sixth and Ninth avenues, where bright, transforming lights shine upon porn theaters and jewel-box playhouses alike *(see* Theater District map). Although the area's busy sidewalks contain more than their share of hustlers and pickpockets, visitors brave them for the playhouses' plentiful delights. Extravagant plans for redevelopment of the Times Square area continue to ricochet from marquee to marquee; within the last year four major hotels sprung up in this area. With every thud of the wrecker's ball, theater devotees pray for the survival of the essential character of Broadway—as Paul Goldberger put it in *The New York Times*, "the world of memory, the magical Times Square of old, the lively, glittering district of theaters, restaurants, cabarets, hotels, and neon signs that was in many ways the city's symbolic heart."

Historically speaking, the nation's entertainment capital was once composed of almost 50 theaters, which sprang up between 1899 and 1925 near the intersection of Broadway and 42nd Street. Many of those original showplaces have been gutted or turned into movie houses. The legitimate theaters that remain are squeezed into side streets in such tight spaces that from the outside it's often hard to imagine that there's room inside for an audience, much less a stage.

Some of the old playhouses are as interesting for their history as for their current offerings: the **St. James** (246 W. 44th St.) is where Lauren Bacall served as an usherette in the '40s, and a sleeper of a musical called *Oklahoma!* woke up as a hit; the **Lyceum** (149 W. 45th St.) is New York's oldest still-functioning theater, built in 1903 with a posh apartment on top that now holds the Shubert Archive (open to scholars by appointment only); the **Shubert Theatre** (225 W. 44th St.) is where Barbra Streisand made her 1962 Broadway debut, and the long-run record-breaker, *A Chorus Line,* played for 15 years; and the **Martin Beck Theatre** (302 W. 45th St.), built in 1924 in Byzantine style, is the stage that served up premieres of Eugene O'Neill's *The Iceman Cometh* and Maxwell Anderson's *Winterset.*

As you stroll around the theater district, you may also see: **Shubert Alley,** a shortcut between 44th and 45th streets where theater moguls used to park their limousines, today site of a jam-packed Great White Way memorabilia store called One Shubert Alley; **Actors' Equity** (165 W. 46th St.), home of the stage actor's union, and a crashing place for auditionees between cattle calls; **Manhattan Plaza,** a subsidized apartment complex at Ninth Avenue and 42nd Street inhabited largely by theater people, whose rent in hard times is assessed at a quarter of their income (whatever that comes to); **Theatre Row** (42nd St. between 9th and 10th Aves.), a convivial collection of six 9-seat Off-Broadway theaters; and **Restaurant Row** (46th St. between 8th and 9th Aves.), which offers plenty of choices for dining before or after a show. For a deeper drink of the district, take a **Backstage on Broadway tour** (tel. 212/575-8065), guided by a professional actor, director, stage manager, or designer.

Theater District

Recent seasons have brought their requisite gloomy specula-
tion about the future of commercial theater. British imports,
sessions with stand-up comics, and revivals of old standards often seem to outnumber riskier productions of new plays. Serious drama still has a hard time finding serious audiences, but
has been faring pretty well of late with the recent successes of
the Pulitzer Prize-winning *The Heidi Chronicles* and the *Piano
Lesson*, as well as the Steppenwolf production of *The Grapes of
Wrath* and Lincoln Center's *Six Degrees of Separation*. Can
Broadway compete with the new fad for "sensaround drama"
(*Tamara* and *Tony 'n' Tina's Wedding*), in which dinner is offered along with the play? Is the American musical gone with
the Andrew Lloyd Webber wind from London, which blew in
hits like *The Phantom of the Opera*? While the answers to such
questions wait in the wings, New York's splendid invalid, the
Broadway theater, carries on.

In determining which Broadway show to see, first consider the
long-running hits: *Cats*, *Les Misérables*, *The Phantom of the
Opera*, *The Fantastiks* (downtown), and others, which most
magazine and newspaper listings helpfully point out. Then look
beyond the marquees for both tomorrow's hits and today's re-
sounding flops. Remember, there's something special about
catching a show in previews or seeing a harshly reviewed play
before it bites the dust. A lousy review can quickly close a
show, even though discriminating audience members often dis-
agree with the critics.

Beyond Broadway Ten years ago it was relatively simple to categorize the New
York stage beyond Broadway. It was divided into Off-Broad-
way and Off-Off-Broadway, depending on a variety of factors that included theatrical contract type, location, and ticket
price. Today such distinctions seem strained, as Off-Broadway
prices have risen and the quality of some Off-Off-Broadway
productions has improved markedly. Off- and Off-Off-Broadway is where Eric Bogosian and Laurie Anderson make their
home. It's the land where such plays as *Nunsense*, *Driving
Miss Daisy*, and *Other People's Money* enjoy long runs. To com-
plicate matters further, scores of established companies hop
from one theater to another, or go underground for a season or
two and then reemerge in new quarters. Unremitting rent
hikes have become the bane of such smaller theaters' existence.
As a study undertaken by the Alliance of Resident Theatres/
New York recently pointed out, small theaters often venture
into marginal neighborhoods and revivify them, only to be
forced out by gentrification.

Name actors appear in top-flight productions at **Lincoln Center's** two theaters: the **Vivian Beaumont** and the more intimate
Mitzi E. Newhouse (65th St. and Broadway, tel. for both 212/
362–7600). Strong new management there led by Gregory
Mosher has scored some startling successes—witness the long
runs of John Guare's *The House of Blue Leaves* and the vintage
Cole Porter musical *Anything Goes*. Downtown at the **Public
Theater** (425 Lafayette St., tel. 212/598–7150) New York's premier *homme de theatre*, Joseph Papp, mounts new and classic
plays, along with film series, dance concerts, and musical
events. This Shakespeare marathon, currently in its fourth of
six years, will present all the Bard's works with a roster of big-
name stars. In the summertime, Papp's Shakespeare Festival

raises its sets in Central Park's open-air Delacorte Theater, while the **Festival Latino** takes over the building at Astor Place.

One of the major Off-Broadway enclaves is **Theatre Row,** a collection of small houses (100 seats or less)—such as the John Houseman and Douglas Fairbanks theaters, Playwrights' Horizons, or the Harold Clurman Theatre—on the downtown side of 42nd Street between Ninth and Tenth avenues. Another Off-Broadway neighborhood lies in Greenwich Village, around Sheridan Square. Its theaters include **Circle Rep** (161 6th Ave., tel. 212/807–1326), a showcase for new playwrights; **Circle-in-the-Square Downtown** (159 Bleecker St., tel. 212/254–6330); the **Lucille Lortel Theater** (121 Christopher St., tel. 212/924–8782); the **Cherry Lane Theater** (38 Commerce St., tel. 212/989–2020); and the **Provincetown Playhouse** (133 MacDougal St., tel. 212/477–5048). Other estimable Off-Broadway theaters are flung across the Manhattan map: the **Promenade Theatre** (Broadway at 76th St., tel. 212/580–1313); the **Roundabout** (100 E. 17th St., tel. 212/420–1883), specializing in revivals of the classics; and the **Manhattan Theatre Club** (at City Center, 131 W. 55th St., tel. 212/581–7907).

Here are a few other Off- and Off-Off-Broadway theater groups to keep your eye on:

The Classic Stage Company (136 E. 13th St., tel. 212/677–4210), providing a showcase for the classics—some arcane, others European.
The Ensemble Studio Theatre (549 W. 52nd St., tel. 212/247–4982), with its tried-and-true company of players, stressing new dramatic works.
Equity Library Theatre (performances held in various venues throughout the city, tel. 212/663–2880), offering mostly revivals of both plays and musicals, performed by unsalaried actors working for exposure.
The Jewish Repertory Theatre (344 E. 14th St., tel. 212/505–2667), begun 15 years ago, producing plays about Jewish life; one recent offering, *Crossing Delancey*, was turned into a hit film.
Manhattan Punch Line (410 W. 42nd St., tel. 212/239–0827), devoted to comedy for the past 10 years.
Musical Theatre Works (St. Peter's Church, corner of 54th St. and Lexington Ave., tel. 212/688–6022), for musical comedy experiments.
The Negro Ensemble Company (Theatre Four, 424 W. 55th St., tel. 212/246–8545), for high-caliber black drama.
The New Theatre of Brooklyn (465 Dean St., Brooklyn, tel. 718/230–3366), off Flatbush Avenue (on the outskirts of Park Slope), offering new plays and neglected classics.
The Pan Asian Repertory Theatre (Playhouse 46, 423 W. 46th St., tel. 212/245–2660), a center for Asian and Asian-American artists, producing new works or adapted Western plays.
Perry Street Theatre Co. (31 Perry St., tel. 212/255–7190), presenting innovative new plays.
Repertorio Español (Gramercy Arts Theatre, 138 E. 27th St., tel. 212/889–2850), an Obie-award-winning Spanish arts repertory theater whose productions are in Spanish.
Riverside Shakespeare Company (performing in parks throughout the five boroughs, tel. 212/877–6810), a 14-year-old troupe producing the Bard's works and other classical plays.
The Second Stage (the Promenade Theatre, Broadway at W.

76th St., tel. 212/873–6103), producing recent plays that may not have been given a fair shake their first time around.

The Soho Rep (Greenwich House, 27 Barrow St., tel. 212/925–2588), dedicated to contemporary plays on controversial issues.

TWEED (c/o 496 Hudson St., tel. 212/741–0812), a decidedly downtown company that explores contemporary themes through various theatrical forms.

Avant-Garde Last, but not at all least, is New York's fabled theatrical avant-garde. The "experimental theater" movement's founders may no longer be the long-haired hippies they were when they first started doing mixed-media productions and promoting off-center playwrights (such as Sam Shepard) 20 years ago, but they continue at the forefront. Take Ellen Stewart, also known, simply and elegantly, as "LaMama." Over the past two decades, her East Village organization has branched out to import European innovators and has grown physically as well. **La MaMa E.T.C.** (74A E. 4th St., tel. 212/475–7710) now encompasses a First Floor Theater, an Annex theater, and a club. At these you'll see African fables, New Wave opera, reinterpretations of the Greeks (assisted by the likes of director Andrei Serban and composer Elizabeth Swados), and novels adapted for the stage.

Another chief player in the theatrical avant-garde is **Mabou Mines** (150 1st Ave., tel. 212/473–0559), a peripatetic troupe whose trademarks are the innovative use of stage technology and the repeated exploration (some call it "deconstruction") of Samuel Beckett's texts. Still thriving is the **Ridiculous Theatrical Company** (1 Sheridan Sq., tel. 212/691–2271), despite the death of its inspired founder, Charles Ludlum, in 1987. This theater has been around since 1972, honing its unique performance style—a blend of classical acting and high camp.

Performance Art At the vanishing point of the avant-garde is that curious mélange of artistic disciplines known as performance art. Intentionally difficult to categorize, it blends music and sound, dance, video and lights, words, and whatever else comes to the performance artist's mind, to produce events of erratic success—sometimes fascinating, sometimes deadening. Performance art is almost exclusively a downtown endeavor, though it is also showcased in the outer boroughs, especially Brooklyn, where the **Brooklyn Academy of Music** (30 Lafayette Ave., Brooklyn, tel. 718/636–4100) has built its considerable reputation on an annual Next Wave Festival of performance works. To BAM have come the performance-art elite, including Philip Glass, Laurie Anderson, and David Byrne.

Other performance–art showcases are:

Franklin Furnace (112 Franklin St., tel. 212/925–4671), since 1976 a supporter of off-center arts—this is where Eric Bogosian (recently seen in the movies *Funhouse* and *Talk Radio)* got his start.

The Kitchen (512 W. 19th St., tel. 212/255–5793) in new Chelsea digs, perhaps *the* Manhattan center for performance art, although video, dance, and music have their moments here, too.

Performance Space 122, or **P.S. 122** (150 1st Ave., tel. 212/477–5288), called by *The Village Voice* "the petri dish of downtown culture." Occupying a former public school that was comedian George Burns's alma mater, P.S. 122 presents exhibits and productions that come and go quickly but seldom fail in freshness. Look especially for its annual marathon in February, in which scores of dazzling downtowners take part.

BACA Downtown (111 Willoughby St., Brooklyn, tel. 718/596–2222), another Brooklyn outpost of the avant-garde, featuring up-and-comers and imported acts.

P.S. 1 (46–01 21st St., Queens, tel. 718/784–2084), a contemporary art museum in lively Long Island City, Queens, featuring occasional theatrical events.

Music

"Gentlemen," conductor Serge Koussevitzky once told the assembled Boston Symphony Orchestra, "maybe it's good enough for Cleveland or Cincinnati, but it's not good enough for New York." That's New York's place in the musical world, in a nutshell; quite simply, it's the top, for performers and music lovers alike.

New York possesses not only the country's oldest symphony, the New York Philharmonic, but also three renowned conservatories—The Juilliard School, The Manhattan School of Music, and Mannes College of Music—plus myriad musical performance groups. Since the turn of the century, the world's great orchestras and soloists have made Manhattan a principal stopping point. Over the past 10 years, live TV and radio broadcasts have brought the music played in New York to millions more listeners across the North American continent.

To those who visit the city for its music, New York opens like a Stradivarius case. In an average week, between 50 and 150 events—everything from zydeco to Debussy, Cole Porter, Kurt Weill, and reggae—appear in newspaper and magazine listings, and weekly concert calendars are published in all of the major newspapers. Record and music shops, such as the cavernous **Tower Records** (692 Broadway, tel. 212/505–1500, and 1965 Broadway, tel. 212/799–2500), the reliable **Bleecker Bob's Golden Oldies** (118 W. 3rd St., tel. 212/475–9677), and the classy **Patelson's** (160 W. 56th St., tel. 212/582–5840), serve as music information centers, too, as do the city's radio stations. WNYC (FM 96.4) updates listeners on current musical events in its "Around New York" show, Fridays from 4 to 5 PM, and WNCN (FM 104) broadcasts concert capsules daily, plus a "New York Magazine" on Monday nights, 8–9. Both of these classical music stations also publish monthly program guides *(Wavelength* and *Keynote,* respectively), with extensive concert listings. The **Bryant Park Music and Dance Discount Ticket Booth** (42nd St. just east of 6th Ave., tel. 212/382–2323) also lists music around town.

In recent seasons, the city has been fevered by a mania for composer marathons. Early music, often performed on historic instruments, has caught the New York public's ear, too. Up from downtown wafts the sound of New Music, played by such masters as saxophonist John Zorn, the Kronos Quartet, and Peter Gordon's Love of Life Orchestra, and, increasingly, the uptown establishment halls, including Carnegie and Avery Fisher, are expanding their repertoires to accommodate them. Recently, infusions of Third World music—the Big Apple calls it World Beat—have thickened the city's musical stew, with smaller concert halls and alternative venues featuring the melodies of Cuba, Ghana, and other countries you'd need an atlas to locate.

Classical Music **Lincoln Center** (W. 62nd St. and Broadway) remains the city's musical nerve center, especially when it comes to the classics. The 150-year-old **New York Philharmonic** performs in its Avery Fisher Hall (tel. 212/874–2424), as does the **American Philharmonic Orchestra.** In summer, the popular **Mostly Mozart** concert series presents an impressive roster of classical performers. Avery Fisher, designed by Max Abramovitz, opened in 1961 as Philharmonic Hall, but underwent drastic renovation in 1976 to improve the acoustics (at a price tag of $5 million). The result is an auditorium that follows the classic European rectangular pattern. To its stage come the world's great musicians; to its boxes, the black-tie-and-diamond-tiara set.

A note for New York Philharmonic devotees: The orchestra rehearses Thursday mornings at 9:45. In season (September–May), and when conductors and soloists are amenable, rehearsals are open to the public for $5.00. Call 212/874–2424 for information.

Near Avery Fisher is Alice Tully Hall (tel. 212/362–1911), an intimate "little white box," considered as acoustically perfect as concert houses get. Here the **Chamber Music Society of Lincoln Center** tunes up, along with promising Juilliard students and famous guest artists and concert groups. Lincoln Center's outdoor Damrosch Park, and Bruno Walter Auditorium (in the Library of the Performing Arts, tel. 212/870–1630) often offer free concerts; two new summer programs, **Serious Fun** and **Classical Jazz,** have recently been added to the Lincoln Center bill as well.

While Lincoln Center is only 30 years old, another famous classical music palace—**Carnegie Hall** (887 7th Ave., tel. 212/247–7800)—is about to celebrate its 100th birthday. This is the place where the great pianist Paderewski was attacked by ebullient crowds (who claimed kisses and locks of his hair) after a performance in 1891; where young Leonard Bernstein, standing in for New York Philharmonic conductor Bruno Walter, made his triumphant debut in 1943; where Jack Benny and Isaac Stern played violin duets; and where the Beatles played one of their first U.S. concerts. When threats of the wrecker's ball loomed large in 1960, a consortium of Carnegie loyalists (headed by Isaac Stern) rose to save it; an eventual multimillion-dollar renovation in 1986 left Carnegie's Main Concert Hall and Weill Recital Hall in better physical shape than ever. Public tours are conducted on Tuesdays and Thursdays; for information, call 212/247–7800.

Because Carnegie Hall's 1990–91 season marks its 100th birthday, it will be an extravagant year-long fete, with appearances by such artists as Marilyn Horne, specially commissioned works by Ned Rorem and Sir Michael Tippett, and a 10-day celebration (April 26–May 5, 1991) culminating in a gala performance by the New York Philharmonic. Meanwhile, at Weill Recital Hall, the "Cabaret Comes to Carnegie" series and "Festival of Folk Music of the Americas" will continue.

Other prime classical music locales are:

Aaron Davis Hall at City College (W. 134th St. at Covent Ave., tel. 212/690–4100), uptown scene of iconoclastic musical events staged by the World Music Institute and a variety of classical concerts.
Grace Rainey Rogers Auditorium at the Metropolitan Museum

of Art (5th Ave. at 82nd St., tel. 212/570–3949), providing classical music in classic surroundings.

Merkin Concert Hall at the Abraham Goodman House (129 W. 67th St., tel. 212/362–8719), almost as prestigious as the concert halls at Lincoln Center.

Kaufman Concert Hall at the 92nd St. Y (1395 Lexington Ave., tel. 212/415–5440), with the mixed ensemble Musical Elements in residence, plus scores of guest performers.

Bargemusic at the Fulton Ferry Landing in Brooklyn (tel. 718/624–4061), with chamber music bubbling from an old Erie Lackawanna coffee barge tethered on the murky East River.

Brooklyn Academy of Music (30 Lafayette Ave., tel. 718/636–4100), ever experimenting with new and old musical styles, and still a showcase for the Brooklyn Symphony.

Outdoor Concerts Weather permitting, the city's great out-of-doors becomes one wide concert hall. Each August, the plaza around Lincoln Center explodes with the **Lincoln Center Out-of-Doors** series. In the summertime, both the **Metropolitan Opera** and the **New York Philharmonic** decamp to municipal parks, rocking the greenswards with the thunder of the *1812 Overture* or the trills of *La Bohème*. These occasions are free, which explains why on one balmy summer night in 1986, the Philharmonic made *The Guinness Book of World Records* by entertaining a crowd of 800,000. (For information call Lincoln Center, tel. 212/877–2011, or the City Parks Events Hotline, tel. 212/360–1333.) A **Jazzmobile** (tel. 212/866–4900) trucks jazz and Latin music to parks throughout the five boroughs, and Prospect Park comes alive with the sounds of its annual **Celebrate Brooklyn Concert Series** (tel. 718/788–0055). Starlit Saturday evenings at South Street Seaport turn Pier 16 into **Summerpier** (tel. 212/669–9400), featuring a range of musical styles and plenty of pretzels and beer.

Lunchtime Concerts During the work week, more and more, lunchtime concerts provide musical midday breaks at public atriums all over the city. Events are generally free, and bag-lunching is encouraged. Check out the **Continental Insurance Atrium** (180 Maiden Ln.); the **World Financial Center's Winter Garden Atrium** (across the West Side Highway from the World Trade Center); and the **Citicorp Center Marketplace** (54th St. and Lexington Ave.). And, of course, everywhere—in parks, on street corners, and down under in the subway—aspiring musicians of all kinds hold forth, with their instrument cases thrown open for contributions. True, some are hacks, but others are bona fide professionals: moonlighting violinists, Broadway chorus members indulging their love of the barbershop quartet, or horn players prowling up from clubs to take in the fresh air.

Downtown, the venerable **Trinity Church** (Broadway and Wall St., tel. 212/602–0760) presents free lunchtime concerts of mostly classical music. On Tuesdays, concerts are at 12:45; on Mondays and Thursdays, they're at 12:10 up the street in St. Paul's Chapel (Fulton St. and Broadway).

A midtown music break can be found at **St. Peter's Lutheran Church** (619 Lexington Ave., at the Citicorp Ctr., tel. 212/935–2200), with its Wednesday series of lunchtime jazz and its Sunday jazz vespers.

Opera

The past decade has sharply intensified the public's apprecia-
tion for grand opera—partly because of the charismatic personalities of such great singers as Placido Domingo and Beverly
Sills, and partly because of the efforts of New York's magnetic
Metropolitan Opera Company. A Met premiere draws the rich
and famous, the critics, and the connoisseurs. At the Met's elegant Lincoln Center home, with its Marc Chagall murals and
weighty Austrian-crystal chandeliers, the super charged atmosphere gives audiences a sense that something special is going to happen, even before the curtain goes up. Luciano
Pavarotti put it best: "When it comes to classical music, New
York can truly be called a beacon of light—with that special
quality that makes it *'unico in mondo,'* unique in the world."

The Metropolitan Opera (tel. 212/362–6000) performs its vaunt-
ed repertoire from September to mid-April, and though tickets
can cost as much as $75 apiece, standing room is available for
far less if you're willing to join the line that forms at 10 AM on
the day of a performance. The Met's 1990–91 season will open
with a revival of *La Bohème* directed by Franco Zefferelli. The
season continues with new productions featuring Luciano
Pavarotti (*Un Ballo in Maschera*) and Jesse Norman (*Par-
sival*).).

Meanwhile, the **New York City Opera,** which performs in Lincoln Center's New York State Theater (tel. 212/870–5570), has
faced the departure of its famous general director, Beverly
Sills. But it persists in its "tradition of taking chances on unfa-
miliar works, old and new" (in the words of *New York Times*
critic Donal Henahan). City Opera recently widened its repertoire to include several classic musical comedies, such as
Brigadoon, South Pacific, and *The Sound of Music,* and it continues its ingenious practice of "supertitling"—electronically
displaying line-by-line translations into English for foreign-
language operas. Recent seasons have included such time-
tested favorites as *Street Scene, Madama Butterfly,* and
Rigoletto.

Opera aficionados should also keep track of the **Carnegie Hall**
schedule (tel. 212/247–7800) for debuting singers, and pay
close attention to new developments at the **Brooklyn Academy
of Music** (tel. 718/636–4100), which last year kicked off its BAM
Opera project with the Theatre Royal de la Monnaie's production of Mozart's rarely performed *La Finta Giardiniera.* BAM
plans to coproduce a number of new works with the Met, to be
staged at its handsomely renovated **Majestic Theatre** beginning
in 1991. **City Center** (tel. 212/581–7907) is a good place to catch
opera, too. Periodically the center hosts the New Sadler's Wells
Opera (specializing in Gilbert and Sullivan) and premiers
works produced by the **New York Opera Repertory Theater.**

Other city opera groups include:

Amato Opera Theatre (319 Bowery, tel. 212/228–8200), a showcase for rising singers.
New York Gilbert and Sullivan Players (251 W. 91st St., Apt.
4C, tel. 212/769–1000), performing G & S classics at Christmastime.

Opera Ebony (2109 Broadway, Suite 1418, tel. 212/690–4100), a
black company performing major and minor works.

Repertorio Español (138 E. 27th St., tel. 212/889–2850), whose
performers sing in Spanish.

True devotees might consider a New York opera theme tour—
several days of concentrated immersion, usually conducted by
an expert. Check *Opera Monthly* magazine (Box 816, Madison
Square Station, 10159, tel. 212/627–2120) for the names of tour
firms.

Dance

Ballet Visiting balletomanes live out their dreams in New York,
where two powerhouse companies—the New York City Ballet,
directed by Jerome Robbins and Peter Martins, and the American Ballet Theatre, led until October 1989 by Mikhail Baryshnikov—continue to please and astonish.

The **New York City Ballet,** a hallmark troupe for over 40 years,
recently presented a festival of Jerome Robbins's Ballets, high-
lighting some of the successful choreographer's best works.
NYCB has long been famous for its repertoire of Balanchine,
and now Peter Martins is breaking new ground with his series
of dances inspired by the avant-garde music of Michael Torke.
The company performs in Lincoln Center's New York State
Theater (tel. 212/496–0600). Its season runs from November to
February—with December set aside for the beloved annual
production of *The Nutcracker*—and from April to June.

Founded by Lincoln Kirstein and George Balanchine in 1948,
NYCB continues to stress dance as a whole above individual
ballet stars, though that hasn't stopped a number of prima ballerinas (such as Patricia McBride, Kyra Nichols, and Darci
Kistler) from standing out. The company contains 110 dancers
altogether, and maintains a repertoire of 20th-century works
unmatched in the world.

Across the plaza at Lincoln Center, the Metropolitan Opera
House (tel. 212/362–6000) is home for the **American Ballet Theatre,** noted especially for its brilliant renditions of story ballets
and its lyrical style, as well as its world renowned featured
dancers. Its season runs from October to November and from
April to June.

Part of Lincoln Center's dance vitality is accounted for by the
presence of the **School of American Ballet,** the focus for the
dreams of young dancers across the country. Some 2,000 of
them vie for spots in SAB's summer session, and a talented
handful of the 200 who make it into the summer group go on to
join the school. Here the Balanchine legacy lives on, and
soulful-eyed baby dancers are molded into professional performers. You can see SAB students dashing across 67th and
Broadway with leotard-stuffed bags slung over their shoulders, or congregating in **The Ballet Shop** (1887 Broadway, tel.
212/581–7990).

When the ABT and NYCB take a break from performing, Lincoln Center acts as impresario for dozens of world-renowned
companies, such as the Bolshoi and Stuttgart ballets.

The varied bill at **City Center** (131 W. 55th St., tel. 212/581–
7907) often includes touring ballet companies; recently the Ba-

sel Ballet performed there. The **Brooklyn Academy of Music** (30 Lafayette Ave., tel. 718/636–4100) holds an **American Ballet Festival** from October to June that features interesting American companies.

Modern Dance At City Center (131 W. 55th St., tel. 212/581–7907), the moderns hold sway. In seasons past, the New York–based **Martha Graham Dance Company,** the **Paul Taylor Dance Company,** the **Harlem Dance Theater,** and the **Merce Cunningham Dance Company** have performed here.

A growing modern dance center is the **Joyce Theatre** (175 8th Ave., tel. 212/242–0800), permanent home of the **Feld Ballet,** founded 15 years ago by an upstart ABT dancer who went on to become a principal fixture on the dance scene. The loony acrobats of **Pilobolus** and the avant-garde **Zeromoving Company** have also performed at the Joyce, which is housed in a renovated Art Moderne movie theater. Every year the **Moiseyev Dance Company,** with its 135 Moscovite dancers and musicians, settles into Radio City Music Hall (50th St. and 6th Ave., tel. 212/757–3100) for a popular series. At Symphony Space (2537 Broadway, tel. 212/864–1414), the bill features ethnic dance.

Here's a sampling of other, mostly experimental and avant-garde, dance forums:

Dance Theater Workshop (219 W. 19th St., tel. 212/691–6500), one of New York's most successful laboratories for new dance.
Danspace Project (at St. Mark's Church in the Bowery, 10th St. and 2nd Ave., tel. 212/674–8112), with a series of avant-garde choreography that runs from October to June.
Nikolai/Louis Choreospace (38 E. 19th St., tel. 212/777–1120), a showcase for modern-dance masters.
P.S. 122 (150 1st Ave., tel. 212/477–5288), where dance events border on performance art; among others, Meredith Monk occasionally cavorts here.
Repertorio Español (138 E. 27th St., tel. 212/889–2850), oft-visited by the famed Spanish stylist Pilar Rioja.
Riverside Dance Festival (at Riverside Church, 490 Riverside Dr., tel. 212/864–2929), for classical, jazz, modern, and ethnic dance.
Washington Square Church (137 W. 4th St., tel. 212/924–9299), where dancers and visual artists join forces.

Film

On any given week, New York City seems a kind of film archive featuring all the major new releases, classics renowned and arcane, unusual foreign offerings, small independent flicks, and cutting-edge experimental works. Because you don't usually need to buy tickets in advance, movie-going is a great spur-of-the-moment way to rest from the rigors of sightseeing. You may have to stand a while in a line that winds around the block, but even that can be entertaining—conversations overheard in such queues are generally just as good as the previews of coming attractions. Note, however, that these lines are generally for people who have already bought their tickets; be sure, as you approach the theater, to ask if there are separate lines for ticket *holders* and ticket *buyers.*

Festivals New York's numero uno film program remains the **New York Film Festival,** conducted by the Film Society of New York every

September at Alice Tully and Avery Fisher halls (tel. 212/877–1800). Its program includes 25–50 hot independent movies, most of them never seen before in the United States; the festival's hits usually make their way into local movie houses over the following couple of months. This festival has presented the U.S. premieres of such memorable movies as Martin Scorsese's *Mean Streets*, François Truffaut's *Day For Night*, Lawrence Kasdan's *The Big Chill*, and Akira Kurosawa's *Ran*. In March the Film Society joins forces with the Museum of Modern Art to produce a **New Directors/New Films** series, where the best works by up-and-coming directors get their moment to flicker. This series is held at MOMA's Roy and Niuta Titus theatres (11 W. 53rd St., tel. 212/877–1800, ext. 489).

Museums   The **Museum of the Moving Image** (36–01 35th Ave., Queens, tel. 718/784–0077 or 784–4520), housed in a building belonging to the historic Kaufman Astoria Studios, offers multiple galleries that are a movie buff's paradise, as are its 195-seat Riklis Theatre and 60-seat Warner Communications Screening Room. The museum presents more than 700 programs annually, including major artist-oriented retrospectives, Hollywood classics, experimental videos, and TV documentaries.

In midtown Manhattan, the **Museum of Broadcasting** (1 E. 53rd St., tel. 212/752–7684) has a gigantic collection of 37,000 radio and TV shows, including everything from *The Patty Duke Show* to *Soap*, *Cheers*, and *Taxi*. The museum's library provides 23 consoles, where you can watch whatever you wish for up to an hour at a time. It also offers noontime "comedy breaks," featuring classic side-splitters from radio and TV, and a series of Saturday morning screenings for children.

First-Run Houses   Film traditionalists rue the current multiplexing craze that has turned the city's big-screen, single-show theaters into warrens where as many as six movies play concurrently; a firm called Cineplex Odeon seems to be moving toward a monopoly in this area. Just in 1989, multiscreen complexes opened up all over town: at Worldwide Plaza (320 W. 50th St.), in Chelsea (260 W. 23rd St.), in Gramercy Park (890 Broadway at Loew's 19th St.), on the Upper East Side (123 E. 86th St.), and in SoHo (Houston and Mercer Sts.)—whose construction moved the *New York Times* to wonder, "Is a multiplex just too, shudder, suburban for SoHo?" The 1990s should bring several multi-screen houses farther downtown. Whether this increase in the number of cinemas will ease lines at the box office remains to be seen. Extensive first-run film information can be obtained by dialing 212/777–FILM, the Movie Phone sponsored by WPLJ and *New York* magazine.

In 1989, lavish restorations of the big-screen movie classics *Gone with the Wind* and *Lawrence of Arabia* were brought to the two New York theaters best equipped to handle such extravaganzas: The **Ziegfeld** (141 W. 54th St., west of 6th Ave., tel. 212/765–7600), with its awesome sound system, and **Radio City Music Hall** (1260 6th Ave., tel. 212/247–4777), with its 34-foot-high screen and 4,500-watt projector.

The Times Square area is still a movie mecca, though action and porn flicks prevail on 42nd Street, and viewers should be warned to sit tight and hold on to their purses. Posh East Side first-run theaters line Third Avenue between 57th and 60th streets and continue up Second Avenue into the 60s. Another group is clustered around East 34th Street.

Midnight Movies   At a handful of Greenwich Village theaters, midnight madness continues with late and late-late showings of eccentric classics such as *King of Hearts*, *The Rocky Horror Picture Show*, and *The Texas Chainsaw Massacre*. **East Side Cinema** (919 3rd Ave., tel. 212/755–3020), the **New Quad Cinema** (13th St. between 5th and 6th Aves., tel. 212/255–8800), the **Angelika Film Center** (Houston and Mercer Sts., tel. 212/995–2000), and the **Waverly Twin** (323 6th Ave., tel. 212/929–8037) are the theaters to check out for these.

Revival Houses   Cineplex Odeon ignited a firestorm of protest in 1988 when it transformed one of New York's most cherished old revival houses, the **Regency** (Broadway at 67th St., tel. 212/724–3700) into a first-run theater. When it threatened to do the same thing to the **Biograph Cinema** (225 W. 57th St., tel. 212/582–4582), 30,000 signatures were gathered to block the conversion. Today, the Biograph remains a revival island in a sea of first-run theaters. America's first revival repertory cinema, the **Thalia** closed in 1987, but the new **Thalia Soho** (15 Vandam St., tel. 212/675–0498) carries on the tradition. Revivals can also be found at:

Cinema Village (3rd Ave., between 11th and 12th Sts., tel. 212/924–3363), often offering as many as three sets of double features a week.

Film Forum (209 W. Houston St., tel. 212/431–1590) in a brand new building, has series based on movie genres, directors, and other film artists.

Theatre 80 St. Mark's (80 St. Mark's Pl., tel. 212/254–7400), small and shabby but convivial, sports double-features from the '30s and '40s and a welcoming coffee bar.

Foreign Films   New York film lovers are used to reading subtitles. Between the interest generated by the Film Festival, the city's population of foreign executives and diplomats, and a large contingent of cosmopolitan *cinéastes*, there's always an audience here for foreign films. New Yorkers saw the French *Three Men and a Cradle* long before it was Americanized into *Three Men and a Baby;* such recent movies as the Swedish *My Life As a Dog*, the Japanese *Tampopo*, and the Italian *Cinema Paradiso* were long-running hits in this city. The following cinemas more or less specialize in foreign films:

Carnegie Screening Room (887 7th Ave. between 56th and 57th Sts., tel. 212/757–2131), an adjunct of the tony Carnegie Hall Cinema.

The Plaza (42 E. 58th St., tel. 212/355–3320), a showcase for some of the most talked-about foreign entries.

Lincoln Plaza (Broadway between 62nd and 63rd Sts., tel. 212/757–2280), three subterranean cinemas playing long-run foreign hits.

68th Street Playhouse (68th St. at 3rd Ave., tel. 212/734–0302), with exclusive extended runs of foreign discoveries.

New Quad Cinema (13th St. between 5th and 6th Aves., tel. 212/255–8800), with first-run art and foreign films.

Foreign films also run at art societies and museums around town, including:

African-American Institute (833 United Nations Plaza, tel. 212/949–5666).
Asia Society (725 Park Ave., tel. 212/517–2742).
French Institute-Alliance Française (22 E. 60th St., tel. 212/355–6100).
Goethe House (1014 5th Ave., tel. 212/972–3960).
International Center of Photography (1130 5th Ave., tel. 212/860–1777).
Japan Society (333 E. 47th St., tel. 212/752–3015).
The Museum of Modern Art (11 W. 53rd St., tel. 212/708–9490).

Avant-Garde Films The **Public Theater** (425 Lafayette St., tel. 212/598–7171) is one of the city's most reliable forums for experimental and independent film. Many of its series focus on politics and social issues, or are tributes to nonmainstream artists. **The Collective for Living Cinema** (41 White St., tel. 212/505–5181), **Anthology Film Archives** (32–34 2nd Ave., tel. 212/477–2714), and **Millennium Film Workshop** (66 E. 4th St., tel. 212/ 673–0090) showcase more off-center works, old and new, American and foreign.

Readings and Lectures

New York is, of course, the center of the American publishing world, and as a result most writers—however reclusive—eventually find reason to come here. The Writers Guild headquarters and the U.S. offices of P.E.N. International are in Manhattan; the National Book Awards are presented here annually in the grand foyer of the New York Public Library.

If you're interested in the written word (and in stealing a look at the people who create it), a New York fiction or poetry reading is a good idea. They spring up all over the city—in bookstores, libraries, museums, bars, and legitimate theaters—drawing some of the top names in contemporary literature, writers such as Russell Banks, Kurt Vonnegut, Tom Wolfe, Mary Gordon, Louise Ehrdrich, and Margaret Atwood, as well as debuting talents.

A major reading and talk series held at the **Lincoln Center Library for the Performing Arts** (tel. 212/870–1630) specializes in musicians, directors, singers, and actors. In fact, the entire **New York Public Library** system (tel. 212/930–0571) is a wide-open field for reading events, as is the **Brooklyn Public Library** network (tel. 718/780–7700).

At the **Metropolitan Museum of Art** (5th Ave. at 82nd St., tel. 212/535–7710 or 535–3949), seasonal lectures regularly draw sell-out crowds. Artist such as David Hockney hold forth here, as do the world's eminent art historians.

Authors, poets, lyricists, and travelogue-spinners take the stage at the **92nd St. Y** (1395 Lexington Ave., tel. 212/996–1100), while the **West Side YMCA** (5 W. 63rd St., tel. 212/787–6557) offers readings by major novelists, poets, and humorists in a series called "The Writer's Voice."

Many Manhattan bookstores organize evening readings by authors or recently published books. Best bets are **Books & Co.** (939 Madison Ave. near 74th St., tel. 212/737–1450), **Endicott Booksellers** (450 Columbus Ave. near 81st St., tel. 212/787–6300), **Three Lives & Co.** (154 W. 10th St., tel. 212/741–2069),

and the **Pomander Bookshop** (955 West End Ave. at 107th St.,
tel. 212/866–1777).

The Arts for Kids

In the seemingly endless argument over whether or not to raise
kids in this city, New York parents consistently point out the
advantages of being able to expose their offspring to the city's
cultural treasures. Precocious Manhattan toddlers cut their
teeth on outings to the Metropolitan Museum, puppet plays in
Central Park, holiday spectaculars at Radio City, and traditional Christmas performances of *The Nutcracker* ballet. Many
performing arts groups cater specifically to children, including:

The Big Apple Circus (35 W. 35th St., tel. 212/268–2500), whose
three-ring escapades charm the toughest New Yorkers during
the summer months.

Don Quijote Experimental Children's Theatre (Lincoln Square
Theater, 250 W. 65th St., tel. 212/496–8009), which exposes
city kids to realistic theater exploring topics such as literacy
and aging.

52nd St. Project's Triple Play Club (549 W. 52nd St., tel. 212/
247–4982), presenting plays, written by children and performed by professionals, in February.

4th Wall Repertory Company, Truck & Warehouse Theatre (79
E. 4th St., tel. 212/254–5060), producers of musical circus
shows, with plenty of audience participation.

Hartley House Theatre (413 W. 46th St., tel. 212/666–1716),
featuring adaptations of classic fairy tales and such.

Henry Street Settlement Louis Abrono Arts for Living Center
(466 Grand St., tel. 212/598–0400), founded by a nurse to care
for the sick and disadvantaged, now bringing the arts to kids
and families with the Arts for Family series every Sunday.

The Little Orchestra Society (220 W. 42nd St., tel. 212/704–
2100), with concert series that introduce classical music con-
cepts to children ages 3–5 or 6–12, usually at Lincoln Center.

Little People's Theatre Company (The Courtyard Playhouse, 39
Grove St., tel. 212/765–9540), where audiences participate in
such classics as *Hansel and Gretel*, Sundays at 1:30 and 3PM.

The Paper Bag Players (tel. 212/677–5959), which frequently
performs at Symphony Space and Town Hall, featuring original
plays such as *I Won't Take a Bath*.

Theater of the Open Eye (270 W. 89th St., tel. 212/769–4141),
offering both classic and new plays.

Theatreworks/USA (at the Promenade Theatre, Broadway and
76th St., tel. 212/677–5959), for their polished productions
about historical figures and events.

Thirteenth Street Repertory Company (50 W. 13th St., tel. 212/
675–6677), which directs its performances to children ages two
to ten.

Vineyard Theater (108 E. 15th St. and 309 E. 26th St., tel. 212/
353–3366), presenting children's events, during the winter holiday season.

11 Nightlife

by Susan Spano Wells

Okay, so you've taken the Staten Island Ferry, you've lunched at the Plaza, and you've visited the Met. But don't tuck yourself in just yet. Instead, get yourself truly attuned to the Big Apple's schedule, which runs more by New York nocturnal than by eastern standard time. Even if you're not a night owl by habit, it's worth staying up late at least once, for by night, Manhattan takes on a whole new identity.

Clubs and Entertainment

New York nightlife really started to swing in 1914, when a pair of ballroom dancers, Florence and Maurice Walton, took over management of the Parisian Room, in what is today's theater district. At Chez Maurice, as the new club was called, the city's café society learned a sensual dance at "Tango Teas." Forty years later, night spots mushroomed in Greenwich Village, Harlem, and the east 50s. Along 52nd Street in those years, recalls columnist Pete Hamill, "you could walk down a single block and hear Art Tatum, Billie Holiday, and Charlie Parker. And you could go to the Latin quarter and see girls running around with bananas on their heads. On the other hand, Babe Ruth doesn't play for the Yankees anymore, either."

But Keith Hernandez and Dwight Gooden do play for the Mets, and the old Copacabana Club has been reincarnated as a trendy discotheque. *Plus ça change* . . . In truth, the current nightclub scene is probably more varied and vital than it ever was, but in different ways. To begin with, it has moved downtown— along with just about everything else— to dead-looking East Village dives that come alive nightly, to classic jazz joints in the West Village, to sleekly decorated TriBeCa see-and-be-seen traps, and to preppy hangouts around Wall Street.

There are enough dedicated club-hoppers here to support night spots for almost every idiosyncratic taste. But keep in mind that *when* you go is just as important as where you go in clubland. Clubs vary their themes every night of the week. Depending on where you go, an appropriate costume for a night on the town could include anything from blue suede shoes to an Armani coat to a Balenciaga gown; anything from an orange fright wig to leather and chains to a vintage pink poodle skirt.

That doesn't mean that "anything goes," however, for exclusivity is the name of the game. At certain clubs, gimlet-eyed door staff zealously guard the barrier of velvet rope outside, selecting customers according to arbitrary standards. For a new crop of gypsy clubs, only those in the know can even find out where the group is meeting this week.

On Friday, *The New York Times's* "Weekend" section carries a "Sounds Around Town" column that can give you a picture of what's in the air, as can the *Village Voice*, which probably has more nightclub ads than any rag in the world. Or stop by Tower Records (692 Broadway, tel. 212/505–1500, and 1695 Broadway, tel. 212/799–2500), where fliers about coming events and club passes are stacked outside. You may also get good tips from your cab driver or waitress—they hear and see more than most people do—or from a suitably au courant hotel concierge. Just remember that what's hot and what's not changes almost weekly in this city, so visitors are at a distinct disadvantage. We've tried to give you a rounded sample of reliable hangouts—

establishments that are likely to be still in business by the time you use this book—but clubs come and go as fast as spawning tsetse flies, so phone ahead to make sure your target night spot hasn't closed or turned into a polka hall. Most will charge a cover of at least $10 a head; some go as high as $20–$50 (nobody said catting around was going to be cheap!). Take cash because many places don't accept plastic. *Et maintenant, mesdames et messieurs*, what's your choice?

Putting On the Ritz

You and your date are wearing Oscar de la Renta and Armani finery; your transport's a white stretch limo; and you've just come from dinner at Lutèce or Regine's. Just remember to hide this guidebook in your tux pocket or your rhinestone clutch so people won't guess you're not regulars at:

The Ballroom (253 W. 28th St., tel. 212/244–3005). This very hip Chelsea spot has an extensive tapas bar and a nightclub where some of the great chanteuses—including Peggy Lee and Helen Schneider—rhapsodize.

Café Society (915 Broadway, tel. 212/529–8282). Whoosh through the revolving doors to astonishment: soaring ceilings, pink art deco decor, a long, inviting bar, and dinner dancing. The quixotic entrepreneur who owns Café Society also runs Society Billiards next door.

The Carlyle (35 E. 76th St., tel. 212/744–1600). The hotel's discreetly sophisticated Café Carlyle is where Bobby Short plays when he's in town; Bemelman's Bar, with murals by the author of the Madeleine books, regularly stars jazz pianist Barbara Carroll.

The Edwardian Room (at the Plaza Hotel, 5th Ave. at 59th St., tel. 212/759–3000). With "Trumped-up" digs for dinner and dancing, this place caters especially to the over-40 set.

Nell's (246 W. 14th St., tel. 212/675–1567). Back in vogue, Nell Campbell (of *Rocky Horror* fame) reintroduced sophistication to nightlife with her club. The tone in the upstairs jazz salon is Victorian; downstairs is for tête-à-têtes and dancing.

The Oak Room (at the Algonquin Hotel, 59 W. 44th St., tel. 212/840–6800). Please don't gawk at the famous writers as you come in. Just head straight for the long, narrow club-cum-watering hole; at the piano you'll find, perhaps, singer Julie Wilson, the hopelessly romantic Andrea Marcovicci, or heartthrob jazzman Harry Connick, Jr.

The Rainbow Room and **Rainbow and Stars Club** (30 Rockefeller Plaza, tel. 212/632–5000). You can find two kinds of heaven high up on Rockefeller Center's 65th floor. The Rainbow Room serves dinner (*see* Chapter 8), and dancing begins at 7:30 on a floor right out of an Astaire/Rogers musical. At the intimate new Rainbow and Stars Club, singers such as Tony Bennett and Liliane Montevecchi entertain, backlit by a view of the twinkling lights of the city.

Regine's (502 Park Ave., tel. 212/806–0990). As upscale as the restaurant of the same name, this spot attracts the international set for dancing and listening to a variety of contemporary sounds.

Stringfellows (35 E. 21st St., tel. 212/254–2444). At this British import for the jet-and-blank-check set, you can order a Dom Perignon cocktail and pay $500 for your bubbly pleasure. At 11, mirrored panels unveil a dance floor, where commodities traders, TV commentators, and famous fashion designers invade each other's personal space.

Boogie and Be Seen

The city's busiest dance floors are seeing all kinds of styles revived, from "Vogue-ing" to the Twist to bebop swings and lifts. Revelers come to socialize, to find romance, to scream business deals over the music, to show off their glad rags, or to be photographed rubbing shoulders with stars.

Bolido (3 W. 18th St., tel. 212/463–8898). A swank showcase for the Italian design style known as Bolidismo, this club is described by its creator as a "George Jetson fantasy." There are dancing opportunities on two floors, and dining in a mezzanine restaurant.

Chevy's (27 W. 20th St., tel. 212/924–0205). Offering dance workouts for the 9-to-5 crowd, this joint starts to hop earlier than most. Nostalgia is perpetuated by a vintage red Chevrolet beached at the door and by endless retro music.

d Station (220 12th Ave., tel. 212/529–6324). This cavernous, multilevel club is generally crowded, despite being erratic on the music side. Outside you get views of New Jersey; inside, high-energy disportment.

Dukie's (in the Gold Bar, 345 E. 9th St., no phone). This classic East Village neighborhood bar is transformed into a dance club on Friday nights. Interior design is not Dukie's trademark—unless you're inspired by the silver toilet seat over the bar. The crowd is interesting; the music, discs from the past.

Heartbreak (179 Varick St., tel. 212/691–2388). Homage to the '50s is carried out with a bust of the King on the bar, a linoleum dance floor, a luncheonette, and kitschy touches everywhere. Come wearing bobby sox and you'll fit right in.

Juke Box NYC (304 E. 39th St., tel. 212/685–1556). More 1950s and early '60s nostalgia is offered here in what looks like a high school gym. The mood is that of a nonstop giddy graduation prom, where guests revive their teenage selves, happily singing and bopping along to a variety of rock 'n' roll.

Limelight (47 W. 20th St., tel. 212/807–7850). In this transformed Chelsea church, the stained-glass windows endure amid catwalks, spiral staircases, and energetic dancers getting down. Although it's no longer at the cutting edge in terms of its pretty-people draw, this is still a great place for garrulousness and gyration.

M.K. (204 5th Ave., tel. 212/779–1340). Located across from the Flatiron building, the SoHo-chic design attracts a celebrity crowd to this supperclub noted for its number of film premiere parties.

Mars (10th Ave. at 13th St., tel. 212/691–6262). This spot is still hot after over a year as *the* place to go. Take your pick among five levels here (the basement theme is "Afrotech"). The door staff is *very* particular.

Private Eyes, Inc. (12 W. 21st St., tel. 212/206–7770). This quality video palace caters to a varied but generally hip Manhattan crowd. The dance floor is smallish, but the style is never cramped.

The Red Zone (440 W. 54th St., tel. 212/582–2222). Opened in January 1989, this 14,000-square-foot discotheque features huge movie screens where images of water-lapped beaches and the Wild West are projected. Upstairs is a restaurant and bar.

Roseland (239 W. 52nd St., tel. 212/247–0200). This famous old ballroom-dance floor goes disco on weekends. A dollar buys you a dance lesson with a resident host or hostess.

Roxy (515 W. 18th St., tel. 212/645–5156). This place wins the award for the city's most cavernous club to date. Although the design is plain, the club remains enjoyable and popular.

Shout! (124 W. 43rd St., tel. 212/869–2088). In the converted Henry Miller Theater, the disc jockey spins '60s hits from the orchestra seats. This is the place for serious dancing and, on Wednesday nights, live music—such vintage acts as Lou Christie and the Shondells have claimed the spotlight here.

The Surf Club (415 E. 91st St., tel. 212/410–1360). Younger members of the East Side upper crust let down their hair here (while managing, even in the heat of the moment, to remain impeccably coiffed). Patio tables with umbrellas and stuffed sharks set an island mood.

Woody's in the Village (82 E. 4th St., tel. 212/982–3686). Rolling Stone Ron Wood's place is fast becoming an East Village landmark for rockers. The adjacent gallery for musicians-turned-artists is a must-see.

Jazz Notes

Jazz players always come home to Manhattan. Somehow, the city evokes their sound. Greenwich Village is still the mecca, with more than 12 jazz nightclubs, although plenty of others are strewn around town. Here are some classics:

The Angry Squire (217 7th Ave., tel. 212/242–9066). This Chelsea jazz outpost cooks with live jazz seven nights a week.

Arthur's Tavern (57 Grove St., tel. 212/675–6879). The place starts to cook late (say 1 or 2 AM) and eschews all fancy trappings. It attracts a mixed crowd and offers jazz on the steamy side.

Birdland (2745 Broadway, tel. 212/749–2228). Although way up on the West Side (at 105th St.), this spot is still close to the Village at heart. You'll find lots of up-and-coming groups here, as well as the requisite thick atmosphere.

The Blue Note (131 W. 3rd St., tel. 212/475–8592). This club may be the jazz capital of the world. Just an average week could bring Irma Thomas, the Modern Jazz Quartet, and Dizzy Gillespie. If jazz is your thing, make a beeline to the Blue Note.

Bradley's (70 University Pl., tel. 212/228–6440). With brighter-than-usual lighting and, generally, jazz piano, this is a spot for serious fans of jazz and blues.

Carlos I (432 6th Ave., tel. 212/982–3260). Another major Village jazz establishment, this club offers everything from boogie-woogie to blues.

Dan Lynch Bar and Restaurant (221 2nd Ave., tel. 212/677–0911). This jazz surprise in the East Village bustles, especially on Sunday afternoons.

Fat Tuesday's (190 3rd Ave., tel. 212/533–7902). Two sets are p ayed here every night of the week in an intimate basement; there's a popular restaurant/bar upstairs.

Fortune Garden Pavilion (209 E. 49th St., tel. 212/753–0101). Jazz and Chinese food create the Fortune Garden's celestial duo. Two shows are played nightly, Tuesday–Sunday.

Indigo Blues (221 W. 46th St., tel. 212/221–0033). A club that opens headlining Miles Davis is serious about its booking policy. This one doesn't disappoint. The stylishly decorated room seats 200.

The Kitchen (512 W. 19th St., tel. 212/255–5793). The home of the downtown arts features jazz mixed with a little New Music and World Beat.

The Knitting Factory (47 E. Houston St., tel. 212/219–3055). It looks seedy on the outside, but inside there's often fine avant-gardish jazz.

Mikell's (760 Columbus Ave., tel. 212/864–8832). This uptown jazz café/bistro, airier than most, is often visited by show-stopping singers—seven years ago you might have caught Whitney Houston backing up her headlining mama.

Red Blazer Too (349 W. 46th St., tel. 212/262–3112). Roaring '20s, Dixieland, and above all swing music are on tap here. It's a hot spot for after the theater.

Sweet Basil (88 7th Ave. S, tel. 212/242–1785). A little ritzy, though reliable, this night spot presents a range that runs from swing to fusion.

Tramps (45 W. 21st St., tel. 212/727–7788). The place just celebrated 15 years on the scene with the likes of Albert Collins and Buster Poindexter. Come here for a little Chicago blues in the big city.

Upstairs at Greene Street (105 Greene St., tel. 212/925–2415). The restaurant has smashing surroundings converted from a three-story parking garage. Greene Street spent a long time looking for its niche, but it seems to have found it with free jazz and ultracool environs.

The Village Gate (160 Bleecker St., tel. 212/475–5120). This is another of the classic Village jazz joints. Music starts at 9:30 PM. Upstairs there's a cabaret theater.

The Village Vanguard (178 7th Ave. S, tel. 212/255–4037). This old Thelonius Monk haunt lives on in a smoky cellar until recently presided over by the late jazz impresario Max Gordon. It's pricey, but worth every penny.

Rock Around the Clock

The roots of rock may lie in America's heartland, but New York has added its own spin. Crowds at the Big Apple's rocketerias are young, enthusiastic, and hungry; the noise is often deafening, but you can catch many a rising star in this lively scene. Here's where to go:

The Bitter End (147 Bleecker St., tel. 212/673–7030). This old Village standby still serves up its share of new talent, such as Joan Armatrading and Warren Zevon.

The Cat Club (76 E. 13th St., tel. 212/505–0090). Another place with a big dance floor, this one specializes in heavy metal music, but occasionally throws in swing—just to keep you on your toes.

CBGB & OMFUG (315 Bowery, tel. 212/982–4052). American punk rock was born here, in this long black tunnel of a club featuring bands with inventive names: Blind Idiot God, Rude Buddhas, Chemical Wedding. Repair your ears and your appetites at the Pizza Boutique next door.

Maxwell's (1039 Washington St., Hoboken, NJ, tel. 201/656–9632). If you're adventurous enough to cross the Hudson, take the PATH train to Hoboken, a low-rent outpost for young artistic types. Musicians know Maxwell's, even if most Manhattanites don't; it offers up a mix of New Music and rock.

Palladium (126 E. 14th St., tel. 212/473–7171). Here you'll find the world's biggest dance floor, fashioned from the gutted hulk of a theater, along a New Wave/oriental '60s-psychedelic theme. Home to the V.I.P. Mike Todd room, Lambada fever, and Club MTV, this place is to clubland what Macy's is to shopping.

Pyramid Club (101 Ave. A, tel. 212/420–1590). Dancing transvestites might greet you at the bar; in the back, different kinds of music are played every night, all at a decibel level high enough to qualify as rock.

The Ritz (254 W. 54th St., tel. 212/541–8900). There must be something magical about the former site of Studio 54; this club is just as popular but not quite as infamous as its predecessor. Weeknight shows begin at 9 PM; the main floor is for dancing, with seating in the balcony.

The Rock 'n' Roll Café (149 Bleecker St., tel. 212/677–7630). A week's worth of band names should clue you in: War Babies, Mixed Media, the Down Town Boys, and Hell Hounds.

Spo-Dee-O-Dee (565 W. 23rd St., tel. 212/206–1990). This Chelsea haunt alternates jazz and rock performances in a cozy, publike setting.

Wetlands Preserve (161 Hudson St., tel. 212/966–4225). Billed as a "watering hole for activists," this relative newcomer specializes in psychedelic rock. There are Grateful Dead nights on Tuesdays, and "Eco-Saloons" on Sundays.

The Latin and Island Beat

Next to dependable jazz, Latin music is the sound of the moment in New York clubs. Salsa, samba, merengue—all offer an exotic counterpoint to the city's rhythms, and Big Apple musicians have found ways to integrate the Latin strain with indigenous styles. Check them out at:

Club Broadway (2551 Broadway, tel. 212/864–7600). This Upper West Side club is a tradition on the Latin music scene.

Club Paradise (15 Waverly Pl., tel. 212/533–3048). The owners bill this night spot thusly: "Hottest tropical bar on the island; top tropical bands nightly." At 2 AM on Fridays and Saturdays, Club Paradise serves, fittingly, a free tropical buffet.

Corso (205 E. 86th St., tel. 212/534–4964). An institution on the Latin scene, Corso features plenty of mirrors, accomplished dancing, and music from points south.

The Great American Clubhouse (333 E. 60th St., tel. 212/724–6632). Reggae comes to midtown.

Island Club (285 W. Broadway, tel. 212/226–4598). This is another reliable place to hear reggae music.

Kilimanjaro (531 W. 19th St., tel. 212/627–2333). S.O.B.'s (*see* below) has got major competition with this brand-new large club, riding on the success of the DC original; it features world beat music.

S.O.B.'s (204 Varick St., tel. 212/243–4940). Since 1982, this has been the—and we mean *the*—place for reggae, Trinidadian carnival, zydeco, African, and Caribbean funk. The initials Stand for Sound of Brazil, just in case you wondered. The decor is à la Tropicana; the favored drink, a Brazilian *caipirinha*.

The Village Gate (160 Bleecker St., tel. 212/475–5120). Monday at this jazz club is Latin night; the line starts forming early to hear the likes of Ruben Blades.

Down-Home Sounds

The Bottom Line (15 W. 4th St., tel. 212/228–7880). Clubs come and go, but this granddaddy has stayed around since 1974. Its reputation is for showcasing talents on their way up, as it did for both Stevie Wonder and Bruce Springsteen. There's no way to categorize the Bottom Line bill, except to say that folk has headlined consistently—recently with such acts as Suzanne Vega, the McGarrigle Sisters, and the Roches. The sound system is swell, but don't go for the first set and expect to stay for the next—they round up all you little doggies and herd you out through the door.

Delta 88 (332 8th Ave., tel. 212/924–3499). This Chelsea joint was described by the *New Yorker* as having a "white-trash-chicken-shack theme." R & B is the mainstay, along with a dash of hillbilly, zydeco, and blues.

Eagle Tavern (355 W. 14th St., tel. 212/924–0275). Come here for Irish folk music, with a little bluegrass and comedy thrown in.

The Lone Star Roadhouse (240 W. 52nd St., tel. 212/245–2950). In the heart of the theater district, this offspring of a recently closed downtown landmark is an anomaly—but a welcome one. Inhabiting a heady two-story space, it has a long bar for picking up long drinks. The food runs to chili and deep-fried crayfish; the music from doo-wop to gospel.

O'Lunney's (915 2nd Ave., tel. 212/751–5470). Red-checked tablecloths and the smell of stale beer accompany real country music every night. Irish music is often featured, too.

Rodeo Bar (375 3rd Ave., tel. 212/683–6500). Next door to the Abilene Café, this night spot lets loose jamming fiddles and accordions, as well as a comic country band called the Surreal McCoys.

Speakeasy (107 MacDougal St., tel. 212/598–9670). Pure folk is found here, Wednesday–Monday.

Comic Relief

The *Village Voice* covers the comedy scene well, and it's worth checking its listings because lots of music clubs book comedians for periods between sets. Some cabarets and music spots that often bring in stand-ups are Eighty-eight's, Michael's Pub, the Duplex (*see* The Show's the Thing, below), and the Village Gate (*see* Jazz Notes, above). Several clubs, however, are exclusively devoted to comedy acts:

The Boston Comedy Club (82 W. 3rd St., tel. 212/477–1000). Beantown comedians come here to test their stuff in the Big Apple.

Caroline's (332 8th Ave., tel. 212/924–3499, and 89 South St. Seaport, tel. 212/233–4900). The Chelsea location is a classic comedy club—small, drab, but packed with aspiring jokesters; the Seaport spot offers more commodious surroundings and established stars.

Catch a Rising Star (1487 1st Ave., tel. 212/794–1906). Johnny Carson got his start here, and his talent scouts still show up to test the comic current. This place is neither trendy nor cutting edge, but it is reliable.

Chicago City Limits (351 E. 74th St., tel. 212/772–8707). This troupe's been doing improvisational comedy for a long time, and it seldom fails to whip its mostly youngish audiences into a laughing frenzy. Chicago City Limits performs in an East Side church and is very strong on audience participation.

Comedy Cellar (117 MacDougal St., tel. 212/254–3630). This spot has been running for eight years beneath the Olive Tree Café, with a bill that's a good barometer of who's hot.

Comedy U (55 Grand St., tel. 212/431–4022). Popular with downtowners and student comedians, this club offers a wild Marathon Night on Fridays and a comedy jam on Sundays.

The Comic Strip (1568 2nd Ave., tel. 212/861–9386). The atmosphere here is strictly corner bar. The stage is brilliantly lit but minuscule (8 by 10 feet); the bill, unpredictable but worth checking out.

Dangerfield's (1118 1st Ave., tel. 212/593–1650). Since 1969, this has been an important showcase for prime comic talent. It's owned and frequently visited by comedian Rodney Dangerfield himself.

The Original Improvisation (358 W. 44th St., tel. 212/765–8268). The Improv is to comedy what the Blue Note is to jazz. Lots of now-famous comedians got their first laughs here, among them Richard Pryor and Robin Williams. It gets crowded, especially on weekends; there are two shows on Fridays and three on Saturday nights.

Rags to Riches (226 E. 54th St., tel. 212/688–5577). A newcomer to the New York comedy scene, this club features some pleasant innovations, such as roominess (the place seats 300) and weeknight happy hours from 5 to 8, made happier still by the low cover charge.

Stand Up N.Y. (236 W. 78th St., tel. 212/595–0850). A 175-seat Upper West Side option for comedy devotees, this club books lots of bright faces coming off recent TV gigs, and occasional drop-ins by stars. Monday is political-satire night.

The Show's the Thing

Cabaret takes many forms in New York City, from a lone crooner at the piano to a full-fledged song-and-dance revue. Various night spots have stages; here are some of the most consistently entertaining.

Broadway Baby (407 Amsterdam Ave., tel. 212/724–6868). This Upper West Side contribution to the cabaret scene features show-stopping, energetic performers guaranteed to make you smile.

Cafe Arielle (432 W. 42nd St., tel. 212/714–2442). Cabaret and chamber musical comedy are performed at this new 75-seat hall above one of Theatre Row's tried-and-true restaurants.

Danny's Skylight Room (346 W. 46th St., tel. 212/265–8130). Danny's is housed in the Grand Sea Palace, a fixture on Restaurant Row. It offers a little bit of everything: jazz, crooners, ivory-tinklers, and monologuists.

Don't Tell Mama (343 W. 46th St., tel. 212/757–0788). At this convivial theater district spot, composer/lyricist hopefuls show their stuff. Extroverts will be tempted by the open mike policy of the piano bar in front.

The Duplex (61 Christopher St., tel. 212/255–5438). This longtime Village favorite has moved to great new digs on the corner of Sheridan Square. Catch a singing luminary-on-the-rise in the upstairs cabaret, or join the happy crowd downstairs by the piano for a Broadway sing-along.

Eighty-eight's (228 W. 10th St., tel. 212/924–0088). Come here to hear songs by the best of Broadway's tunesmiths (among other things) and inventively assembled programs.

Jan Wallman's (49 W. 44th St., tel. 212/764–8930). Located in the lobby of the Hotel Iroquois, this club is known for singing pianists in the Michael Feinstein mold.

Michael's Pub (211 E. 55th St., tel. 212/758–2272). Guess which underweight, bespectacled Jewish comedian-writer-actor-director often moonlights on the clarinet here on Monday nights? On other evenings, other fine performers take the stage. The crowd is very monied, very uptown.

One Fifth (1 5th Ave., tel. 212/260–3434). This New York steak house serves up other choice cuts as well—comedians, musicians, and singers, such as the multitalented Phoebe Légère.

Steve McGraw's (158 W. 72nd St., tel. 212/595–7400). This West Side supper club and bar presents sophisticated comedy revues.

West Bank Café (407 W. 42nd St., tel. 212/695–6906). In an attractive bistro-type restaurant across from Theatre Row, moonlighting musical-comedy triple threats (actor/singer/dancers) show off; on occasion, new plays are read.

Bars

While the health-club craze may have hit New York hard, there's little danger that Manhattanites will abandon their bars. Drinking establishments thrive and multiply, particularly in TriBeCa, where it appears bar design has become a minor art. The city's liquor laws allow bars to stay open until 4 AM, so it's easy to add on a watering stop at the end of an evening's merriment.

Vintage Classics

The Algonquin Hotel Lounge (59 W. 44th St., tel. 212/840–6800). This is a venerable spot, not only because it was the site of the fabled literary Round Table, but also for its elegant tone. A fabulous grandfather clock tolls the passing hours, while noted writers still come and go (*see also* The Oak Room in Putting on the Ritz, above).

Café des Artistes (1 W. 67th St., tel. 212/877–3500). This restaurant, as well known for its glorious Beaux Art murals as for its food (*see* Chapter 8), has a small, warm bar where interesting strangers tell their life stories and the house drink is pear champagne.

Elaine's (1703 2nd Ave., tel. 212/534–8103). The food's nothing special, and you will be relegated to an inferior table, but go to crane your neck and gawk. Woody Allen's favorite table is by the cappuccino machine. It's best to visit late, when the stars rise in Elaine's firmament.

The Four Seasons (99 E. 52nd St., tel. 212/754–9494). Miró tapestries greet you as you enter this power bar through the Grill Room (*see* Chapter 8). Watch for Kissingers and Trumps.

The Jockey Club (112 Central Park S, tel. 212/664–7700). Dressy and traditional, this is a slice of upper-crust New York in the lobby of The Ritz-Carlton. It's a very double-martini sort of place.

The Oak Bar (at the Plaza Hotel, 5th Ave. and 59th St., tel. 212/759–3000). With its plummy, dark-wood furnishings, this old favorite continues to age well. Its great location draws sophisticates and high rollers, shoppers, tourists in the know, and stars.

The River Café (1 Water St., Brooklyn, tel. 718/522–5200). An eminently romantic spot, hidden at the foot of the Brooklyn Bridge, this restaurant offers smashing views of Wall Street and the East River. Tables are set up on a terrace when it's warm (*see* Chapter 8).

Top of the Tower (3 Mitchell Pl., tel. 212/355–7300). There are other, higher hotel-top lounges, but this one on the 26th floor of the Beekman Hotel still feels like it's halfway to heaven. The atmosphere is elegant and subdued, with piano arpeggios in the background.

"21" Club (21 W. 52nd St., tel. 212/582–7200). Famous for its old-time club atmosphere even before it was filmed in *All about Eve*, this isn't exactly a swinging joint, but its conservative environs evoke a sense of connections, power, and prestige. It's tough to get in unless you plan to eat here, too (*see* Chapter 8).

Windows on the World (1 World Trade Center, tel. 212/938–1111). To borrow Cole Porter's words: "You're a Botticelli, you're Keats, you're Shelley . . . you're the top." Here, you'll be 107 stories up, drinking in your favorite poison and the outstanding view (*see* Chapter 8).

Drinking Spots Around Town

South of Houston Street

The Bridge Café (279 Water St., tel. 212/227–3344). This busy little fish restaurant flanks the Brooklyn Bridge, a hop, skip, and a jump from South Street Seaport. The bar is abridged, but between lunch and dinner you can pass a pleasant afternoon sipping a good selection of wines at a table.

Ear Inn (326 Spring St., tel. 212/226–9060). There's nothing fancy here, though it inhabits an 1817 Federal house. It's the artsy crowd that makes the place, along with Saturday afternoon fiction readings—they call them "lunch for the ear."

Fanelli's (94 Prince St., tel. 212/226–9412). This is a casual SoHo neighborhood bar, where many come on Sundays with the fat *New York Times* under their arms.

I Tre Merli (463 W. Broadway, tel. 212/254–8699). The sound of happy drinkers spills out of the massive doors of this wide, inviting restaurant/bar. Wine by the glass is a favorite here—16 different varieties are offered.

The Manhattan Brewing Company (42 Thompson St., tel. 212/219–9250). Manhattan's only brewery is six years old and includes a bar that attracts a cheerful, noisy crowd. Try a "brown and tan"—half amber, half light ale.

Raoul's (179 Prince St., tel. 212/674–0708). The decor is 1950s chic; the clientele, upscale downtown.

South Street Seaport (Water and Fulton Sts., tel. 212/732–7678). There's no dearth of drinking opportunities at this major New York attraction: **Fluties, Roeblings,** the **Fulton Street Café,** and **McDuffy's Irish Coffee House,** to mention only a few. On warm Friday evenings, the Seaport is transformed into a gigantic college mixer, where apprentice Wall Streeters go to meet others from the Ivy League.

The Sporting Club (99 Hudson St., tel. 212/219–0900). Lots of TV monitors here stay tuned to the evening's major sports event. Aficionados come in after punching out on Wall Street.

Spring Street Bar and Restaurant (162 Spring St., tel. 212/219–0157). At the heart of trendy SoHo, this spot possesses a sleek bar with Japanese overtones and an artsy clientele.

Chelsea and the Village

America (9 E. 18th St., tel. 212/505–2110). Outside, a lone neon star tells you you've found the place. Inside, there's a vast and stunning skylit room, with an oval bar situated beyond and above the tables.

Bayamo (705 Broadway, tel. 212/475–5151). If you can't get in at the Caliente Cab Company (*see* below), try this handsome, paper-palm-shaded spot nearby. The food is Chinese-Cuban.

Cadillac Bar (15 W. 21st St., tel. 212/645–7220). A full Chelsea block long, this lively bar has graffiti-slathered walls, Tex-Mex food, and many warm bodies happily packing in margaritas.

Caliente Cab Company (61 7th Ave. S, tel. 212/243–8517). The party never seems to stop at this roomy Tex-Mex restaurant/bar. You'll find pleasant outside seating and plenty of tequila.

Cedar Tavern (82 University Pl., tel. 212/243–9355). Here's a very informal, warm spot for a post-double-feature beer. Years ago, this was the hangout of choice for a generation of New York painters.

Chumley's (86 Bedford St., tel. 212/675–4449). There's no sign to help you find this place—they took it down during Chumley's speakeasy days. A fireplace warms this relaxed spot where the burgers are hearty, and the kitchen stays open until 11:30 PM.

Downtown Beirut I (156 1st Ave., tel. 212/777–9011). This electrified East Village hangout attracts artists and student types. Occasionally, live music is played by local rock bands.

Downtown Beirut II (157 E. Houston, tel. 212/614–9040). This club picks up where I left off with live entertainment.

Harvey's Chelsea Restaurant (108 W. 18th St., tel. 212/243–5644). Here is one of the last remaining traditional enclaves in this increasingly trendy neighborhood. Booths and a long bar offer solace and booze downstairs.

McSorley's Old Ale House (15 E. 7th St., tel. 212/473–9148). One of New York's oldest saloons (opened in 1854), this place has its own satisfying label of ale. Weekend nights are boisterous; on Sunday afternoons McSorley's offers quaint surroundings for reading the paper and munching on a plate of the house specialty, onions and cheese.

Peter MacManus Café (152 7th Ave., tel. 212/929–9691). It's known simply as MacManus's to the regulars, who like this bar's unpretentiousness. Among them are lots of actors, fresh from acting classes in the neighborhood.

Metropolis Café (31 Union Sq. W, tel. 212/675–2300). Soaring ceilings and lots of white marble distinguish this pretty Yuppie drink palace—it's so pretty, in fact, that it's often used as a backdrop for movies and commercials.

Old Town Bar and Restaurant (45 E. 18th St., tel. 212/473–8874). Tawdry and proudly unpretentious, this bar posts signs announcing "quiche not served here," and "the coffee is only four hours old." The Old Town has been around since 1897, long before the trendy set discovered Chelsea.

Peculiar Pub (145 Bleecker St., tel. 212/691–8667). Here, in the heart of the Village, you'll find 250 brands of beer, from Aass to Zyweic.

Pete's Tavern (129 E. 18th St., tel. 212/473–7676). This saloon is famous as the place where O. Henry wrote "The Gift of the Magi." These days, it's ever crowded with noisy, friendly souls.

The White Horse Tavern (567 Hudson St., tel. 212/243–9260). Famous among the literati, this is the place where Dylan Thomas drained his last cup to the dregs. From April to October, there's outdoor café drinking.

Midtown and the Theater District

Barrymore's (267 W. 45th St., tel. 212/391–8400). This is a pleasantly downscale theater-district spot, with the requisite show posters on the wall. Listen in to the conversations at the bar and you'll hear the tawdry, true stories of what goes on behind gilt prosceniums.

Café Un Deux Trois (123 W. 44th St., tel. 212/354–4148). This old hotel lobby, charmingly converted, is chicly peopled. The bar itself is small, but it's a hot spot after the theater.

Century Café (132 W. 43rd St., tel. 212/398–1988). An immense vintage neon sign lights up the bar at this trendy, friendly theater-district bistro.

Charley O's (on Shubert Alley, between 44th and 45th Sts., tel. 212/840–2964). Its seemingly endless bar is conveniently located for quick intermission pit stops during dull shows.

Hard Rock Café (221 W. 57th St., tel. 212/489–6565). Embraced by the kids of stars—in fact, its clientele seems eternally prepubescent—this place is big, popular, and far too noisy for talk.

Houlihan's (49th St. and 7th Ave., tel. 212/575–2012). Great happy hours attract a congenial, post-college crowd. This is a safe bet for before- and after-showtime fare.

Joe Allen (326 W. 46th St., tel. 212/581–6464). At this old reliable on Restaurant Row, everybody's on their way to or from a show.

The Landmark Tavern (626 11th Ave., tel. 212/757–8595). This aged pub (opened in 1868) is blessed by the glow of warming fireplaces.

Lavin's (23 W. 39th St., tel. 212/921–1288). Brass and lace curtains adorn the windows; inside, you can order many wines by the glass. This is a popular after-work spot, especially with Garment District execs.

Raga (57 W. 48th St., tel. 212/757–3450). In this fine midtown Indian restaurant, a comfortable, deep-chaired lounge hosts a pleasant happy hour.

Sardi's (234 W. 44th St., tel. 212/221–8440). If you care for the theater, don't leave New York without visiting this establishment, which is as much a fixture in the theater district as the playhouses themselves. Tatty elegance is the trademark—it looks like some grande dame of the theater, wrinkled beneath her pancake makeup.

Top of the Sixes (666 5th Ave., tel. 212/757–6662). This bar has an impressive nighttime view, from 39 stories up above Fifth Avenue.

East Side

Ciao Bella (1311 3rd Ave., tel. 212/288–2555). This postmodern Italian restaurant/bar, like its well-heeled clients, keeps trying very hard to be in style, and generally succeeds.

Jim McMullen's (1341 3rd Ave., tel. 212/861–4700). A young, quintessential Upper East Side watering hole, McMullen's has a large, busy bar decked with bouquets of fresh flowers. Here you'll find lots of Gold Cards, tennis talk, and alumni fund gathering.

La Famille (2017 5th Ave., tel. 212/722–9806). The cuisine is southern at this 27-year-old Harlem favorite, where you'll find a warm drinking lounge downstairs.

P.J. Clarke's (915 3rd Ave., tel. 212/759–1650). New York's most famous Irish bar, this bar comes complete with the requisite mirrors and polished wood. Lots of after-workers like unwinding here, in a place that recalls the days of Tammany Hall.

The Polo Lounge (at the Westbury Hotel, 15 E. 69th St., tel.

212/535–9141). This place is, in a word, classy; it's frequented by European royalty and Knickerbocker New York.

Rusty's (1271 3rd Ave., tel. 212/861–4518). This casual restaurant, owned by former Mets right fielder Rusty Staub, is beloved by members of the Big Apple's professional teams and Central Park leagues alike. The ambience is pleasant enough to win you, even if baseball is not your thing.

The Water Club (500 Waterside Dr., tel. 212/683–3333). Right on the East River, with a pleasing outside deck, this is a special-occasion kind of place—especially for those who've already been to all the special landlocked spots in town.

The Terrace (at the Hotel Inter-Continental, 111 E. 48th St., tel. 212/755–5900). A gilded, gargantuan birdcage greets you as you enter. To your left is a spacious lounge, with a pianist reinforcing the sophisticated atmosphere.

Third Avenue Sports Bar (497 3rd Ave., tel. 212/686–8422). This pub is popular with the same crowd that spends Saturday afternoons glued to "The Wide World of Sports." Mets posters cover the walls, and there are TVs galore.

Tuba City Truck Stop (1700 2nd Ave., tel. 212/996–6200). Though Route 66 never passed by a joint like this one, Tuba City's ersatz southwestern aura still charms. There are battered license plates on the wall and tire treads printed on the white place mats. The place attracts a nicer-than-average crowd, whose lips turn blueish as they down the turquoise margaritas.

West Side **The Conservatory** (at the Mayflower Hotel, 15 Central Park West, tel. 212/581–1293). Furnished, perhaps, out of a Bloomingdale's window, this is reputedly the haunt of Hollywood movie barons in town to cut deals. Beyond all that, it's a pleasant, quiet place in which to talk and drink.

Dublin House (225 W. 79th St., tel. 212/874–9528). Above the door glows a small neon harp; inside you'll find lots of very young professionals, Columbia students, and softball teams throwing back two-bit drafts.

The Ginger Man (51 W. 64th St., tel. 212/724–7272). This old reliable in the Lincoln Center area offers a seemingly endless warren of rooms, handsome Tiffany lamps, and famous faces from ABC-TV (several blocks uptown).

J. G. Melon (340 Amsterdam Ave., tel. 212/877–2220). A quiet corner pub near the busy intersection of 72nd Street and Broadway, this spot has a small but comfortable bar and additional table space in the back room. Pictures of melons—the fruit—are everywhere you look. The East Side branch is at 1291 Third Avenue.

Lucy's Restaurant (503 Columbus Ave., tel. 212/787–3009). This Tex-Mex hangout is a hit with young Upper Westsiders, who pack themselves into the bar area and sometimes even manage to dance. The decor is playful Gulf beach hut.

Museum Café (366 Columbus Ave., tel. 212/799–0150). Trendy, overdesigned joints on Columbus Avenue come and go, but this one across from the American Museum of Natural History endures thanks to nice streetside windows and high, airy ceilings. Split a homemade pizza as you drink.

The Saloon (1920 Broadway, tel. 212/874–1500). The menu goes on and on; the bar is large and informal; and the waitresses and waiters cruise around on roller skates. It may be gimmicky, but the spirit of fun is infectious.

Gay Bars

The Bar (68 2nd Ave., tel. 212/674–9714). This classic East Village gay bar is a bit seamy to look at, but an unforced and convivial atmosphere prevails. Late weekend nights—after 1 AM—are best.

Crazy Nanny (21 7th Ave. S., tel. 212/366–6312). Even in wide-open New York, women's bars aren't easy to find. This one's small, but that doesn't discourage the die-hard jukebox dancers.

The Eagle's Nest (142 11th Ave., tel. 212/691–8451). The hormones are always running at this favorite cruise bar, attracting a balanced mix of types, including pool players and dancing fools (there's a DJ on board).

Julius (159 W. 10th St., tel. 212/929–9672). Warm, friendly, and low-key, Julius was one of the first bars on the gay scene; it's renowned for its beefy "Julius Burger." The crowd's a little older now, but the place still offers respite from more frenetic atmospheres.

Marie's Crisis (59 Grove St., tel. 212/243–9323). You've got to love it for its name, and for its ecstatic piano sing-alongs—everybody seems to know all the words to Stephen Sondheim's musical *Sunday in the Park with George*.

Uncle Charlie's Downtown (56 Greenwich Ave., tel. 212/255–8787). This extremely popular Village gay bar is visited by stylish young men and distinguished-looking professionals. Happy hour on weeknights between 5 and 8 packs them in.

12 Excursions from New York City

by David Laskin

Freelance writer David Laskin is the author of Eastern Islands: Accessible Islands of the Atlantic East Coast. *His articles about travel and other subjects have appeared in* The New York Times, Travel & Leisure, *and* Esquire.

The pleasures of New York may be inexhaustible, but the city itself can be exhausting, and after a few days of full-tilt touring you may need a break from the concrete, the noise, the hubbub, and the congestion. Here are three destinations within easy striking distance of Manhattan: a beach resort at the eastern end of Long Island; a quintessential New England village near the coast of Connecticut; and two historic mansions overlooking the Hudson River. In any of these spots, you will find clean air, lots of space in which to wander, green and rural landscapes, and escape from the pressures of the city. Each is close enough to the city to be seen in a day trip, but you may prefer an overnight or weekend visit to explore these towns at greater leisure.

Montauk

As the easternmost point in New York State, the last village of the Hamptons, and the tip of fish-shaped Long Island's tail, Montauk has the double allure of extremity and the sea. To get as far out into the ocean as you can without leaving dry land, make the trip not only to Montauk Village, but out to Montauk Point, where the 1795 lighthouse decreed by George Washington confronts the raging Atlantic from an eroding bluff.

Montauk is often lumped together with the trendy Hamptons, but actually it is quite distinct both in history and in atmosphere from that string of South Shore towns to its west. Named for the Montaukett Indians, Montauk (old-timers put the accent on the second syllable, but most people emphasize the first) was America's first ranch, serving as the open cattle range for South Shore farmers from Colonial days until the late 19th century. There was really no settlement here, aside from the three houses built for the cattle keepers. In stark contrast to East Hampton with its elegant Colonial homes and inns, Montauk is a 20th-century village, dominated by beach motels, undistinguished storefronts, and 1950s suburban-style housing.

But then, you don't go to Montauk for the architecture—you go for the beaches; the wild, rolling moors of Hither Hills; and the lighthouse at the Point. Despite the oceanfront development of the past two decades, Montauk retains the feel of the open range it used to be, and has the delightful bonus of miles and miles of superb white sand beaches on the Atlantic.

Tourist Information The **Montauk Chamber of Commerce** (tel. 516/668–2428) is located on Main Street, on the Plaza in the center of town.

Getting Around Although you can get to Montauk from New York City by train (the Long Island Railroad from New York's Penn Station, tel. 516/758–5477) or by bus (the Hampton Jitney from 41st St. between Lexington and 3rd Aves., tel. 212/936–0440 or 516/283–4600; reservations required), a car gives you the most freedom and flexibility for a day trip. From New York City, the Midtown Tunnel will take you to the Long Island Expressway (Rte. 495); follow it to Exit 70 (Manorville Rd.), then follow the signs to Route 27 (Sunrise Hwy.). Route 27 changes its name to the Montauk Highway and goes all the way out to Montauk Point. You can park your car on the street in town or at the IGA parking lot on the western edge of town.

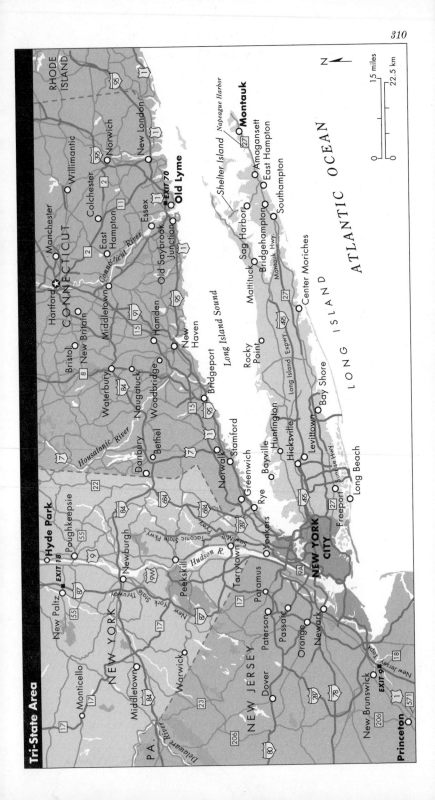

Tri-State Area

310

Exploring The landscape between Amagansett and Montauk is almost lu-
The Village nar: flat, windswept, and scrubby, with glimpses of ocean to
the south and Napeague Harbor to the north. You know you're
approaching Montauk Village when beach motels featuring the
inevitable watery names—Wavecrest, Driftwood, Seascape,
Seacrest—start coming thick and fast beside the road.

Just east of the convergence of Montauk Highway and Old Montauk Highway, you come to the **Second House,** Montauk's oldest standing dwelling, which was built in 1797 to replace a
house built in 1746. (The First House, near the entrance to
Hither Hills Park, burned down in 1909; the Third House, 3
miles east of the village at Montauk County Park, dates from
1804.) Originally the home of summertime livestock herders,
the Second House is now a museum run by the Historical Society, with exhibits of antique tools and furniture. *Rte. 27, tel.
516/668–5340. Admission: $1 adults, 50¢ children. Open daily
in summer 10–2:30.*

At the center of Montauk Village is a traffic circle known as the
Plaza. Here stands Montauk's most bizarre and incongruous
building—a seven-story Tudor-style office tower that looks
about as much at home in Montauk as a sand dune would look on
Fifth Avenue. This and the palatial Montauk Manor off Edgemere Avenue are about all that remain of developer Carl Fisher's elaborate (and fortunately failed) scheme in the 1920s to
turn Montauk into "the Miami of the North." Fisher built the
tower as his office building; it was recently converted to
condos.

Time Out **Plaza Restaurant** (on the Plaza, tel. 516/668–4687) serves
breakfast all day, along with burgers, salads, sandwiches, and
desserts.

If you follow Edgemere Avenue from the Plaza out of town until
it runs into Flamingo Road, and then follow that until it inter-
sects with West Lake Drive, you'll arrive at **Montauk Harbor** on
Lake Montauk, headquarters for a large commercial fishing
fleet as well as charter fishing boats. The deck at Gosman's
Dock (*see* Dining, below) is a choice spot to nurse a drink and
watch the fishermen come home to port with swordfish, tuna,
bluefish, cod, and pollack.

From the harbor, take West Lake Drive south past Star Island,
site of the posh Montauk Yacht Club and the U.S. Coast Guard
Station, until you hit Montauk Highway again. Turn left and
drive to the highway's end at Montauk Point. Here, at the edge
of the ocean, stands the **Montauk Lighthouse,** Long Island's
oldest, commissioned by President George Washington in 1790
and built of red sandstone in 1796. When the light was first kin-
dled in 1797, the lighthouse stood nearly 300 feet from the
ocean; today, the ocean nibbles at the shore within 50 feet of the
base. A small museum housed in the old keeper's quarters displays photographs and maps as well as the immense Fresnel
lenses that once refracted the light. For years the tower was
closed to visitors, but today you can climb up the 137 steps for a
sweeping view on a clear day of the East End, Gardiners Island, the distant shore of Connecticut, and Block Island off the
coast of Rhode Island. *Rte. 27, tel. 516/668–2544. Admission:
$2 adults, $1 children 6–12. Open Martin Luther King and
Washington's Birthday weekends 11–4; March–Apr., week-*

ends and May, Fri.–Mon. 10:30–4:30; Memorial Day–Labor Day, daily 10:30–6; Sept. daily, Oct. Fri.–Mon., Nov. weekends, and Thanksgiving 10:30–4:30. Closed Dec.

The 724-acre state park surrounding the lighthouse has hiking trails, surf fishing, picnic tables, and a refreshment stand; there are beaches on both the ocean and Long Island Sound, but heavy surf and submerged rocks make swimming hazardous here. *Open daily, sunrise–sunset.*

The Beaches Montauk has some of the finest beaches on an island renowned for fine beaches, but the trick is getting access to them. If you've come by car, your best bet is **Hither Hills State Park,** a 1,750-acre oceanfront park a few miles west of Montauk Village; this is the only official public beach in Montauk where you can park without a town permit. Hither Hills has a bathhouse, surf fishing, oceanfront camping, a picnic area, hiking through pitch pine and scrub oak forests, a central shower building, a playground, and a refreshment stand and store that are open in summer. *Rte. 27, tel. 516/668–2493. Admission: $4 per car (free after Labor Day and until Memorial Day). Open first week of Apr.–mid-Oct., daily sunrise–sunset; Camping by advance reservation only (tel. 800/456–CAMP).*

You can also reach the ocean by walking to the south end of just about any street in town. The roar of the surf drowns out the sound of the highway traffic, the dunes block out most of the town buildings, and the breeze brings you the heady salt scent of the sea.

Dining *Price categories are the same as in the Dining chapter for New York City.*

★ **Gosman's.** Gosman's has everything you could ever hope for in a classy fish restaurant: a spectacular location at the entrance to Montauk Harbor, indoor and outdoor dining, and the freshest possible fish, since Gosman's is also a wholesale and retail fish supplier. The one catch is its size—it seats 400 between its indoor dining room, two deck dining areas, and waterside patio. It is hugely popular, though, and since it takes no reservations, you may have to wait some time to be seated in peak season. Try the broiled fluke, which is not available at many places outside Montauk, or the broiled tuna. The Cajun-style blackfish and weakfish are both excellent, and lobster is very popular. The chocolate torte dessert was designed expressly for chocoholics. *West Lake Dr., tel. 516/668–5330. No reservations. Dress: casual (no jogging shorts). MC, V. Closed mid-Oct.–mid-Apr. Closed Tues. mid-Apr.–Memorial Day and Labor Day–mid-Oct. Moderate.*

The Inn at Napeague. Despite its tacky-looking building, this restaurant actually serves some of the best seafood and Continental dishes in town, including bouillabaisse, grilled mako, swordfish, and tuna, and steak au poivre. The cozy, unpretentious dining room has a nautical theme, with shiny wood tables and fish nets hanging from the ceiling. *Montauk Hwy. at Napeague Harbor, tel. 516/267–3332. Reservations advised. Dress: casual. AE. Dinner only; closed Nov.–mid-Apr. Moderate.*

Windjammer Restaurant. One of the few restaurants in Montauk Village that is open year-round, the Windjammer has a dining room that feels about as big as a football field (but much more comfortable), with tables set well apart and spectacular views of Fort Pond through large picture windows. Specialties include flounder baked in parchment, poached salmon with lobster caviar, bouillabaisse, and such Continental dishes as sautéed breast of chicken with artichoke, and veal with crabmeat and hollandaise sauce. *Edgemere Rd., tel. 516/668–2872. Reservations suggested. Dress: casual. AE, MC, V. Closed Tues. mid-Nov.–mid-Mar. Moderate.*

Lodging The following chart establishes price categories for all of the lodgings listed in this chapter. In towns such as Montauk that have a "season" (generally Memorial Day to Labor Day), these categories reflect in-season prices; off-season prices are considerably lower.

Highly recommended accommodations are indicated by a star ★.

Category	Cost*
Very Expensive	over $120
Expensive	$90–$120
Moderate	$50–$90
Inexpensive	under $50

*All prices are for a standard double room; excluding tax and gratuities.

The following credit card abbreviations are used: AE, American Express, CB, Carte Blanche; DC, Diners Club; MC, MasterCard; V, Visa.

★ **Gurney's Inn Resort and Spa.** This resort has long been popular for its fabulous location high on a bluff overlooking 1,000 feet of private ocean beach; in recent years it has become even more famous for the International Health and Beauty Spa at Gurney's Inn—one of America's only Marino therapeutic spas, a European therapy that features the use of seawater and sea plants. The large, luxurious rooms, all with ocean views, have refrigerators and room service, and guests have the choice of modified-American meal plans (breakfast and dinner) or spa cuisine (three meals). The oceanview restaurant features French cuisine, and spa cuisine is served in a separate oceanview dining room. The indoor pool, nearly Olympic size, has heated sea water. *Old Montauk Hwy., 11954, tel. 516/668–2345. 125 rooms with bath. Facilities: restaurant, bar, health club, exercise equipment and classes, Roman bath, recreation room, indoor pool, meeting rooms, golf and tennis nearby. AE, DC, MC, V. Very Expensive.*

Shepherd's Neck Inn. This country inn gives you a real feel for the simple, unpretentious seagoing style that sets Montauk apart from the trendier Hamptons to the west. Located right in the village, it has 5 acres of quiet grounds and the rooms are spacious. Furnishings are simple—a step up from motel-drab but with no valuable antiques or breakables—so the inn is well suited for families with young children. Guests choose between two meal plans: bed-and-breakfast or modified American (breakfast and dinner). Golf, beaches, and boats are nearby. *Second House Rd., Box 639, 11954, tel. 516/668–2105. 70 rooms with bath. Facilities: restaurant, bar, heated pool, tennis, AV* *and VCR equipment, meeting rooms, card room, movie room with nightly features. MC, V. Moderate–Expensive.*

Old Lyme

With its classic white Congregational church, clapboard mansions, and gracious country inns, **Old Lyme** is redolent of the old Yankee spirit of New England. Situated near Long Island Sound, at the mouth of the Connecticut River, the town rose to prominence as a shipbuilding center in the mid-19th century, but it declined with the advent of steamships in the late 1880s (the local waters were too shallow for the deeper-draft steam-powered vessels). Old Lyme's loss was our gain, for the town remains much as it was in the days of the clipper ships, when 60 sea captains lived in its fine Federal, Georgian, and Greek Revival houses. Many of these homes still stand on Lyme Street, their tall arched windows and fanlighted doors gazing serenely down on wide lawns and tidy gardens. Behind them runs the marshy Lieutenant River, part of which is protected as a nature reserve for waterfowl.

Old Lyme achieved new prominence as an art colony around 1900, when Florence Griswold, daughter of a sea captain, opened her father's mansion as a boardinghouse for artists. For nearly three decades, the leading painters of the American Impressionist school came to stay with Miss Florence and paint in the open air.

Tourist Information Contact the **Selectman's Office** in the Old Lyme Town Hall (Lyme Street, 06371, tel. 203/434–1605).

A brochure outlining a self-guided walking (or driving) tour of historic Old Lyme is available at the Griswold Museum (*see* Exploring, below).

Getting Around The only way to travel directly from New York to Old Lyme is by car. Take I–95 north to Exit 70; at the bottom of the ramp turn left, and at the first traffic light make a right onto Route 1. After about half a mile, you'll come to another light: This is Lyme Street. A left turn here takes you to the inns and the Griswold Museum; a right turn leads you to the Town Hall and the Congregational church.

Amtrak (tel. 800/872–7245) has frequent service out of Penn Station to Old Saybrook Junction, Connecticut, a 20-minute taxi ride from Old Lyme.

Exploring A tour of Old Lyme should begin at the **Florence Griswold Museum,** an imposing lemon-yellow mansion built in 1817 with a broad portico supported by four white columns. Miss Florence opened the house to artists around 1900, and her generous support made it a kind of summer headquarters for the American Barbizon and Impressionist movements. Such painters as Childe Hassam, Henry Ranger, William Chadwick, and Walter Griffin came here to capture the soft, bright Connecticut landscape.

Today the Griswold Museum gives visitors a wonderful opportunity to see paintings exhibited in the house in which they were painted. Some of the best works were painted not just *in* but *on* the house—to repay Miss Florence for her hospitality, artists decorated her wood paneling and doorways. The dining room panels have some especially fine landscapes. The downstairs of the house, furnished with period pieces, contains such masterpieces as Charles Ebert's *Monhegan Headlands* and William Chadwick's *On the Porch*, as well as exhibits of bird-cages, dollhouses, and toys. Upstairs are galleries with changing displays of the works of painters who worked in Old Lyme. *96 Lyme St., tel. 203/434-5542. Admission: $2 adults, children under 12 free. Open Nov.-May, Wed.-Sun. 1-5; June-Oct., Tues.-Sat. 10-5 and Sun. 1-5.*

Next door to the Griswold Museum is the **Lyme Art Association,** founded by members of the Old Lyme art colony in 1914 and housed in a simple shingled building designed by Charles Platt in 1921. The association galleries present changing art shows. *90 Lyme Street, tel. 203/434-7802. Suggested donation: $3. Open May-Oct., Tues.-Sat. noon-5, Sun. 1-5.*

A walk up and down Lyme Street will take you past a number of fine old homes. A few doors north of the Griswold Museum is the **Ely-Noyes House,** which has wide eaves, a flat roof, a columned porch, and large barns on well-maintained grounds. South of the museum you'll find the **John Sill House,** a nobly proportioned late-Georgian structure sitting behind a formal wrought-iron gate, and now the home of the **Lyme Academy of Fine Arts** (open weekdays 9-4:30). Walk a few steps farther to the **Deming-Avery House,** built in 1726 with a low gambrel roof, black shutters, and a white rail fence.

The **First Congregational Church** is a replica of the 1817 church designed by Samuel Belcher that burned down in 1907 (an even earlier church on the site was hit by lightning in 1815). It is a picture-postcard New England church, with a grand portico supported by four soaring white columns, a square clock tower, and a tapering steeple surmounted by a weather vane.

Time Out Head east on Route 156 to find the **Hall Mark Ice Cream Place,** noted for its freshly made ice cream; sandwiches and snacks are also available (open May-Oct.).

To reach the Old Lyme beach on Long Island Sound, follow Route 156 about 1½ miles south of town to Hartford Avenue, where you turn right and continue to the public parking lot, on the right.

Dining and Lodging *For price categories, see the Montauk lodging price chart, above.*

The Old Lyme Inn. Occupying an 1850 farmhouse, with a new wing added in 1985, the Old Lyme Inn is a touch more formal than the Bee and Thistle, and it feels less rural and secluded, being set rather close to the road and next to I-95. But the Old Lyme Inn compensates with the size of its guest rooms, particularly the eight rooms in the new wing, which combine modern bathrooms with antique furniture, including canopied beds, Victorian cut-velvet love seats, and mirrored gentlemen's dressers. The inn's formal main dining room has a high ceiling hung with Victorian etched-glass globes; blue plush chairs, gold brocade wallpaper, and massive oil paintings recall the stately grandeur of the French Empire style. The cuisine is innovative American, and the seasonally changing menu features fresh poached salmon in potato crust, veal with Roquefort butter and braised celery, and, in winter, venison with red-currant sauce. There is also a less formal Grill Room serving a lighter menu. *85 Lyme St., tel. 203/434–2600. 13 rooms. Facilities: restaurant, bar, grill, private dining rooms. AE, DC, MC, V. Closed first 2 wks Jan. Expensive.*

★ **The Bee and Thistle.** This quintessential country inn, housed in a 1756 mansion, was completely and tastefully redecorated seven years ago; both public rooms and guest rooms have been furnished with period antiques. The two downstairs parlors have flower-print Chippendale sofas, comfy wing chairs, and working fireplaces. Each bedroom has a different flowery wallpaper and antique quilts, and many have four-poster beds with hand-knotted fishnet canopies. The 5 acres of rustically landscaped grounds stretch to the Lieutenant River, and the gardens are full of flowers in spring and summer. Four small, cheerful dining rooms overlooking the garden serve a changing menu of sophisticated American country cooking: for lunch there might be chowders, English sausages, crab cakes, and gorgonzola ravioli; dinner standouts may include quail stuffed with sausage and apples, venison with port and cranberry sauce, and rainbow trout grilled with garlic sausage and honey tarragon. *100 Lyme St., tel. 203/434–1667. 11 rooms, 9 with bath. Children under 12 not allowed. Facilities: restaurant, bar. AE, DC, MC, V. Closed Dec. 24–25, first 2 wks. Jan. Moderate–Expensive.*

Hyde Park

The Hudson River is often compared to Germany's Rhine—though its history is not as long, its scenery is just as spectacular: mountains rise from its shores, vineyards are tucked away in the folds of its hills, and lordly estates crown its picturesque promontories. The village of Hyde Park, on the east side of the Hudson, is graced with two of these estates, the Vanderbilt Mansion and the Franklin D. Roosevelt National Historic Site, both owned and operated by the National Park Service. Magnificent houses in their own right, both are also fascinating for their historic importance.

Tourist Information The **Dutchess County Tourism Promotion Agency** is at 532 Albany Post Road in Hyde Park (Box 2025, Hyde Park, NY 12538, tel. 914/229–0033). A regional tourist information center runs May–October in the Carriage House at the FDR home. For more information about either historic house, contact the **National Park Service** (519 Albany Post Rd., 12538, tel. 914/229–9115).

Getting Around The only direct way to reach the Hyde Park historic homes from New York City is to drive. Take the New York State Thruway to Exit 18, New Paltz, and follow signs to the mid-Hudson Bridge. Cross the bridge and pick up Route 9 north. The Roosevelt home is 5 miles north on the left-hand side, the Vanderbilt mansion is 2 miles farther north, also on the left.

An alternative is to take the Henry Hudson Parkway (Rte. 9A) to the Saw Mill River Parkway, and follow that to the Taconic State Parkway. Get off at the exit for Route 55 west (Poughkeepsie), and follow Route 55 to Route 9. Proceed 5 miles north to the house.

Exploring The FDR Historic Site Springwood, the house where Franklin Delano Roosevelt, the nation's 32nd president, was born, was purchased by Roosevelt's father in 1867. In 1915 FDR and his mother, Sara, enlarged the circa 1826 frame house that stood on the grounds, stuccoing over the central section and adding two native blue fieldstone wings; they also added the white colonnaded portico over the front entrance and the balustrade around the terrace, Georgian-style touches that give the house an air of quiet elegance. The house contains the original furniture that FDR's parents collected, including an 18th-century grandfather clock, Chinese porcelains, and the delicate Dresden chandelier and mantel set in the formal Dresden room, which was used as a music room. The office (which FDR called the "Summer White House") is where he and Winston Churchill signed an agreement to pursue the development of the atomic bomb in 1942; his bedroom upstairs still contains his books, family photos, and the blanket and leash of Fala, his famous Scottie.

On the grounds of the Roosevelt estate are the hemlock-hedged rose garden where Eleanor and Franklin Roosevelt are buried and, in a separate building, the Franklin D. Roosevelt Library and Museum, which holds the president's personal papers, books, and some of his ship models. A nature trail winds down the steep slopes that rise above the Hudson.

Though Eleanor lived at Hyde Park after her marriage to Franklin, the house remained very firmly under the control of her steely mother-in-law; Eleanor escaped Sara's rule for picnics at the nearby property of Val-Kill, where in the 1920s she built a stone Dutch-style cottage to a design made by her husband. After FDR's death, Eleanor retired to a small stucco-and-fieldstone building there, now open as the Val-Kill Museum. Visitors to Val-Kill can view a film about Mrs. Roosevelt and the property and tour her cottage, with its knotty pine walls and scores of photographs of family and friends (among them such world leaders as Haile Selassie, Jawaharlal Nehru, and Marshal Tito). *FDR Historic Site, tel. 914/229–9115. Admission: $3.50, children under 16 and senior citizens over 62 free. Open Nov.–Mar., Thurs.–Mon. 9–5; Apr.–Oct., daily 9–5. Closed Thanksgiving, Christmas, New Year's Day. Val-Kill admission free. Open Apr.–Oct., daily 9–5, Mar. and Nov.–Dec., weekends 9–5.*

The Vanderbilt Mansion   The Vanderbilt Mansion, a 54-room Renaissance-style palace encased in brilliant Indiana limestone, is a grand monument of the gilded age. Completed in 1898 to a design by the renowned architectural firm McKim, Mead and White, it was built for Commodore Vanderbilt's grandson Frederick, who came here with his wife Louise in the spring and autumn to pursue his hobbies of gardening, farming, and raising purebred livestock. Though smaller than the Breakers, which was built for Frederick's brother at Newport, Rhode Island, this house is far grander, more formal, and to some minds more pretentious than the Roosevelt home down the road. The interior has a dizzying gilt-and-marble opulence, for Mr. and Mrs. Frederick Vanderbilt ransacked the Orient, the Near East, and Europe to decorate their home. Don't miss Mrs. Vanderbilt's Louis XV–style bedroom, which, like the bedchambers of French queens, has a carved railing around the bed and painted medallions of languidly elegant pastel figures set into the wood-paneled walls. The meticulously landscaped formal parterre garden features a loggia, a pergola, a rose garden, and symmetrical flower beds. Views of the Hudson from the grounds are breathtaking; a road through the 211-acre property leads to a picnic area on the river. *Tel. 914/229–9115. Admission: $2, children* under 16 and senior citizens over 62 free. Open Apr.–Oct., daily 9–5; Nov.–March, Thurs.–Mon. 9–5. Closed Thanksgiving, Christmas, New Year's Day.

Dining *Price categories are the same as in the Dining chapter for New York City.*

★ **Culinary Institute of America.** This renowned school for chefs, housed in a former Jesuit seminary just a short drive from the Roosevelt and Vanderbilt mansions, has four dining rooms where students prepare and serve meals as the grand finale of their 21 months of training. The *Escoffier Room*, named for the great French culinary artist Auguste Escoffier, features classic French cooking in an elegant maroon-and-rose dining room with black chandeliers, cushioned chairs and banquettes, and a window through which you can watch the students cooking. The offerings change every season, and the prix fixe menu ($20 lunch, $40 dinner) changes daily. Entrées might include beef fillet with mushrooms and wine, grilled salmon on a bed of lentils, strips of veal and fillet of sole with dill cream, and couscous with clams. The *American Bounty* dining room, which pioneered the return to regional American cooking a few years back, has a warm and friendly decor with green-cushioned wood chairs, arched windows overlooking a courtyard, and a wonderful display of fresh-baked breads and the local produce in front of the small kitchen, where you can watch students at work on the desserts and pastries. Menus change daily, but entrées might include stuffed breast of chicken with pecans and Kentucky bourbon, fillet of mahimahi in macadamia nuts with fresh pineapple salsa, scallop salad, and shrimp and Cajun sausage with pecan rice. The less expensive menu at the casual *St. Andrew's Café* features nutritionally balanced, low-calorie, low-cholesterol meals in a cheerful 65-seat room enlivened with hanging plants. The smaller *Caterina de Medici* dining room, featuring northern Italian cooking, is primarily for staff and family members of CIA students. The public is welcome to book any remaining tables by calling the school on Tuesday morning at 8:30; reservations are taken three weeks in advance. Typical entrées include braised stuffed veal shank with vegetable sauce, and fillet of sea bass with saffron and basil. Smoking is prohibited in all the restaurants. *Rte. 9, tel. 914/471–6608. Reservations required, booked on a quarterly basis. Jacket required (casual dress only for St. Andrew's Café). AE, DC, MC, V. Escoffier and American Bounty closed Sun. and Mon.; St. Andrew's and Caterina de Medici closed weekends. Inexpensive–Expensive.*

Coppola's Restaurant. Located a half mile from the FDR home, this restaurant features an extensive selection of southern Italian standards along with steaks, chops, and seafood dishes. The decor is exactly what you'd expect from a family-oriented Italian restaurant: crystal chandeliers, red-and-white tablecloths, and pictures and murals of Italy. Popular dishes include veal marsala and Italian seafood plate with clams, mussels, calamari, and shrimp on linguine; there is also a children's menu. The same family runs the adjacent Dutch Patroon Inn, a 34-room motel. *Rte. 9, tel. 914/229–9113. Dress: casual. AE, CB, DC, MC, V. Inexpensive.*

Pepe's. This nice, cozy Italian restaurant convenient to the historic homes may have the inevitable red-checked tablecloths and posters of historic Italy, but it features some imaginative dishes at good prices. Standouts include the linguine topped with fish and shellfish, stuffed artichoke, and fettucine carbonara. The homemade cheesecake is recommended for dessert. *108 Albany Post Rd., tel. 914/229–9050. Dress: casual. MC, V. Inexpensive.*

Lodging *For price categories, see Montauk lodging price chart.*

Village Victorian Inn. Built as a private home in 1860 in an Italianate Victorian style, this pale yellow house was converted to a small inn in 1987. It's furnished throughout with Victorian antiques, including canopy beds, French armoires, marble-topped dressers, and a walnut Hepplewhite dressing table. Full breakfast (included) is served in the cozy dining room, where a fire is lit in winter. *31 Center St., Rhinebeck, 12572, tel. 914/876–8345. 5 rooms. AE, MC, V. Very Expensive.*

The Beekman Arms. A few miles north of the historic homes, this Rhinebeck landmark claims to be the oldest inn in America, dating to 1766, though it has been expanded over the years and now includes several 19th-century buildings. Rooms in the old section feature pine floors and reproductions of Colonial furniture; many have four-poster beds. The Delamater House, down the street, is a Victorian-Gothic-style cottage with an inviting front porch. The furnishings here are reproductions of Victorian pieces, and 20 additional rooms, all with working fireplaces, are located in the newer Delamater Courtyard buildings. The hotel's cozy, low-ceilinged Tap Room serves hearty traditional American fare, such as prime rib or scallops with bacon, cream, and basil. *4 Mill St., Rhinebeck, 12572, tel. 914/876–7077. 54 rooms. Facilities: restaurant, bar. AE, DC, MC, V. Moderate.*

The Super 8 Motel. This Hyde Park branch of the nationwide chain is conveniently located near the entrance to the FDR house and a quarter-mile from the Vanderbilt Mansion. Although clean and new (it was built three years ago), the Super 8 has little to distinguish it from the standard roadside offering. Free Continental breakfast is served. *Rte. 9, Hyde Park, 12538, tel. 914/229–0088. 61 rooms. AE, CB, DC, MC, V. Inexpensive–Moderate.*

Index

The Lion's Dinner
A Play

Paul Shipton

Illustrated by Garry Davies

RIGBY

The Characters

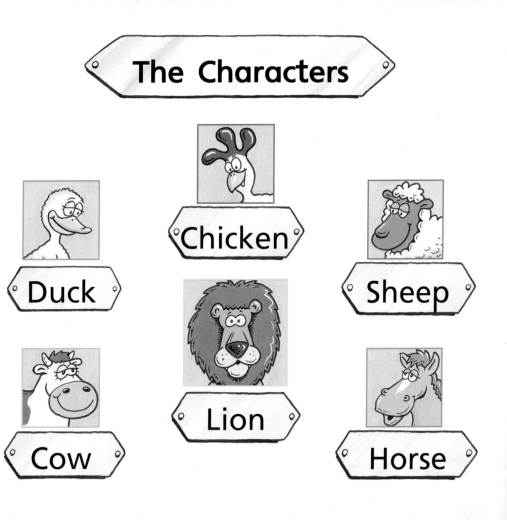

Duck

Chicken

Sheep

Cow

Lion

Horse

Lion:
Hello. I'm a lion.

Sheep:
What do you like to eat?

Lion:
What do **you** eat?

Sheep and Cow:
We eat grass.
Do you like grass?

Lion:
No.

4

Horse:

I like hay.

Do you like hay?

Lion:

No.

6

Chicken:

You can eat some corn.
Do you like corn?

Lion:

No.

9

Duck:

You can eat some bread.
Do you like bread?

Lion:

No.

11

Lion:

I don't like grass and I don't like hay.
I don't like corn and I don't like bread.

Chicken:

What **do** you like to eat?

13

Lion:

I like to eat animals . . .

Lion:

but I've just had my dinner!

Fodor's Travel Guides

U.S. Guides

Alaska
Arizona
Boston
California
Cape Cod
The Carolinas & the
  Georgia Coast
The Chesapeake
  Region
Chicago
Colorado
Disney World & the
  Orlando Area

Florida
Hawaii
Las Vegas
Los Angeles
Maui
Miami & the
  Keys
New England
New Mexico
New Orleans
New York City
New York City
  (Pocket Guide)

New York State
Pacific North Coast
Philadelphia
Puerto Rico
  (Pocket Guide)
The Rockies
San Diego
San Francisco
San Francisco
  (Pocket Guide)
The South
Texas
USA

The Upper Great
  Lakes Region
Vacations on the
  Jersey Shore
Virgin Islands
Virginia & Maryland
Waikiki
Washington, D.C.

Foreign Guides

Acapulco
Amsterdam
Australia
Austria
The Bahamas
The Bahamas
  (Pocket Guide)
Baja & the Pacific
  Coast Resorts
Barbados
Belgium &
  Luxembourg
Bermuda
Brazil
Budget Europe
Canada
Canada's Atlantic
  Provinces
Cancun, Cozumel,
  Yucatan Peninsula
Caribbean
Central America
China
Eastern Europe

Egypt
Europe
Europe's Great
  Cities
France
Germany
Great Britain
Greece
The Himalayan
  Countries
Holland
Hong Kong
India
Ireland
Israel
Italy
Italy 's Great Cities
Jamaica
Japan
Kenya, Tanzania,
  Seychelles
Korea
London
London Companion

London
  (Pocket Guide)
Madrid & Barcelona
Mexico
Montreal &
  Quebec City
Morocco
Munich
New Zealand
Paris
Paris (Pocket Guide)
Portugal
Rio de Janeiro
Rome
Saint Martin/
  Sint Maarten
Scandinavia
Scandinavian Cities
Scotland
Singapore
South America
South Pacific
Southeast Asia
Soviet Union

Spain
Sweden
Switzerland
Thailand
Tokyo
Toronto
Turkey
Vienna
Yugoslavia

Special-Interest Guides

Cruises and Ports
  of Call

Smart Shopper's
  Guide to London
Healthy Escapes

Shopping in Europe
Skiing in North
  America

Addresses

Name	*Name*
Address	*Address*
Telephone	*Telephone*
Name	*Name*
Address	*Address*
Telephone	*Telephone*
Name	*Name*
Address	*Address*
Telephone	*Telephone*
Name	*Name*
Address	*Address*
Telephone	*Telephone*
Name	*Name*
Address	*Address*
Telephone	*Telephone*
Name	*Name*
Address	*Address*
Telephone	*Telephone*
Name	*Name*
Address	*Address*
Telephone	*Telephone*
Name	*Name*
Address	*Address*
Telephone	*Telephone*

Personal Itinerary

Arrival *Date* *Time*

Departure *Date* *Time*

Transportation

Accommodations

Arrival *Date* *Time*

Departure *Date* *Time*

Transportation

Accommodations

Arrival *Date* *Time*

Departure *Date* *Time*

Transportation

Accommodations

Arrival *Date* *Time*

Departure *Date* *Time*

Transportation

Accommodations

Personal Itinerary

Departure *Date*

Time

Transportation

Arrival *Date* *Time*

Departure *Date* *Time*

Transportation

Accommodations

Arrival *Date* *Time*

Departure *Date* *Time*

Transportation

Accommodations

Arrival *Date* *Time*

Departure *Date* *Time*

Transportation

Accommodations